ANC

Trevor Bryce is an Honorary Professor and Research Consultant in the University of Queensland, and an Emeritus Professor of the University of New England, Australia, where he was Professor of Classics and Ancient History. He is also a Fellow of the Australian Academy of the Humanities and has been awarded an Australian Centenary Medal for services to History. Although trained as a classicist (primarily in Latin language and literature) most of his research has been conducted in the field of Near Eastern history and civilization, with some emphasis also on the links between the Classical and near Eastern worlds. He is the author of numerous books and articles on Near Eastern history, including most recently *Babylonia: A Very Short Introduction* (2016, also published by Oxford University Press).

Praise for *Ancient Syria*

'This book can be thoroughly recommended for anyone wishing to gain a broad overview of the history of ancient Syria.'

Adam John Fraser, *Palestine Exploration Quarterly*

'Bryce has outdone himself; a marvellous achievement. Reads as smoothly as a novel, but packed as full of facts as an encyclopedia. Bryce weaves together the threads of disparate cultures and centuries of civilization, creating the very fabric of history itself.'

Eric H. Cline, The George Washington University, and author of *Biblical Archaeology: A Very Short Introduction*

'sketches the history of Syria in a lively and fluid style.'

Bibliotheca Orientalis

'The author is an engaging writer and one quickly gets the impression that he has enjoyed researching and writing this book... Professor Trevor Bryce's publication provides a lucid account that assists our understanding of Syria's historical importance and continuing strategic location.'

Andrew Jamieson, *Ancient Near Eastern Studies*

'*Ancient Syria* should be read, studied or consulted by those who want to deepen their knowledge about an amazing country, cradles of cultures and civilizations. I really appreciated Bryce's effort to convey in a single book such a vast material. It has not been done before in such a comprehensive way. One must be grateful that the multiple fascinating (hi)stories of ancient Syria are now accessible to a wider audience.'

Matteo Vigo, *Bryn Mawr Classical Review*

ANCIENT SYRIA

A THREE THOUSAND
YEAR HISTORY

TREVOR BRYCE

OXFORD
UNIVERSITY PRESS

OXFORD
UNIVERSITY PRESS

Great Clarendon Street, Oxford, OX2 6DP,
United Kingdom

Oxford University Press is a department of the University of Oxford.
It furthers the University's objective of excellence in research, scholarship,
and education by publishing worldwide. Oxford is a registered trade mark of
Oxford University Press in the UK and in certain other countries

© Trevor Bryce 2014

The moral rights of the author have been asserted

First published in hardback 2014
First published in paperback 2019

Impression: 1

Published in the United States of America by Oxford University Press
198 Madison Avenue, New York, NY 10016, United States of America

British Library Cataloguing in Publication Data
Data available

Library of Congress Cataloging in Publication Data
Data available

ISBN 978–0–19–964667–8 (Hbk.)
ISBN 978–0–19–882890–7 (Pbk.)

Printed and bound in Great Britain by
Clays Ltd, Elcograf S.p.A.

Links to third party websites are provided by Oxford in good faith and
for information only. Oxford disclaims any responsibility for the materials
contained in any third party website referenced in this work.

Acknowledgements

It has been a pleasure to work with OUP's editorial staff, particularly Luciana O'Flaherty and Matthew Cotton. And I would like to thank Dorothy McCarthy for her meticulous work on the copy-editing process and David Pelteret for his thorough proofreading and many valuable suggestions. My sincere thanks are due also to Geoff Tully for his important contributions to the preparation of the maps, and to the School of History, Philosophy, Religion and Classics, University of Queensland, for its valuable infrastructural support. I am also most grateful to OUP's anonymous external reviewer, from whose comments I have gained much benefit in preparing the final manuscript of this book. The idea for writing this book arose partly from lectures I gave during a cruise to Egypt and Syria on the ship *Aegean Odyssey*.

Trevor Bryce
University of Queensland

Contents

PART IV. SYRIA UNDER ROMAN RULE

PART V. THE RISE AND FALL OF PALMYRA

List of Maps

List of Figures

Abbreviations

<dl>

ABC A. K. Grayson (1975), *Assyrian and Babylonian Chronicles*, New York: J. J. Augustin. (Specific references are made to both the Chronicle (Chron.) number and the relevant pages in Grayson's edition.)

ANET J. B. Pritchard (1969), *Ancient Near Eastern Texts relating to the Old Testament*, 3rd edn, Princeton: Princeton University Press.

ARAB D. D. Luckenbill (1928), *Ancient Records of Assyria and Babylonia* (2 vols.), Chicago: University of Chicago Press (repr. Greenwood Press: New York, 1968).

Aust. M. Austin (2006), *The Hellenistic World from Alexander to the Roman Conquest*, 2nd edn, Cambridge: Cambridge University Press.

Beck. G. Beckman (1999), *Hittite Diplomatic* Texts, 2nd edn, Atlanta: Scholars Press.

CAH *Cambridge Ancient History.*

CANE J. M. Sasson (ed.) (1995), *Civilizations of the Ancient Near East* (4 vols.), New York: Charles Scribner's Sons.

CS (I, II, III) W. W. Hallo and K. L. Younger (eds.) (1997, 2000, 2002), *The Context of Scripture* (3 vols.), Leiden, New York, and Cologne: Brill.

DCM F. Joannès (ed.) (2001), *Dictionnaire de la civilisation mésopotamienne*, Paris: Éditions Robert Laffont.

DL M. H. Dodgeon and S. N. C. Lieu (1991), *The Roman Eastern Frontier and the Persian Wars AD 226–363: A Documentary History*, London and New York: Routledge.

EA *The El-Amarna letters*, most recently ed. and transl. by W. Moran (1992), *The Amarna Letters*, Baltimore and London: Johns Hopkins University Press (cited by document nos.).

Eccl. Hist. Eusebius, *Ecclesiastical History.*

Epit. Justin's epitome (i.e. abridged version) of the *Historiae Philippicae* ('Philippic Histories') of Pompeius Trogus.

FGrH F. Jacoby (ed.) (1923–59), *Die Fragmente der griechischen Historiker*, Berlin: Weidmann.

FHG C. Müller (ed.) (1841–70), *Fragmenta Historicorum Graecorum* (5 vols.), Paris: Ambroise Firmin-Didot.

</dl>

HCBD	P. J. Achtemeier (ed.) (1996), *The HarperCollins Bible Dictionary*, New York: HarperCollins.
HA	*Historia Augusta = Scriptores Historiae Augustae.*
JA	Josephus, *Jewish Antiquities.*
JW	Josephus, *Jewish Wars.*
OCD	S. Hornblower and A. Spawforth (eds.) (1996), *Oxford Classical Dictionary*, 3rd edn, Oxford: Oxford University Press.
OEANE	E. M. Meyers (ed.) (1997), *The Oxford Encyclopedia of Archaeology in the Near East*, New York and Oxford: Oxford University Press.
OGIS	*Orientis Graeci Inscriptiones Selectae* (2 vols.), ed. W. Dittenberger (1903–5), Leipzig: Hirzel.
PRU IV	J. Nougayrol (1956), *Le Palais Royal d'Ugarit IV* (Mission de Ras Shamra, Tome IX), Paris: Klincksieck.
RIMA 2	A. K. Grayson (1991), *The Royal Inscriptions of Mesopotamia. Assyrian Periods, Vol. 2. Assyrian Rulers of the Early First Millennium BC I (1114–859 BC)*, Toronto, Buffalo, and London: University of Toronto.
RIMA 3	A. K. Grayson (1996), *The Royal Inscriptions of Mesopotamia. Assyrian Periods, Vol. 3. Assyrian Rulers of the Early First Millennium BC II (858–745 BC)*, Toronto, Buffalo, and London: University of Toronto.
RS	Tablets from Ras Shamra
>	'translated in'

The Tale to be Told

Life's but a walking shadow, a poor player,
That struts and frets his hour upon the stage,
And then is heard no more.
It is a tale told...

(Shakespeare, *Macbeth*)[1]

The purpose of this book is to tell a story, more precisely a series of stories and sometimes stories within stories. All of them are about Syria, have Syria as their focus, or start from or end there. With just one or two exceptions (plus a ghost encounter you can make up your own mind about), our stories are about people who really existed and events that really happened. At least if we can trust the sources from which they come. The tales they tell are woven into a continuous historical narrative that extends over three thousand years—from the Early Bronze Age kingdom of Ebla where excavations have produced written records dating to the 24th century BC and indicate a line of kings going back at least to the 27th, to the reign of the emperor Diocletian, who held sway over the Roman world at the turn of the 3rd–4th century AD. Ebla's records are the earliest documents we have in Syria's history, and thus mark our story's starting-point. Diocletian's reign, though we shall touch only briefly upon it, provides a convenient book-end to the last major period of Syrian history prior to the Byzantine era.[2] Within this period, the city of Palmyra built an empire that for a brief time rivalled the might of Rome. Its rise and fall will be our story's climax.

The nature of the written sources on which ancient Syria's history is based varies greatly. For much of the first half of this history, we have to rely very largely on official documents, notably the often voluminous collections of clay tablets unearthed from the palaces, temples, administrative buildings, and private residences of the sites where they were produced or stored. Other forms of documents include sealings from these and other locations, and also, importantly, inscriptions carved on stone stelae,[3] built walls, and rock-faces. Most of the documents are written in a cuneiform syllabic script, but no small number are in other scripts, including an alphabetic one and the distinctive hieroglyphic script carved on the public monuments that dot the Hittite and Neo-Hittite landscapes. The great advantage of the majority of these documents is that they are *contemporary* records. That is to say, the information they contain and the events they record belong to the actual period of composition. They are in the main official records—produced by or on behalf of an elite administrative class, reflecting the interests of that class, and putting their own political spin on the particular event or set of events they report. There is an obvious downside to this. From the documents themselves, we generally learn very little about the men and women whose personal attributes, with all their strengths and weaknesses, are masked by the official pronouncements made by them or in their names. More we sometimes learn from the collections of letters, of various periods and regimes, that passed between a king and members of his family, a king and his vassal rulers, kings of equal status, and between bureaucrats, merchants, and other beings of a lower order. These letters sometimes have much to tell us about the personalities of their senders and recipients, and the dynamics of their relations with one another—information that is excluded from the decrees, dedications, and records of achievements that are produced for more public display.

Particularly from the period of the Persian Achaemenid empire to the end of our narrative, we are served with a much greater array of written sources. Inscriptions, coin legends, and other forms of official documents continue to provide a valuable repository of contemporary information about their respective periods. But we have an abundance of 'literary' sources as well. These have the advantage of being, for the most part, independent, non-official records, and thus, in theory at least, provide more detached views of the events and the persons whose stories they relate. Of course they are themselves often highly biased, both in the cast they give to particular events and in the motives and behaviour they assign to the persons involved in them; and what they report is often influenced more by a desire to entertain and titillate (sometimes under the guise of moral outrage) than to inform in an objective way. Too, many of the literary sources date many years, sometimes centuries, after the events they deal with. They are themselves dependent on earlier sources which are often no longer extant. On the other hand, we are frequently blessed (sometimes to excess!) with a range of ancient writers from whom we can draw our information on such matters as the internecine squabbles of the Seleucid dynasty, the contests for the imperial succession in the Roman period, particularly as they affected Syria, and the struggles to win sovereignty over Syria—from the Achaemenid through the Roman era. Sometimes multiple sources for a particular episode agree with one another, sometimes they are at complete variance. The historian's task is to assess the credibility of each as a basis for reconstructing the history of the period or periods with which they deal. And indeed the reliability of the various sources has been the subject of much learned research by scholars, in their quest for truth, promotion, and funding for conference travel.

I should single out here one source of which we should be especially wary. It is the one commonly known as the *Scriptores Historiae Augustae* ('the writers of the Augustan History'), or the *Historia Augusta* for short. Supposedly covering the reigns of all Roman emperors from Hadrian to Diocletian's predecessor Numerian (i.e. the period AD 117–284), the work is really a literary concoction put together by one person, who lived probably in the reign of the 4th-century emperor Theodosius I. Much of it is a mixture of pseudo-historical episodes and characters, fake documents (including many letters), and pure fantasy. It has to be said that Edward Gibbon draws extensively on this work for the relevant section of his grand *Decline and Fall*—which means in effect that the Gibbonian masterpiece is based, for a large part of its narrative, on an elaborate ancient literary confidence trick. But amid the dross of pure invention which liberally covers the pages of this reputed history a nugget of genuine fact does sometimes gleam forth. Like all the best hoaxes, literary and otherwise, the *Historia Augusta* contains some half truths or even full truths, so we cannot entirely discount everything it says. Indeed, though lots of disparaging noises are made about the *HA*, it is rare to find a scholar who completely dismisses it. Besides, some of its stories are too temptingly entertaining to discard altogether, fantastic though they may be. Most scholars who refer to these stories, albeit with some scepticism, really do want to have their cake and eat it too. I am no different. I shall be alluding to the *HA* on a number of occasions in my chapters on Roman history, including the section on Palmyra, but always on the understanding that my piece of cake will be seasoned with a good deal more than just the one proverbial grain of salt.

Of course, all historical reconstruction is largely a matter of interpreting and assessing what our original sources tell us, and then piecing together a narrative from the information they contain. So too my history of Syria is based on my interpretation of the relevant sources, and my assessment of how reliable each source is, whether it be an official document on a clay tablet, a sealing or coin legend, a monumental inscription on a rock-face, a passage from the Old Testament,[4] or an item from the literature of the Classical period. The endnotes contain a select number of the ancient sources I have used in compiling my story, the bibliography a selection of the secondary literature, books and articles by modern scholars who have dealt at greater length with the various periods my story covers, and often provide a critical assessment of the sources on which they are based.

It is important to stress that in writing this historical narrative I have confined my attention almost entirely to the political and military events of the periods in question. My focus is above all on the human characters who instigated, participated in, and became the victims of these events. Inevitably, a history of this kind is fairly narrowly based. For the specific individuals who inhabit its pages come from a very select group—those who sat atop the power structures of their societies. It is they who made the news, and had their names and deeds preserved because of it. It is their lives and careers that dominate Syria's recorded history, almost to the exclusion of the ordinary people of Syrian society, who mostly went about their daily affairs unheralded and unheeded—except when they were caught up in the wars that engulfed their communities, or rose up in rebellion, or became the victims of massacres (sometimes all three of these things in rapid succession) as their leaders set about the task of plotting and fighting against and murdering one another.

But when all is said and done, our human characters strut but briefly on life's stage, and often exit it as abruptly as they enter it. The cities they inhabit or conquer generally live much longer, their lifespan sometimes extending across several of the periods traversed by our story, and occasionally across all of them. Some cities flourish, decline, and then rise once more before sinking into oblivion fairly early in our narrative, like Ebla and Mari. Others are more enduring—like Carchemish, which appears first in the Ebla archives, reaches its peak in the Late Bronze Age as a Hittite viceregal kingdom, then re-emerges in the Iron Age as an archetypal Neo-Hittite state before it too disappears forever. Some cities are late starters—like Antioch, born in the early Seleucid period then growing to become one of the greatest cities of the Roman empire. Other cities like Sidon and Tyre remain with us throughout our story. So too Damascus, which waxes and wanes across the ages until in the epilogue to our tale it rises supreme as the capital of the new Muslim empire.

In focusing primarily on the political and military events of the ages covered by this tale, and particularly on the 'big people' who inhabited these ages, I have concentrated on but one aspect of Syria's history. There are other complementary stories to be told—of the great works of art and architecture that were created, of flourishing international trade and commerce in and beyond the Syrian region,[5] of the multifaceted cultures that gave Syria its distinctive character, and of the archaeological investigations that have contributed so much to what we know about Syrian history and the societies of which it was composed. Each of these is important to a full understanding of ancient Syria. On each of them books could be, and have been, written. A fully comprehensive history of the region would embrace them all. That is an ambitious undertaking, well beyond the scope of this book.

Which brings us to the question of what we actually mean by Syria. First attested in Greek in the *Histories* of Herodotus, the name is almost certainly a variant of 'Assyria', the Bronze and Iron Age kingdom based in northern Mesopotamia. In its ancient context, 'Syria' is used by many scholars in a broad geographical sense to cover a conglomerate of lands extending southwards from south-eastern Anatolia to Arabia, through the Amuq plain of modern Turkey, the modern country of Syria west of the Euphrates, and the territories of Israel, Palestine, Lebanon, and Jordan,[6] and eastwards from the Mediterranean littoral to the western fringes of Mesopotamia.[7] It should of course be stressed that ancient Syria as so described excludes the large and economically important triangular area of modern Syria that is delineated by the Euphrates on the west, the Habur river and its tributaries on the east, and the mountain-lands to the north. (In the pages that follow, this area will be included in the region broadly referred to as northern Mesopotamia.) Whatever their compass, the lands comprising 'ancient Syria' retained throughout the ages a high degree of ethnic and cultural homogeneity, despite their populations being intermixed with constant influxes of immigrants into their communities and cities—new settlers sometimes forcibly transplanted from other parts of the Near Eastern world. At different times in its history, and with varying degrees of success, Syria's conquerors tried to impose some degree of administrative coherence upon the cities and kingdoms of the region, like the Hittites and Egyptians in the second millennium BC, and the Assyrians and Babylonians in the first.

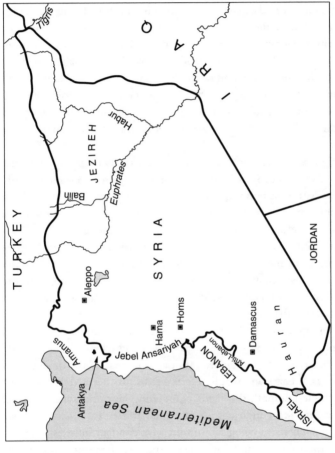

Map 1. Modern Syria and its neighbours (after P. Akkermans and G. Schwartz, *The Archaeology of Syria* (Cambridge: Cambridge University Press, 2003) p. 3)

Syria subsequently became a province of the Persian Achaemenid empire, its governor responsible for an extensive spread of territories which in the west stretched from the Amanus range in south-eastern Anatolia along the coast to the Peninsula of Sinai, and in the east touched upon the Euphrates. In the Roman period, Syria was more narrowly defined when Pompey the Great established a province of this name in 64 BC. The territory then covered by Roman Syria was expanded by later Roman rulers. We shall have more to say about its components in Part IV.

Topographically, Syria in both its ancient and its modern contexts consists of a series of diverse sub-regions, with dramatically contrasting vegetation, rainfall patterns, and temperature-ranges. Its westernmost part, a narrow fertile strip along the Mediterranean coast with a typically Mediterranean climate (up to 1000 mm of rain annually), is separated by mountainous terrain, notably the Jebel Ansariyah range in the north and the anti-Lebanon range south of it, from the region's interior, a dominant feature of which is the vast semi-arid and arid plateau called the Syrian Desert. Yet despite its large tracts of inhospitable terrain, Syria provided what has often been called the crossroads of the Near East, because through it passed some of the most important routes that linked Mesopotamia and lands further east with the land of the Nile, and the lands of the Mediterranean and the western world beyond it. That helps account for the rich cultural melting pot that ancient Syria became, clearly reflected in its archaeological remains as well as in its written records. And it also accounts for the wealth and affluence that characterized many regions and cities of Syria through much of its history. The downside of all this is that Syria provided killing grounds and plunder houses for a succession of rapacious outsiders. And their quest was often not only for booty and plunder. Syria was strategically important. If you wanted to be a Great King in the Near Eastern world, you had to have control of Syria, or at least a good deal of it. That's why so much of Syria's history has to do with outsiders who fought one another over it, like Hittites and Egyptians and Assyrians and Babylonians and Persians and Macedonians and Romans. Syria suffered at least as much as it benefited from its international intruders.

Finally, some words about the book's contents and its division into five parts. Part I covers Syria's story, or stories, throughout the Bronze Ages, from the rise of Ebla in the Early Bronze Age through the ascendancy of Yamhad and Mari in the Middle Bronze Age to the conflicts between the Great Kingdoms of the Late Bronze Age—especially Egypt, Hatti, Mitanni, and Assyria. Part II extends from the dawning of a new age, the so-called Iron

Age, when the Neo-Hittite kingdoms were a marked feature of Syria's political and cultural landscape, through the period of Assyrian domination of the region, followed by the domination in turn of the Babylonian and Persian Achaemenid empires, and the short-lived empire built by Alexander the Great. In Part III, we are once again in a transformed world, the world which began with the death of Alexander and the squabbles among his heirs over the spoils of his empire. Control of Syria was contested by Alexander's Ptolemaic and Seleucid heirs, with the latter finally prevailing. But the Seleucid empire gave way to the Roman when Pompey the Great made Syria a part of the Roman world in 64 BC. In Part IV, Rome becomes the dominant character in Syria's story.

The history of Israel and Judah/Judaea is often closely intertwined with that of Syria in the periods with which we shall be dealing, and a number of episodes of Jewish history figure in this book throughout its ages; notably Israel's participation in the alliance which fought the Neo-Assyrian armies at Qarqar on the Orontes in the 9th century BC, the Jewish rebellions against the Babylonian king Nebuchadnezzar in the early 6th century BC, which led to the destruction of Jerusalem and the beginning of the Jewish exile, the Maccabean rebellion in the 2nd century BC, to which I have given a chapter of its own, the uprising against the Romans in the 1st century AD, leading to the destruction of Jerusalem by Titus, son of the emperor Vespasian, in the year 70, and the Bar Kochba rebellion, near the end of the emperor Hadrian's reign, in the years 131–4 AD.

Part V of our book tells the story of Palmyra. Three chapters are devoted to this story. The desert-city's origins extend back to at least the 19th century BC when as an oasis-settlement called Tadmor it first appears in Assyrian merchant texts. But its most distinguished phase belongs to the Roman imperial era, when it developed as a great metropolis, the wealthy and monumental city Palmyra, now one of the world's finest archaeological treasures. It is to the Roman period of its development that our story of Palmyra is almost entirely confined—indeed very largely to a few years within this era, when its queen Zenobia became one of Rome's most formidable enemies. For a short time, Palmyra co-starred with Rome itself on the international stage. It thus has a special significance in the story of Syria, which throughout its various ages was cast more often in a secondary than in a leading role. For this reason I have devoted a full section to Palmyra, with a special emphasis on its famous leader. The story of Queen Zenobia's triumph and tragedy deserves to be played out in full.

PART
I

The Bronze Ages

I

The First Kingdoms

27th–24th centuries BC

Ebla unearthed

Spectacular things were happening in Mesopotamia in the period we call the Early Bronze Age, particularly in the southern part of it, commonly called Babylonia. It was here that the wealthy, sophisticated Sumerian civilization developed, its growth and prosperity greatly spurred by the invention of writing. A magnificent assortment of beautifully wrought items, like those unearthed from the so-called royal tombs of Ur and now on display in the British Museum, testifies to the high level of craftsmanship of the Sumerian civilization at its zenith. In the wake of the Sumerian Early Dynastic period (*c.*2900–2334), there arose in southern Mesopotamia the first great empire in Near Eastern history—the Akkadian empire (*c.*2334–2193) founded by Sargon, which at its peak extended through the whole of Mesopotamia, and north-westwards into south-eastern Anatolia. Early Bronze Age Mesopotamia's archaeological remains and prolific tablet-finds provided rich and exciting fields of investigation for archaeologists, historians, and linguists alike.

But across the Euphrates in Syria, the picture was much bleaker, so it seemed, if you happened to be any of these. Up until the 1960s, third-millennium Syria was generally thought of as no more than 'an illiterate backwater of small communities far removed from the great developments of civilization occurring in Mesopotamia and Egypt'.[1] But there must have been more to it than this! And indeed it was quite possible that the numerous unexplored mounds (tells) throughout the region did include remains of settlements of various kinds contemporary with the first great civilizations of Mesopotamia. But attention was too much focused on other regions that offered surer prospects of significant finds, in Mesopotamia, Egypt, and Palestine. None the less, an Italian archaeologist, Paolo Matthiae, believed

Map 2. Syria in the Middle and Late Bronze Ages

that Syria should not be entirely neglected. And he selected a site now
called Tell Mardikh in northern Syria, some 60 km south-west of Aleppo,
for further investigation.

Potsherds found scattered over its surface gave an indication of its early
date, and the unusually large dimensions of the tell which marked the site
persuaded Professor Matthiae that it was worth a closer look. The upshot of

this was that in 1964 he led the first of what were to be many campaigns at Tell Mardikh as head of the Italian Archaeological Expedition of the University 'La Sapienza' of Rome. It soon became evident that there was in fact a major settlement on the site at the time of Syria's so-called 'backwater period'. But it took four years before the site could actually be identified. That happened in 1968 when part of a statue was found, with an inscription. The statue was dedicated to the goddess Ishtar, by a man called Ibbit-Lim, king of Ebla. So Tell Mardikh was in fact the ancient city of Ebla—a city already known to us from a wide range of texts. The earliest of them record the conquest of Ebla by Akkadian kings, Sargon and his grandson Naram-Sin, and the city appears later in economic texts of the Ur III empire (i.e. the empire of the Third Dynasty of Ur; 2112–2004). These written records clearly established Ebla's existence as early as the 24th century BC. Its subsequent existence, after the Ur III empire, is attested in texts from Alalah in northern Syria, dating to the 17th and 15th centuries BC, and in the latter century it appears in the list of Syro-Palestinian conquests of the pharaoh Tuthmosis III.

So the site of Ebla had been discovered, and information about it was available from a range of external sources. But could Ebla also speak for

Figure 1. Ebla, Palace G

itself? The answer to that question came in 1974, as Matthiae and his team
worked patiently through the site's layers. Up till then, Ebla had attracted
little interest outside the world of Near Eastern archaeology, and indeed
relatively muted interest within it. The 1974 excavations dramatically
changed all that. Already the year before, Matthiae's team while excavating
on the western slope of the acropolis came upon signs of a major building
complex just below the mound's surface. The full extent and significance of
this complex became clear in the 1974 excavations. It was a large, sprawling
structure, whose walls in parts still reached a height of seven metres, built
around two sides of a large open area now called 'the court of audience',
with a raised dais made of mudbrick against its north wall. Was this the base
of a royal throne? There was no doubt that the building was a royal palace.
It is now called, rather prosaically, 'Palace G', and in archaeological terms it
belongs to what is called the Mardikh (or Ebla) IIB1 period.

   In itself this vast, multi-chambered complex was an important archaeological discovery—the earliest structure of its kind found anywhere in Syria,
clearly distinguishing Ebla as a major regional centre. But the most spectacular aspect of the find was a massive collection of thousands of clay tablets, often in fragments, inscribed with the cuneiform script[2] and located in
various rooms of the palace. Above all else, the tablet finds, excavated
between 1974 and 1976 (there have been only occasional discoveries since),
brought Ebla to world attention. Dating as they do to the 24th century, they
provide us with early evidence for writing in Syria. Particularly interesting
is the fact that many of them are written in a local Semitic language, now
dubbed 'Eblaite', and are thus the oldest significant evidence we have for
any Semitic language in written form. There are also a number of Sumerian
texts, including a hymn, and some lexical lists with Eblaite and Sumerian
equivalents, described as the most ancient dictionaries known.

   The actual contents of the great majority of the tablets are fairly mundane.
Apart from the few 'literary texts' (hymns etc.) and lexical texts, they are very
largely administrative documents, arranged in a number of different archives, to
do with the administration of Ebla and the surrounding region. They indicate
the existence of an enormous royal, highly centralized bureaucracy, employing
thousands of officials, and a broader workforce of artisans and labourers, all
documented in the palace records along with the food rations for their susten-
ance. That much of the wealth of Ebla was agriculturally based is reflected in
the palace records which indicate the large flocks of sheep owned by the king,
and the thriving textile industry associated with wool production. The tablets

tell us of the distribution of these products, both to local officials within the Ebla region and to important foreigners. Mundane though they may be, we learn much from the tablets about the highly efficient organization of the Eblaite state and its strict administrative and social hierarchy.

But the tablets are also important more broadly for what they tell us about social, political, and economic conditions in northern Syria in the mid third millennium,[3] that is to say in the middle of the Early Bronze Age, and the pattern of city-states in the region at this time, with king, royal officials, and 'elders' at the top of the hierarchy. A large assortment of economic, administrative, legal, lexical, literary, diplomatic, and epistolary texts provide valuable insights into the administration, daily life, and culture of Ebla and its relations with its surrounding region during this phase of its existence, including its competition with Mari on the middle Euphrates (to which we shall return). A number of other finds in Palace G provide further evidence of the richness of this phase of Ebla's history. Contacts with Egypt are indicated by fragments of alabaster and diorite vessels from the land of the Nile, and large quantities of lapis lazuli indicate trading links as far afield as Afghanistan. The high level of Eblaite craftsmanship in this period is reflected in a human-headed bull figurine of steatite and gold foil attached to a wooden core, and limestone inlays applied to wooden panels used for wall decoration.[4] Fine works fashioned in gold, lapis lazuli, and ivory found in the palace are Babylonian in origin, or inspiration. More generally, there is no doubt that the development of Ebla as a politically, commercially, and culturally sophisticated centre owed much to its strong cultural links with a number of contemporary cities of Babylonia.

From both written and archaeological sources, we can build up a picture of Ebla as the most politically and commercially powerful kingdom of northern Syria in the Early Bronze Age.[5] Archaeologically, it is extremely important for our understanding of Syria's urban and commercial development in this period. By then, Syria contained a complex of city-states, each ruled by a king, whose relations with the rulers of Ebla are recorded in the Palace G archives. The territory over which Ebla held sway was clearly a substantial one—as it needed to be, given the region's relatively low rainfall and the necessity of having a large area to graze the flocks that produced abundant quantities of wool for a flourishing textile industry. Clearly too, Ebla's wealth and importance derived from its centrality within an international trading network, with links with southern Syria, central Anatolia, Mesopotamia, and regions further to the east. For a brief time, Ebla was a tributary of Mari, but it regained its independence after about fifteen years

and became Mari's chief political and commercial rival. This we learn from
the kingdom's archives, which tell us of three kings who ruled Ebla during
the three-generation period covered by the tablets—Igriš-Halab, Irkab-
Damu, and Išar-Damu. But there were many more Eblaite kings. An
offering-list found in the archives names of ten of them, of whom Irkab-
Damu was the last. There were more names still. Another text from Ebla lists
twenty-six kings, including the group of ten named in the offering-list plus
Ebla's last king (successor to Irkab-Damu) Išar-Damu. This tells us that the
line of Ebla's rulers, and hence the royal city itself, extended back at least
three centuries before the peak of its power in the 24th century. That is to
say, Ebla's history as a royal seat dates back at least to the 27th century BC.

24th–21st centuries BC

The end of this great phase of Ebla's existence was due to its destruction
by an Akkadian king, almost certainly Sargon, though Sargon's grandson
Naram-Sin claimed responsibility. It may well be that one or other of these
rulers believed that the kingdom was getting too powerful, to the point
where it threatened Akkadian territorial ambitions west of the Euphrates, or
at least refused to cooperate with the Akkadians in their western enterprises.
But Ebla's lifespan was far from at an end. It had a first new lease of life when
a modest new settlement, designated Mardikh IIB2, was built on the northern part of the site following the Akkadian destruction. The most significant
building of this phase, now called the 'Archaic Palace', was probably the residence of a new or revived line of local kings, possibly collaborators if not
subordinates of the rulers of the Ur III empire, successor to the Akkadian
empire. But the new city was short-lived. It too was destroyed, about 2000,
around the time the Ur III empire was finished off, and perhaps by the same
agents (see below). Ebla would rise again. As we shall see, it was to have at
least one major regeneration before its final decline and abandonment.

The Amorites

At this point, we should say something about the Amorites, who will figure
prominently, in one way or another, through much of the next part of our
story.[6] They are probably best known today as one of the peoples of the Old
Testament, where they are listed in the Table of Nations amongst the tribal

groups, occupying parts of Canaan, whom God ordered the Israelites to destroy: 'However, in the cities of the Nations the Lord your God is giving you as an inheritance, do not leave anything alive that breathes. Completely destroy them—the Hittites, Amorites, Canaanites, Perizzites, Hivites, and Jebusites—as the Lord your God has commanded you' (Deut. 20:16–17). (We shall come back to other members in this list.) Speakers of a north-west Semitic language, the Amorites consisted originally of a number of nomadic groups who inhabited parts of Syria and Palestine. By the 24th century, some of them had moved to Ebla and settled there, as we know from Amorite names in the city's archives. No doubt the secure, prosperous, and culturally sophisticated environment which Ebla offered, as did places further south like Qatna and Hamath which probably also had Amorite populations at this time, were inducement enough for the traditional pastor-alists to exchange their nomadic lifestyle for a more settled urban one.

But as their tribal cousins were settling into the comforts and security of a Syro-Palestinian urban existence, other Amorite groups who maintained their traditional lifestyle began spreading eastwards into southern Mesopo-tamia. Perhaps drought conditions forced them to seek new pasturelands for their flocks and herds across the Euphrates. As their numbers east of the river grew, so did the threat they posed to the kingdoms and city-states of their new homeland. Amorites now show up in Sumerian texts, under the name MAR.TU, meaning 'west' (that is to say, they came from the west), and the references to them are distinctly hostile. A Sumerian literary composi-tion speaks of them as boorish, rootless, uncultured savages: 'The MAR.TU who know no grain . . . no house nor town, the boors of the mountains. The MAR.TU who digs up truffles . . . who does not bend his knees (to cultivate the land), who eats raw meat, who has no house during his lifetime, who is not buried after his death . . . '.[7]

What the relationship is between the Amorites referred to here and those attested in the Eblaite texts of the same period is unclear. In any case, the Akkadian kings Sargon and Naram-Sin became involved in conflicts with the intruders. Naram-Sin finally defeated them when he quashed the 'Great Revolt', a widespread uprising of his subject cities, at a place called 'the mountain of (the land) Martu' (Basar, modern Jebel Bishri). But the Amor-ite menace persisted. After the fall of the Akkadian empire, Amorite groups consistently pressed upon territories claimed by the new overlords of Babylonia, the kings of the Ur III dynasty. In an attempt to keep their lands free of the Amorites, the kings built a chain of fortifications or watchtowers across northern Babylonia. Their efforts failed. But the Ur III empire was soon to end anyway. Around 2004, it was destroyed—not, as it happened, by the Amorites but by invaders from south-western Iran called the Elamites. The situation was ripe for exploitation. Amorite chieftains moved quickly to fill the power vacuum in the region left by the Elamite victory, setting themselves up as rulers of a number of Babylonian cities formerly subject to the Akkadian and Ur III kings, including Larsa, Babylon, Kish, Marad, and Sippar. Discarding their ancestral nomadic origins, the Amorites had by now completely assimilated to urban society.

20th–18th centuries BC

That brings us to the great Amorite rulers who emerged in the first centuries of the second millennium BC—the Middle Bronze Age—and the kingdoms over which they held sway. The first of these was a man called Samsi-Addu (Akkadian Shamshi-Adad) (1796–1775), who brought to its peak the first great kingdom of Assyria. From the traditional Assyrian capital Ashur on the Tigris river, Samsi-Addu conquered and consolidated the territories between the Tigris and Euphrates rivers into 'the Kingdom of Upper Mesopotamia', and embarked on a series of military campaigns which took him westwards to the Mediterranean coast. In the process, he seized control of the strategically valuable kingdom of Mari on the Euphrates.

Mari and its contemporaries

Before we speak of Mari under Assyrian rule, let us pick up on the kingdom's earlier history. By the middle of the third millennium, Mari had become a wealthy city, due largely to its participation in international trading activities between Babylonia and Syria. It competed with Ebla for dominance over northern Syria, and for a brief time Ebla was Mari's tributary. During the Akkadian period, Mari suffered violent destruction, in circumstances unknown to us, but towards the end of the period it enjoyed a revival under a line of rulers called the Shakkanakku dynasty, initially installed by the Akkadian administration. When the Akkadian empire fell, Mari regained its independence and enjoyed further growth and redevelopment before it declined and sank into obscurity in the late third millennium. It rose to prominence once more with the accession of a king called Yahdun-

Lim (1810–1794), who extended his sway over a broad expanse of territory in the middle Euphrates lands, and led an expedition to the west, to stock up on quantities of the prized timbers of Lebanon.[8]

But Yahdun-Lim had to exercise some caution in his territory-acquiring enterprises on both sides of the Euphrates and his timber-getting expeditions in the west. For the Middle Bronze Age saw the emergence of other kingdoms in these regions, whose territorial ambitions might well lead them into war with Mari. One of the most important of these, and the most direct threat to Mari, was a kingdom called Yamhad.[9] Its rulers were also of Amorite stock. By the beginning of the 18th century, Yamhad had become the major power of northern Syria. Under nine successive kings, it dominated the region for two centuries (c.1800 to 1600), holding sway over a number of the cities and states that lay between the Euphrates and the Orontes rivers. Its capital became one of Syria's most famous cities—Aleppo.

The first of Yamhad's rulers, Sumu-epuh (–1781), was a contemporary of Yahdun-Lim. To begin with, neither king seems to have wanted a test of strength with the other. Northern Syria was big enough for both of them. And so they made a pact, no doubt involving an agreement over where their respective territorial limits lay, which was cemented by a marriage alliance when Yahdun-Lim married a princess of Aleppo. But relations between the kingdoms eventually turned sour—and that was due partly to another group of Amorites, a confederation of nomadic and semi-nomadic tribes called the Yaminites. In their search for suitable grazing lands, the Yaminites had spread over large areas of Mesopotamia and northern Syria. (They also made a habit of raiding local towns and cities in the regions through which they roamed, making the roads unsafe for travel.) But their tribal encampments were located principally in the middle Euphrates region, in the territories over which Yahdun-Lim claimed sovereignty. They were thus subjects of the Mariote king, albeit not particularly willing ones. In one of his inscriptions, Yahdun-Lim reports that three of their chieftains rebelled against him, and had done so with the support of Sumu-epuh.[10] Indeed, Sumu-epuh may have provoked the rebellion. Yahdun-Lim was quick to put it down, in a pitched battle with the three rebel leaders at the town of Samanum, a port city on the middle Euphrates. But there remained a score to settle with Sumu-epuh for his meddling in Mari's affairs.

A possible reason for this interference brings us to another Syrian kingdom to emerge under an Amorite dynasty in the early second millennium.

This was Qatna, located in central Syria just east of the Orontes river, 18 km north-east of modern Homs (Emesa).[11] From early in their history, Aleppo and Qatna became bitter rivals. And any third party who supported either of them was bound to be regarded by the other as his enemy. It may well be that an alliance between Mari and Qatna was established during Yahdun-Lim's reign, as there certainly was after his death. If so, it could have provoked Sumu-epuh into supporting the Yaminite rebellion against Yahdun-Lim, in the hope that the Mariote king would become too preoccupied with the affairs of his own kingdom to take on board any request for assistance from Qatna. Tensions certainly flared between Yamhad and Mari during Yahdun-Lim's reign. But the kingdoms never actually came to blows in this period. And after Yahdun-Lim's death around 1794, his son and successor Sumu-Yamam may have tried to put relations with Sumu-epuh back on a peaceful footing—until deprived of the opportunity by an assassin's hand, within two years of his accession. Suspicion falls upon the man who now seized control of his kingdom as the instigator of his murder, Samsi-Addu, ruler of the Kingdom of Upper Mesopotamia.

After establishing his authority over Mari, Samsi-Addu spent some years redeveloping and refurbishing the palace there, and finally installed one of his sons, Yasmah-Addu, as the city's viceroy. On the international front, Samsi-Addu's relations with the Yamhadite king Sumu-epuh were cordial, to begin with. But they turned hostile as Sumu-epuh became alarmed at the spread of Assyrian influence across the Euphrates, particularly when Samsi-Addu sought out and obtained a peace accord with Yamhad's arch-enemy in the south, Qatna. The king of Qatna, Ishhi-Addu, was no doubt as eager as Samsi-Addu for the accord, which was consolidated by a marriage alliance between his daughter Beltum and Samsi-Addu's son Yasmah-Addu. At Ishhi-Addu's insistence, the bride was to hold the rank of Queen of Mari. The peace agreement gave Mariote shepherds grazing rights in Qatna's territory, in the event of drought in their own land. Of greater moment, it led to Samsi-Addu's direct involvement on the side of Qatna, in Ishhi-Addu's war with Yamhad.

Mari played an extremely important role in Samsi-Addu's kingdom, from a commercial as well as a political and military viewpoint. The extensive clay tablet archives unearthed during French excavations there (more than 22,000 tablets have come to light) provide much information about the city's administration and relations with other states, and include many letters written to the viceroy Yasmah-Addu by his father, and by his brother Ishme-

Dagan, appointed viceroy in the city of Ekallatum further east. Yasmah-Addu cuts a rather poor figure in these letters. His father constantly complains of his idleness, immaturity, and dereliction of duty, taking him to task for giving more attention to women, fast horses, and the contents of his cellar than to the affairs of state. 'Are you a child, not a man, have you no beard on your chin?' rebukes his father. 'Even now when you have reached maturity, you have not set up a home.... While your brother has won a great victory here, you remain there [in Mari], reclining among the women.'[12] Despite his shortcomings, Yasmah-Addu retained his viceregal seat for eight years, until 1775 when the Kingdom of Upper Mesopotamia disintegrated, not long after its founder's death. This first Assyrian kingdom barely out-lived the reign of the king who built it.

Its disintegration paved the way for the return of the family that had ruled Mari before the Assyrians took it over. When Yasmah-Addu was viceroy, one of the members of this family, a child called Zimri-Lim, prob-ably Yahdun-Lim's nephew or grandson, was spirited away from the city by his carers and taken to a place of safety out of Yasmah-Addu's reach. Per-haps Aleppo. Now, Zimri-Lim returned to Mari in triumph, at the head of an army. News of his approach reached the city in time for a panic-stricken Yasmah-Addu to pack his bags and head for the hills. In this way Zimri-Lim reclaimed the throne of 'his father' Yahdun-Lim, and embarked on a reign, very largely successful, lasting thirteen years. His time on the throne is the best documented period in Mari's history, for the majority of tablets found in the palace archives belong to it.[13] The reign was as noteworthy for its diplomatic as it was for its military achievements. One of the impor-tant diplomatic events in it was the conclusion by Zimri-Lim of a peace accord with Yamhad's king Yarim-Lim, son and successor of Sumu-epuh.[14] The accord was cemented with a marriage alliance when one of Yarim-Lim's daughters became Zimri-Lim's bride. Relations between Mari and Qatna also remained peaceful during this period. And east of the Euphra-tes, Zimri-Lim secured an alliance with one of the great rulers of the Near Eastern world, Hammurabi, king of Babylon. Mari was now at the peak of its development. And its wealth, derived in large measure from its central position in an international trading network, enabled Zimri-Lim to com-plete the city's great palace-complex on a scale of unprecedented size and splendour.

It was not to last. Relations between Mari and Babylon suddenly took a turn for the worse, for reasons unknown to us, and the staunch alliance betweeen the two kingdoms gave way to bitter enmity. The outcome was disastrous for Mari. In 1762, Hammurabi attacked, seized, looted, and destroyed the city. It would later be rebuilt, on a modest scale, but Hammurabi's destruction of Mari cost it forever its role as a major player in Near Eastern affairs. Yamhad now became the dominant power of northern Syria, a position for which Yarim-Lim had already paved the way, some years earlier, by concluding an alliance with Hammurabi, and establishing a peaceful relationship with his counterpart in Qatna. Holding sway over some twenty subject rulers, Yarim-Lim was indisputably one of the great kings of the Near Eastern world in its Middle Bronze Age phase. A letter written by an official of Mari provides us with valuable information on the distribution of power in Mesopotamia and Syria during his reign: 'No king is truly powerful just on his own. Ten to fifteen kings follow Hammurabi of Babylon, Rim-Sin of Larsa, Ibal-pi-El of Eshnunna, or Amut-pi-El of Qatna; but twenty kings follow Yarim-Lim of Yamhad.'[15]

We shall be hearing more of Yamhad and its kings in the next episode of Syria's story. For a time it was to flourish as one of the great kingdoms of its age, before becoming locked in a contest-to-the-death with a formidable new military power that descended upon it, via passes in the Taurus mountains, from the Anatolian plateau.

2

The International Intruders

His forces mustered before the walls of Carchemish, Suppiluliuma, king of the Hittites, was preparing for his final assault on this last remaining stronghold of the once great Mitannian empire. But his attention was momentarily diverted by news just received. There was a messenger from Egypt, with an urgent letter from its queen. The message-bearer was brought to the king, and the letter delivered. It was written in Akkadian, the international language of diplomacy. Suppiluliuma bade one of his bilingual scribes read it to him, translating it as he did so into Hittite. As the king heard its contents, his expression, normally impassive, turned to amazement. 'Such a thing has never happened to me in all my life!' he declared. But amazement turned quickly to suspicion. 'Maybe they are deceiving me.' He summoned his vizier. 'Go to Egypt,' he commanded, 'and bring me back the truth.'

So began one of the most extraordinary, and ultimately one of the most tragic personal episodes in ancient Near Eastern history. Dating to the year 1327 BC, it involved three of the Great Kingdoms of the age. All were intruders into Syria—Hatti, kingdom of the Hittites, now reaching the pinnacle of its power in the Near East, Mitanni, now in its final death throes,[1] and Egypt, now facing one of the most serious crises in its monarchy since the united kingdom of Egypt had been established eighteen hundred years earlier.

17th century BC

To set the scene for all this, we need to retrace our steps to the 17th century. At this time, Yamhad was still the dominant power of northern Syria, and Aleppo still its capital. In the second half of the century, the kingdom was ruled by Yarim-Lim (III), a descendant of the first Yamhadite ruler so called.

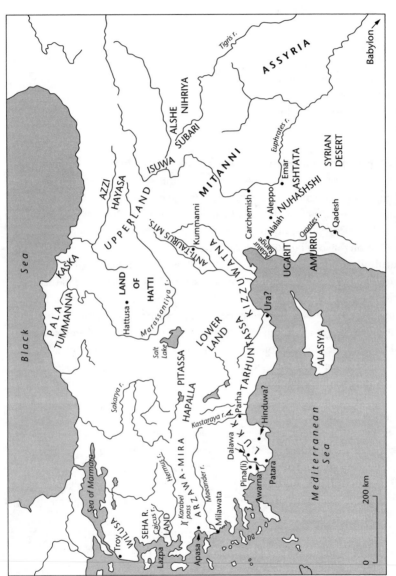

Map 3. Late Bronze Age Anatolia, northern Syria, and northern Mesopotamia

Its subject territories included the vassal kingdom of Alalah, located in the Amuq plain near the mouth of the Orontes river. Alalah's fortified urban centre is revealed to us today in seventeen archaeological levels, extending through the Middle and Late Bronze Ages. Level VII dates to the second half of the 17th century, when the local ruler, subordinate to Yarim-Lim, was a man called Ammitaqum (II). So we learn from tablet archives belonging to this period of the city's history. Some two hundred tablets have survived from these archives, which provide important and otherwise unknown contemporary information about Yamhad and its capital Aleppo, for Aleppo itself has left us no written records of this period.[2]

To the south-west of Aleppo and very likely subject to it, the city of Ebla was enjoying a relatively prosperous existence. Having risen once more from the ashes of its destruction at the end of the third millennium, it had already in the early second millennium been rebuilt on an impressive scale, at a time when many other sites in the region were abandoned or impoverished. In this period (c.2000–1800), Ebla was a well-planned city, laid out on regular lines and protected by a double fortification wall. Sacred and secular buildings were constructed in the lower part of the settlement, and large public buildings on the acropolis. Further building and reconstruction took place in the following period (c.1800–1600). We have no written records for this phase of the city's history. But we can be fairly sure that Ebla was one of the vassal states ruled by Yarim-Lim III, king of Yamhad.

It is now time to turn our attention to Syria's international intruders, beginning with the people we call the Hittites.[3]

The Hittites in Syria

Some time during the Early Bronze Age, three groups of Indo-European-speaking peoples entered the Anatolian peninsula and settled there. One of them, the Palaians, occupied part of the rugged north-central region of Anatolia to the south of the Black Sea. It was called Pala in Hittite texts and Paphlagonia in later times. Another group, the Luwians, spread widely through central, western, and southern Anatolia. A third group, speakers of a language called Nesite, occupied north-central Anatolia, principally the area bounded by the river called the Marassantiya in Hittite texts, the Halys in Classical sources, and the Kızıl Irmak in modern times. Long before the Indo-European migrations, this region was called the Land of Hatti, and its indigenous inhabitants Hattians. By the early 17th century, the Nesite-speakers had established a ruling elite which held sway over Hatti, perhaps still largely populated by its indigenous stock. The new over-lords maintained the region's traditional name; they called themselves, as well as those over whom they ruled, 'the people of the Land of Hatti'. Late 19th-century scholars believed that the people so called in Egyptian and Assyrian texts of the period could be linked or even identified with the Hittites of the Bible. And ever since, we have used the name 'Hittite' to designate the inhab-itants of Late Bronze Age Hatti, an increasingly mixed bag of ethnic groups ruled by kings of Indo-European origin.[4] Through five centuries, from the 17th to the early 12th century BC, Hittite kings built and maintained an international empire, one of the Great Kingdoms of the age.

Syria entered the horizon of Hittite imperial ambitions in the reign of the 17th-century king Hattusili I, perhaps the founder of the Hittite royal capital Hattusa.[5] Following in the footsteps of his predecessor Labarna (probably his grandfather), Hattusili first imposed his authority upon the countries, states, and cities of southern Anatolia between his homeland and the shores of the Great Sea (the eastern Mediterranean). Then he set his sights upon conquests in Syria.[6] What induced him to go there? He already held sway over much of the Anatolian peninsula, and had to ensure that suf-ficient military resources were always on hand to maintain his authority there. What incentives were there for him to take on the costs, and the risks, of leading an army into Syria?

The basic answer is that any Near Eastern ruler who sought to make his kingdom a major power in the international scene needed to exercise some sort of control or influence over Syria, or at least a large part of it, as we have already observed. Unfettered access to the international merchandise that found its way into Syrian markets was a major consideration for any king-dom which claimed or sought international status. Military force may have been necessary to ensure this access—not merely to the many exotic luxury goods which passed through the Syrian world, but also to basic commodities, including in the Bronze Age tin, an essential ingredient in the manufacture of bronze. Most if not all the tin that entered the Hittite world came from distant eastern lands, like Iran or even Afghanistan, probably often passing through Syria on its way.

Defence considerations may also have motivated Hattusili's Syrian cam-paigns. For much of their early history, the Hittites were menaced by groups of peoples based in northern Mesopotamia and known collectively as the Hurrians, who gradually spread through northern Syria and eastern Anatolia, and ultimately threatened Hatti itself. Hittite military enterprises in Syria could help brake their territorial ambitions. Very likely this was one of the prompts for Hattusili's decision to invade Syria. There was also a personal ideological dimension to his enterprises. Royal ideology required that a king be a great warrior, and new kings could be expected to demonstrate their fitness to rule by finding new worlds to conquer. Hattusili had decided that Syria would be his new world. And once he had bedded down his Anatolian conquests, he set out upon his mission, marching his troops across the anti-Taurus ranges into the lands of northern Syria. He quickly met with armed resistance. Not in the first instance from the Hurrians, but from the allies and subjects of the kingdom of Yamhad. Alalah's archives provide the names of a number of these—Carchemish, Urshu, Hassu, Ugarit, Emar, Ebla, Tunip, and Alalah itself. An attack on any one of them was in effect an act of war against all of them, their overlord in particular. The stage was now set for a test of strength between the two great kingdoms, under the banners of their rulers Hattusili and Yarim-Lim III. In the background, the Hurrian problem still lurked. That would be dealt with in time. For the moment, the destruction of Yamhad and its capital Aleppo was the prime objective of Hattusili's Syrian enterprises. The Hittite king undertook at least five campaigns, perhaps many more, in his attempts to achieve this.

His basic strategy was to undermine the kingdom by whittling away its acolytes. And so on his first campaign, he singled out the walled city of Alalah as his main target. Launching the full fury of his army against the city, Hattusili besieged, captured, looted, and destroyed it. Surprisingly, there seems to have been no response from Yarim-Lim. Perhaps the speed and ferocity of the Hittite advance had caught him unawares.[7] But Hattusili had not yet built up sufficient momentum to march upon the Yamhadite capital Aleppo. He was not yet ready to confront Yarim-Lim on his own territory. Instead, he skirted to the north of the capital, and attacked several cities in the Euphrates region north of Carchemish, allies or subjects of Yamhad, before returning home. His first Syrian campaign had been essentially a probing operation. He had tested the strength of enemy resistance on Syrian soil, and in the process destroyed one of its major cities—thus eliminating an important source of support for Yarim-Lim while avoiding conflict with the Yamhadite king himself. On his way home, he picked off a few more of Yamhad's allies and subjects, further reducing its sources of military back-up—in anticipation of the time when the showdown between the two great kingdoms finally came. The Syrian states were left in no doubt that the Hittites would be back.

Not for a while, though. In the year following his first Syrian expedition, Hattusili was obliged to campaign against a troublesome western Anatolian region called Arzawa. But his military operations there were cut short when he received alarming news from home: a crisis had arisen in the heartland of his kingdom that required his immediate response: 'In my rear, the Hurrian enemy entered my land, and all the countries became hostile to me; the city Hattusa alone remained.'[8] The prompt return of the king and his army to their homeland was sufficient to drive the intruders from it and restore order there. But the Hurrians remained a constant menace, and would in the near future provide the Hittites with their most formidable opponent in a series of contests—whose ultimate prize was the domination of Syria.

For the rest of this year and the next, Hattusili was occupied with the suppression of further rebellions in his Anatolian territories. But then he was ready for his second Syrian campaign—and conducted it, he claimed, with the ferocity of a lion on the rampage: 'I marched against and destroyed Zaruna. Then I marched against Hassuwa. The men of Hassuwa came against me in battle, assisted by troops from Aleppo, and I overthrew them. Within a few days I crossed the river Puruna and I overcame Hassuwa like a lion with its paws. I heaped dust upon it, plundered it of all its possessions, and filled Hattusa with them.' Hassuwa lay in the Euphrates region, north of Carchemish. Other cities, Zaruna, Zippasna, and Hahha on the Euphrates, suffered a fate similar to Hassuwa's—they were looted and destroyed when they refused to surrender. Hahha had made a futile gesture of coming to Zippasna's assistance before it too came under siege. Three times Hahha's inhabitants rallied against their attackers before the city finally fell. Then the plunder began. The spoils of the city were loaded onto waggons for transport back to Hattusa. But Hattusili was not done yet. There was one final indignity to be inflicted upon the kings of Hassuwa and Hahha. They were hitched to one of the plunder-laden waggons and made to pull it to Hattusa.

17th–15th centuries BC

In Hattusili's account of his Syrian conquests, the kingdom of Yamhad itself receives almost no mention. But continued Hittite military successes in the Syrian region must have placed its very existence in jeopardy. We can be fairly certain that Hattusili made a number of attempts to seize its capital

Aleppo during his Syrian campaigns, and thereby deal a death blow to the kingdom. Nevertheless, at the end of his reign Aleppo remained intact, and the kingdom of Yamhad, though shorn of many of its subject states and allies, unsubdued. Its capital's massive fortifications were probably the chief obstacle to a comprehensive Hittite conquest of it. Like other campaigning armies, the Hittites found that laying siege to a well-fortified and well-stocked city could prove a long, costly, and ultimately unsuccessful operation. Indeed, it is possible that a last attempt by Hattusili to capture Aleppo ultimately cost him his life—a conclusion that *may* be drawn from a curious statement made by his successor.

To provide context for this, we need to go to a city called Kussara in the anti-Taurus region of south-eastern Anatolia. It was the ancestral home of the Hittite royal family, though the seat of the kingdom had later been shifted to Hattusa. The scene is set in Kussara's palace, in a room where a man lies dying. It is King Hattusili. Around his bed the dignitaries and military officers of the kingdom have gathered, for their overlord, his end near, has something important to say to them. There is a looming crisis in the succession. With a scribe at hand to record his every word, Hattusili tells the gathering that his nephew, the man designated for his throne, is to be rejected; he has been treacherous and disloyal, and is thus unfit for royal office. So it had been with the king's own sons! In what may have been his final moments, Hattusili announces a new heir to the throne, his grandson Mursili, now adopted as his son. Mursili is still a child, but there is no longer anyone else. The king's officials must ensure the stability of the kingdom by supporting the new king, nurturing him during his childhood years, and preparing him for the responsibilities of rule, giving him battle experience but protecting him in the battle's midst.[9]

The king's wishes were honoured, and Mursili inherited his throne. Then, when he reached manhood, he achieved what his grandfather had not—the conquest of Aleppo and the destruction of the kingdom of Yamhad. The record of this achievement survives in just two texts, each frustratingly brief. One is from the reign of a later Hittite king, Telipinu: 'Mursili went to the city of Aleppo (Halpa). He destroyed Aleppo, and brought Aleppo's deportees and its spoils to Hattusa.'[10] The other text reports the same victory, but contains the enigmatic statement: 'Mursili set out against Aleppo *to avenge his father's blood.* Hattusili had assigned Aleppo to his (grand-)son (to deal with). And to him the king of Aleppo made atonement.'[11] Mursili thus carried out his grandfather's legacy. But what does the expression 'avenge his

father's blood' mean precisely? Here is a hypothesis. It is possible that Hattusili's death resulted from a wound inflicted on him as he laid siege to
Aleppo in a final attempt to capture the city and bring down the kingdom.
The attempt was unsuccessful, and the wounded king's condition grew
worse. He was taken home to die. But his final days were spent not in his
capital Hattusa, but in his ancestral home Kussara. Was this his own choice—
to breathe his last and be buried in the home of his ancestors? Or was he
taken directly to Kussara, which must have lain on the quickest route back
to the Hittite homeland, because it was feared that he would not live to
reach Hattusa? In any case, the curious statement made in the second text
may add a dimension of personal revenge to Mursili's final onslaught on
Aleppo. The city was destroyed, and its king was captured and 'made atonement' to Mursili. The specific form this atonement took must be left to the
imagination.

But whatever we choose to imagine, there is no doubt that Mursili's victory over Aleppo was a decisive one. With the capture and destruction of its
capital, the kingdom of Yamhad was at an end. We hear no more of it in our
records. But Aleppo survived its destruction and was rebuilt. It was to play a
prominent role within the history of the Hittite kingdom—and in later
times too, as illustrated by an exciting discovery recently made on the city's
mound. We shall come to that in due course. For the moment, let us return
to Mursili. His conquest of Aleppo was not all he accomplished on this mission. While the city's ashes were still warm, he followed through with his
second main objective—the conquest of Babylon. An 800-kilometre march,
from Aleppo east to the Euphrates and then along the river, brought him to
the Babylonian capital. Mursili captured and sacked the city. Thus, abruptly
and violently, the first major epoch in Babylonian history was brought to an
end (c.1595). Its king at the time was a man called Samsuditana, the last in
the line of a royal dynasty whose most illustrious member was the Great
King Hammurabi.[12]

Mursili's army now returned home, laden with its treasures. At this point
in their history, the Hittites made no attempt to incorporate the lands they
had conquered into their sovereign territory. That would come later. In
Babylonia, the demise of Hammurabi's line left a power vacuum that would
eventually be filled by another royal dynasty, of Kassite origin.[13] But what of
the void left in Syria by the demise of Yamhad? On his way to or from
Babylon, Mursili had a military encounter with a group of people we have
already met—the Hurrians, who had attacked and occupied the Hittite

homeland during Hattusili's reign. We now meet them in a Syrian context, once more as enemies of the Hittites. They bring us in fact to the next stage in our story of Syria, and will for a time play a big part in it.

But let us first tie up a loose end. Around the time of Mursili's expedition to Aleppo and Babylon, the city of Ebla was once more destroyed. It had bounced back from earlier destructions, and though it never regained the political status it had enjoyed in the third millennium, it did experience several periods of prosperity and redevelopment in the first centuries of the second. Then, around the beginning of the 16th century, it suffered a further destruction, on a massive scale. The culprit is not identified, but we can be fairly sure that it was the Hittite king Mursili, who may well have taken the opportunity to sack it during his Aleppo and Babylon campaigns. There was limited resettlement on the site in later periods, from the Late Bronze Age onwards, with more substantial growth and development in the first millennium BC. But the tell appears to have been completely abandoned in the 2nd century BC, while other parts of the site continued to be sparsely occupied until at least the 3rd century AD, and perhaps through much of the first millennium.

The rise of Mitanni

To return to the Hurrians. Identified in our written sources by a common language called Hurrian, the peoples so designated had by the end of the third millennium formed a number of small principalities in northern and eastern Mesopotamia. For a time, they were subject to both the Akkadian and the Ur III empires. But after the collapse of these empires, they became increasingly ambitious and aggressive as they spread ever further westwards, through northern Syria and into the eastern part of the Anatolian plateau. They had clashed with the Hittites in both Hattusili's and Mursili's reigns, but appear to have accepted the sovereignty of Yamhad over much of northern Syria, and may indeed have established diplomatic relations with it. None the less, Mursili's destruction of Yamhad provided them with a welcome power vacuum in northern Syria. Particularly since the Hittites failed to follow up their military successes there. Mursili was assassinated a few years after his campaigns against Aleppo and Babylon, and a long period of instability within Hatti ruled out any prospect of a Hittite return to Syria in the foreseeable future. That enabled the Hurrians to consolidate their presence in the region. By the end of the century, a powerful confederation

of Hurrian states had emerged—the kingdom of Mitanni, to become the
Hittites' fiercest rival for control of northern Syria and eastern Anatolia.[14]

Meantime, however, the Hittites' temporary withdrawal from the contest over Syria was offset by another stumbling block to Mitanni's bid for
power in the region—an enterprising pharaoh of the vigorous and still
relatively new Eighteenth Dynasty of Egypt—Tuthmosis I (1504–1492).
Fifty years earlier, the founder of this dynasty, Ahmose (1550–1525), had
expelled from Egypt a line of foreign kings of Syro-Palestinian origin
called the Hyksos, driving them back to their own lands and inflicting
further defeats on them there. Tuthmosis followed up his military enterprises with fresh campaigns in the northerners' countries, conquering Palestine and subsequently leading his army to the Euphrates, where he
erected a victory stele.[15] Thus while the Hittites were trying to sort themselves out at home, a contest was in the making between Egypt and Mitanni
for control over the lands between the Euphrates and the Mediterranean.
But it never came to a showdown, and the pharaoh's son and successor
Tuthmosis II showed no interest in pursuing his father's Syro-Palestinian
ventures. Nor did the next effective ruler of Egypt. When the second
Tuthmosis died, his successor Tuthmosis III was still a minor, and the powers
of kingship were taken over by his stepmother Hatshepsut. Mere regency
proved insufficient to satisfy her ambitions, and after seven years of it, she
assumed the throne in her own right (1473–1458). By and large she enjoyed
a peaceful reign, placing much emphasis on her kingdom's commercial
development and trade-links. Military action in Syria was simply not on
her agenda. In fact, she abandoned most of Tuthmosis I's conquests there,
and withdrew Egypt's forces from all parts of Syria and Palestine except for
the southern part of Palestine. That provided an excellent opportunity
for the first major westward expansion of Mitannian power—in the first
half of the 15th century under the third known Mitannian king, a man
called Parrattarna.

Parrattarna clearly identified his first objective—Aleppo. The kingdom of
which it had been capital, Yamhad, had disappeared for all time. But in
the decades that followed, Aleppo had recovered from its destruction by the
Hittites and re-established itself under a new line of kings—we know the
names of three of them: Sarra-el, Abba-el, and Ilim-ilimma—and had also
imposed its sovereignty over a number of nearby states, including Niya (Nii),
Ama'u (Amae), and Mukish. The stage looked set for the rise of a new great
kingdom in northern Syria based again on the city of Aleppo. And that

clearly posed a major threat to any ideas Mitanni entertained for expansion into Syria. Aleppo had to be conquered!

The Idrimi affair

In one of the Syro-Palestinian rooms in the British Museum, there is a white statue, just over a metre high, depicting a short, squat man with a very large head. He is seated on what appears to be an armchair. In fact, the chair is the remnant of a throne, once flanked by lions and mounted on a stone pedestal. Its occupant is a glum-looking fellow, bearded and wearing a close-fitting skull-cap. As he moodily surveys the scene before him, he places his right hand on his heart, his left hand in his lap. The British archaeologist Sir Leonard Woolley unearthed him during excavations at Tell Atchana. We have already encountered this site under its ancient name Alalah. Woolley found the statue in one of the chambers of a temple at Alalah, dating to the

Figure 2. Idrimi, king of Alalah

city's last phase, which ended in destruction early in the 12th century. But the statue is much older than this. It belongs to the first half of the 15th century, to Alalah IV in archaeological terms. It was carved in this period, and though the city was later destroyed by the Hittites, who then rebuilt it (level III), the image was carefully preserved, in pieces, and finally deposited in the precincts of the city's main temple. It clearly had a revered status of long standing in the city. Woolley observed that it was treated like a god!

The statue is that of a king of Alalah called Idrimi. This we know from the 104-line cuneiform inscription written in Akkadian and carved across the front of it.[16] The inscription tells the story of Idrimi's career. Its narrator is allegedly Idrimi himself, and we must allow for some dramatic licence in the telling of it. But taken at face value, this glum-faced man's narrative provides us with one of the most fascinating adventure tales, of personal enterprise and daring, in the repertoire of ancient Near Eastern literature.

It begins in Aleppo, with the overthrow of King Ilim-ilimma in a coup staged by an unnamed enemy, and the flight of his sons from the city, in fear for their lives. Idrimi was the youngest of these sons, one of whom might reasonably have expected to inherit his father's throne. The brothers went to Emar on the Euphrates, where their mother's relatives lived, and found safe refuge there. Very likely the Mitannian king Parrattarna had engineered their father's death, and now moved quickly to establish his sovereignty over the entire former kingdom of Aleppo, where no doubt he installed a puppet ruler.

Idrimi quickly grew restless in exile. If his brothers were no longer interested in winning back the throne of Aleppo, he certainly was—and thus by default he became his father's heir. But achieving his goal meant drumming up support among those of his father's former subjects who had rejected the new regime in Aleppo. Word reached him that a number of them were now living in a city called Ammiya, in the region of Canaan along the Phoenician coast, about 160 km south of Aleppo. This might be a good place to begin his campaign. So he decided to travel to Canaan. But when he urged his brothers to join him, his plea fell on deaf ears. Perfectly happy with where they were, they showed no interest in supporting his bid to claim his 'rightful' inheritance. Nor were they at all enthusiastic about the prospect of leaving the safety of Emar and embarking on a dangerous trek across the desert to Canaan.

So Idrimi departed without them. Taking his horse and chariot and accompanied only by his faithful groom, he left Emar and headed south-westwards across the Syrian wilderness, in his quest to gain support for his claim to the throne of Aleppo. The enterprise was hazardous in the extreme. Aside from the natural perils facing travellers who braved the desert's harsh natural environment, there was always the risk of attack by bandits. Even large merchant caravans or other groups with military escorts were not entirely proof against the brigands of the desert. What chance did a single traveller and his servant have if confronted by them? This must have been one of Idrimi's worst fears. Not without reason, it seemed, when the traveller, now well into his journey, suddenly encountered a band of the dreaded bedouin tribe called the Sutaeans, probably of Amorite origin and notorious as marauders and cut-throats. Idrimi no doubt believed that his last moments had come. Maybe his brothers were right after all in refusing to budge from Emar. But then a seeming miracle occurred, for which our inscription provides no explanation. Far from robbing and killing Idrimi, the Sutaeans welcomed him into their midst. Scarcely believing his luck, Idrimi erected a canopy over his chariot and spent a peaceful night (or more) among his unlikely hosts before continuing his journey to the land of Canaan. Once there, he proceeded immediately to the city of Ammiya, where he met former inhabitants of Aleppo and its subject territories, including Mukish, Niya, and Amae. All had fled south after the death of Ilim-ilimma, and now (if we have correctly interpreted a difficult sentence in the inscription) pledged their support for Idrimi in his bid for the Aleppan throne.

But the time was not yet ripe for action. The king-in-waiting tells us that for seven years he lived among troops of the Habiru, landless outlaws whose support could be won if the payment was right or the promises of rich rewards convincing enough. No doubt Idrimi built himself a support base among them, while preparing his move to seize the throne that he believed was rightfully his. But there would be no action, he declared, without divine approval. And that took seven years of omen-taking to achieve. Finally, the sign was given, by no less an authority than Teshub himself, god-in-chief. By this time, Idrimi had mustered a formidable fighting force. He promptly loaded it onto a fleet of ships, built while he had been awaiting the divine nod, and sailed north. As soon as the fleet had reached a suitable landing-spot on the coast of Mukish, probably near the mouth of the Orontes river, Idrimi gave the disembarkation order. News of his return spread quickly. The peoples of Niya, Amae, Mukish, and Alalah flocked to his standard and proclaimed him their lord.

Then came the big question. Would he try to reclaim Aleppo, and thus provoke head-on conflict with Parrattarna? He was already Parrattarna's enemy, and had been, he tells us, for seven years—probably the period between his flight from Aleppo and his landing in Mukish.[17] What would the final outcome be? *Realpolitik* now came into play. Knowing that he had no chance of defeating Parrattarna in an all-out military confrontation, but aware that he was negotiating from a position of some strength, Idrimi tried the diplomatic route. Through his envoys, he approached Parrattarna in a conciliatory manner, reminding him of the peaceful links between former Hurrian kings and his own royal ancestors. Parrattarna responded positively, and a treaty was drawn up between the pair. It meant compromise on Idrimi's part. Idrimi was installed as a king—but as vassal of Parrattarna, and with authority over only the western parts of the former kingdom of Aleppo (Niya, Amae, and Mukish). Alalah, not Aleppo, was to be his royal seat. Parrattarna granted virtual autonomous status to the rest of the territories comprising the old kingdom of Aleppo. Idrimi had certainly gained a kingdom for himself, albeit one rather less grand than he had originally hoped. (And his appointment seems to have roused the ire of a number of rulers in the surrounding territories, who rose up against him, and were put down by brute force.) But the agreement clearly favoured Parrattarna, who had thus effectively consolidated Mitannian control over the region where the kingdom of Aleppo once held sway.

Idrimi may well have continued to feel that he had been done out of his birthright. Perhaps that is why he stares so lugubriously at us when we visit him in the British Museum.

Mitanni to the fore

Mitanni had now surged to political dominance in northern Syria and south-eastern Anatolia, through its network of compliant vassal states—and thanks too to a still relatively weak Hatti, whose rulers down to the end of the 15th century had neither the will nor the capacity to campaign afresh in Syria. But the Mitannians were not to get it all their own way. Egypt was once more on the move. The death of Hatshepsut in 1458 paved the way for a new phase in Egypt's international ambitions, when her stepson and co-regent Tuthmosis III became pharaoh in his own right. Chafing at the bit to renew Egypt's imperial enterprises, he wasted no time after his stepmother's death in setting about the task. He began by leading a large Egyptian force into Palestine and Syria, where he inflicted a devastating defeat on a coalition of Syrian forces at Megiddo in northern Palestine. Next, setting his sights on northern Syria, he followed in the footsteps of his great ancestor and namesake Tuthmosis I and carried Egyptian arms once more to the Euphrates, conquering Mitanni's subject territories along the way.[18]

Mitannian influence and authority in Syria had rapidly taken a turn for the worse. And several of the Near Eastern kingdoms made haste to acknowledge the pharaoh as the region's new overlord. They sought diplomatic relations with him, and sent him gifts and tribute. Notable among them were Assyria, Babylon, and Hatti. The more obvious reason for their conciliatory overtures was that they were seeking to buy the pharaoh off, to dissuade him from attacking their own lands. But Mitanni had posed a much greater direct threat to their kingdoms, and the pharaoh's advance into Syria may well have been welcomed as a check to Mitannian aggression. As it turned out, Tuthmosis' Asiatic ventures imposed no more than a temporary setback upon Mitanni, and gave Egypt no significant permanent control over the conquered Syro-Palestinian states. Egyptian influence declined in the region following Tuthmosis' campaigns, while Mitannian influence was once more on the rise, under a new king, Saushtatar. The kingdom was to reach its peak during his occupancy of its throne. Egypt on the other hand was winding down its Asiatic operations. Tuthmosis' seventeenth campaign in Syria and Palestine, directed against the central Syrian cities Tunip and Qadesh which had rebelled against him, was to be his last. Very likely the rebels had Mitannian support. Already, Saushtatar had seized upon Egypt's withdrawal from northern Syria to re-establish his sovereignty there. And he did so knowing that Egypt's ally Hatti could safely be ignored. Its rulers were still too preoccupied with problems in their own kingdom to think about returning to Syria and taking him on.

But Saushtatar did have another worry—the possibility of a resurgent Assyria, whose territory lay east of Mitanni. Though the Old Assyrian empire had been effectively finished off by Hammurabi around 1762, an Assyrian state, albeit of much reduced proportions, still survived, and might become a threat to Mitannian territory while Saushtatar was engaged in operations in the west. That placed Assyria at risk of a pre-emptive attack by Mitanni, prompting it to seek an anti-Mitannian alliance with Tuthmosis. Nothing came of it. And once the threat of an Egyptian offensive against him had gone, Saushtatar turned his attention to bringing his hostile neighbour to heel. Which he did by invading Assyria and sacking and looting

Ashur, its traditional capital. Assyria was now absorbed within the Mitannian realm as a vassal state of Saushtatar. And that left the Mitannian king free to pursue his territorial ambitions in Syria. Sweeping across the northern regions, he imposed his control over everything in his path, between the Euphrates and the Mediterranean. All the northern territories formerly subject to Parrattarna had Mitannian sovereignty imposed upon them afresh, including Alalah.

Late 15th–14th centuries

The Hittites return to Syria

Perhaps at this time too Saushtatar made an alliance with the king of Qadesh on the Orontes, who was acknowledged as overlord of Syrian territory south of Alalah (probably between the Orontes valley and the coast). A developing situation elsewhere may well have persuaded Saushtatar that a diplomatic settlement with Qadesh was the wisest course to take. For his newly acquired northern Syrian territories had suddenly come under threat. Across the Taurus, the fortunes of Hatti had taken a dramatic turn for the better. A new era in its history had begun, with the accession of a vigorous and enterprising ruler called Tudhaliya. After conspiracy and armed conflict had paved his way to the Hittite throne, Tudhaliya had first established his authority over much of the Anatolian peninsula, and was now intent on restoring Hatti's status as a major power in the wider Near Eastern world.[19] That meant a resumption of Hittite campaigns in Syria. And one of Tudhaliya's prime objectives was the city Aleppo!

Aleppo was no longer as important as it once was. In fact, it had recently been reduced to the status of a subsidiary of Alalah, handed over by Saushtatar to Alalah's ruler Niqmepa. Even so, it was upon Aleppo that Tudhaliya had his sights firmly set. News of his approach placed the local ruler in a dilemma[20]—of a kind faced by many vassals whose loyalties were contested by the great powers of the day. If he maintained his allegiance to Saushtatar, he could expect savage reprisals from the rapidly advancing Hittite army. But if he broke it, he could expect equally savage reprisals from Saushtatar if things did not go the Hittites' way. The trick was to decide which of the two Great Kings would prevail. To begin with, he decided Tudhaliya was the better bet, and declared his allegiance to him. But he must have done so while the Hittite army was still some distance away, for Saushtatar pressured him into changing his mind and redeclaring his allegiance to Mitanni. Then the Hittites arrived. Furious at Aleppo's about-face, Tudhaliya destroyed the city and killed its king. So we are told in the Hittite account, which further informs us that Tudhaliya went on to destroy the king of Mitanni and the kingdom itself (here called Hanigalbat). This must be a gross exaggeration.[21] We do not know what happened to Saushtatar in the aftermath of the Aleppo campaign. But Mitanni certainly continued to exist, even though much of its territory, particularly the northern Syrian part of it, was probably taken over by the Hittites. But a reinvigorated Mitanni was soon to rise again, under a new king, Artatama, successor and probably son of Saushtatar. One of Artatama's chief objectives was almost certainly to regain any Mitannian territories lost to the Hittites, and above all to reclaim sovereignty over his kingdom's former subject lands in Syria.

Problems experienced by the Hittites in maintaining their authority over their Anatolian subjects—distracting them for a time from new threats posed by Mitanni—provided an opportunity for this. But Artatama was careful not to risk too precipitate a move upon the northern Syrian states. A premature attempt by him to seize them might well prompt the return of Hittite forces to the region, despite continuing volatility closer to their homeland, and a showdown which Mitanni could well lose. There was also the matter of Egypt. Egyptian influence in Syria and Palestine had declined since Tuthmosis III's campaigns, but Egypt still retained an active interest in the region. This was illustrated by (at least) two campaigns which Tuthmosis' son and successor Amenhotep II conducted there, and a subsequent campaign by his grandson Tuthmosis IV. Egypt and Mitanni had never resolved their differences, and were still virtually on a war footing. But compromise between them was possible. Mitanni's territorial interests west of the Euphrates were focused primarily on the northern Syrian states, and these it would always fiercely contest with Hatti. Here there was no room for compromise. It was a 'winner-take-all' situation.

But central and southern Syria and Palestine were more remote from Mitannian interests. A treaty which conceded them to Egypt, while Egypt allowed Mitanni a free hand in northern Syria, might well satisfy the territorial ambitions of both kingdoms, besides providing the basis for an alliance between them against a third power—Hatti. An accord was reached between Artatama and Tuthmosis IV, and a frontier in Syria established between their territories. The precise location of this frontier is not certain.

But it seems that much of the region south and west of the Orontes (including Qadesh on the river itself) went to Egypt, and everything north and east of it to Mitanni. That effectively locked the Hittites entirely out of the Syrian region; if Hatti ventured to reclaim the territories of either treaty-partner, it would risk war with both.

But the Hittites had far more to worry about in Anatolia than their kingdom's exclusion from Syria. Indeed, uprisings throughout the Anatolian peninsula led to a crisis that threatened Hatti's very existence. All around the homeland, enemy forces massed—Kaska peoples from the north, Arzawans from the south and south-west, intruders from the lands of Isuwa and Azzi to the east and north-east. The homeland was invaded and occupied, and Hattusa looted and destroyed. The royal family escaped just in time, and established a temporary residence at a place called Samuha further east. From there, it began the task of winning its lands back from the enemy. Operation Recovery was outstandingly successful—thanks largely to the young Hittite prince Suppiluliuma, almost certainly the principal architect of his kingdom's restoration. Especially as his father (Tudhaliya III) suffered recurring bouts of illness during the exile, and may well have died before the restoration was complete. As the king lay on his sickbed, Suppiluliuma no doubt got to thinking about his throne. Its designated successor was another of the king's sons. But that was not a major obstacle. After the king's death, the heir was eliminated in a palace conspiracy, and Suppiluliuma became the next Great King of Hatti. The greatest Great King of them all, some would argue, for Suppiluliuma succeeded in bringing his kingdom back from the brink of extinction, and was soon to make it the supreme political and military power of the age. This he achieved by setting his sights on a final resolution of the Mitanni problem—the destruction of the kingdom of Mitanni, and its replacement by Hatti as the overlord of all its Syrian possessions.[22]

Undeterred by Mitanni's friendly relations with Egypt (which may recently have cooled somewhat), and fully aware that a Hittite attack might bring Egypt into the conflict on its ally's side, Suppiluliuma pushed on with his plans to confront and destroy the Mitannian empire. He was encouraged in his enterprise by news he received from Mitanni around the time of his accession. The recent death of its king Artatama had led to an outbreak of dynastic squabbles over his throne. Following the short-lived reigns of Artatama's first two successors, the ultimate winner of the dynastic contests was a man called Tushratta, one of Artatama's grandsons. Tushratta now seated himself upon the Mitannian throne. But he was not altogether secure upon it, for he had another contender to deal with. This was a second Artatama, who declared that *he* was the rightful king of Mitanni, apparently with the support of a large part of the Mitannian population. Suppiluliuma saw that the situation was ripe for exploitation. In what was essentially a probing operation, he led an expedition across the Euphrates into the land of Isuwa, which lay between Hittite and Mitannian territory. Formerly subject territory of Hatti, Isuwa was now aligned with Mitanni, and Suppiluliuma sought to win it back. This led to a direct confrontation with Tushratta in which, according to a letter Tushratta wrote to the pharaoh Amenhotep III, the Mitannian won a decisive victory.[23] To prove it, he sent a gift to the pharaoh, extracted from the plunder taken from the Hittites: one chariot, two horses, one male and one female servant. Little enough, it seems, and hardly evidence of a devastating defeat of the Hittite army.

None the less, the Mitannian victory was sufficient to send Suppiluliuma back home, if not exactly with his tail between his legs at least sufficiently chastened by the experience to be aware that in Tushratta he had found a formidable adversary. To be sure of defeating him and destroying his empire, Suppiluliuma needed to devise a more comprehensive set of strategies, involving politics as well as military force. Adopting a 'divide and conquer' approach, he sought to isolate Tushratta from his major sources of support by a series of diplomatic alliances. Included amongst these was a treaty he drew up with the Mitannian pretender Artatama. The treaty itself has not survived, but it no doubt contained an agreement that Suppiluliuma would recognize Artatama as the rightful Mitannian king (he must have had his fingers firmly crossed behind his back in making such an agreement)—if he supported him, or at least remained benevolently neutral, in the Hittites' upcoming war with Tushratta.

More importantly, Suppiluliuma wanted to keep the pharaoh out of the conflict, by making it clear that he had no quarrel with him, nor any intention of extending his military operations against Mitanni into pharaonic territory in southern Syria and Palestine. At this time, Egypt's throne was occupied by Amenhotep IV, the so-called heretic king who renamed himself Akhenaten after his god Aten. Suppiluliuma claimed that his relationship with Akhenaten was of the warmest and most cooperative kind. He said this in a letter he wrote to the pharaoh's immediate successor, Smenkhkare: 'Neither my messengers, whom I had sent to your father, nor the request which your father had made in these terms: "Let us establish between ourselves nothing but the friendliest of relations"—I have not refused these.

I did absolutely everything your father asked of me. And my own request, that I made to your father, he never refused it; he gave me absolutely every-thing.'[24] Suppiluliuma's relationship with Akhenaten was probably not as cordial as this letter would have us believe. Particularly after the Hittite king had finished with Tushratta. But that is something to which we shall return.

In the meantime, Suppiluliuma prepared for a final, decisive showdown with Mitanni. Four or five years after his accession, his preparations were complete. He was now ready to embark on what was to prove one of the defining events of his reign, a comprehensive one-year campaign against Mitanni and its Syrian subjects, commonly referred to as the Great Syrian War (c.1345).[25] There were two main objectives to his campaign: the destruc-tion of Mitanni's heartland in northern Mesopotamia, and the conquest of the states in Syria that had bound themselves to Mitanni as subjects or allies; these states would almost certainly range themselves alongside their over-lord in an all-out contest with Hatti.

There was, however, one important state that Suppiluliuma did win over, eventually, by diplomacy rather than by force. This was the kingdom of Ugarit, located in north-western Syria, within the northernmost bend of the Orontes river. Ugarit was a prosperous land, noted for its thickly wooded mountains from which large quantities of valuable timber were extracted, its fertile steppes and plains which provided excellent grazing and agricultural lands, its thriving manufacturing and crafts industries, and its excellent sea-ports. It was never an important kingdom militarily, but its wealth and stra-tegic location attracted the keen interest of the great powers of the age.[26] For a time, it had remained independent of any of these powers. But its king Ammishtamru found himself in a quandary when Mitanni went to war with Hatti. If he sided with Mitanni in the conflict, and Suppiluliuma got the upper hand, his kingdom would surely be seized by the Hittites during their sweep through the territories of Mitanni's allies in Syria. If, on the other hand, he threw in his lot with Suppiluliuma (as Suppiluliuma tried to get him to do) and Tushratta drove the Hittites out of Syria, reprisals from Mitanni were bound to follow. Better to support neither side in the conflict. But that in itself was risky. Neutrality could well render Ammishtamru liable to attack by either of the great powers, without any reasonable prospect of the other coming to his assistance.

He had, he believed, only one viable course of action: to declare allegiance to the pharaoh.[27] It was a clever political move. Mitanni was unlikely to risk its alliance with Egypt by attacking a state which had pledged loyalty to the pharaoh. On the other hand, Suppiluliuma was unlikely to jeopardize his cordial relations with the pharaoh by wresting from him his recently declared subject-ally. And so Ammishtamru felt safe in both distancing himself from Mitanni and rejecting Suppiluliuma's advances. But when he died shortly afterwards, Suppiluliuma made fresh overtures to his son and successor Niqmaddu II, this time successfully, in a very eloquently and persuasively written letter.[28] Niqmaddu became his ally—but not without cost. His neighbours, the kings of Mukish and Nuhashshi, both allies of Mitanni, attacked and plundered his lands to punish him, before Suppiluliuma had had a chance to respond to his appeal for assistance. When he did respond, he drove the invaders from his new ally's kingdom, and restored to Niqmaddu the booty they had taken. Niqmaddu was further rewarded for joining the Hittites when Suppiluliuma handed over to him a significant slice of his neighbours' territories.

To return to the broader scene, Suppiluliuma's strategy in his 'Great War' was first of all to cross the Euphrates and strike at the heart of Mitannian power, occupying Tushratta's homeland before his adversary had time to prepare an adequate defence against him. Everything went according to plan—almost. Washshuganni, the Mitannian capital, fell to the Hittites and was plundered. But Tushratta himself managed to escape before it fell, taking with him whatever troops he could muster. He would have other opportunities to confront the Hittites. So he hoped. Suppiluliuma made no attempt to pursue him, but immediately turned back, recrossing the Euphrates into Syria where, in a series of rapid operations, he imposed his authority over all the local kingdoms formerly subject to Mitanni, from the Euphrates to the Mediterranean coast. His conquests included Aleppo, Mukish, Niya, Arahtu, Qatna, and Nuhashshi, and regions south to the frontiers of Damascus—where Egyptian territory began. Not trusting the current rulers of any of these states, who had sworn allegiance to Mitanni, he deposed them all and deported them and their families to Hattusa. It was a spectacularly successful campaign—but not an entirely comprehensive one. There was still one major Mitannian stronghold west of the Euphrates to be subdued—the city of Carchemish. So long as Carchemish remained defiant and Tushratta remained at large, Suppiluliuma's victory was incomplete. The Great Syrian War was fought about 1345, as we have noted. It was to be many more years before Carchemish was taken. Around the time of its fall, Tushratta was executed. But Suppiluliuma was denied the satisfaction of pronouncing the death sentence himself; the Mitannian king was murdered by a group of his fellow-countrymen, among whom was his own son Shattiwaza.

Figure 3. Ankhesenamun and Tutankhamun on the lid of a box from Tutankhamun's tomb

Finally, the episode before the walls of Carchemish. In 1327 Suppiluliuma laid siege to the city. And it was just at this time that he received from Her Majesty Queen Ankhesenamun, wife of Tutankhamun, the letter that had so astonished him. Its contents were blunt and to the point: 'My husband has died, and I have no son. They say that you have many sons. If you will give me one of your sons, he will become my husband. I do not wish to choose a subject of mine and make him my husband.'[29] The death of the pharaoh, still little more than a child, had left his young queen in a desperate position.

Her kingdom was on the verge of crisis, for Tutankhamun, the last member of his ruling line, had died without issue. Now his widow was seeking a Hittite prince to take his place—as her husband, and as ruler of Egypt. For, she declared, she would never marry a commoner. Better that a prince of foreign blood should become the next pharaoh! Suppiluliuma's initial reaction to the request is understandable. Foreign princesses were often sent to Egypt to wed one of the pharaohs. But never before had marriage into the Egyptian royal family been offered to a foreign prince, let alone Egypt's throne! For that reason alone, Ankhesenamun's request was cause for surprise. But there was another very compelling reason for Suppiluliuma's astonishment and suspicion. What was it?

Before finding out, we should take a closer look at Egypt's role in Syro-Palestinian affairs in the period leading up to the fall of Carchemish, the middle years of the 14th century, when the throne of Egypt was occupied by Amenhotep III (died 1352) and then by his son Amenhotep IV, soon to be known as Akhenaten (1352–1336).

3

The Amorite Warrior-Chiefs

Mid 14th century BC

Abdi-Ashirta's reign of terror

While the kingdom of Hatti was embroiled in conflict with Mitanni, both sides sought to maintain peace with Egypt, at that time ruled by Akhenaten. Soon after his accession in 1352, Akhenaten had built himself a new capital, Akhetaten ('Horizon of (the sun-god) Aten') on the site now called el-Amarna, 300 km south of modern Cairo. The city had but a brief lifespan, barely surviving Akhenaten's reign. But it lived long enough to leave us one of our most valuable sources of information on international relations in the Late Bronze Age. This is the cache of tablets known as the Amarna archive, discovered quite by accident in 1887. The great majority of its contents are letters, or copies of letters, exchanged by Akhenaten and his predecessor Amenhotep III with their foreign peers and vassal rulers. Figuring prominently in the vassal letters are a land called Amurru and the thugs who ruled over it in the 14th century—ostensibly as loyal subjects of Egypt.

In earlier times, 'Amurru' was a name broadly applied to a large expanse of territory, inhabited by Amorites, extending through much of the region occupied by modern Syria. In the Late Bronze Age, the term was used in a more restricted sense, of the territory lying between the Orontes river and the central Levantine coast. This territory became part of the Egyptian empire during Tuthmosis III's Syrian campaigns in the 15th century. But its ties to Egypt were very loose. It was a wild and anarchic region, infested by predatory bands of semi-nomadic outcasts and outlaws known collectively as the Habiru (whom we met briefly in the story of Idrimi). The name 'Habiru' has often been connected with the word

'Hebrew' ('ibri in Hebrew), and it is possible that the peoples later identified as Hebrews arose out of the Habiru groups, or at least had some connection with them. But 'Habiru' does not designate a specific people. Rather, it is a term covering a large assortment of persons and groups from a variety of ethnic backgrounds, living for the most part a roving existence outside organized society. They were one of the scourges of their age, swooping on merchants and other travellers who passed through their territories, and sometimes attacking towns and cities, plundering them and carrying off their crops before vanishing into their mountain lairs.

They were effective enough when operating as independent groups, often small in size. What if they were combined into a single fighting force under one leader? That was the ambition, and the achievement, of a local Amorite (more specifically Amurrite) chief called Abdi-Ashirta, a man who first comes to our attention in the reign of Amenhotep III. He was a brilliant organizer and military leader, and just as importantly, a consummate politician. To unite the anarchic rabble of Habiru bands under his leadership was no mean feat. The incentives offered to them, in terms of power and material rewards, must have been very great indeed. But the region of Amurru over which Abdi-Ashirta had appointed himself as warrior-in-chief was actually the pharaoh's subject territory. And Abdi-Ashirta had no desire to provoke Egypt—which he risked doing if his Habiru bands were continually let loose on the peoples and cities of the region. They were, after all, attacking the property of the pharaoh. On the other hand, Abdi-Ashirta well knew that his troops' allegiance depended on his providing them, as their leader, with the means of constantly enriching themselves—from the pharaoh's subject lands and cities, and therefore at the pharaoh's expense. How could he reconcile this with his protestations of loyalty to Egypt? That was the challenge! The way he handled it was to represent himself as the pharaoh's faithful servant, and his cut-throats' plundering expeditions as actions undertaken to defend the pharaoh against his enemies; any opposition he did encounter was due to the disloyalty and treachery of his overlord's own officials and subjects. That at least was the spin Abdi-Ashirta put upon his actions in his letters to Amenhotep. All the time he was building his power base in Amurru. And his troops always wanted more. The bigger the cities they captured or terrorized into submission, the more ambitious their demands—and their leader's aspirations.

Driven by such factors, Abdi-Ashirta engaged in an act which seemed certain to provoke Egyptian retaliation. After seizing the cities of Ardata and

Irqata in southern Amurru, he marched upon the strategically important fortified city Sumur in the north, which Amenhotep had placed under the command of an Egyptian resident commissioner called Pahhanate. As it happened, Pahhanate was away from Sumur when Abdi-Ashirta moved against and occupied the city, almost certainly timing his attack to coincide with the commissioner's absence.

News of this seizure of one of Egypt's most important bases in Syria, by a supposedly loyal subject, spread rapidly. Letters of protest were sent to Egypt, most notably by the king of Byblos, Rib-Hadda. 'Why did you hold back and not speak to the king?' he wrote to one of Amenhotep's chief officials. 'He would then have sent archers to (re)capture Sumur.'[1] In another letter, to the pharaoh himself, Rib-Hadda complained that the Amurrite chieftain had actually slept in the royal bedchamber of Sumur's palace and broken into the royal treasury![2] These was surely not the acts of a loyal subject who was merely trying to protect the city against the pharaoh's enemies! Of course none of this reflected at all well on Sumur's supposedly residential commissioner Pahhanate. Embarrassed at his loss of the city entrusted to him by the pharaoh, the commissioner wrote angrily to Abdi-Ashirta denouncing him as a traitor and enemy of Egypt. Abdi-Ashirta responded that he had entered Sumur merely to protect it when it had been left defenceless. He then wrote to the pharaoh, personally assuring him of his undying support and proclaiming himself the defender—albeit a self-appointed one—not only of Sumur, but of the whole of Amurru. He also raised the bogey of foreign intervention in Egypt's subject territories in the region. 'All the rulers subject to the king of the Hurrians are trying to wrest your lands from you,' he declared. But the pharaoh had no need to worry: '*I'm* guarding your lands for you,' he assured him.[3] Egypt's fear of foreign aggression in Syria could readily be exploited. It provided the lords of Amurru, Abdi-Ashirta and his successors, with a useful card to play from time to time. And they did so with consummate skill and considerable success.

Abdi-Ashirta retained his control over Sumur, apparently with Amenhotep's approval, and thus gained for himself a valuable base for his future operations. He now moved to occupy other cities in the region, until he had made himself master of the entire land of Amurru. But he was always the obedient servant of his sovereign Amenhotep, acting merely to secure the pharaoh's lands against his enemies, especially the Hurrians and the wicked Hittites. So he claimed. And it seems that the pharaoh believed him.

The constant stream of protests from other local rulers about what he was really up to were ignored. Leading these protests was the king of Byblos, particularly when Abdi-Ashirta began unleashing his Habiru bands on cities and towns and mountain villages in Rib-Hadda's own kingdom! So severe and thorough was their looting, Rib-Hadda complained, that his kingdom was close to starvation: 'Our sons and daughters are gone, sold in the land of Yarimuta for provisions to keep us alive,' Rib-Hadda informed the pharaoh. 'For lack of a cultivator, my field is like a woman without a husband.'[4]

One of the most alarming aspects of Abdi-Ashirta's enterprises was that with each victory, his military strength grew, as ever-increasing numbers flocked to join his ranks. Partly because those who refused were ruthlessly cut down—in the interests of peace and unity, so Abdi-Ashirta maintained. Other letters written by Rib-Hadda to the pharaoh warned repeatedly of the unbridled ambitions of the Amurrite warlord. He had reduced the kingdom of Byblos to the verge of total collapse. But he would not stop there. Ultimately, Abdi-Ashirta would seek to join the select ranks of the Great Kings of the Near Eastern world—not only at the pharaoh's expense, but as his replacement! 'Who is Abdi-Ashirta, the dog, that he seeks to take all the cities of the king, the Sun, for himself? Is he the king of Mitanni, or the king of the Kassites, that he seeks to take the land of the king (of Egypt) for himself?'[5]

Amenhotep must have been concerned at the course events were taking in the north, even allowing for some exaggeration by his vassal rulers there. But he decided to take no action against Abdi-Ashirta, yet. The Amurrite chieftain had succeeded in establishing his authority throughout a land whose terrain and unruly population elements made it extremely difficult to control—it was a task beyond the capacity of the pharaoh's own officials and military commanders in the region—and had allegedly done so as the pharaoh's loyal subject, even if he hadn't asked him first. He had also undertaken to keep the land secure against external predators, an important consideration given that Amurru was within easy access of the foreign powers that fought for control over the rest of northern Syria. All in all, it was probably best to put up with Abdi-Ashirta and give tacit approval to the enterprises that had so alarmed his neighbours, and were now allegedly doing serious damage to their own lands. At least for the time being.

Thus Abdi-Ashirta was able to proceed with his campaigns, particularly against Amurru's neighbours to the south, unimpeded by any threat from

Egypt. Part of his strategy was to target individual city rulers. Some were slaughtered by his Habiru warriors, others by their fellow-citizens, at Abdi-Ashirta's prompting. 'Kill your lord so that you may be like us and at peace', the Amurrite allegedly urged the inhabitants of one of the cities he approached. 'They were won over by his words,' said Rib-Hadda, 'and became like Habiru.'[6] Fear of savage reprisals from Abdi-Ashirta gave them little choice. In reporting this to the pharaoh, Rib-Hadda again appealed to him for action. The rebels would quickly abandon Abdi-Ashirta, he declared, if only His Majesty would send troops to deal with him. He went on to say that even the people of Amurru no longer supported Abdi-Ashirta. They would welcome a force of Egyptian archers and would join them if they came—to get rid of the self-appointed warlord.

Rib-Hadda's own situation was becoming increasingly desperate. One by one his cities fell to the Amurrite. Soon only two cities remained, Batruna and his royal capital Byblos. But then Batruna fell. And the king's capital stood alone. Once more, Rib-Hadda wrote to the pharaoh, begging even at this eleventh hour for military assistance. He could hold out for just a little longer. He sent an express delegation to Egypt with the appeal. It returned empty-handed. There was but one glimmer of hope left. Amenhotep had finally written to the kings of Beirut, Sidon, and Tyre, informing them that they would soon receive a request from Rib-Hadda for an auxiliary force, and ordering them to respond by sending troops to his support. These cities lay on the coast south of Byblos. Their remoteness from the regions where Abdi-Ashirta operated would surely make them proof against Amurrite aggression. Tyre was the furthermost south, and for that reason the most secure. As Abdi-Ashirta's forces moved ever closer to his capital, Rib-Hadda sent his sister and her children to Tyre as a safe haven. He now felt a little better about the situation, and after receiving Amenhotep's letter wrote to the rulers of Beirut, Sidon, and Tyre, as advised. But the speed and ferocity of Abdi-Ashirta's advance had been seriously underestimated. By the time Rib-Hadda's appeal reached the cities, all three were already in the hands of Abdi-Ashirta's supporters! Yapah-Hadda, ruler of Beirut, and Zimredda, ruler of Sidon, had both surrendered to the Amurrite. Then from Tyre, a city with which Rib-Hadda had particularly close bonds, came chilling news. Its ruler was dead, murdered by his own citizens after he had refused to join Abdi-Ashirta's ranks. Along with him Rib-Hadda's sister and her children had been slaughtered. All hope now seemed at an end.

Figure 4. Byblos (Bronze Age Gubla)

Rib-Hadda's royal capital still stood. But Abdi-Ashirta intensified his attacks upon it, and prepared for a final assault. He sent out a message to all his troops: 'Assemble in the temple of Ninurta(?),[7] and then let us attack Byblos. See! No one will save it from us!'[8] Soon the whole kingdom of Byblos would be absorbed into Abdi-Ashirta's realm. He would be ruler of all the territories stretching from the northernmost end of Amurru to the city of Tyre. Rib-Hadda sent one more desperate appeal to the pharaoh: 'I am very, very fearful, for there is no one to save me from them. Like a bird in a trap, so I am in Byblos!' Even in his own city, he was the victim of disloyalty and treachery. 'All the men you gave me', he wrote to the pharaoh, 'have fled.' Abdi-Ashirta attempted to seize control of the capital by putting pressure on its inhabitants to kill their king and join him. Many of Rib-Hadda's subjects were won over. 'In this way,' Rib-Hadda said, 'my own people became traitors.' He barely survived an assassination attempt: 'A man with a bronze dagger struck me nine times, but I killed him.'[9] There would undoubtedly be other attempts.

Then Rib-Hadda tried another ploy. He presented the pharaoh with an ultimatum: 'Either send me word that you have despatched a garrison and horses, or I will abandon the city and take my loyal supporters with me.

Or like the mayors of Sidon and Beirut I will make an alliance with Abdi-Ashirta!'[10] He tried a further line as well. Perhaps Abdi-Ashirta could be bought off: 'Why not pay him a thousand (shekels of) silver and 100 (shekels of gold), so that he will go away from me?'[11]

Then finally, when all hope seemed at an end, the pharaoh took action. But probably not out of sympathy with Rib-Hadda, whose incessant stream of letters may have tried his patience beyond endurance. His main concern, very likely, was that the loss of Byblos city would threaten Egypt's entire network of Syrian territories, once Abdi-Ashirta controlled all the coastal states from Sumur south. Byblos would fill the last remaining gap. Amenhotep sent a large force into Syria against Abdi-Ashirta. And that brought the Amurrite warlord's career abruptly to an end. But his fate remains uncertain. It is possible that he was assassinated by his own countrymen, or was summarily executed by Egyptian troops once he had fallen into their hands, or was deported to Egypt and executed there. All these possibilities have been suggested. In any case, he was out of the way. Once more Rib-Hadda and his city and many other terrorized populations of western Syria could feel secure. So they hoped.

Alas, there was worse in store for them.

In his father's footsteps

After Abdi-Ashirta's elimination, the power vacuum he left was quickly filled—by his sons. Amurru was now controlled by a family dynasty of tribal warlords. As Rib-Hadda soon discovered, the sons of Abdi-Ashirta were as bad—or even worse—than their father! Once again Rib-Hadda poured forth his grievances to the pharaoh, now Amenhotep's son Akhenaten. 'The enmity of Abdi-Ashirta's sons against me is severe,' he wrote. 'They have occupied the land of Amurru and the entire country is theirs!'[12] One after another the cities and regions previously occupied by Abdi-Ashirta now fell to his sons, who used the same tactics as their father—first try to persuade the local rulers to join them, incite their subjects to assassinate them if they refused, then if necessary destroy the local garrisons and storm the cities. Again, the northern stronghold of Sumur came under siege from the Amurrite warlords. They attacked it by day and by night, by land and by sea. The beleaguered Egyptian commissioner in Sumur appealed for assistance. Ironically, Akhenaten wrote to Rib-Hadda instructing him to go to Sumur's assistance and to remain there until reinforcements arrived from Egypt. Rib-Hadda protested that he simply could not do so, partly because his own capital was again threatened by Amurrite forces, and Habiru bands had resumed their raids on his farmlands. What made his situation even worse was that the city had become a centre for refugees from regions already occupied by the Amurrites. Further, Rib-Hadda had not been able to secure support from the rulers of Sidon and Beirut for a relief expedition—not surprisingly, since these men too had refused requests for assistance from the beleaguered Egyptian governor in Sumur.

For Sumur, lacking military support from any quarter, the siege ended disastrously. Its governor was killed, probably assassinated by one of his own people under pressure from the besiegers, and the city surrendered. Almost certainly the architect of the Sumur campaign was a man called Aziru, one of the sons of Abdi-Ashirta. Aziru now makes regular appearances in Rib-Hadda's correspondence, as the king's new arch-enemy. He was a man in his father's mould, a ruthless warrior-brigand who terrorized, plundered, and

Figure 5. Akhenaten, from the temple of Aten at Karnak

occupied the neighbouring lands while protesting his loyalty to the pharaoh. Once Sumur was firmly in his grasp, he wrote to the pharaoh: 'Right
from the beginning, My Lord, I have sought to devote myself to the service
of the king, My Lord, but the high officials of Sumur have not allowed me.
Yet I am innocent of the slightest offence against the king, My Lord. The
king, My Lord, knows who the real offenders are. I will truly comply with
all that the king, My Lord, asks of me.'[13] Aziru wanted the best of both
worlds. Formal acknowledgement as the pharaoh's vassal, and the licence to
continue attacking and plundering the pharaoh's subject territories. Akhenaten knew full well how treacherous this man was, and if he ever needed
reminding of it, the constant stream of complaints from his Syrian vassals,
especially Rib-Hadda, made sure that the Amurrite was never far from his
thoughts. Why should he even think of trusting Aziru? Why not get rid of
him for all time by despatching a sizeable Egyptian force to the region
against him? That was easier said than done. For Aziru was holding an
important bargaining counter!

The Mitannian empire was at this time in its dying stages. Hatti's king
Suppiluliuma had all but finished it off and was the master of his enemy's
former subject territories in northern Syria east of the Orontes. The treaty
between Mitanni and Egypt which had apportioned Syrian territory
between the two kingdoms was now obsolete. To be sure, Suppiluliuma had
so far steered clear of Egyptian territory in his Syrian conquests. But now
he had achieved dominance over Mitanni and swept all its states beneath his
sway, could he be trusted not to continue his momentum and try to take
over Egypt's Syro-Palestinian subject territories as well? That possibility
must have preyed on Akhenaten's mind, and Aziru made haste to stoke up
his concerns, again representing himself as the champion of the pharaoh's
interests in the region: 'If the king of Hatti takes hostile action against me,
may the king, My Lord, send me troops and chariots to support me, and
I will defend the land of the king, My Lord.'[14] Aziru had worries of his own
about what might happen to him if the Hittites did invade his land, which
lay just across the Orontes from their own newly acquired possessions. So
he was looking out for himself, as much as he claimed he was protecting
the pharaoh's interests, in asking his overlord for military support against a
possible Hittite attack. Of course, if the pharaoh complied and sent him
troops, that would greatly strengthen his military position and lessen his
dependence on the ill-disciplined and unpredictable Habiru bands who
made up the bulk of his forces.

Akhenaten can have had no illusions about the self-serving motives behind Aziru's proposal. But Egypt might just benefit from these. If the Amurrite could be relied on to hold his kingdom together and use it, reinforced by troops from Egypt, as a buffer against Hittite encroachment into Egyptian territory, he might well prove a more effective agent of Egyptian interests in the region than the pharaoh's more trustworthy subjects there, or the king's own officials. Yet supposing he did agree to Aziru's proposal and send him troops? How sure could he be that his Syro-Palestinian subjects would not be even more imperilled than they were now by the boost Aziru's military capabilities would thus receive? There was only one way to make an informed decision, Akhenaten concluded, and that was to summon Aziru to Egypt for face-to-face talks. That would give him a better idea of how much his wayward 'subject' really could be trusted. So the summons went out to Aziru: 'Come to Egypt!' Aziru complied, leaving the affairs of his land in the hands of two trusted followers (probably family members) while he was away.

He had little choice but to accept the pharaoh's summons. Refusal might well have provoked speedy retaliation and an abrupt end to his career. (He hadn't forgotten his father's fate!) Of course, going to Egypt was also a risk. The journey to and from the land of the Nile and the time spent there would have occupied many months. Many more if the pharaoh decided to prolong his guest's stay. It was not unknown for envoys of foreign kings to be detained in Egypt for very lengthy periods, sometimes years, before the pharaoh granted them their release. Akhenaten could well try to resolve the Aziru problem by holding his guest in indefinite detention. Still, keeping Aziru in Egypt might have created bigger problems for him. There was no known suitable alternative to his leadership in Amurru. Like his father, he had demonstrated his ability to keep the land in order, ostensibly as Egypt's loyal vassal. And he might well act as a useful deterrent to any attempts made by Suppiluliuma to invade Egypt's northern subject territories. Even so, the pharaoh was yet to be convinced that Aziru could be trusted once he returned home. He really didn't know what to do with his guest. So he kept him in Egypt while he tried to make up his mind.

Back in Amurru, Aziru's family became increasingly concerned about his absence. One of his sons wrote to the pharaoh's local official Tutu, reporting that he had been accused by the kings of Nuhashshi of selling his father to the pharaoh for gold. It was now widely rumoured that Aziru would never be allowed to return. These rumours, said the son, were creating dangerous

instability in the region, which would quickly be exploited by Aziru's enemies. Most alarming was the news from Amurru's caretakers. They wrote
to Aziru that Hittite troops had captured cities in the land of Amka, which
lay south of Amurru in the Biqa' valley, and a massive Hittite force, allegedly
of 90,000 troops, had arrived in Nuhashshi, which lay just across the Orontes. Nuhashshi was now under Hittite control, and might well be used as a
base for launching attacks on Egyptian territories. Amurru, along with other
Egyptian subject lands in the region, was now under severe threat of a
Hittite invasion. The number of troops specified was almost certainly exaggerated, but there is little doubt that the Hittite threat was real—and that
the letter addressed to Aziru was intended as much for the pharaoh as for its
actual recipient. Akhenaten was persuaded, finally, to let Aziru go back
home, as its formally recognized Egyptian vassal ruler. But strict conditions
were imposed upon him, including the stipulation that he submit to regular
inspections by Akhenaten's roving ambassador Hani.

Whatever promises Aziru may have given the pharaoh, he had absolutely
no intention of keeping them; his actions and policies would be determined
purely by his own ambitions and self-interest. Above all else, it quickly
became clear to him that an alliance with the Hittite king had more to offer,
in terms of his kingdom's and his own personal security, than continuing
allegiance to the pharaoh. But he took his time in declaring this. Outwardly,
he maintained a show of loyalty to Egypt. Secretly, he began building alliances with rulers of local states now firmly in the Hittite camp, including
the king of Qadesh, which bordered Amurru on the Orontes river in the
south-east, and the king of Ugarit, which lay immediately north of Amurru.
At the same time, he began communicating with the Great King of Hatti
himself. Back in Egypt, Akhenaten grew increasingly anxious about Aziru's
failure to fulfil a number of obligations he had imposed upon him. Including the reconstruction of Sumur. One of the most important of Egypt's
northern strongholds, Sumur had been left in considerable disrepair after
Aziru and his brothers had besieged, captured, and looted it. Particularly in
view of the looming Hittite threat, it was essential that it be rebuilt and
refortified. Why had Aziru not done this?

Aziru responded reassuringly. His Majesty's own officials were partly to
blame for the delay; and he had also been distracted by a war with his next-
door neighbours, the Hittite-aligned kings of Nuhashshi. But, he said, he
would attend forthwith to the rebuilding of Sumur. The pharaoh had
another serious complaint to make. In direct violation of the conditions

imposed upon him before he left Egypt, Aziru had snubbed the Egyptian ambassador Hani when he came to Amurru on one of his inspection tours. Aziru wasn't there to meet him. Akhenaten accused him of 'hiding' from his representative. But Aziru had a ready excuse: 'My Lord, I was living in Tunip (at that time), and was unaware that he had arrived. The moment I heard, I came after him, (but he had already left and) I failed to catch up with him.'[15] It was a lame excuse, as the pharaoh well knew. His anger was scarcely assuaged by Aziru's assurance that his brothers had taken good care of the Egyptian visitor during his time in Amurru, and provided him with horses and asses for his homeward journey.

Aziru had no wish to meet the Egyptian ambassador. If he had, he would have found it difficult to explain to the pharaoh's agent a number of his recent actions. One of these was his occupation of Tunip, a city adjacent to Amurrite territory on the west bank of the Orontes. Tunip had been a subject and important stronghold of Egypt since the campaigns of Tuthmosis III. The city was left leaderless when its king Aki-Teshub died, and his son had been sent to Egypt for 're-education' and held there as a virtual hostage. Appeals to Akhenaten for his return went unanswered. This was too good an opportunity for Aziru to pass up—precisely what Tunip's citizens feared. After seizing what was left of the kingdom of Niya further to the north, following Suppiluliuma's transferral of most of its territory to neighbouring Ugarit, Aziru occupied Tunip and set up one of his royal residences in the city. There was a sinister ulterior motive behind his action. Tunip brought him very close to Hittite subject territory, and indeed to the Hittite king himself, who was at that time in Nuhashshi, just two days' journey to the north.[16] To be fair to Aziru, he did openly admit to Akhenaten his contacts with the Hittite king, and at that time Hatti and Egypt were still nominally on friendly terms. None the less, diplomatic communications between two Great Kingdoms were matters for the kings' own official envoys, not their vassal rulers! Even if we put the most charitable spin on them, Aziru's approaches to Suppiluliuma as Egypt's self-appointed representative were presumptuous in the extreme.

Aziru may already have decided by the time he returned from his stay with the pharaoh that his interests were best served by abandoning Egypt and aligning himself with Hatti. But he had to be very careful about the timing of his 'coming out'. Especially while Egypt and Hatti were still theoretically at peace. He could not be sure that if he openly declared loyalty to Suppiluliuma, the Hittite king would accept his defection at this time and thus rupture his relations with Egypt. And even if Suppiluliuma did receive him into the Hittite fold, he might not retain him on his throne, which had been in theory a gift from Akhenaten. So careful probing and careful negotiations were needed before he made his move, and preferably from a base close to Hittite territory—a purpose which Tunip admirably served.

That brings us to the final episode in Rib-Hadda's career. In the process of gobbling up his neighbours, Aziru had, like his father, acquired all the territory of Byblos, except the royal capital: 'Aziru has seized all my cities! My capital is all that is left to me! If Aziru's troops march against it, they will seize it!'[17] As he had done so often in the past, Rib-Hadda appealed repeatedly to the pharaoh for military support. But like his father Amenhotep, Akhenaten lost patience with his vassal: 'Why does Rib-Hadda keep sending a tablet in this way to the palace?', he exclaimed wearily as yet another letter arrived from Byblos.[18] Yet despite his threats to abandon his city and join forces with the Amurrite, as many of his neighbours had done, Rib-Hadda remained loyal to Egypt, often against what appear to have been insuperable odds. And this too despite repeated urgings from his subjects and his own family to come to terms with Aziru: 'The people of Byblos, and my own household, my own wife, kept saying to me: "Join the son of Abdi-Ashirta and let us make peace!" But I refused. I gave no heed to them.'[19]

Finally, when all hopes of a positive response from Egypt had been exhausted, Rib-Hadda made a last-ditch effort to get local support. He went to Beirut where he met with the city's ruler Ammunira. Ammunira listened sympathetically. But that was all he did. He was either unwilling or unable to provide any material assistance. With that final straw of hope for external support gone, Rib-Hadda's own family lost patience with the king. And his younger brother Ilirabih moved against him. Rib-Hadda might be willing to stick to his principles, remain loyal to the pharaoh, and die a martyr, but Ilirabih certainly wasn't. He seized Rib-Hadda's throne, and banned the ex-king from the city. Then he handed Rib-Hadda's sons over to the Amurrites, as a gesture of goodwill. Deprived of his kingdom and his capital, Rib-Hadda went back to Beirut and was granted asylum by Ammunira.

One more time, from his place of exile, Rib-Hadda wrote to the pharaoh begging his assistance for an attempt to regain his throne, capture the traitors who had seized it from him, and ensure that the city did not fall into the hands of Aziru and his brothers. He would have made his appeal in person, he said, but ill health and old age prevented him from undertaking the arduous journey to Egypt. So he entrusted the mission to one of his sons who had escaped Aziru's clutches. Nothing came of it. Now, with all assistance denied him, his own city barred to him, and nowhere else to go, Rib-Hadda took a final step that brought his long and brave career to a humiliating end. Finding temporary residence in Sidon, he threw himself on the mercy of his arch-enemy Aziru, and offered him a substantial bribe for restoring him to Byblos.[20] What was Aziru's response? Unfortunately, that's not altogether clear. Aziru reported the matter in a letter he wrote to Akhenaten. The pharaoh refers to it in his reply to Aziru, and makes a brief, enigmatic mention of what Aziru eventually did to Rib-Hadda.[21] The relevant words have been translated: 'you gave him to (some) mayors', and alternatively 'you gave (appointed) him for mayoralty'. The first alternative has been taken to mean that Aziru handed over the ex-king of Byblos to a cruel end at the hands of the rulers of Sidon, the second that Aziru showed him mercy and gave him a mayoral appoinment, enabling him to see out his days in a relatively comfortable sinecure.

Whatever Rib-Hadda's fate, Akhenaten reacted angrily to Aziru's treatment of him. But this was only one of the many grievances that the pharaoh listed in his reply to his treacherous vassal's letter. All Aziru's protestations of loyalty were now seen for what they really were. The vassal could no longer be trusted: 'Everything you wrote to me was lies!' the pharaoh declared. What particularly infuriated him was Aziru's hob-nobbing with the ruler of Qadesh, who had been expanding his own territory at the expense of Egypt's other subject states: 'You are at peace with the ruler of Qadesh. The two of you take food and strong drink together. Why do you act so? Why are you at peace with a ruler with whom the king is fighting?' We can perhaps take this to mean that Aziru had concluded a treaty with Aitakkama, who was now Egypt's enemy, marking the occasion with a celebratory banquet.[22]

Then came a dire threat from Akhenaten: 'If for any reason whatsoever you prefer to do evil, and if you plot evil, treacherous things, then you, together with your entire family, shall die by the axe of the king!' The threat had followed a demand from the pharaoh that Aziru return to Egypt, or send his son as his representative, no doubt to answer all the charges that had piled up against him. Aziru had no illusions about the outcome if he complied. But he needed more time before openly defying the pharaoh. So he had avoided a final reckoning by requesting a year's extension. Akhenaten had granted this. The year was now up, and no further extensions would be

allowed. It was time for Aziru to make clear where he stood. And so he did.
His alliances with the kings of Ugarit and Qadesh were now firmly in place,
and when he received the pharaoh's ultimatum, he immediately broke off
his relations with Egypt and declared his loyalty to Suppiluliuma. He drew
up with him a treaty of vassalhood,[23] and from then until his death, he
remained a loyal Hittite subject. The warrior-chieftains of Amurru had at
last gained respectability.

The pharaoh prepares for war

How did the pharaoh respond to Aziru's defection? No doubt with considerable alarm, particularly since the defector took with him into the
Hittite realm the whole of the land of Amurru. Other Egyptian territories
in the region were now severely at risk. War between Egypt and Hatti
seemed imminent. And indeed, Akhenaten may have begun preparations
for war—a possibility raised by a fragmentary letter found in 1956 in
Ugarit. The letter was written by a Hittite field commander and addressed
to a king whose name is now lost. Its author is a man called Sumi[-] (only
the first part of his name is preserved). From what survives of the letter, it
seems that Sumi[-] and his men had the task of defending an important
frontier region in southern Amurru, between Mt Lebanon and the sea,
against incursions by Egyptian forces. They had already spent five months
on active frontline duty.

Tensions in the region were high, for Egypt was determined to get
Amurru back. The pharaoh's forces launched repeated attacks on Sumi[-]'s
troops, who beat them back time and again. But winter had now set in, and
the harsh weather conditions were taking a serious toll on the Hittites.
Sumi[-] had already written several times to his king with an urgent appeal
for reinforcements and fresh supplies. But apparently he received no reply.
He wrote again, highlighting the desperateness of his position: 'My Lord,
what is my outlet from here? Now for five months the cold has been gnaw-
ing me, my chariots are broken, my horses are dead, and my troops are
lost!'[24] The enemy had launched a series of night assaults. They had breached
the Hittite defences and were now fighting the defenders within their own
fortress. Finally, after fierce fighting and heavy casualties, they were repulsed.
One of the enemy was taken prisoner, and under interrogation revealed an
alarming piece of news: the pharaoh himself was preparing to come to the
region. Which meant that almost certainly a major Egyptian campaign was

being planned, under the pharaoh's personal command. That is what Sumi[-] feared: 'Heaven forbid that the king of Egypt should arrive quickly; for we shall not be able to overpower him by force. Heaven forbid that the king of Egypt should come forth!'

This frustratingly incomplete epistle raises a number of questions. To whom was it addressed? To a local Syrian vassal ruler, or to the Great King of Hatti himself? The latter is much more likely. If so, which Great King? The letter was found in an archive of 335 tablets unearthed from a private house in Ugarit. Almost the entire cache of tablets can be dated to the 13th century. But this particular letter may be earlier, and perhaps belongs to the Amarna period, i.e. the mid 14th century.[25] If so, and if its intended recipient was a Hittite Great King, then the king in question was almost certainly Suppiluliuma. In this case, the events to which it refers probably belong to the period after Aziru's defection and his reappearance on the Hittite side. That would mean that Akhenaten was the pharaoh in question.

This so-called heretic, allegedly obsessed with the worship of his god Aten, is commonly portrayed as a king who took little interest in his country's affairs, especially its international ones. But if our letter does in fact belong to this period, it shows the pharaoh in a rather different light, as a military leader prepared to lead his forces in person against his powerful Hittite adversary and risk all-out conflict with Hatti. War was avoided when the pharaoh died suddenly, in 1336, before the launch of his campaign. But tensions between Egypt and Hatti continued to mount. Sixty years later, they would culminate in a final showdown between the Great Kingdoms, at Qadesh on the Orontes river.

4

The Empires Collide

Third quarter 14th century BC

The kingdom of Qadesh (modern Tell Nebi Mend) on the Orontes river lay in a kind of frontier zone between northern and southern Syria. First appearing in our records as an ally of Mitanni, it frequently crops up in the power struggles between the Great Kingdoms of the age. It had been one of the Syrian kingdoms to fall to Tuthmosis III at the battle of Megiddo, and Tuthmosis incorporated it into Egyptian subject territory during a later campaign in the region. Suppiluliuma was happy to leave things that way, acknowledging Qadesh as Egyptian territory and keeping clear of it during his Syrian campaigns. But despite its Egyptian vassal status, there was a strong pro-Mitannian element in the city, led by its king Shuttarna, who attacked Hittite troops as they passed through the region. Suppiluliuma quickly retaliated, marching against and conquering the city, then deporting its king and leading citizens to Hatti. Included among the prisoners was the king's son, Aitakkama. Suppiluliuma decided to send him back to Qadesh as its new ruler, on the understanding that he would conduct the affairs of his city-kingdom in Hatti's interests. Though in one of the letters in the Amarna archive, Aitakkama expresses allegiance to the pharaoh,[1] other letters make it clear that he was effectively a Hittite vassal.

That must have rankled with the pharaoh, doubtless Akhenaten, especially when Aitakkama allied himself with the turncoat Aziru and began expanding his territory at the expense of other loyal Egyptian states in his region. But for the time being, Egypt left Qadesh alone—until the reign of Akhenaten's second successor Tutankhamun. Completely out of the blue, it seems, Tutankhamun despatched an expeditionary force to attack Qadesh. Suppiluliuma was furious. What did the young pharaoh think he was doing? Didn't he know that Qadesh now belonged to the Hittites? To teach him a lesson, Suppiluliuma ordered a retaliatory attack on the Egyptian subject state Amka, located in the Biqa' valley of southern Syria. And that began a new era in the relations between Hatti and Egypt. The thin façade of their friendship had now been completely shattered. For this Tutankhamun must take a large share of the blame. What could have induced him to provoke the wrath of the most powerful warrior-king of the age, now at his very peak, in the knowledge that retaliation was inevitable? Was this fledgling pharaoh seeking to prove that despite his tender years he was a great warrior in the mould of his most illustrious predecessors, like Tuthmosis III? Circumstances unknown to us may have forced upon him the need to demonstrate his fitness to rule with a bold new enterprise in the northern lands. In so doing, he made an implacable enemy of Suppiluliuma.

The outcome of the widow's letter

That provides us with the context for the letter Tutankhamun's widow Ankhesenamun wrote to Suppiluliuma, which reached its recipient while he was laying siege to Carchemish, probably in late August of the year 1327. It explains his flabbergasted reaction. Egypt and Hatti had but shortly before been on a war footing. And now Suppiluliuma was being offered not only a marriage alliance with Egypt, but Egypt's throne for the son he chose as the bridegroom. His suspicion was understandable. Still, if the request was genuine, the opportunity it provided was too good to pass up. A Hittite prince could be installed as pharaoh of Egypt without a single drop of Hittite blood being spilt. So the king sent his vizier to Egypt to check out Ankhesenamun's proposition. In the meantime, Suppiluliuma completed his siege of Carchemish, within a week, thus bringing the Mitannian empire finally and decisively to an end.[2] He returned home to Hattusa, to await the report of his envoy's visit to Egypt.

The vizier had plenty of time to carry out his investigations in Egypt, because the year was now well advanced and he had to wait until the following spring, when the winter snows on the Anatolian plateau had thawed, before he could return to Hattusa. He was accompanied by a man we have already met, Egypt's most distinguished diplomat, Hani. Hani brought with him a furious letter from his young queen: 'Why did you say "they deceive me" in that way? Had I a son, would I have written about my own and my land's embarrassing predicament to a foreign land? You did not believe me, and have dared to speak this way to me! My husband has died, and I have

no son. I do not wish to take one of my subjects and make him my husband.
I have written to no other land, only to you. They say you have many sons.
Well then, give me one of them. To me he will be husband, but in Egypt he
will be king!'[3]

Egyptian tradition demanded that a new king conduct his predecessor's
final burial rites. These must be carried out after a seventy-day mourning
period, not a day more nor less. But all that was thrown awry by the delay
caused by Suppiluliuma's suspicions. Ankhesenamun had indeed told the
truth. With her husband's death, the royal line of Egypt, the great Eighteenth Dynasty, had ended. The future terrified her, she freely admitted. But
she was resolute. She would never stoop to marrying a commoner. Her new
husband, the new king of Egypt, had to have royal blood in his veins, even
foreign blood. And so, she would break with tradition and postpone her
husband's burial until the right person could be found to replace him. But
the delay in consigning the dead king to his tomb and installing a new one
on his throne exposed her to enormous risks, from her own countrymen as
well as her kingdom's enemies. These were risks she had to take; they would
be justified—if the Hittite king could now be persuaded to supply her with
one of his sons, as bridegroom and new pharaoh. She was furious that his
initial response had forced this situation upon her. And she left him in no
doubt about this. But Suppiluliuma was in no mood for a rebuke and delivered one of his own: 'I myself was friendly, but you, you suddenly did me
evil and attacked my land Qadesh.' You were treacherous then, he declared.
Why should I entrust a son of mine to you now? You'll probably make him
your hostage, not your king!

That prompted the silver-tongued Egyptian ambassador Hani to step
forward. 'Oh my Lord! This is our country's humiliation! If we had a son
of the king at all, would we have come to a foreign land and kept asking
for a lord for ourselves? Niphururiya (= Tutankhamun)[4] who was our lord
has died. He has no son. Our lord's wife is childless. We are seeking a son
of yours for the kingship in Egypt. And for the woman, our lady, we seek
him as her husband! Furthermore, we went to no other country. We only
came here. Now, oh our Lord, give us one of your sons.' His words were
backed up by Suppiluliuma's own representative. Yes, the queen was indeed
telling the truth. There was no one in Egypt to succeed her husband, at
least no one important enough. She really did want to settle differences
with Hatti and put a Hittite prince on her kingdom's throne, with herself
thrown in as his wife. Suppiluliuma was finally won over. 'Since my father

was kind-hearted,' his biographer-son Mursili tells us, 'he granted the woman's wish and set about choosing the son he would send.' Of his five sons, there was but one available for marrying the queen, a young man called Zannanza. Suppiluliuma summoned him, and told him to pack his bags for Egypt. And off he went, across the Taurus, and along a route which led through Syria and Palestine and across the Sinai peninsula into the land of the Nile. Suppiluliuma waited anxiously for news of his safe arrival.

When news finally came, it was the worst possible. 'Your son is dead!' the messenger flatly announced to Suppiluliuma. Alas, the text which tells us this becomes fragmentary at this point, and we do not know the circumstances of the prince's death. Was his party ambushed somewhere in Syria-Palestine on its way to Egypt—he must have had a substantial military escort of both Egyptian and Hittite troops—and was he then assassinated? If so, was it by a dissident or rival group in Egypt who fiercely opposed the action taken by the queen in seeking out a foreigner, an Asiatic at that, to take her husband's place? Answers to these questions may forever elude us. All that is certain is that the young queen's hopes and plans had come to naught. Her kingdom's throne was now assumed in haste by a seventy-year-old man called Ay who had long been influential in the Egyptian court. He was perhaps related to the royal family, and may have been Ankhesenamun's grandfather. In any case, Ay quickly completed the burial rites—a scene from Tutankhamun's tomb depicts him doing this—and ascended the throne as the new pharaoh. Ankhesenamun probably became his wife. But from this time on she fades into obscurity.

Whatever the truth of the matter, Suppiluliuma held the Egyptians reponsible for his son's death. His fury knew no bounds: 'Oh Gods! I did no evil, but the people of Egypt did this to me!' Ay wrote to him, denying any involvement in the tragedy, and seeking to renew the former ties of friendship between their kingdoms. But Suppiluliuma was not to be placated. He launched a savage reprisal attack on Egyptian territory in the Syro-Palestinian region. Many thousands of Egypt's subjects were taken prisoner and brought back to Hatti. Ironically, they brought with them a plague that was to devastate the Hittite homeland for the next twenty years, carrying off among its victims both Suppiluliuma and his first son and short-lived successor Arnuwanda.

The full truth of the Ankhesenamun affair may never be known. And in the manner of all good murder mysteries, there is a fair chance that the chief suspect, the new pharaoh Ay, was in fact as innocent as he claimed. What is certain is that this episode marked the beginning of a period of increasing tensions between Egypt and Hatti, which were to culminate five decades later in one of the most famous and best documented conflicts of the ancient world—the battle of Qadesh, fought on the Orontes river in Syria.

Hittite rule in Syria

Following his conquest of Carchemish, Suppiluliuma took a step unprecedented in the history of the Hittite kingdom. He made Carchemish the centre of a viceregal state and appointed his son Sharri-Kushuh as its first viceroy. To the south along the west bank of the Euphrates, the kingdom called Ashtata was incorporated into Sharri-Kushuh's domain. Its administrative centre was the city of Emar. During the French excavations of the site, around 800 cuneiform tablets were unearthed, in the residence of the local ruler.[5] Some were written in Hurrian and Hittite, but the great majority were in Akkadian and Sumerian. Their contents cover economic and legal activities, prescriptions for festivals and ritual practices, and a few lexical, omen, and literary texts (including a fragmentary version of the Gilgamesh epic). After the Amarna letters and the archives of Ugarit, they are our most important source of contemporary written information about Syria during the second half of the Late Bronze Age. To the south-west of Carchemish, Suppiluliuma made Aleppo into another viceregal centre. He appointed another of his sons, Telipinu, as its viceroy. Between them the viceroys in Syria exercised the most important functions of the Great King himself— political, military, judicial, and religious—in the regions over which they had sway, and which they ruled in the name of the Great King. Thus Suppiluliuma established direct Hittite rule over a large part of northern Syria, which lasted until the empire's final days.

Elsewhere in the Great King's Syrian domains, local kingdoms remained under local regimes, and were allowed a relatively high degree of autonomy, subject to the obligations imposed upon them by Hittite overlordship. After its king Niqmaddu II was won over by Suppiluliuma, Ugarit remained a loyal vassal state, for the time being. Across the Orontes, the Nuhashshi lands had been brought by Suppiluliuma under Hittite control, and a man called Tette was appointed as their vassal ruler. (We shall be hearing further about him.) The Nuhashshi lands had been strong allies of Mitanni and bowed to Hittite sovereignty with no small degree of reluctance. To the south of Nuhashshi, the land of Tunip, formerly an important Egyptian stronghold, had been occupied by the Amurrite Aziru and used by him as a base for his subsequent negotiations with Suppiluliuma. It may thus for a time have been an ally or subject of Hatti. But it was later recaptured by the pharaoh Ramesses II during a campaign which he conducted into Syro-Palestinian territory in 1271. We have noted that Amurru became a subject-ally of Hatti when Aziru finally deserted his allegiance to Akhenaten and concluded a formal treaty with Suppiluliuma, which still survives. Also extant is a treaty between Aziru's grandson Duppi-Teshub and Suppiluliu-ma's son and second successor Mursili II.[6] But control over Amurru remained a source of dispute in the decades following Suppiluliuma's death, and pro-vided one of the two main catalysts for the showdowns between Egypt and Hatti during the reigns of the pharaohs Seti I and Ramesses II. Qadesh pro-vided the second catalyst. It too lay in the frontier area between Egyptian and Hittite territory.

Overall, Suppiluliuma's achievements in Syria had been considerable. But his successes were not unqualified ones. By eliminating the Mitannian empire, he also made smooth the way for Assyria to fill the large power vacuum which its demise left east of the Euphrates. A resurgent Assyrian kingdom did this with alacrity, and then posed a threat to Hittite and ulti-mately Egyptian subject territories west of the Euphrates. Tensions between Egypt and Hatti remained high throughout Suppiluliuma's final years and the reigns of his successors, eventually to culminate in all-out war which would irreparably weaken both kingdoms. Further, major uprisings in the king's western Anatolian lands demonstrated the fragility of Suppiluliuma's hold over this region, no doubt due in large measure to his preoccupation with Syrian affairs. And the Egyptian-transmitted plague which carried off Suppiluliuma, six years after his conquest of Carchemish, and then his son and first successor Arnuwanda, seriously jeopardized the Hittites' sover-eignty over their Syrian territories as well as other parts of their realm.

Late 14th–early 13th centuries BC

With Arnuwanda's death after only two years (at most) on his throne, Great Kingship was suddenly thrust upon the king's younger brother Mursili (II), barely out of his teens. As Mursili himself tells us, his enemies initially treated him with contempt: 'You are a child; you know nothing and instil no fear in me. Your land is now in ruins, and your infantry and chariotry are few.

Against your infantry, I have many infantry; against your chariotry I have many chariotry. Your father had many infantry and chariotry. But you, who are a child, how can you match him?'[7] Their contempt was premature. Within four years of his accession, Mursili had crushed the rebellions that broke out in the west, then took decisive action against rebel and enemy states to the north and east of his kingdom. During these early critical years he was fortunate in having the unqualified loyalty of his two elder brothers, Sharri-Kushuh and Telipinu, the viceroys of Carchemish and Aleppo. Sharri-Kushuh in particular proved a major source of support to the young king, joining him with reinforcements from Carchemish for his campaign against the rebel states in western Anatolia. And both viceroys no doubt contributed significantly to the maintenance of peace and stability in Syria at this time.

But then early in Mursili's seventh regnal year, trouble flared in the region. It had to do with Tette, whom Suppiluliuma had appointed as ruler of the Nuhashshi lands. Tette now decided it was time to establish his independence, and led his kingdom in rebellion against Hittite rule. Preoccupied with other matters, Mursili was reluctant to commit his forces to a major operation in Syria against the rebels. There might in fact be another way to deal with the situation. The king's intelligence sources revealed that Tette's action did not have the wholehearted support of his family. That was a situation worth exploiting. Negotiations were secretly conducted with Shummittara, Tette's brother, probably by Sharri-Kushuh on Mursili's behalf. Shummittara was urged to depose his brother, either by assassinating him or taking him prisoner and handing him over to the Hittites. Either way, Shummittara could then assume the throne for himself, with Hittite backing—provided of course he acknowledged Hittite overlordship.

Initially, things went according to plan. The coup took place, Tette was deposed and held under house arrest, and Shummittara became king. Just to tidy things up, Mursili took time out from his northern campaigns to conduct a brief expedition into Syria, to eliminate a minor troublesome king who had supported Tette. Amazingly, Mursili did not take custody of Tette while he was in Syria. That proved a bad mistake. Shortly after his departure, Tette staged a counter-coup and got his throne back. Under his leadership, rebellion in the Nuhashshi lands broke out afresh, before Mursili had troops available to prevent it. The situation was made worse when an expeditionary force arrived from Egypt, then ruled by Ay's successor Horemheb, to support the rebels. The main responsibility for crushing the uprising fell on

Sharri-Kushuh. But the viceroy seriously doubted that he had the resources to defeat the rebels, particularly now that they had been strengthened by reinforcements from Egypt. This was probably the context in which he sought an alliance with the king of Ugarit, Niqmaddu II, who had previously drawn up a treaty with Suppiluliuma, and seems to have remained loyal to it. Niqmaddu may well have agreed to support Sharri-Kushuh, but he died before the agreement could be implemented. He was succeeded, perhaps even before his death, by his son Arhalba, who sought to establish his kingdom's independence and entered into negotiations with Horemheb. Yet though the odds were stacked against him, Sharri-Kushuh, his army swelled by an expeditionary force sent by Mursili, defeated and expelled Tette's Egyptian reinforcements. Whether or not he also managed to bring Tette's reign to an end remains unknown. What we do know is that within two years rebellion had broken out afresh in Nuhashshi, with or without Tette as its leader.[8]

Troubles in the north-eastern part of his kingdom kept Mursili fully occupied with campaigns there for the next two years. But in his ninth year, he took time out to go to a city called Kummanni, an important cult centre in the land of Kizzuwadna in south-eastern Anatolia. A major festival was being celebrated there in honour of the goddess Hepat. Mursili's presence was deemed particularly important, for his father had neglected the festival, at the risk of considerable divine displeasure. Mursili's pilgrimage had a further purpose. While in Kummanni, he summoned his brother Sharri-Kushuh for an urgent meeting, almost certainly to discuss the mounting problems in the Syrian region, and how best to deal with them. Pressing matters included the as yet unresolved situation in Nuhashshi, the increasing threat of Assyria, and the menace posed by the renewal of Egypt's territorial claims in Syria under the pharaoh Horemheb. Another matter to be dealt with was the recent death of Mursili's other brother Telipinu, viceroy at Aleppo. Telipinu's son had been installed as the new viceroy, but no doubt Mursili wanted to discuss with Sharri-Kushuh his role in supporting the new man, particularly in view of the increasing volatility of the whole Syrian region.

There was much to discuss between the two brothers at Kummanni. But then came an unexpected and enormous blow for Mursili. While at Kummanni, Sharri-Kushuh suddenly fell ill and died. His death would undoubtedly place further strain on the Hittite regime's efforts to maintain its authority in Syria—with the loss within a few months of both its viceroys. The Nuhashshi lands were quick to take advantage of the situation, and once more rose in revolt. Qadesh's ruler Aitakkama, installed as vassal by Suppiluliuma, also seized the opportunity to rebel against Mursili. Even more serious, the news of Sharri-Kushuh's death prompted the Assyrians to cross the Euphrates and invade and occupy the now leaderless kingdom of Carchemish. And at the same time all this was happening, the ruler of the large vassal kingdom Azzi-Hayasa in the north-east of the Hittite realm broke his Hittite allegiance and attacked and ravaged the Hittite buffer zone called the Upper Land.

Mursili could not afford the slightest delay in dealing with these crises. And so he despatched one of his generals to deal with the Syrian vassal rebellions, he sent another to expel the Azzi-Hayasan enemy from the Upper Land, and he himself set out for Ashtata on the Euphrates to make preparations for driving the Assyrians from Carchemish. It took two years to restore Hittite authority over Azzi-Hayasa. But the Syrian crisis was sorted out more quickly. Little time was needed to crush the rebellion in Nuhashshi, which the victorious Hittite commander Kuruntiya followed up with reprisals in its territory. He also re-established Hittite control over Qadesh. But not too much credit should be given to him for this. The rebel state was handed to him on a plate, so to speak. Its king Aitakkama was assassinated by his eldest son Niqmaddu, who then pledged his allegiance to Hatti. Father and son must have disagreed about where their kingdom's future lay. The fact that the son favoured Hatti probably means that his father wanted to re-establish an alliance with Egypt. Complete independence for any of the small Syrian kingdoms was simply not an option. In any case, the assassin was brought before Mursili. This created something of a dilemma for the Great King. Reputedly the most pious and conscience-driven of all Hittite rulers, Mursili found the act of patricide abhorrent, even though in this case he himself had benefited from it. The crime was about as serious as a crime could get—and now its perpetrator wanted to be rewarded with his father-victim's throne! At first, Mursili angrily rejected him: 'Under these circumstances, I did not accept Niqmaddu into vassalage.' But later on, he had second thoughts. Political considerations finally prevailed over moral ones. The son was formally installed on his father's throne.

Mursili dealt in person with the Assyrian occupation of Carchemish. The Assyrian king had probably not sent a large force to occupy the city, and Mursili succeeded in dislodging it and driving it back across the Euphrates with apparently little effort. Before leaving Carchemish, he replaced the deceased viceroy Sharri-Kushuh with one of his sons, and then went to Aleppo to install a new viceroy there, likewise a son of his predecessor. Next, to consolidate Hittite control further over northern Syria, he put a new king Niqmepa on the throne of Ugarit, in place of his older brother Arhalba who had broken his ties with Hatti and negotiated with Egypt. Henceforth, Ugarit appears to have remained loyal to its Hittite allegiance almost to the end of its existence. But as we shall see, its obligations to Hatti were met with increasing reluctance as its final days drew ever closer.

Mursili could be well satisfied with his Syrian enterprises. He had reaffirmed his control over all the territories won by his father. And for the time being Assyria had been held in check. But there were dark clouds gathering. Egypt was to loom ever larger and more menacingly on Hatti's southern horizon.

First half of the 13th century BC

Qadesh!

With the death of Tutankhamun and the end of the Eighteenth Dynasty, Egypt had lost all but token influence in Syria. Things had begun to improve when Tutankhamun's successor Ay died after a four-year reign and was replaced by Horemheb, who paved the way for an Egyptian resurgence under a new dynasty. This, the Nineteenth or Ramesside Dynasty, was founded in 1295 by a king called Ramesses I. But it was Ramesses' co-regent and successor Seti I (1294–1279) who developed an aggressive new programme of imperial expansion, intent on re-establishing his kingdom as a great international power. Tuthmosis III was his model and source of inspiration. A successful expedition in his first regnal year against bedouin groups in Canaan was followed a year or so later by another campaign further north in the region, which led to the defeat and submission of a coalition of local rulers. Then he set his sights on a more ambitious undertaking—the reconquest of the kingdoms of Qadesh and Amurru.

And he succeeded! Both kingdoms fell to the pharaoh. The die was cast. By seizing what were hitherto Hittite subject states, Seti was in effect declaring war on Hatti. At that time, the Hittite throne was occupied by Mursili's son and successor Muwattalli II. Muwattalli was fully aware that all-out conflict with Egypt was now very close. But he did not yet have sufficient troops mustered in Syria to repel a large-scale Egyptian attack, and had been caught off guard by Seti's sudden seizure of Qadesh and Amurru. So a showdown was postponed for the time being. Seti withdrew to Egypt and undertook a successful campaign against the Libyans. Then he returned to Syria, ready for fresh conquests and a test of strength with Muwattalli in defence of the states he had taken from him. This time, Muwattalli was ready for his adversary. The forces met near Qadesh. In an account of the battle on Seti's war monument at Karnak in Egypt, the pharaoh claims a resounding victory: '...mighty Bull, [ready]-horned, [mighty]-hearted, smiting the Asiatics, beating down the Hittites, slaying their chiefs, overthrown in their blood, charging among them like a tongue of fire, making them as that which is not... Chiefs of the countries that knew not Egypt, whom his Majesty brought as living captives... The victor returns, when he has devastated the countries. He has smitten the land of Hatti, causing the cowardly rebels to cease.'[9] As far as we can sift through all this bombast, it does seem that Seti won a decisive victory, and thus confirmed his hold over Qadesh and Amurru. But Muwattalli was far from finished with Egypt. His encounter with Seti was but a prelude to the much better known 'second' battle of Qadesh, which he fought a few years later, in 1274, with Seti's son and successor Ramesses II.[10]

No doubt learning much from his first defeat, Muwattalli made extensive preparations for this second confrontation, assembling from all parts of his realm, and beyond it, an army so large that his victory was assured—so he believed. But his efforts were matched by those of the new pharaoh Ramesses, fully determined to maintain and indeed expand Egypt's control over its hard-won Syrian territories, and as primed as his Hittite adversary for all-out war. The first three years of Ramesses' reign had been taken up largely with internal matters. But by the summer of his fourth year, he was ready for Syria. In 1275, he led a preliminary operation into the region, and the following year the campaign that brought him into head-on conflict with the Hittites.

Qadesh provided the arena where the conflicting claims of Egypt and Hatti would at last be resolved. Following Seti's capture of it, the kingdom had later reverted to Hittite control, for it was once more on the Hittite side by the early years of Ramesses' reign. But the matter was far from settled. Ramesses' version of the contest that finally determined Qadesh's fate is recorded on the walls of five Egyptian temples, both in pictorial form, depicting various episodes in the campaign, and also in a so-called 'Literary

Figure 6. Ramesses II, Abu Simbel

Record', which provides us with a written account of it, at least from the Egyptian point of view. (We have no corresponding Hittite version of the battle.) Usefully, the Egyptian record contains not only details of the battle itself, but also the events leading up to it, including the progress of the four Egyptian divisions, recruited from four Egyptian cities and each named after an Egyptian god—from Thebes the army of Amun, from Heliopolis of Re, from Memphis of Ptah, and probably from Tanis the army of Sutekh. They all mustered in the pharaoh's capital Pi-Ramesse in the Delta. Ramesses led the way into the northern lands at the head of the Amun division. In Syria, Muwattalli's core Hittite forces were swelled by a large assemblage of troops from the subject states, and, according to Ramesses' account, a massive horde of mercenaries, the Hittite king stripping his country of everything he could to pay for their services. If we are to believe the Egyptian figures, the Hittite force totalled 47,500 warriors, including 3,500 chariot teams-of-three and 37,000 infantry. Ramesses' four divisions probably equalled this number. One of the largest military engagements so far in the history of the ancient world was about to take place.

Despite what Ramesses would have us believe, things did not go at all well for the Egyptians. Poor planning and poor reconnaissance character- ized their progress throughout the campaign. As they marched northwards, their four divisions became spread out over a considerable distance, with the pharaoh's own Amun division advancing far ahead of the other three. But Ramesses seems to have been quite unaware of his increasingly vulnerable position. Indeed, his confidence in victory received a considerable boost when two bedouins, alleged defectors from the Hittite army, came to him and declared that the entire Hittite army was far to the north, in the Land of Aleppo; its commander Muwattalli was too scared to come south to meet the pharaoh's army. It was a trick, but the report reinforced Ramesses' delu- sions about the fear he inspired in his enemy. He accepted what he was told at face value, without any further investigation or even token reconnais- sance. After crossing a ford on the Orontes south of Qadesh, he started set- ting up his camp, in leisurely fashion, to the north-west of the city as he prepared to lay siege to it. Then came a severe shock. Two Hittite scouts sent by Muwattalli to find out the exact position of the Egyptian army were caught, and under torture revealed the horrifying truth. Far from being way up north, Muwattalli's army was in a concealed position on the other side of Qadesh, poised to attack! Ramesses roundly abused his officers for their disastrous intelligence failure, and then sent two of his officials south with urgent orders for the Re and Ptah divisions to proceed post-haste to Qadesh to meet the Hittite attack. The Sutekh division was too far off to worry about. The Re division rushed north as quickly as possible. But as it crossed the Orontes, it was caught by the charge of the Hittite army and broke apart. Its troops fled in panic to the camp still being set up by Ramesses and his Amun division—with the Hittite chariotry in hot pursuit. A rout looked inevitable!

But then Ramesses showed his true mettle, with a remarkable display of courage and coolness in the face of overwhelming odds. Well, at least that is what he himself tells us. As the Hittite three-man chariot teams surrounded his forces in an ever-tightening circle, he launched a desperate counter- attack: 'Then His Majesty started forth at a gallop, and entered into the host

Figure 7. Hittite warriors at Qadesh, from temple of Luxor

of the fallen ones of Hatti, being alone by himself and none other with him.... And he found 2,500 chariots hemming him in on his outer side, consisting of all the fallen ones of Hatti with the many foreign countries which were with them... I called to you, My Father Amun, when I was in the midst of multitudes I knew not. All foreign countries were combined against me, I being alone by myself, none other with me, my numerous infantry having abandoned me, not one looking at me of my chariotry. I kept on shouting to them, but none of them hearkened to me as I called.... I found Amun come when I called him; he gave me his hand and I rejoiced.... All that I did came to pass. I was like Mont. I shot to my right and captured to my left.... I found the 2,500 chariots, in whose midst I was, sprawling before my horse. Not one of them found his hand to fight.... I caused them to plunge into the water even as crocodiles plunge, fallen upon their faces one upon the other. I killed among them according as I willed.'[11]

Let us do a reality check. While we should in no way doubt the pharaoh's courage, the resounding victory he claimed, depicting his opponent Muwat-talli ('the wretched ruler of Hatti') paying homage to him and begging for mercy, is so much nonsense. Ramesses survived the battle, but by the skin of his teeth! Two factors in particular seem to have saved him and his army

from annihilation: the timely arrival of reinforcements from the west, perhaps a contingent from Amurru, and a breakdown in discipline among the
Hittite troops, especially the mercenaries among them, who had set about
looting the Egyptian camp before the victory was secured. Early the following day, Ramesses attacked the Hittites once more. Muwattalli's forces
held firm against the onslaught, though they were unable to launch a
successful counterattack. The contest thus ended in a stalemate, with neither side emerging as its winner. But that did not stop Ramesses claiming
victory, and proclaiming his 'triumph' on the walls of five temples. In the
long term, however, the Hittites could justifiably be regarded as the victors in the contest. For they regained the disputed territories Qadesh and
Amurru, and retained them until the end of the empire. And Egypt conceded to them all territories in Syria north of Damascus. Indeed, after the
battle, Damascus itself was for a time occupied by Hittite forces, under
the command of the future king Hattusili III until he was recalled by his
brother Muwattalli. On his homeward journey, he met and married, in
the city Lawazantiya in the land of Kizzuwadna, the daughter of a Hurrian priest. Her name was Puduhepa. We shall be meeting Puduhepa
again on several occasions. A formidable power behind the throne, and
indeed sometimes (metaphorically speaking) *on* the throne beside her
husband, she was to have a profound influence on Hattusili for the rest of
his career, on the entire Hittite royal family, and on the affairs of the
kingdom at large.

Tensions continued for a time between Hatti and Egypt,[12] but the
Qadesh engagement had taken a heavy toll on both sides. Indeed, it had
so drained their resources that neither could ever again think of conflict
on such a scale. There was also the Assyrian question. The resurgent
kingdom's aggressive new rulers might well set their sights on extending
their conquests west of the Euphrates, all the way to the Mediterranean
Sea. If so, then Egyptian as well as Hittite territories in the region could
very well be lost. This may have been one of the prompts for the establishment of a peace accord between Egypt and Hatti. After many
exchanges of correspondence and many ambassadorial visits between the
two royal courts, the famous document known as the 'Eternal Treaty' was
finally drawn up, in 1259. Written on tablets of silver with versions in
both Egyptian and Akkadian, the treaty signalled peace for all time
between the Great Kingdoms. Its signatories were Ramesses II and the
current king Hattusili III.[13]

The elusive ex-king

Hattusili was the brother of Ramesses' opponent Muwattalli, as we have noted. When Muwattalli died *c.*1272, his throne had first passed to his son Urhi-Teshub. But Hattusili had other plans. Despite an initial show of cooperation with his brother's son, he fell out with him after a few years, seized his throne, and exiled him to the Nuhashshi lands in Syria. To keep him out of mischief, he made him governor of some cities there. But that did not work. Urhi-Teshub was determined to get his throne back, and devoted the rest of his life to his mission. From his place of exile, he sent appeals for assistance not only to his former vassals, but also to foreign kings—the rulers of Assyria, Babylon, and Egypt. Hattusili countered by sending his own appeals to these kings, demanding that they acknowledge *him* as the true sovereign of Hatti. The Babylonian and Assyrian kings initially snubbed him, and so he set much store by his alliance with the pharaoh. This was one of the reasons, perhaps the main one, why his treaty with Ramesses was so important to him. It provided him with explicit pharaonic acknowledgement of his right to occupy the Hittite throne. What made this acknowledgement all the more pressing was that Urhi-Teshub had fled his place of exile in Syria and was apparently now somewhere in Egypt. His finding safe haven there could well be construed as Egyptian support for him. Hattusili sent a stream of letters to Ramesses demanding his extradition.

We are not sure about the chronology of Urhi-Teshub's movements, or how long he enjoyed the pharaoh's (unwitting?) hospitality. But it seems likely that he absconded to Egypt before the treaty was drawn up, and may have stayed there some twenty years, including the period after the treaty had been signed and sealed. In any case, Hattusili wanted Ramesses to take him into custody. And once the treaty was in place, he could invoke its extradition clauses, which obliged each of the signatories to hand back to the other any fugitives from his lands. Still, Hattusili was willing to compromise; if the pharaoh did take custody of Urhi-Teshub, he could keep him in Egypt, somewhere out of harm's way. That was all very well. But Urhi-Teshub had to be found first. The question was, *where* was he in Egypt? Ramesses protested that he did not know. And he may have been telling the truth. Even so, Hattusili could still call upon him, under the terms of the treaty, to spare no expense in tracking the fugitive down, bribing his supporters if necessary. Hattusili's queen

Puduhepa also wrote to Ramesses, reminding him of her husband's request, and likewise urging him to make every effort to apprehend Urhi-Teshub.

Of course it all depended on whether the ex-king was still in Egypt or one of its subject territories. And on that score, Ramesses had bad news for his royal brother. Despite all his efforts, he had failed to run Urhi-Teshub to ground—for the very good reason that he was no longer in Egypt! He was back in Hattusili's own lands! 'He has flown (there) like a bird,' the pharaoh announced. In a spirit of friendly cooperation, he suggested some of the Hittite lands where his royal brother might find him. Perhaps he was in Syria, in the land of Aleppo or Qadesh; perhaps he was in south-eastern Anatolia, in the land of Kizzuwadna. Egypt was still available as a place of exile for Urhi-Teshub. But it was now up to his uncle to catch him first.

Hattusili was outraged. To claim that the fugitive was back in his own territory, without his even knowing it, was an insult. 'Urhi-Teshub is not in Aleppo or Qadesh or Kizzuwadna!' he wrote angrily to the pharaoh. 'Otherwise my own subjects would have told me!' 'Your subjects are not to be trusted,' sniffed the pharaoh in reply.[14]

In fact, Urhi-Teshub very likely *was* back in Hittite territory. From what we can piece together of the remains of two parallel letters which Ramesses wrote to Hattusili and Puduhepa, it seems that Hattusili had instructed one of his sons, the prince Nerikkaili, to collaborate with Ramesses in locating Urhi-Teshub. Nerikkaili was the son-in-law of the king of Amurru, and may at that time have been acting as his father's agent or representative in the Amurrite region. The fragmentary letters suggest that Urhi-Teshub had in fact managed to elude his Egyptian pursuers by crossing the frontier in southern Syria back into Hittite-controlled territory. And here, probably in the country of Amurru, he had fallen into Nerikkaili's hands. But his run of good fortune had not yet ended. Nerikkaili apparently died before having a chance to notify his father that he had apprehended the fugitive. Urhi-Teshub managed to bribe his guards to set him free. Once again he was on the loose!

What eventually happened to him? We'll probably never know for sure. But there is a possibility that he did re-establish himself and his family in Syria or south-eastern Anatolia, and that a kingdom ruled by his descendants emerged somewhere in these regions in the centuries following the fall of the Hittite empire.

The royal visit that never was[15]

Apart from the Urhi-Teshub episode, relations between Egypt and Hatti remained relatively cordial (though sometimes strained). This is reflected in the correspondence exchanged between members of the royal courts, notably the letters that passed between Ramesses and Hattusili, and Puduhepa and Ramesses. In one of these, Ramesses issued an invitation to his royal brother to visit Egypt. Hattusili allegedly accepted the invitation. Ramesses was delighted, and wrote enthusiastically to him about arrangements for his journey. Egyptian officials would meet him halfway between their kingdoms, in the Hittite–Egyptian frontier region north of Damascus, and escort him to the pharaoh who would be awaiting him in the land of Canaan. Thence the Great Kings would proceed together to Ramesses' capital Pi-Ramesse in the Delta, where the pharaoh would present his brother to his subjects and give him a tour of the great monuments of his land.

The visit never took place. Ramesses had clearly misinterpreted Hattusili's response to his invitation. Indeed, it is inconceivable that Hattusili would ever have gone to Egypt. To begin with, he was far too occupied with events, often verging on crises, within his own kingdom to contemplate taking time out for an extended period away, far to the south in Egypt. In the second place, it was simply not the done thing for one Great King to visit another in the latter's own country. Visits were made by one's envoys to a fellow-king's lands. For a Great King to go himself would have been seen as an act of subservience to his royal brother. And we can be sure that if Hattusili had in fact made such a visit, the pharaoh would have extracted maximum political capital out of it, parading his guest around the temples which proclaimed his alleged victory at Qadesh, and making clear to his subjects that 'the wretched ruler of Hatti's' visit was in fact an act of submission. A third factor that must have dissuaded Hattusili from even thinking about a visit to Egypt was his state of health. He was now well advanced in years, some ten years older than Ramesses, and was afflicted with an ailment which his queen Puduhepa describes in a prayer for him as 'fire-of-the-feet'. From this still surviving text, a Turkish medical expert has concluded that Hattusili was afflicted by a painful condition called neuropathy.[16] To make things worse, he also suffered from a chronic eye-disease. With problems affecting both ends of his anatomy, the possibility of a Hittite royal visit to Egypt could never have been seriously entertained, even if all other things had been equal—and Puduhepa had given her consent.

In any case, peaceful relations between Hatti and Egypt remained in place after the treaty for the rest of the Late Bronze Age, and were consolidated by a marriage alliance between the two Great Kings, when one of Hattusili's daughters was sent to Egypt to wed the pharaoh, and a second one some years later. Arrangements for at least the first of these were not without acrimony, as indicated by the pre-marriage correspondence that passed between Puduhepa and Ramesses. But that is a story for another time. The two royal families were united by marriage, and remained at peace until the collapse of Hatti at the end of the Late Bronze Age.

The ties that unbind

Let us return to the immediate post-war scene in Syria. For Muwattalli, the reacquisition of the kingdom of Amurru had been one of the most important outcomes of his showdown with Ramesses. Control of it was the key to the security of Hittite territories in northern Syria. Its capture by Seti I in the first battle of Qadesh had put at serious risk all of Hatti's Syrian lands. Getting it back must have been high on Muwattalli's list of reasons for engaging the Egyptians a second time at Qadesh. In the aftermath of the battle, Benteshina, son of Duppi-Teshub and now the current ruler of Amurru, was held responsible for the loss of his kingdom to Egypt. This was probably unfair. He had indeed gone over to the pharaoh. But he had done so only when Egyptian forces were already on his border. Without military back-up from Hatti, he had no option but to surrender. This cut no ice with Muwattalli. Immediately after the battle he had Benteshina arrested and deported to Hatti, replacing him in Amurru with a man called Shapili.

Back in the Hittite homeland, Benteshina had the good fortune to find favour with Hattusili, who managed to persuade his brother that the ex-king really had been the victim of forces beyond his control. Hattusili had him assigned to his personal charge in the city Hakpissa, capital of the northern part of the Hittite homeland. Hattusili ruled there on special appointment from his brother. And in Hakpissa Benteshina lived in considerable style and comfort. For a time. After Muwattalli's death, and probably during the early part of Urhi-Teshub's reign before relations between the king and his uncle deteriorated, he was restored to the throne of Amurru. Almost certainly he owed his reinstatement to Hattusili. With his eye on the future, Hattusili had long marked out his protégé as a valuable ally and source of intelligence in the Syrian region, once he was back on his throne.

We do not know what happened to his predecessor Shapili. He may well have been eliminated by Hattusili's agents to make way for Benteshina's return.

Probably not long after his coup against Urhi-Teshub, and in the context of his attempts to win endorsement from both foreign rulers and his own subjects, Hattusili formalized his relationship with Benteshina by drawing up a treaty with him.[17] Benteshina had asked for the treaty, but we can be sure that Hattusili was only too willing to oblige. It was a handy prop for his flaky kingship. He further strengthened his relationship with the vassal by arranging a double marriage alliance with him; his daughter Gassuliyawiya wed Benteshina himself, and his son Nerikkaili (whom we have already met) wed Benteshina's daughter. Hattusili also united himself with the royal house of Babylon by a double marriage, provided two of his daughters as brides for Ramesses, and wed another daughter to the vassal king of Isuwa in northern Mesopotamia. He does seem to have had an inexhaustible supply of offspring available for such purposes. Indeed, during the reign of his son Tudhaliya (IV), yet another of his daughters was wed to Benteshina's son and successor in Amurru, a man called Shaushgamuwa. Political marriages were a long-established means of consolidating alliances between royal families. But those of Hattusili's reign took on a particular significance, in so far as they helped establish the usurper's status among his peers and vassal rulers as the true king of Hatti.

Third quarter of the 13th century BC

Like all other marriages, high-level diplomatic ones did not always work out. And if such a marriage turned sour, the consequent fallout could be severe—as illustrated by a marriage-gone-wrong that linked the royal houses of Amurru and Ugarit. In an effort to bind these Hittite vassal kingdoms more closely together, one of Benteshina's daughters had been wed to a young man called Ammishtamru II, who had recently occupied the throne of Ugarit. The marriage ended in divorce—apparently because of a serious offence committed by the princess, perhaps adultery. The princess returned to her homeland in disgrace, leaving in Ugarit all the possessions she had acquired since her marriage, in accordance with standard divorce provisions. She was, however, allowed to take her original dowry with her. But after her departure, her ex-husband continued to brood over his grievances, and convinced himself that she had got off too lightly. He now demanded that she be sent back to Ugarit for appropriate punishment, and declared that he was prepared to go to war with Amurru to enforce his demand.

At first, the current Amurrite king Shaushgamuwa refused, knowing that if he returned the princess (who was his sister) to Ugarit, he would in effect be signing her death warrant. He backed up his refusal by declaring that if Ammishtamru invaded his kingdom by land or by sea in pursuit of his demand, he would be met with force. A serious impasse had arisen. All-out conflict between the vassals seemed inevitable! And that prompted hasty intervention by the Hittite king Tudhaliya. The last thing he could have wanted was a war between two of his key subjects in Syria. Yet there were serious risks involved if he took the side of one against the other. What to do? Clearly Ammishtamru was the aggrieved party. His wife had wronged and disgraced him, and no doubt caused him much loss of face. What made things more difficult for him was that his position on his throne was not entirely secure. He had quarrelled with his two brothers, very likely over the succession. And at the instigation of his mother Ahat-milku, who had been regent for a short time following the death of her husband Niqmepa, he had sent them into exile. Tudhaliya had supported this action. But now the young king's credibility had been seriously undermined in the eyes of his subjects. How could he rule his kingdom effectively if he couldn't rule his own wife?

Protracted negotiations followed as Tudhaliya tried to sort the matter out. In the process, he called upon the assistance of his cousin Ini-Teshub, the current viceroy at Carchemish, who had overall responsibility for the Hittites' Syrian affairs. Ammishtamru refused to budge from his position, and Tudhaliya acknowledged that he had right on his side. So the Hittite king took what he believed was the only course possible. He made it clear to Shaushgamuwa that if he refused to deliver up his sister and Ammish-tamru sent troops to fetch her back to Amurru, he must not resist them: 'If Shaushgamuwa, son of Benteshina, king of Amurru, does violence to Ammishtamru, son of Niqmepa, king of Ugarit, or does violence to the boats or the soldiers who go to retrieve the daughter of the Great Lady, Heaven and the Earth will know it... (A list of deities follows.) May these gods do him violence, may they make him disappear from the house of his father and from the country of his father, and from the throne of his fathers!'[18] But compromise is the essence of all good diplomacy. Tudhaliya managed to extract from both parties an agreeement to the effect that if

Shaushgamuwa surrendered his sister to the king of Ugarit, the latter would pay him 1,400 shekels of gold by way of compensation. The agreement stipulated that this was a one-off arrangement, thus anticipating any demand Shaushgamuwa might subsequently have made for more money to help soothe his grief at the loss of his sister. And so Shaushgamuwa reluctantly farewelled the wayward princess, in the knowledge that he was sending her to what would almost certainly be a humiliating and painful death.

Assyria and Hatti in conflict

We have noted the involvement of Ini-Teshub in this affair. As viceroy of Carchemish, Ini-Teshub proved a highly competent administrator and an invaluable support to the Great King by his efficient governance of his own kingdom, and more broadly by the vital role he played in maintaining stability within Hatti's Syrian territories—particularly at this time when fears were mounting of renewed Assyrian aggression. Tudhaliya's father Hattusili had tried to cultivate good relations with the Assyrian king Shalmaneser I (c.1263–1234),[19] and for a time there was peace between the Great Kingdoms. But tensions returned and escalated sharply during Tudhaliya's reign, especially when Shalmaneser invaded and destroyed the Hittite-backed kingdom of Hanigalbat, the final remnant of the fomer Mitannian empire. Hanigalbat's territory had extended to the east bank of the Euphrates. By conquering it, Shalmaneser expanded his power to a mere river's breadth away from Hittite territory. An Assyrian invasion of Tudhaliya's Syrian states seemed imminent. Then came news of Shalmaneser's death and his replacement on the Assyrian throne by his young son Tukulti-Ninurta. Tudhaliya wrote to the new king in cordial terms, congratulating him on his accession, and praising the exploits of his father—a necessary piece of diplomatic hypocrisy. He made an explicit offer of friendship to the new king, who wrote a warm letter in reply, expressing his own desire for friendship. Perhaps this would mark the beginning of a new era of peace between Hatti and Assyria.

It was too good to be true. Tukulti-Ninurta had barely mounted his throne before he began preparations for a major offensive against a number of Hurrian states in northern Mesopotamia. This was alarming news for Tudhaliya. For an Assyrian conquest of the region would give Tukulti-Ninurta control of the major routes leading across the Euphrates into Hittite territory in Anatolia. Already his subject lands along the river's east bank provided him with immediate access to Syria. The time for diplomatic posturing was over, and Tudhaliya declared the Assyrian king his enemy. This we learn from a treaty he drew up with the Amurrite king Shaushgamuwa.[20] Hatti and Assyria were now at war, he informed his vassal. Bans were to be imposed on all commercial dealings between Amurru and Assyria: 'As the king of Assyria is the enemy of My Sun, so must he also be your enemy. No merchant of yours is to go to the Land of Assyria, and you must allow no merchant of Assyria to enter your land or pass through your land. If, however, an Assyrian merchant comes to your land, seize him and send him to My Sun. Let this be your obligation under divine oath! And because I, My Sun, am at war with the king of Assyria, when I call up troops and chariotry you must do likewise.'

A showdown between the two Great Kings was now inevitable. It took place in the region of Nihriya in north-eastern Mesopotamia, probably north or north-east of modern Diyabakır. In a letter to the king of Ugarit, Tukulti-Ninurta described the conflict, disclaiming all responsibility for initiating it.[21] He had no wish for war with Hatti, he declared. His campaign had been directed primarily at a region called the Nairi lands, which had nothing to do with the Hittites. Tudhaliya saw things differently. The Assyrian campaign in the region was but one more stage in the continuing expansion of the Assyrian empire which ultimately threatened Hatti, and he made the decision to confront the Assyrian forces there and then, outside Hittite territory and in support of the local kings who were the object of the Assyrian offensive. Tukulti-Ninurta sent an ultimatum to Tudhaliya to back off and withdraw from Nihriya. When Tudhaliya ignored it and continued his advance, Tukulti-Ninurta ordered his forces to attack. If we are to believe the account he gives in his letter to the Ugaritic king, the Hittite forces were routed. It was one of the very few occasions in the history of the Late Bronze Age that two of the Great Kingdoms ever met in an all-out pitched battle. And though we have only the Assyrian version of the engagement, almost certainly the Hittites were heavily defeated. With their defence forces now substantially weakened, all looked set for an Assyrian invasion across the Euphrates. Indeed, two later inscriptions from Tukulti-Ninurta's reign may indicate that the Assyrians did attack Hittite territory at this time. The inscriptions refer to the capture of 28,800 troops 'of Hatti' from across the Euphrates. But most scholars think that the figure is highly exaggerated, and the whole episode indicative of no more than a minor border clash. None the less, there is little doubt that after the Assyrian victory in Nihriya, Tudhaliya feared a comprehensive Assyrian invasion of his kingdom—and there was little he could have done to prevent it.

Then came news that led him to breathe a huge sigh of relief. Inexplicably, at least to us, Tukulti-Ninurta suddenly changed direction. Instead of launching an invasion west of the Euphrates, he turned against his southern neighbour Babylon, and spent much of the rest of his career locked in conflict with the Babylonians. Hatti was spared the ravages of an Assyrian invasion.

But the end was in sight anyhow, for the world as the Hittites and their subjects knew it. This phase of Syria's history is almost played out.

5

The End of an Era

Late 13th–12th centuries BC

The disintegration begins

We are now entering the final years of the Late Bronze Age. This doom-fraught period, the early decades of the 12th century, witnessed the collapse and disappearance of one of the era's great super-powers, the Anatolian-based kingdom of Hatti, and the decline of two of the others, Egypt and Babylon. Assyria appears to have survived the period relatively unscathed, and one of its kings, Tiglath-pileser I (1114–1076), carried out fresh conquests west of the Euphrates (as we shall see in Chapter 7). But his campaigns in the west had no lasting impact there, and after his death Assyria also suffered significant decline, for the next 150 years. No longer were the Syrian peoples subject to imperial overlords, Great Kings whose sovereignty over them had not been altogether without its advantages. The loss of independence and the obligations and costs which vassalhood had entailed were in many cases offset by the benefits that came from the protective umbrella that their overlords extended over them (albeit sometimes unreliably and spasmodically). To be sure, they often became caught up in the contests between rival Great Kings. But some of them managed very well in turning these contests to their benefit. All that was about to change. The increasingly anarchic conditions that resulted from the weakening and disappearance of Syria's last overlords, Hatti and Egypt, profoundly affected the local regions, states, and cities from which they withdrew. Some like Ugarit's capital in north-western Syria suffered total destruction and were never rebuilt. The kingdom of Amurru vanished entirely. Other city-states like Qadesh and Qatna were reoccupied in the succeeding age, but remained insignificant. But others again, like Tyre and Sidon on the Levantine coast, and Carchemish

Figure 8. Postern gate, Ugarit

on the Euphrates, not only survived the upheavals of the age but re-emerged all the stronger and flourished anew in the age that followed.

What happened in the last decades of the Late Bronze Age to bring all this about, particularly in the Syro-Palestinian region? Our search for answers takes us to several places, including the archives of the kingdom of Ugarit, where archaeologists have unearthed a rich repository of correspondence dating from the late 13th and early 12th century BC. These archives appear to have a direct bearing on our quest. Ugarit proved, *almost* always, a loyal vassal to Hatti, ever since Suppiluliuma had won over its ruler Niqmaddu II during his contest with Mitanni. Though it seems never to have made much of a contribution to Hatti's military enterprises, its rich coffers must have helped finance the Hittites' war efforts, through regular tribute payment, and its grainfields became an increasingly important source of food for the Hittite homeland in the empire's final decades. The kingdom's several ports along the Mediterranean coastline played a valuable role in the international trade network, and served as major points of departure for grain shipments to Anatolia's south-eastern coast, whence the grain was transported by donkey caravans into the heartland of the Hittite world. Ugarit as a source of food for the Hittite homeland assumed ever greater significance as grain supplies from Egypt began to run out. Egypt had almost certainly provided Hatti with large consignments of grain via the sea lanes of the eastern Mediterranean between Cyprus and the Levantine and Syrian coasts, following a deal concluded by Hittite authorities with the pharaoh, no doubt in the wake of the 'Eternal Treaty', and consequent negotiations by one of Hattusili's envoys to Egypt, the prince Hishmi-Sharrumma.

Hatti was finding it increasingly difficult in this period to produce enough food to sustain its population. The mounting crisis was in large measure due to an insufficient labour force whose numbers were continually reduced as they were deployed to the ever-more difficult task of defending the kingdom's extensive territories, against both external enemies and rebel leaders. Grain shipments from Egypt were probably despatched to Hatti on a regular basis now, until the last decades of the Late Bronze Age, when imports from this source of supply dwindled and eventually stopped altogether. So too, shipments from Ugarit and other places on the Levantine coast became smaller and more spasmodic. Hatti's position grew more and more desperate. The homeland was fast running out of food. Its plight is reflected in a letter sent from the Hittite court to the Ugaritic king, either Niqmaddu, the second to last king, or his successor Ammurapi. The letter demands a ship and crew for the export of 450 tonnes of grain from the region to be taken by ship to Ura, a port on the south-eastern Anatolian coast, for immediate transportation overland to the Hittite homeland. The urgency of the demand is highlighted in the letter's last words: 'It is a matter of life or death!'[1]

Without doubt, the crisis in Hatti was exacerbated if not directly caused by the transfer of many of its basic food-producers to military duties, often in regions remote from their homeland. But there was little choice. Peter had to be robbed to pay Paul. The defence forces needed boosting, for protection against a tide of enemy predators—but primarily against the Great King's own subjects. From the reign of Tudhaliya IV ($c.$1237–1209), the last kings of Hatti were faced with increasing disturbances and uprisings amongst their subject states throughout their realm, from western Anatolia to the vassal states of Syria. Matters were not helped by the still-festering divisions within the Hittite royal dynasty, with the family of the deposed Urhi-Teshub taking over Tarhuntassa, an important Hittite sub-kingdom in southern Anatolia. Almost certainly Urhi-Teshub's followers and heirs used

Tarhuntassa as a base for winning local support in their attempts to get back the Hittite crown. All this at a time when the empire was in serious trouble anyhow. To judge from correspondence in the Ugarit archive, the Syrian vassals, at least the Ugaritic ones, were rapidly losing confidence in their overlord's ability to protect them, and rapidly gaining confidence in their ability to defy him, or least ignore his requests, with impunity.

Thus a new vassal, Ibiranu (c.1230–1210), who came to the throne of Ugarit as its third-to-last ruler during the reign of Tudhaliya IV, failed to acknowledge Tudhaliya as his overlord, prompting a stern letter of rebuke from a high-ranking Hittite official Pihawalwi: 'Since you have assumed royal power in Ugarit, why have you not come before His Majesty? And why have you not regularly sent messengers? This has made His Majesty very angry. So send messengers to His Majesty with all haste, and see that gifts are brought for the king along with my gifts.'[2] The fact that the new vassal had neglected one of his first obligations on mounting his throne sent a chill warning to the Hittite administration. Ibiranu's failure to acknowledge his overlord was not merely a breach of protocol; it raised serious concerns about his kingdom's future loyalties. Grudgingly, Ibiranu sent some gifts as requested. But they were paltry, prompting another letter of rebuke. This one came from Talmi-Teshub, the Hittite viceroy in Carchemish; Ibiranu was directly responsible to him as the Great King's representative in northern Syria: 'Your messenger which you have sent to Hatti, and the presents which you have had conveyed to the Great Men are quite inadequate,' Talmi-Teshub angrily declared. 'Did I not write to you in these terms: "Send to the Chief of the Tablets a gift of outstanding quality"? So why have you not shown him the respect to which he is due by sending him such a gift? Why have you acted thus?'[3] Ibiranu's neglect of the formalities expected of him was cause enough for concern. Even more concerning was his failure to send a contingent of troops for service in the Hittite army, now desperately in need of reinforcements. This prompted a review of his entire defence establishment by officials from Carchemish. Their findings were clear. Ibiranu had no excuse for welshing on his military obligations, and a second demand for troops was sent to him. He had no option but to comply. But the half-hearted way in which he did so stirred Talmi-Teshub's anger even more: 'The charioteers you sent me are of inferior quality and their horses half-starved!' was but one of the viceroy's complaints when he surveyed the pathetic array of troops and animals provided by his vassal.[4]

Ibiranu's reluctance to contribute troops and equipment to the Hittite army, despite his treaty obligations, is understandable. The kingdom had always been averse to committing its military resources to campaigns by its overlord or to the defence of his territories outside Ugarit itself. And in the past, Hatti had been content to receive large payments of gold and other tribute from the kingdom in lieu of military service. But Hatti could no longer afford to accept tribute from its vassals in place of troops. That greatly worried Ibiranu. As the political and military situation in Syria became increasingly unstable and the threats to Ugarit itself grew ever more severe, he had no wish to weaken further his country's defence forces by sending any of them, let alone the pick of them as his overlord demanded, outside his own territory. The clearer it became to Ibiranu that he could no longer expect his overlord's protection in the event of an attack on Ugaritic territory, either by land or by sea, the more he realized the necessity of keeping the best of his forces at home, for the defence of his own land.

Invaders from the sea

The biggest threat to it and indeed to the whole Syrian and Levantine coast—and for that matter, to the southern Anatolian coast, Cyprus, and the Egyptian Delta—came from the sea. Throughout the Late Bronze Age, and in many earlier and later periods as well, the eastern Mediterranean was a dangerous place for travel. That was partly because of the natural hazards of sudden storms, which left many a merchant ship and other vessels at the bottom of it. But also because of piracy. In the mid 14th century, Akhenaten had written to the king of Alasiya (= Cyprus or part thereof) complaining about the seabooting activities of the notorious Lukka people operating from bases on the southern Anatolian coast and attacking cities on the shores of Egypt. He accused the Alasiyan king and his subjects of complicity in the attacks. The Alasiyan king objected strongly. His cities too, he declared, had suffered annual raids by pirates.[5] We also hear of raids upon the Egyptian coast by buccaneers called Sherden, in the reigns of Amenhotep III and Ramesses II. And in the last years of the Late Bronze Age, what was almost certainly another pirate group, called 'the Shikila who live on boats', appears in a letter sent by a Hittite king (probably the last one, Suppiluliuma II) to a Ugaritic king (probably the last one, Ammurapi).[6] The letter shows deep interest in these boat-people. Its author had learnt that a citizen of Ugarit called Ibnadushu had been captured by them, but was subsequently released or escaped his captivity. He requested that Ibnadushu be sent to Hatti for debriefing, with the promise that he would be returned home safely afterwards. The Great King was understandably anxious to find out more about the size and the movements of pirate operations in the eastern Mediterranean. Largely, it must be, because of the serious threat they posed to the safety of transport ships in the waters of this region and the increasingly vital role these ships were playing in the struggle 'to keep alive the land of Hatti'.[7]

Ugarit's final days provide a microcosm of the forces of upheaval and destruction that engulfed much of the Near Eastern world in the late 13th and early 12th centuries. For the Syrian coastal kingdom, the dangers came particularly from the sea. Ammurapi kept a squad of coastwatchers on constant alert, scanning the horizon. Then came the news he most feared: enemy ships had come into view just off his kingdom's shores and were heading directly for the capital. Ammurapi wrote to the Carchemish viceroy, Talmi-Teshub, begging for assistance. Perhaps out of pique for Ugarit's earlier lack of cooperation, but more likely now because he had no choice, Talmi-Teshub wrote back offering nothing but advice: 'As for what you have written to me: "Ships of the enemy have been seen at sea!" Well, you must remain firm. Indeed for your part, where are your troops, your chariots stationed? Are they not stationed near you? No? Behind the enemy, who press upon you? Surround your towns with ramparts. Have your troops and chariots enter there, and await the enemy with great resolution.'[8] In other words, you're on your own. Make the best of what resources you already have. These were little enough. We have noted that Ammurapi had responded positively to a Hittite demand to send his troops and chariots to Hatti, even though what he sent was considered inadequate and second-rate. And after a second demand was made of him, by Suppiluliuma II, he had sent his fleet to the coast of Lukka in south-western Anatolia— for reasons scholars are still debating. We can understand the desperateness of Ammurapi's appeal to the viceroy.

It was to no avail. Ammurapi was left defenceless. With part of his land forces and all his navy elsewhere, he had no chance of repelling the seaborne marauders now rapidly descending upon his kingdom. He wrote to the king of Alasiya, with whom he seems to have had close ties, describing how critically dangerous his situation was: 'My father, the enemy's ships have been coming and burning my cities and doing terrible things in my country. All my troops and chariots are in the land of Hatti, and all my ships are in Lukka. My land has been left defenceless!'[9] Though the letter's precise date is uncertain, its words of despair and abandonment could have been among the very last Ammurapi put to tablet. Indeed, so sudden was the final enemy onslaught upon his kingdom that letters ready for despatch from the capital, including this one, may never have left it. Unless they were copies of originals already sent, they provide graphic evidence of the city's abrupt end. Ammurapi's royal seat, centre of one of the most prosperous kingdoms of Late Bronze Age Syria, was looted and abandoned. There was no Iron Age successor. Ugarit would never rise from its ashes.

Its destruction belongs within the context of the general waves of upheavals and devastations that brought the Late Bronze Age civilizations to an end in both the Aegean and the Near Eastern worlds. Environmental catastrophes (earthquakes, prolonged droughts, and the like), new waves of invaders from the north, the collapse of central administrations, disruption of international trading links, and economic meltdown (to give a modern ring to our tale) have all been suggested as factors contributing to the disintegration of the Bronze Age world. These possibilities will no doubt continue to be debated by

Figure 9. Sea Peoples, Temple of Ramesses III, Medinet Habu

scholars, inconclusively and endlessly. But Egyptian records, supported to some extent by archaeological data, specifically associate the devastations with large groups called 'peoples from the sea', a motley conglomerate of marauders who travelled by land as well as by sea as they swept across and destroyed much of the Near Eastern world early in the 12th century. Already in the reign of the pharaoh Merneptah (1213–1203), groups of invaders called Sherden, Shekelesh, Lukka, Ekwesh, and Teresh had attacked the coast of Egypt.

Merneptah managed to repel the intruders, but their attacks on Egypt were merely a prelude to the invasions of the eastern Mediterranean countries during Ramesses III's reign (1184–1153). On the walls of his funerary temple at Medinet Habu at Thebes in Uppper Egypt, Ramesses graphically records the trail of ruin left by these peoples: 'The foreign countries made a conspiracy in their islands. All at once the lands were removed and scattered in the fray. No land could stand before their arms, from Hatti, Qode, Carchemish, Arzawa and Alasiya on, being cut off at one time. A camp was set up in one place in Amurru. They desolated its people, and its land was like that which has never come into being. They were coming forward toward Egypt, while the flame was prepared before them. Their confederation was the Peleset, Tjeker, Shekelesh, Denyen, and Weshesh, lands united. They laid their hands upon the land as far as the circuit of the earth, their hearts confident and trusting: "Our plans will succeed!"'[10]

These invasions were not simply or even primarily military operations. They involved mass movements, both by land and by sea, of peoples who were most likely the victims rather than the causes of the disasters that brought about the collapse of the Late Bronze Age civilizations. Displaced from their homelands, they had sought new lands to settle, taking on a marauding character as they did so. What happened to them after they were beaten off by Ramesses III? Some like the Shekelesh, the Sherden, and the Teresh may have gone west, perhaps to Sicily, Sardinia, and Italy. A proportion of the Sherden may have stayed on in Egypt, becoming mercenaries in the pharaoh's armies. Another group, the Peleset, almost certainly became the people well known from biblical sources as the Philistines. We shall have more to say about them in the next chapter.

The calm before the storm

An interesting aspect of Syria's history in these final years is that in contrast to the apocalyptic scenario depicted in the Ugaritic tablets we referred to above, a number of contemporary letters from Ugarit's archives give the impression of business as usual in the Syrian region. Perhaps right up to the last days. This is particularly evident in the correspondence which deals with trade matters and business transactions, indicative of peaceful commercial interactions among various Syrian states. Letters that passed between the kings of Ugarit and Sidon, and the king of Beirut and a high-ranking official in Ugarit, reflect cordial and cooperative relations between the Levantine kingdoms in these last years. Ugarit seems also to have had close links with Emar on the Euphrates. By the 12th century, it had established a trading office in Emar, and sent a man called Dagan-belu to manage it. Letters which Dagan-belu exchanged with officials back in Ugarit, including Shipti-Ba'al, son-in-law of King Ammurapi, contain no hint of the disasters soon to reduce to ruins both Emar and Ugarit. On the contrary, the correspondence has very much the feel of peaceful normality about it. Thus in one of his letters, Dagan-belu assures Shipti-Ba'al that all is well in Emar, and packs some plants to go with the letter to him. In return, he asks Shipti-Ba'al to send him some oil and a large linen garment of good quality with the next messenger he despatches to Emar.[11] No sense of doom and gloom here.

But these letters belong to a world that was now close to extinction. The gathering forces of destruction and change would very soon engulf it and pave the way for the next great epoch in the history of the Near East.

PART II

From the Iron Age to the Macedonian Conquest

6

The Age of Iron

12th–7th centuries BC

The misadventures of a sea-merchant

It seemed a simple enough mission. The Egyptian merchant Wenamun had been summoned before Herihor, chief priest of the god Amun in Karnak. This was during the reign of the pharaoh Ramesses XI (1099–1069), last ruler of Egypt's Twentieth Dynasty. But at the time of Wenamun's summons, power in Egypt was effectively shared between Herihor in the south and a man called Smendes in the north who ruled from his base at Tanis in the Egyptian Delta. Wenamun was instructed by Herihor to go to Byblos on the Levantine coast and acquire from its king Zakar-Baal timber cut from the forests of Lebanon, for the construction of a ship to transport the sacred image of the god Amun. There would be no charge for the timber— at least there never had been in the past. So Wenamun set out on his journey, proceeding first down the Nile to Tanis where he paid his respects to Smendes and acquainted him with his mission. Smendes provided him with a ship and captain for the journey to Byblos. They stopped en route at the port of Dor on the coast of northern Palestine. The city was then ruled by Prince Beder, leader of the Tjeker tribe. Otherwise known to us as one of the Sea Peoples, the Tjeker had apparently seized control of Dor during their sweep through the Syro-Palestinian region. The visit went well to begin with, and Beder ferried out to the merchant food and drink while his vessel lay at anchor in Dor's harbour. But all the goodwill evaporated when one of Wenamun's crew stole some money from the ship and fled. Wenamun held the Tjeker chief responsible, on the grounds that the theft had happened in his harbour, and demanded that he track down the thief and return the money. Beder quite reasonably pointed out that since the money had been stolen by one of Wenamun's own men on his own ship, the responsibility was his. None the less, he ordered a search to be made for the thief. To no avail.

When after nine days the miscreant was still at large, Wenamun lost patience and set sail for Byblos. On the way, he encountered a ship of Dor, ordered it to be boarded, and seized from it a sum of money which, he informed the ship's owners, he would keep until the cash stolen from him at Dor had been found and handed back. Then he proceeded to Byblos. No hand of welcome was extended to him here. In fact his reception was an extremely hostile one, and the Byblite king Zakar-Baal ordered him to depart immediately; he had probably received reports about the merchant's earlier churlish behaviour. But then he had a change of heart and granted him an audience. In the course of their meeting, Wenamun asked for the timber. Zakar-Baal agreed to provide it, but insisted on payment—despite protests that in the past the timber had been provided free of charge. Wenamun had no choice but to send to Smendes for the necessary funds. These duly arrived, the deal was done, the timbers were felled in winter, and in the following summer dragged to the sea for shipping to Egypt. But just as Wenamun was preparing to sail, eleven shiploads of Tjeker men from Dor suddenly appeared. Their leaders demanded that Zakar-Baal hand Wenamun over to them for the crime he had committed on his way to Byblos. To Wenamun's great relief, Zakar-Baal refused, and allowed the merchant's safe departure. But Wenamun's troubles were not yet over. Strong winds blew him off course onto the coast of Cyprus, where he was set upon violently by hostile townspeople, until rescued by the local princess Hatiba.

With that, our story comes abruptly to a halt. The rest of it was perhaps lost, but it may simply be that its Egyptian composer[1] had done with it, and left the reader to finish his tale. In any case, we can assume that from here on, it was plain sailing, so to speak, and that Wenamun actually did, in the end, complete his mission successfully.

The story has a ring of historical authenticity about it, and scholars long believed that it actually *is* based on historical fact. But careful literary analysis carried out over thirty years has demonstrated that the work is probably fiction. None the less, it does reflect a number of characteristics of its era.[2] The humiliating treatment of an Egyptian merchant sent on an official Egyptian mission is in itself a reflection of Egypt's loss of international status in this new age; the demand for payment for the timber which had in the past been provided free, in the days of Byblos' status as an Egyptian tributary, was no

small part of this humiliation. Byblos had survived the upheavals at the end
of the Late Bronze Age, and flourished in the following era, becoming one
of the wealthiest and most important cities of the region which the Greeks
called Phoenicia. To this we shall return.

Map 4. The Iron Age kingdoms of northern Syria and south-eastern Anatolia

The dawn of the new era

We have now embarked on a five-century time-span which will take us from the 12th century BC through to the end of the 7th century, up to the fall of the Neo-Assyrian empire. This covers much of the period commonly dubbed the Iron Age by archaeologists and historians.[3] The period has been so called because during it iron was widely used for the production of tools, weapons, and other artefacts (though the softer copper–tin alloy we call bronze, the hallmark of the preceding era, continued in use as well), once the techniques for smelting the ore at the required high temperatures had been mastered. In Syria and Palestine, the 'era of iron' saw profound changes in the region's geopolitical configuration. New cities and small kingdoms developed, sometimes on sites close to or upon their predecessors, sometimes on quite different locations. A number of cities with a Bronze Age pedigree rose again in the new age, like Byblos and Dor, some becoming major political and/or commercial centres. But one of the most distinctive features of the new era was the appearance of new population groups, most notably the Aramaeans. These were to have a profound effect on the history, culture, and ethnic composition of the states, cities, and peoples of Syria and Palestine. One thing clear is that the early Iron Age communities were able to develop free from the intervention of any major powers seeking to impose their dominance over them. They had the luxury of independence and self-determination—hence the pattern of small, autonomous Iron Age states and tribal groups distributed through the Syrian-Palestinian landscape— up until the early first millennium. Then, once more, a Great Kingdom emerged which sought to impose its authority over them.

The Neo-Hittite kingdoms[4]

Prominent among the new states to emerge during the early Iron Age were a group we now refer to as the Neo-Hittite kingdoms. Ranging in size from a few square kilometres to several thousand, these kingdoms arose in south-eastern Anatolia and northern Syria. They are called Neo-Hittite because they maintained a number of important traditions associated with the Late Bronze Age Hittites. One of these was their continuing use of a hiero-glyphic script, written in the Luwian language for recording on their public monuments the accomplishments of their kings and the blessings bestowed by their gods (and other things of note besides). By the end of the Late

Bronze Age, Luwian-speakers had almost certainly become the most populous ethnic group of the Hittite empire; and in the empire's last century, Hittite kings regularly used the Luwian hieroglyphic script for proclaiming their achievements, and their endorsement by various gods, on monuments intended for public display. So the use of the Luwian hieroglyphic script on the monuments of the Neo-Hittite kingdoms preserved a royal epigraphic tradition established by their Late Bronze Age royal Hittite predecessors.

Most of these New-Hittite kingdoms occupied the region called Hatti in Iron Age Assyrian, Urartian, and Hebrew texts. This too perpetuated the name of the Late Bronze Age Hittite kingdom, though in the Iron Age, the region so called had shrunk to the eastern part of the former empire, especially to south-eastern Anatolia and northern Syria. Many of the Neo-Hittite kingdoms were components of Iron Age Hatti. But their inhabitants would never have identified themselves as peoples of the Land of Hatti, as their Late Bronze Age predecessors had. At least not in a political or ethnic sense. The name was purely a geographical one, used mainly by outsiders to refer to a broad expanse of territories, primarily in northern Syria, which also included several Aramaean states. Another feature of the Neo-Hittite kingdoms is that their royal dynasties often included the names of famous Hittite kings of the past: Suppiluliuma, Arnuwanda, Tudhaliya, Hattusili, Muwattalli. Quite possibly, the retention of these names by some of the Neo-Hittite kings reflects actual family links with the rulers of imperial Hatti, or at least with one of the many branches of their family. Hittite artistic and architectural traditions also resurface, in a modified form, in a number of Neo-Hittite kingdoms, though Assyrian and Syrian elements are often intermixed with them. The states where blends of these kinds occur are sometimes referred to as Syro-Hittite kingdoms (though this term is also used more broadly of all the Neo-Hittite kingdoms). Significantly, there is no evidence that the imperial official Hittite language, called Nesite by those who wrote and spoke it, survived in either written or spoken form beyond the end of the Late Bronze Age.

The earliest and the most important of the Neo-Hittite states was Carchemish on the Euphrates. This name is well known to us from the records of the Late Bronze Age Hittites, particularly from the mid 14th century when the Euphrates city became one of the Hittite empire's two vice-regal seats in Syria. (The other was Aleppo.) With the fall of Hattusa in the early 12th century, Carchemish became the last important bastion of imperial Hatti. Its ruler at the time, Kuzi-Teshub, was the son of Carchemish's last

Figure 10. Storm God, Carchemish

known viceroy Talmi-Teshub. Kuzi-Teshub now assumed control of what was left of the Hittite world, and took on the title of Great King, reflecting a status hitherto borne only by the occupant of Hattusa's throne. For a time Kuzi-Teshub may have presided over the last remnants of the Hittite empire in the east, and begun a programme of rebuilding the territories devastated or abandoned because of the upheavals which brought the Late Bronze Age to an end. But perhaps even within his own lifetime, what was left of the Hittite world fragmented into smaller units, becoming the independent kingdoms of the Neo-Hittite era.

That brings us to a couple of intriguing enigmas. It was long believed that Hattusa's fall was rather like Constantinople's twenty-six centuries later, when the Byzantine city was besieged, captured, and sacked by the Turks, its last emperor, Constantine XI, perishing as his city went up in flames around him. But a recent director of excavations at Hattusa, Dr Jürgen Seeher, has presented a different and rather more puzzling scenario for Hattusa's end. Far from perishing in his capital before it was destroyed, the last Hittite king, Suppiluliuma II, organized a systematic evacuation of it, at least of the palace quarter, taking with him everything of value and simply departing his city one day, accompanied by a heavy military escort, his royal family, and a large entourage, never to return. He probably left behind much of the city's population, now defenceless and leaderless. Then, within months, if not weeks or even days, the city was finally reduced to ruins, perhaps by outside enemy forces, perhaps by its remnant population who scavenged anything of value to them and destroyed everything else. Henceforth the site became largely derelict until a Phrygian settlement was built on it three centuries later.

Two obvious questions to arise from this scenario are (1) Why did the king abandon his city? and (2) Where did he go? The first question is one for another place and another time. As for the second, Suppiluliuma is hardly likely to have set off into the wilds of Anatolia with no idea of where he would end up. He must have decided on an alternative place of residence before he abandoned Hattusa. If so, where? Could one of the Neo-Hittite kingdoms have begun life as the residence-in-exile of the last Great King of imperial Hatti?

We can identify fifteen of these Neo-Hittite kingdoms, spread through south-eastern Anatolia and northern Syria. The most important of them were Carchemish, Malatya, and Kummuh in the Euphrates region, Patin/ Unqi (Assyrian names; = Luwian Palistin/Walistin) and Hamath in north-western Syria and the Orontes valley, and Tabal in south-central Anatolia. We really cannot be sure how or when these kingdoms originated (except for Carchemish), or for that matter who precisely their inhabitants were. A fairly common view is that during the upheavals at the end of the Bronze Age a large number of population groups from the Anatolian lands subject to the Hittites fled south-eastwards and became the basic stock of the Neo-Hittite kingdoms; many of the refugees, perhaps the majority of them, were probably Luwian-speakers, since that was the language inscribed on the public monuments of these kingdoms. So the general view goes.

But I think it likely that already in the Late Bronze Age many Luwian-speaking peoples had settled in northern Syria, particularly from the time of the Hittite king Suppiluliuma I (c.1350–1322) onwards, when Hittite vice-regal kingdoms were set up at Carchemish and Aleppo. The new adminis-trative arrangements for direct rule in Syria may well have resulted in large numbers of scribes and clerks and other administrative personnel being imported from the established bureaucracies of the central Hittite world. And along with them, large numbers of troops to boost the region's defence forces—a matter of particular importance once the territories under direct Hittite rule extended to the western bank of the Euphrates; the Hittites now shared a boundary with their increasingly aggressive Assyrian neigh-bours just across the river. And many of the 'immigrants' may well have been Luwians. We know from our Hittite texts that Luwian peoples taken in Hittite campaigns as part of the spoils of conquest were regularly used to build up populations in areas that were underpopulated or whose defences needed strengthening. I believe that already in the Late Bronze Age many Anatolians, including Luwian-speakers, had settled either voluntarily or compulsorily in Syria at the time the viceregal kingdoms were established there. And the flow of administrative and military personnel into Syria was very likely accompanied by a steady stream of ancillary populations as well, to take advantage of the new opportunities offered by the expansion of direct Hittite authority in the south-east, particularly perhaps in the fields of trade and commerce. So too new trading and commercial opportunities may have been opened up for enterprising Anatolians, including Luwian-speakers, by the peace accord between Egypt and Hatti concluded in 1269. The 'eternal treaty' formalized the end of hostiles between the two Great Kingdoms, and considerably boosted more peaceful enterprises in a region now made much more politically stable.

This is not of course to say that there were not further immigrations into Syria from the Anatolian peninusula at the end of the Late Bronze Age. There may well have been. But in general terms I think it likely that the Neo-Hittite kingdoms evolved largely out of populations already present in Syria and south-eastern Anatolia during the Late Bronze Age. A significant number of these could have contained Luwian elements, or at least Luwian-speaking elements, supplemented by remnants of other Anatolian peoples, including those who spoke Hittite.[5] Many of their kings may have had links with the royal family of imperial Hatti. We know for sure that the new ruling dynasty at Carchemish was, at least to begin with, a continuation of the old Hittite imperial line. And the administrative elites of other Neo-Hittite kingdoms may have been installed by Carchemish's first Neo-Hittite ruler, the Great King Kuzi-Teshub, who probably established dynasties with Hittite royal blood in them in other parts of what was left of the old Hittite world—like Malatya and Kummuh which lay to the north of Carchemish.

Ruling elites elsewhere in Syria may have emerged out of the bureaucracies established earlier by Suppiluliuma I when he made new arrangements for the administration of the Syrian region following his victories over Mitanni. And it is just possible that one of the Neo-Hittite kingdoms began life as the place of refuge of the last Great King of imperial Hatti, Suppiluliuma II. Of course, ruling dynasties in many of the kingdoms may have changed, perhaps several times, throughout the course of their kingdoms' history. But even when they did, the new rulers or ruling lines preserved the old traditions of royalty, as a means of legitimizing their authority. That included states like Hamath and Masuwari/Til Barsip (see the following chapter on these), where Aramaean rulers replaced earlier lines of 'traditional' Neo-Hittite rulers. Old traditions of royalty were maintained by all the rulers, irrespective of their ethnic origins, until the last of the Neo-Hittite kingdoms had disappeared.

At this point a warning should be sounded. We cannot assume as a matter of course that the ethnic origins of a particular state's ruling class were the same as those of the bulk of its population. Various groups of Anatolians and recently arrived Aramaeans may well have made up significant components of this population. But the majority of those who inhabited the Neo-Hittite kingdoms, as all other territories and city-states and communities in Syria and Palestine, were very likely indigenes of the region—above all, Semitic-speaking peoples, including the Amorites and other groups who had already occupied parts of Syria, from at least the early second millennium and probably much earlier.

But it is time now to say a little more about the peoples we have identified as relative newcomers to Syria—'desert intruders' who were to play a major role in Syrian history, during the Iron Age and well beyond it.

The Aramaeans [6]

> I have crossed the Euphrates twenty-eight times, twice in one year, in pursuit of the *ahlamû*-Aramaeans. I brought about their defeat from the city Tadmor of the Land of Amurru, Anat of the Land Suhu, as far as the city Rapiqu of Karduniash (Babylonia). I brought their booty and possessions to my city Ashur.
>
> (Records of Tiglath-pileser I, *RIMA* 2:43)

Assyrian sources depict the Aramaeans as hordes of fierce, wide-roaming desert-dwellers who preyed on hapless travellers and bands of merchants, desecrated religious sanctuaries, and terrorized and plundered whole towns and cities. But other ancient sources give a more balanced, more positive view of the Aramaean peoples. Originally tribal pastoral groups, now commonly believed to be indigenous elements from the region of northern Syria, the Aramaeans spread widely through the Near Eastern world during the Iron Age. They spoke a West Semitic language called Aramaic. By the end of the second millennium, many Aramaean peoples had begun to adopt a more settled way of life, particularly in parts of Mesopotamia, Syria, and eastern Anatolia. Here, a number of Aramaean states emerged, later to have a major impact on the history of the regions where they were established. Bit-Zamani, Bit-Bahiani, Bit-Adini, Bit-Agusi, Aram-Damascus, and Sam'al (Zincirli) were among the most important of the Aramaean states. The prefix 'Bit'—'House (of)'—reflects their tribal origins. Aramaean and Hittite elements became closely blended in a number of Syrian states, and in several of them Aramaean ruling dynasties were (as we have noted) established after a line of earlier 'Neo-Hittite' rulers.

The widespread dispersal of the Aramaeans in later centuries was due in large measure to their forcible resettlement, by their Assyrian conquerors, in many parts of the Assyrian empire. This helps explain how Aramaic became the lingua franca of the Near Eastern world in the first millennium BC. But despite the wide distribution of their language, we learn little about the Aramaeans from their own written sources. Much of what we do know comes from Assyrian and biblical texts. These texts too have their limitations. While they provide valuable information about the more important Aramaean states, they have left us few details of the many Aramaean tribes who lived outside an urban context, or, more generally, of Aramaean tribal structures and the customs and ideals which underpinned their society.

Israel

The kingdom of Israel, located south of Syria in the region called Palestine, also developed in the Iron Age and became deeply involved in Syrian affairs, politically and militarily, culturally and commercially. Our earliest reference to Israel appears in an inscription on a granite stele of the pharaoh Merneptah (1213–1203).[7] It was discovered in 1896 by Sir Flinders Petrie in Merneptah's mortuary temple at Thebes, the chief city of upper Egypt. The 'people of Israel' are listed among Merneptah's Asiatic conquests. They are referred to here not as a nation, but as an ethnic group. It was probably not until the end of the second millennium BC that a nation-state called Israel began to emerge. In biblical tradition, a king called Saul, whose reign is dated on the basis of biblical chronology to c.1020 to 1000, was the founder of a united kingdom of Israel. His reign ended with his suicide after he had suffered a decisive defeat by the Philistines. Then, our biblical sources inform us, David became king of Israel, inheriting from his predecessor his conflict with the Philistines and conducting war against them with considerable success. By the end of his reign, he had effectively destroyed their military power. More infamously, David figures in biblical tradition as the seducer of the beautiful Bathsheba, whose husband Uriah he sent to his death on the battlefield, by ordering him to to take up a front-line position in the fighting where he knew he couldn't survive; thus he removed an inconvenient obstacle to his access to the ill-fated man's wife.

When he was not fighting the Philistines or indulging in fleshly pleasures, David turned his attention to more constructive matters. Amongst these, he settled upon the already long-established city of Jerusalem in the land of Judah as the site of his royal capital. Jerusalem has henceforth become known as 'David's city'. It certainly owed its major growth as one of the great cities of the Near Eastern world, for millennia to come, to its initial reconstruction under King David, if we follow biblical tradition. And also to David's son and successor Solomon (960–922). Under Solomon, Israel reached its peak of cultural and commercial development, due largely to the king's promotion of close links with foreign countries, including the kingdoms and cities of his Syrian and Arabian neighbours. One of the most famous episodes in ancient Near Eastern tradition is the Queen of Sheba's visit to Solomon, conducted with much pomp and splendour, as so often depicted in art and literature. But politically, Solomon's reign was rather less successful. During it, tensions mounted and squabbles broke out between the northern and southern tribes of Israel. Solomon was unable to put a stop to these, or too preoccupied with other matters to try. On his death, full-scale inter-tribal conflict broke out, leading to a complete split between the tribes and the establishment of two separate kingdoms, Israel in the north, with its capital at Samaria, and Judah in the south, with its capital at Jerusalem.

According to Egyptian records, a pharaoh called Sheshonq I (aka Shoshenq), founder of Egypt's Twenty-Second Dynasty, took advantage of the troubles in the region by leading to it a major expedition *c.*925, in an attempt to re-establish his kingdom's long-lost control there. His campaign was resoundingly successful, to judge from his own account: on the so-called Bubastite Gate of the temple of Karnak in Egypt, he has left us a list of well over one hundred cities of Israel, Judah, and southern Palestine which he allegedly conquered during the campaign.[8] And if, as generally believed, he is to be identified with the biblical pharaoh called Shishak, he seized Jerusalem as well, carrying off the treasures of its temple.[9] But Sheshonq was no trail-blazing Tuthmosis. He died shortly after returning home, his northern venture proving to be no more than the proverbial 'flash in the pan'.[10] For more than three centuries to come, Egypt showed no further interest in the

Syro-Palestinian lands. (As we shall see, that was to change dramatically in the reign of the late 7th–6th century pharaoh Necho II.)

I should at this point make clear that apart from the Egyptian account of Sheshonq's campaign, we have no *contemporary* written sources for the history of Israel up to, including, and immediately after Solomon's reign, and almost no archaeological evidence, or at least very little that can definitely be attributed to this early period in Israel's history. Our reconstruction of the period is based almost entirely on biblical sources, and some scholars are reluctant to accept, or totally reject, any information about early Israel that cannot be backed up with independent contemporary evidence. Indeed doubts have been expressed as to whether David and Solomon, let alone Saul, and for that matter the Queen of Sheba, existed at all; they belong to the realms of literature and folklore, not history. This is probably going too far. We do in fact now have a small piece of evidence for an Israelite tribal leader called David. It is an Aramaic inscription mentioning David, found in 1993 in the city of Dan on modern Israel's northern border.[11] Similar evidence for Solomon may also one day emerge. But in any case, David's and Solomon's kingdom must have been a good deal smaller than our biblical sources indicate. And there are those who doubt whether there ever was a united kingdom of Israel, at least not in the 10th century, let alone the 11th century.

If such a united kingdom did exist, many scholars prefer to assign it to a 9th-century ruler of Israel called Omri (*c.*876–869). Allegedly Israel's sixth king, Omri established a royal line known as the Omride dynasty, with Samaria as his capital. According to traditional reckoning, the dynasty may have lasted only about thirty-five years, through the reigns of Omri and three successors, ending with the death of the last of these, Jehoram (Joram) *c.*842. But some think it lasted longer, and for what it is worth, the Assyrians referred to Israelite kings for the next hundred years as 'sons of Omri', and Israel itself as belonging to the house of Omri. In any case, it is with the second Omride king, Ahab, son of Omri, that we can begin correlating information from contemporary foreign records with biblical sources; the latter are preserved by scribes and scholars who mostly lived some centuries after the events to which the biblical texts refer. As we shall see, Ahab figures in Assyrian sources as one of the members of an anti-Assyrian alliance which first confronted Shalmaneser III in a battle on the Orontes river in 853. And henceforth Israel and its kings make frequent appearances in Assyrian and other records.

The Philistines

'An uneducated or unenlightened person; one indifferent or hostile to culture.' Thus the *Shorter Oxford English Dictionary* defines the term 'Philistine' as we use it today. In so doing, it provides a classic example of the

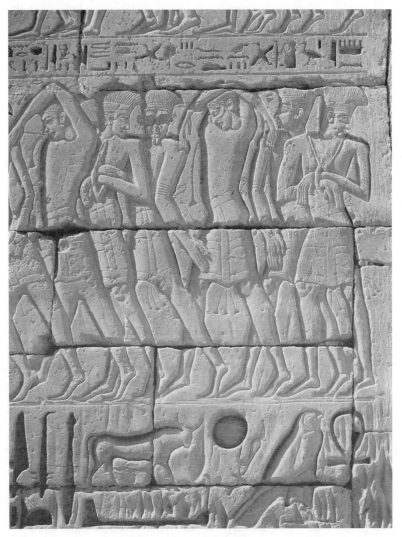

Figure 11. Philistine prisoners, Medinet Habu Temple of Ramesses III

powerful influence the Bible has exercised on Western civilization's vocabu-
lary and ways of thinking. The Philistines figure prominently in biblical
tradition as the archetypal enemies of the early Israelite rulers. Their origins
can be firmly linked to the historical record, for their ancestors, called the
Peleset in Egyptian records, were among the Sea Peoples who pillaged their
way through much of the Near Eastern world before being stopped by the
pharaoh Ramesses III. In Egyptian reliefs from Ramesses' reign, the Peleset
are depicted wearing tasselled kilts and what appear to be feathered head-
dresses. After the Sea Peoples' break-up and dispersal, these proto-Philistines
finally settled in south-western Palestine, on that part of the southern coastal
plain that came to be called Philistia. Five cities, the so-called Philistine
Pentapolis, provided the focal points of Philistine civilization. They were
Ashdod, Ashkelon, Ekron, Gaza, and Gath.

It is not surprising that the Philistines, the Israelites' arch-enemies and a
people who in their victories could be as brutal and destructive as any of
their contemporaries, should get a bad press in our biblical sources. But to
portray them as crude, uncivilized barbarians really flies in the face of the
facts. The material remains of their civilization provide ample evidence that
they were a highly cultured people, with advanced architectural, engineer-
ing, and technological skills, and a high level of attainment in the arts and
crafts. It was perhaps partly their refined, urban-based civilization that
roused the moralistic ire of the Israelites. Especially those Israelites who had
led an ascetic existence in the hill-country of Palestine before descending
on the plains, where they sought a more secure, settled way of life. In the
process, they came into conflict with the Philistines—and the Canaanites.

We haven't yet talked about the Canaanites and I shall return to them in
a moment. But first, I'd like to mention a very interesting discovery of the
last few years, which raises some fresh questions about the Philistines. The
discovery was made in Aleppo. We recall that this city had been the royal
seat of Yamhad, the most powerful kingdom in Syria during the Middle
Bronze Age. It had been destroyed by the Hittite king Mursili I c.1595, but
soon rose again, first as the centre of an independent kingdom, and subsequently as a subject state of the Mitannian empire. When the Hittite king
Suppiluliuma I destroyed Mitanni in the 14th century, he gave Aleppo a new
lease of life by making it a Hittite viceregal kingdom, a status which it
retained until the collapse of the Hittite empire a century and a half later.
Aleppo then seems to have faded into insignificance. It continued to exist,
but at best as a regional sub-kingdom of larger powers.

All this information about Aleppo comes from other places. The city itself tells us very little about its past, since practically nothing from any of its ancient levels survives—due to the constant rebuilding over these in later times. For this reason, the recent discovery there has generated considerable interest.

In 2003, the German archaeologist K. Kohlmeyer was excavating a temple of the Storm God Hadad on Aleppo's citadel-mound when he unearthed two well-preserved statues, facing each other. One depicted the Storm God, the other a king. Alongside the king's statue, an eleven-line inscription in Luwian hieroglyphs had been carved. The first two lines of the inscription are translated thus by the Luwian expert David Hawkins: 'King Taita (am) I, Palistin-ean King. For my lord the Halabean (Aleppan) Storm-God I honoured the image.'[12] 'Palistinean' is the latest reading, confirmed by other experts, of the name applied to a land previously read by Hawkins as PaDAsatini or WaDAsatini. The name is known from several other Luwian inscriptions as well as the Aleppo one. It appears, along with the king's name Taita, in inscriptions on the sites of Meharde and Sheizar located on a crossing of the Orontes river. Both inscriptions have to do with Taita's wife Kupapiya. The first is dedicated to her and calls her 'Queen of the land', the second, her funerary monument, tells us that she lived one hundred years. One further reference to Palistini occurs in an inscription discovered on the site of Tell Tayinat, in the Amuq plain of north-western Syria. In later texts, this site belonged to the Neo-Hittite kingdom Patin (Luwian Palistin, later Walistin), and was probably its capital Kinalua. Hawkins suggests that here too was the capital of Taita, before the kingdom of Patin arose. He proposes a date in or around the 11th century for Taita's inscriptions. To judge from the spread of the inscriptions, Taita's land was a relatively extensive one, reaching from at least Aleppo in the north-east, down into the Orontes valley and probably to the Mediterranean coast.

That brings us to our questions. First, if the reading 'Palistinean' is correct, was this 'Palistinean king' called Taita (Hawkins now thinks there may have been at least two kings so called) connected with the Philistines? If so, how do we explain his presence so far to the north of the region called Philistia *in southern Palestine*, where the Philistine cities of the so-called Pentapolis were located? Does Taita's presence in north-western Syria indicate a Philistine population in this region at that time? And why did a Philistine king use the Luwian hieroglyphic script for his and his family's public monuments? Further excavations may one day provide at least some of the answers to these questions.

Canaanites and Phoenicians

Let us return to the Canaanites.[13] These were the unfortunate occupants, in biblical tradition, of the 'Promised Land', the land vouchsafed by God to the Israelites after their return from Egypt, as recorded in the biblical story of the Exodus. It lay in the region covered in part by modern Israel and Lebanon. With the go-ahead given by God, the returning Israelites virtually obliterated the Canaanites to provide themselves with their own living space, bringing them, as a consequence, into contact and conflict with the Philistines. In a broad sense, the term 'Canaanite' is sometimes used to refer to all the ancient peoples of the Levant, up to the last decades of the 4th century BC. But these peoples were divided into a number of tribal groups, city-states, and kingdoms, each of which developed its own political and social structures, and a number of its own distinctive cultural traits. They identified themselves, and were almost always identified by others, not as Canaanites but by the names of the specific tribal and political units to which they belonged. This explains why in the ancient sources 'Canaanite' is rarely used as a generic designation for them, outside the Bible. The first clearly attested use of the term occurs in the 18th-century archives of Mari on the Euphrates, and there are occasional references to Canaan and Canaanites in later Bronze Age texts; for example, we have seen that Canaan was the place of exile of Idrimi, later king of Alalah, while he was on the run after fleeing his city Aleppo. Canaanites were among the prisoners-of-war deported to Egypt by the 15th-century pharaoh Amenhotep II, and in the following century, Canaan appears several times in the Amarna letters. Subsequently Canaanites are attested in biblical sources as the pre-Israelite occupants of the 'Promised Land'. Some scholars have argued that the Israelites themselves, despite their 'biblical' loathing for every aspect of Canaanite culture, were in fact a sub-branch of the Canaanite peoples who withdrew to the Palestinian hill-country during the unsettled conditions in Syria-Palestine and elsewhere at the end of the Late Bronze Age.

That brings us to the Phoenicians.[14] Phoenicia is the Greek name applied to a region which extended along part of the Syro-Palestinian coast and inland to the Lebanon and anti-Lebanon ranges. Most scholars believe that it is derived from Greek *phoinix*, 'crimson-red/purple', and suggest several explanations for it. One is that it reflects the copper colour of the hair and skin of the people so called. But the most popular explanation derives it from the famous purple dye that was extracted from the murex shellfish found in the region's coastal waters. Phoenicia was an affluent area, deriving much of its wealth from its international sea-trading enterprises, which took Phoenician merchants far into the western Mediterranean, where they established numerous colonies, especially in Sicily, Spain, and north Africa. The most famous of these was Carthage. The city was founded according to legendary tradition by a queen of Tyre called Dido, after she had been forced to flee her home kingdom following the murder of her husband Sychaeus, Tyre's previous ruler, by her wicked brother Pygmalion. Tyre was one of the wealthiest and most important cities of Phoenicia. We have already spoken of it and its fortunes in the Late Bronze Age, when it was an Egyptian vassal; it appears briefly in the tale of Wenamun, and we shall meet it again when we travel into later periods of Syrian history. Its Iron Age phase was one of the most flourishing in its existence. It figures prominently in biblical sources, notably under a king called Hiram who provided the Israelite king David with cedars and craftsmen (e.g. 2 Samuel 5:11), and his son and successor Solomon with assistance in building his temple in Jerusalem (e.g. 1 Kings 7:13–46). Other important Phoenician cities were Byblos, which plays a prominent role in Wenamun's story, and Sidon, which also appears in the story, in a reference to fifty merchant ships in its harbour. Sidon's merchant enterprises were complemented by its craft industries, for which the city was renowned. A reference in Homer's *Iliad* (6.289–92) to the elaborately wrought robes which the Trojan prince Paris brought back from Sidon provides a literary allusion to the reputation of the city's craftsmen. The products of the city's gold-, silver-, and copper-smiths, as well as its weavers, were highly prized in foreign markets and contributed much to this reputation.

If the inhabitants of these Phoenician cities used any generic name at all to refer to themselves, they would probably have called themselves Canaanites. Indeed, they were in many respects the Canaanites' Iron Age descendants, in terms of their language and many aspects of their material culture, and their religion. 'Phoenicia' is purely a term of convenience applied by outsiders to these latter-day Canaanites, who never had any form of common identity, political or otherwise, beyond a broad ethno-cultural one.

7

The Wolf upon the Fold: The Neo-Assyrian Invasions

The Assyrian came down like a wolf on the fold,
And his cohorts were gleaming in purple and gold;
And the sheen of their spears were like stars on the sea,
When the blue wave rolls nightly on deep Galilee.

(Byron, Destruction of Sennacherib)

The treasure amassed for the Great King was impressive. Twenty talents of silver, one of gold, one hundred of tin, and one hundred of iron were heaped up before him.[1] And that was just the entrée. A thousand oxen and ten thousand sheep were mustered and sectioned off for His Majesty. A thousand linen garments of the finest quality, with multi-coloured trim, decorated couches and beds of boxwood, dishes of ivory and an abundance of other exquisitely wrought items from the local ruler's palace further swelled the gift-array. There was yet more: ten female singers, and the gift-giver's own niece, made even sweeter by the rich dowry that accompanied her. Ducks and a large female monkey topped off the list. His Majesty declared himself satisfied, almost, with his gifts, and promised to be merciful to the local ruler and his land: he would spare them the brutalities of Assyrian sack and plunder. But this magnanimous gesture required a further show of gratitude. Chariotry, infantry, and cavalry were demanded for the Assyrian army, and hostages were taken, to ensure that the tributary remained loyal once his overlord had moved on to fresh plundering fields.

We have twice before encountered the Assyrians. First, in the Middle Bronze Age when the Old Assyrian king Samsi-Addu crossed the Euphrates, on campaigns which took him westwards to the Mediterranean coast.

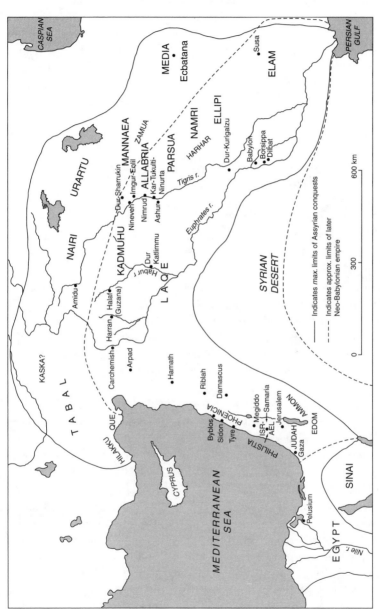

Map 5. The Neo-Assyrian World

Second, in the Late Bronze Age, when Assyrian troops again crossed the river, this time occupying the Hittite viceregal capital Carchemish, and later *allegedly* capturing thousands of Hittite troops stationed in the Carchemish region. Through all periods of Assyria's long history, to conquer and subjugate the lands between the Euphrates and the Mediterranean was the cherished ambition of the most enterprising of its kings. It was an ambition only fully achieved by the Great Kings of the third and most aggressive period in Assyria's history, the era of the Neo-Assyrian empire.

Late 12th–10th centuries BC

To the west once more

One of these kings' early Iron Age predecessors, Tiglath-pileser I (1114–1076), had blazed a trail for them. Tiglath-pileser occupied Assyria's throne not long after the decline and collapse of many other centres of civilization in the Near Eastern world. His kingdom suffered little if at all from the upheavals of the period, and remained a formidable power in the Near East, still retaining control over a substantial part of northern Mesopotamia. But Tiglath-pileser's interests extended well beyond Mesopotamia. Rekindling the aspirations of his most illustrious predecessors, he led an expedition across the Euphrates to the Mediterranean coast; on the way he conquered the entire land of Amurru (which included the Phoenician cities along the Levantine coast and extended inland as far as the city of Tadmor in the Syrian Desert), and received tribute from the cities Arwad, Byblos, and Sidon.[2] Rich spoils flowed into the royal Assyrian treasury from all these conquests. But there was an additional incentive for Tiglath-pileser's and later Assyrian kings' western campaigns—the access they provided to the forests of Lebanon and other Syro-Palestinian regions. Timbers from these regions featured prominently in the royal construction projects of the Assyrian homeland.

As far as we can tell from our sources, Tiglath-pileser's 'conquests' in Syria and Palestine involved no actual conflict. Rulers of the lands through which he passed simply handed over the tribute demanded of them, and were thus spared the ravages of Assyrian pillage and destruction. Indeed in some respects, Tiglath-pileser's campaign took on the character of a royal tour. It included a boat trip, from the island of Arwad to the city Samuru, in the course of which the Great King hunted a sea creature called a *nahiru*. In such a manner, Tiglath-pileser came and went, making no lasting impact on the regions through which he marched. Two centuries passed before his countrymen reappeared west of the Euphrates. For on his death, Assyria suffered a long period of decline, and a substantial reduction in its territories. Things improved in the last decades of the 10th century, when Ashur-dan (II) (934–911) mounted the throne and began the process of winning back Assyria's lost territories. With his reign, we embark on the Neo-Assyrian era. But it was his great-grandson, Ashurnasirpal II (883–859), who turned Assyria's attention once more to the lands west of the Euphrates.[3]

9th century BC

Ashurnasirpal's plans for his western enterprise were bedevilled by a troublesome Aramaean called Ahuni, ruler of Bit-Adini. This was a land in the middle Euphrates region, east of the river but extending across it into northeastern Syria. Ahuni had supported an anti-Assyrian uprising by several Assyrian subject states in the region. The rebellion had been put down, but Ahuni had yet to pay for his interference. Probably in the following year, Ashurnasirpal marched into his kingdom, captured and destroyed one of his fortress cities, Kaprabu, a towering city that 'hovered like a cloud in the sky', and rounded off his conquest by massacring or deporting a large part of the city's population. Ahuni saved his land further devastation by paying the tribute Ashurnasirpal demanded of him, and bowing to Assyrian sovereignty. But only for the time being. In the years ahead, down into the reign of Ashurnasirpal's son and successor Shalmaneser III, he would play a major role in further uprisings against the Assyrians—until the final day of reckoning came.

In the meantime, Ashurnasirpal continued his campaign west of the Euphrates. On rafts made of inflated goatskins, he ferried his troops across the river, downstream of Carchemish. For Carchemish was the invader's first major objective. But no blows were exchanged. Ashurnasirpal's reputation had preceded him, and the threatened city's ruler Sangara knew that resistance was pointless. So he humbly surrendered to the Assyrian, and paid him a rich tribute, including two hundred adolescent girls; these would provide 'comfort' for the king and his officers as their campaign took them ever further from home. Before leaving Sangara's land, Ashurnasirpal made the usual demand, from his new tributary, of chariotry, infantry, and cavalry. In this manner, he ensured a constant supply of fresh troops for his army as it passed through the lands along his route. His passage was an easy one. The speed with which news of Sangara's capitulation spread was matched only by the haste with which all the other local rulers in the region came before the Great King and submitted to him.

Ashurnasirpal now began his descent upon Syria's coastal cities. First the kingdom of Patin (Walistin). Crossing its northern frontier, the Assyrians arrived after a two-day march at the Patinite capital Kinalua, where His Local Majesty, King Lubarna, was in residence. Initially, Lubarna may have attempted resistance, by ordering that his city's gates be bolted against the invader. If so, Ashurnasirpal wasted no time on negotiations, or even preparations for a siege. Instead, he massed his troops outside Kinalua's walls, and instructed them to make a fierce show of their weapons, brandishing their spears and striking their swords upon their shields, in a dazzling, deafening, intimidatory display of Assyrian might. That was sufficient to induce the terrified Patinite king to throw his gates open and welcome the Assyrians inside.[4] Ashurnasirpal graciously accepted his hospitality. He also accepted the enormous tribute I referred to at the beginning of this chapter. It was the price the Patinite had to pay to keep alive his city, his kingdom, and himself.

So far, Ashurnasirpal's progress through Syria had been a bloodless one, like Tiglath-pileser's a quarter of a millennium earlier. Every city and kingdom on his campaign route had surrendered without a fight. But then one kingdom, Luash, held out. These were the circumstances. Ashurnasirpal had set up an Assyrian base in the southern Patinite city called Aribua, and paused there for a time to hold a celebratory banquet in its palace. Aribua's population had no doubt been swelled by the Assyrian personnel who would remain there after his departure. To provision the city, Ashurnasirpal sent an expeditionary force into neighbouring Luash to raid its grainlands. Despite overwhelming odds, the people of Luash tried to drive the invaders out. They paid dearly for their courage. The invasion turned into a comprehensive rout of their forces, and the destruction of the cities they sought vainly to defend. Many Luashites were put to the sword, but some were spared death—long enough to be impaled alive on stakes erected before the smouldering ruins of their cities. It was an exemplary lesson on what lay in store for those who defied Assyrian authority.

No other state or city dared do so, as Ashurnasirpal marched along the Levantine coast to Mt Lebanon. The rulers of the Phoenician cities in the region, from Arwad southwards through Byblos and Sidon to Tyre, made their peace with him, and did so with lavish tribute-offerings. Ashurnasirpal thus became the first Assyrian king after Tiglath-pileser to reach the Mediterranean, and he marked his achievement with a ritual cleansing of his weapons in its waters and sacrifices to the gods. An extensive timber-gathering expedition in the Amanus range, in Syria's north-western corner, concluded the king's campaign. The felled trees were transported to Assyria for building projects in his new capital Nimrud (Assyrian Kalhu, biblical Calah) and other Assyrian cities. As a permanent memorial to himself, Ashurnasirpal ordered a stele to be set up on the range, recording his western campaign's successes. They had proved highly profitable, not least because they opened up channels for an ongoing flow of western tribute into Assyria's royal treasuries, palaces, and warehouses.

Ashurnasirpal himself never returned to Syria. Payments from the western states no doubt continued for a time. But as the years passed, these probably became more sporadic, or ceased altogether as the prospect of a return of Assyrian armies seemed increasingly remote. Perhaps the Assyrians would never return.

A new spirit of resistance

All such hopes were dashed with the news that there was a new monarch on the Assyrian throne, Ashurnasirpal's son and successor Shalmaneser III (858–824), ambitious, aggressive, and eager to lead his kingdom's armies back into their Syrian looting grounds. Shalmaneser's long reign saw a vigorous reassertion of Assyrian sovereignty over the cities and kingdoms west of the Euphrates.[5] He embarked on new ventures there, a fresh series of invasions that put his father's single western operation well and truly into the shade. His campaigns into the region, and into the lands of south-eastern Anatolia, were far more comprehensive than his father's had been, far more numerous, and far more bloodthirsty. No fewer than nineteen of Shalmaneser's known military enterprises were conducted west of the Euphrates. But he met with greater resistance than his father had done. After their earlier submission to Ashurnasirpal, some (though by no means all) of the trans-Euphrates states had now resolved to band together against his successor.

Prominent among their leaders was a man we have already met—Ahuni, ruler of Bit-Adini. Ahuni's kingdom provided the initial focus of resistance to Assyria. And Bit-Adini became Shalmaneser's first major western target. Control of it was an important key to the success of Assyrian campaigns across the river; and for the sake of Shalmaneser's credibility in the west, there was a pressing need to eliminate its troublesome king Ahuni. So within a year of his accession, Shalmaneser marched westwards and invaded Ahuni's kingdom. First, he attacked and burnt a city called Lalatu on the eastern frontier. Then he marched on Ahuni's capital Til Barsip. Ahuni was proof against intimidation. He knew his city was well fortified and could withstand enemy siege. But instead of simply holing up in it, he led his troops outside its walls for a showdown with Shalmaneser. It was a quixotic display of defiance. Ahuni's troops were quickly defeated. But their leader managed to get both himself and probably most of his troops back inside his city. Shalmaneser now abandoned his attack upon the capital, a well-nigh impregnable fortress-establishment. Instead, he moved on to another of Ahuni's cities, Burmarina, which he captured after a short siege, and put to the torch, slaughtering three hundred of its fighting men and making a tower of their corpses before the ruins of their city. That was sufficient to intimidate the neighbouring small Aramaean states into submission. Meanwhile, safe within his capital, Ahuni remained unsubdued, and as defiant as ever.

But the Assyrian had other matters to attend to, for the time being. He was eager to move against the states across the Euphrates, confident that this his first Syrian venture would be little more than a bloodless progress to the Mediterranean, with lots of opportunities for picking up rich tribute along the way. That had been his father's experience. Indeed, he did receive the submission of a king called Hattusili, ruler of the Neo-Hittite kingdom Kummuh, to the north of Carchemish. But one of Ahuni's cities, Paqarhubunu, located on the west bank of the Euphrates, held out against him. The city was captured and destroyed, along with 1,300 of its troops. That seemed lesson enough for Ahuni's neighbours. When the Assyrian marched westwards into the Neo-Hittite kingdom Gurgum, its ruler Muwattalli meekly submitted to him, handing over a tribute of silver, gold, oxen, sheep, and wine, plus his daughter and a rich dowry.

Shalmaneser no doubt expected a similar response from other states as he proceeded westwards to the coast. But it was not to be. When he marched upon the small Aramaean state Sam'al on the eastern slope of the Amanus range, he was met not by a submissive local ruler but by a coalition army mustered from the kings of the region. They included Ahuni, king of

Bit-Adini. After his earlier set-to with the Assyrians, Ahuni had met secretly with his fellow-rulers in Carchemish, Patin, and Sam'al to form an alliance against the invaders. Alas, things did not go their way. All their forces combined could not match the enemy's might. Shalmaneser boasted a massive slaughter of them, filling a large plain with their corpses, dyeing a mountain red with their blood, and erecting towers of their heads around the ruins of their sacked cities. To be sure, this is standard Assyrian battle-rhetoric. But the day was undoubtedly won by the Assyrians. And Shalmaneser's victory did remove a troublesome obstacle on his advance to the Mediterranean coast. Even so, the coalition leaders and most of their forces survived, despite what the Assyrian would have us believe, and remained free. Soon after, they regrouped, ready for another confrontation.

This time it was Patin's king Suppiluliuma who summoned the allies, when his fortified city Alimush came under threat from the invaders. The coalition forces were swelled by contingents brought by other rulers to the alliance—Kate, king of Adanawa, Pihirim, king of Hilakku (both lands lay in the region of Classical Cilicia along the south-eastern Anatolian coast), Burannati from the northern Arabian tribal state Yasbuq, and Adanu from the Aramaean state Yahan. Once more, the allies were defeated. But their spirit of resistance was unbroken. And their leaders remained alive and at large. Including Ahuni, king of Bit-Adini. This sent a clear message to the Assyrians. Neither Shalmaneser nor any of his successors could expect that campaigns in the west would henceforth be easily won. The world had changed since Ashurnasirpal's unimpeded progress through the region.

The contest with Ahuni

Ahuni remained a sharp thorn in the Assyrian side. His relentless defiance of Assyrian authority was both a serious embarrassment to Shalmaneser, and a continuing inspiration to other rulers in the region. Three times he had defied Assyrian authority and got away with it. Shalmaneser was determined there would not be a fourth. So again, in 857, he marched into Bit-Adini and advanced upon its capital Til Barsip. Once more Ahuni led his troops outside the city to defend it. Once more he was defeated and eluded his conqueror by retreating behind his walls. And once more, Shalmaneser was forced to abandon his attack. To console himself, he captured and plundered six other fortified cities within Bit-Adini and massacred their inhabitants. Indeed he claims to have reduced to ashes more than two hundred cities in the land. But Til Barsip could not be taken and Bit-Adini's ruler was still free. Shalmaneser had no option but to fall back on his earlier policy of whittling away the rest of the kingdom, leaving its capital in isolation. Then he sought to cut Ahuni off from all his allies. He marched westwards to the kingdom of Carchemish, seizing and destroying a walled city called Sazabu near its frontier. This display of force was enough to bring to heel all the local rulers of Hatti—formerly Shalmaneser's enemies. They came before the Assyrian to declare their submission, bringing handsome tribute payments with them—Sangara, king of Carchemish, Hayyanu, king of Sam'al, Halparuntiya, king of Patin, Arame, king of Bit-Agusi, Hattusili, king of Kummuh. All were courteously received, mercifully treated, and allowed to retain their thrones as the Great King's tributaries.

But Ahuni's defiance called for action of a different kind. Repeatedly, from the reign of Shalmaneser's father on, this man had taken up arms against the Assyrians, and defied all efforts to capture him. Shalmaneser respected him for it, albeit grudgingly: he spoke of him as 'the man of Bit-Adini, who had fought with might and main since the days of the kings my fathers'.[6] Now, in 856, Shalmaneser launched a fresh assault upon his kingdom. He brought all his resources to bear in a massive attack on the capital, bombarding it with a fire-storm of flaming arrows. Finally, the Assyrians smashed their way in. Til Barsip, royal seat of Ahuni, king of Bit-Adini, had fallen!

Then came the bad news for Shalmaneser. His arch-enemy was no longer there! While the Assyrians were busy breaking into his city, Ahuni had managed to slip out of it, taking flight west across the Euphrates, and gathering together, once more, a large force of infantry, chariotry, and cavalry. The contest was far from over! But Shalmaneser had another matter to attend to before resuming it. Til Barsip occupied a strategic location on one of the Euphrates' most important crossings. The Great King now converted it into an Assyrian stronghold, renaming it Kar-Shalmaneser ('Port Shalmaneser'). He built a palace there to serve as one of his royal residences, and swelled the city's population with new settlers from Assyria. Kar-Shalmaneser became the administrative centre of a region which later, in the reign of Tiglath-pileser III (745–727), became an Assyrian province with the old name Til Barsip restored.

To return to Ahuni. The hunted king had lost virtually all his cities, including his royal capital. But he was not yet finished. With his newly assembled army, he had taken refuge in a lofty, precipitous mountain stronghold called Shittamrat, a natural fortress 'suspended from heaven like a cloud'.[7] The year after Til Barsip's fall, Shalmaneser returned with his army and marched to the foot of the mountain. Caution was essential. Never before had any Assyrian army penetrated the fastnesses of Shittamrat. Shalmaneser had defeated Ahuni in all their previous encounters, but these had been fought on open ground, on terms favourable to the Assyrians. Now he faced the danger of being lured into difficult mountain terrain, to take on an enemy who still numbered in the thousands and would fight him on their own terms. The risk of the Assyrians being caught in an ambush and their forces destroyed was not inconsiderable. Well aware of this, Shalmaneser held back from an immediate attack. Instead, he spent three days on reconnaissance, sending out scouting parties to locate the enemy and check all places where Ahuni might stage an ambush. When satisfied with the information brought to him, he ordered a swift advance up the mountainside.

As the Assyrians approached, Ahuni ordered his men to break cover and attack. But the location and manner of their assault had been anticipated. The element of surprise was lost, and Ahuni's forces were routed. Many were beheaded, many fell from the cliff-tops as they fled. Ahuni himself had nowhere to go. He was cornered, captured, and taken back to the Assyrian homeland, along with his surviving forces—some 17,500 of them according to Shalmaneser. When suitably disciplined and trained, these valiant troops would be a valuable addition to the Assyrian army. As for their leader? We do not know what his eventual fate was. Perhaps this longstanding, resourceful enemy of the Assyrians, respected and admired by the Great King, was treated mercifully and accorded an honoured place in the Assyrian court. That is of course an Arabian Nights-type, 'feel-good' ending. But perhaps not too far from the truth. Shalmaneser may well have decided that such a man, courageous, cunning, and with long experience of conditions in the west, would be more useful to him alive than dead.

The southern alliance

Northern Syria was now firmly under Assyrian overlordship. But the Great King wanted more. There were still rich pickings to be had from the southwestern Syrian states and the lands and cities along the Syro-Palestinian coast. This provided the incentive for the expedition which Shalmaneser launched in his sixth regnal year, 853. It took him into western Syria and along the Orontes valley into the kingdom of Hamath and the lands beyond.

When he had begun his operations across the Euphrates six years earlier, these southern lands must have realized that an Assyrian onslaught upon them would come sooner or later. Nor can they have had any doubt of the fate in store for them as news arrived of the havoc wreaked by Assyrian armies in the north. The dilemma confronting them was simple: Submit to the Assyrian and pay him whatever tribute he demanded as he marched through their lands, as they had done in his father's reign? Or combine their resources and fight, and risk the inevitably horrible consequences of defeat?

Urhilina, ruler of Hamath, decided they should fight, and promptly sought an alliance with his neighbour Hadadezer (Assyrian Adad-idri), ruler of Damascus. Hadadezer readily agreed to partner him at the head of a new coalition army. Indeed for years to come, Damascus was to prove a powerful and resolute enemy of the Assyrians. Between them the two kings mustered a formidable fighting force. According to Assyrian records, Urhilina gathered 10,000 infantry, 700 chariots, and 700 cavalry, and Hadadezer brought to the alliance double his partner's infantry plus 1,200 chariots and 1,200 cavalry. They were joined by Ahab, the king of Israel, reportedly with 2,000 chariots and 10,000 troops. Many other states also flocked to their standards, including Byblos, which despatched 500 troops, and the island-city of Arwad, which sent another 200. Further support came from the pharaoh Osorkon II, who supplied 1,000 Egyptian infantry. It was in his kingdom's interests to do so; if the Assyrians swept through the Syro-Palestinian region, the land of the Nile would no longer be beyond their reach (as later conquerors were indeed to prove). Best for the pharaoh to support the war effort now, even if only with a token armed force.

The enemy numbers recorded by Assyrian scribes may be exaggerated. None the less, the combined army confronting Shalmaneser probably totalled at least 40,000 infantry, 3,000 chariotry, and close to 2,000 cavalry. It was a force comparable in size to that of the Hittite king Muwattalli in his showdown with Ramesses II at Qadesh more than four hundred years earlier. But a new element was added by an Arab chieftain called Gindibu, who provided the alliance with 1,000 camels. These animals had become increasingly important in the Iron Age. They were used not for fighting but for transporting equipment and baggage supplies, in this case providing valuable logistical support for a large army who had to march many kilometres over large tracts of inhospitable desert terrain to reach the battlefield.

For the allied leaders decided they would first assemble all their forces in the territory of Damascus (or perhaps southern Hamath), and then march north along the Orontes valley to meet the enemy. The further north they managed to advance, the less territory the Assyrians would have to plunder and despoil before they were confronted. Finally, the armies met outside the city of Qarqar on the Orontes, probably the site now called Tell Qarqur. The fate of the whole of southern Syria and Palestine hung in the balance. Details of the battle are unknown, beyond Shalmaneser's gloating, rhetorically charged report of its outcome: 'With the supreme forces granted me by Ashur, my lord, I fought with them and defeated them from the city Qarqar as far as the city Gilzau. I felled with the sword 14,000 troops, and rained down destruction upon them. I filled the plain with their corpses and flooded the wadis with their blood. There was not enough room on the plain to lay out their bodies flat. I dammed up the Orontes river with their bodies like a bridge. In the midst of the battle I took away from them chariots, cavalry, and teams of horse.'[8] In other words, Shalmaneser claimed victory. Despite its size, and perhaps partly because of its diversity, the alliance army was no match for the highly disciplined, battle-hardened Assyrians, who had but one supreme commander. But their defeat was far from decisive. All the allied leaders survived to fight another day, and the alliance which they led was to form again to continue its resistance to Shalmaneser.

For the time being, however, the Assyrians had gained the upper hand, and the defeated Syro-Palestinian states were forced to accept tributary status. But Shalmaneser's hold over his subject lands west of the Euphrates remained shaky, and his preoccupation with campaigns in southern Mesopotamia over the next three years (852–850) prompted fresh uprisings in the western territories. In the north Sangara, ruler of Carchemish, and Arame, ruler of Bit-Agusi, were at the forefront. Shalmaneser responded as soon as his Mesopotamian enterprises were completed, crossing the Euphrates once more, attacking and burning many of Sangara's cities, then moving on to Bit-Agusi, whose royal capital Arne he demolished. Henceforth Arpad became the capital of Bit-Agusi. Its name was often used for the kingdom as a whole. The unrest in the western states spread south in the same year (849) and saw a revival of the coalition that had confronted Shalmaneser at Qarqar in 853. Shalmaneser marched to the region without delay, and claimed another decisive victory. But the following year, uprisings broke out afresh in the defeated lands. Many of Shalmaneser's victims showed remarkable resilience to the devastation inflicted on them, and many cities apparently reduced to charred ruins seem to have miraculously resurrected themselves, just in time to be destroyed all over again the following year.

Assyrian kings were far from being the only warlords, past and more recent, to make sometimes extravagant claims about the extent of the damage they inflicted upon their enemies. Yet such claims often had substance. There is no doubt that Assyrian armies regularly left trails of devastation and ruin throughout the countries where they campaigned. Nor is there any doubt that some of the cities and countries so afflicted never recovered. But some did, despite the worst the Assyrians could do to them.

Twice more, in 848 and 845, the states forming the anti-Assyrian southern alliance reassembled for further attempts to cast off the Assyrian yoke. And twice more, Shalmaneser claims to have defeated them. But the very fact of his having to do so—repeatedly—demonstrates how limited and short-term his success really was in imposing his authority throughout the Syro-Palestinian region. Indeed, what ended the alliance was not Assyrian force of arms but its own implosion. This happened with the death of the Damascene king Hadadezer, some time between 845 and 841. His throne was now occupied by Hazael, one of his officers. Shalmaneser speaks contemptuously of the new king as 'the son of a nobody'. According to the biblical report, Hazael seized the throne of Damascus in a coup, smothering his predecessor with a thick cloth soaked in water (2 Kings 8:7–15).[9] Whether or not this is true, Hazael proved no less committed than Hadadezer to the achievement of the alliance's objective—the repulse of the Assyrians. Unfortunately, this was not enough to prevent the loss of his kingdom's two main coalition partners. The rulers of Hamath and Israel now broke free from the alliance. Probably, they had no desire to be associated with the upstart commoner-become-king who, they may well have believed, had assassinated their long-term comrade-in-arms.

Damascus had now to face alone the might of the Assyrians. In 841, Shalmaneser crossed the Euphrates for the sixteenth time, with Damascus as his specific target. In the confrontation that followed, the Great King claimed a crushing victory over his opponent Hazael, putting 16,000 of his troops to the sword and seizing 1,121 of his chariotry and 470 of his infantry. Hazael himself fled the battlefield and took refuge in his capital, where Shalmaneser blockaded him. Damascus held firm, withstanding all the invaders could throw at it, and Shalmaneser could do no more than capture and subjugate four other cities belonging to the king. Even so, Damascus was now completely isolated. Other former alliance partners, including Israel and the Phoenician cities Tyre, Sidon, and Byblos, had by now returned to the Assyrian fold as tribute-paying states. It seemed but a matter of time before

Hazael would follow suit. But he was made of sterner stuff. Humble though his origins may have been, he was to prove one of Damascus' greatest kings, enjoying a reign of perhaps forty years, despite all the Assyrians' efforts to cut it short. Throughout his regnal career, he not only maintained Damascus' independence, but went on to build around it a small empire, which incorporated large parts of Palestine, including Judah, Israel, and Philistia, and perhaps also parts of northern Syria.

In Shalmaneser's wake

In the 830s, Shalmaneser conducted a number of campaigns into the Anatolian peninsula. There, he imposed his sovereignty upon the Neo-Hittite kingdoms in the region called Tabal, which lay south of the Halys river, and the kingdom called Adanawa (aka Hiyawa, Assyrian Que) on the southeastern coast. But he never returned to Syria. In the final years of his reign, he entrusted the conduct of foreign enterprises to his deputies. Notable among these was a man called Dayyan-Ashur, appointed commander-in-chief of all His Majesty's armies. Dayyan-Ashur quickly proved his worth in an expedition he led into the eastern Anatolian kingdom called Urartu, where he won a decisive victory over the local king Sarduri I (c.832). Urartu would continue to pose a serious threat to Assyria and its subject lands. But while the Assyrians ensured that their territories most vulnerable to Urartian attacks were kept secure, they remained fully committed to maintaining, with force if need be, their authority in the west.

A test case arose when the throne of the kingdom Patin, occupied by a loyal Assyrian tributary called Lubarna (the second Patinite king of that name), was seized by a usurper Surri and Lubarna was killed. By this coup, Surri was effectively thumbing his nose at Assyrian overlordship. Immediate action was called for. Aware of the importance of sending a clear and unequivocal message to all his tributaries in the west, Shalmaneser despatched Dayyan-Ashur to Patin to remove the interloper. Dayyan-Ashur marched his troops across the Euphrates and headed directly to Patin's capital Kinalua. Surri was in residence. Panic swept through the city as the Assyrians massed outside Kinalua's walls, their swords flashing blindingly in the sunlight. Surri concluded, quite rightly, that all was lost, and committed suicide. 'Overwhelmed by fear of the radiance of (the god) Ashur,' the Assyrian record reports, 'he departed this life.'[10] Now leaderless, and terror-stricken at the prospect of brutal reprisals for the coup, his abandoned subjects herded together the usurper's sons and troops and handed them over to Dayyan-Ashur. It was a desperate ploy to save their own skins, and it worked. Everyone was spared—bar those who had been delivered up to the Assyrians. These unfortunate wretches were duly impaled on stakes planted around the city. Dayyan-Ashur's mission was now just about finished. He rounded it off by putting his own appointee on Kinalua's throne, and by setting up a colossal statue of Shalmaneser within the city's precincts; it would be a permanent reminder to the Patinites of who their overlord really was. Then he set off home, taking with him a substantial tribute of silver, gold, tin, bronze, and elephant ivory.

We know of no further Assyrian campaigns west of the Euphrates during Shalmaneser's reign. Assyria itself was beset with political upheavals at the end of it, and the continuation of these into the early regnal years of his son Shamshi-Adad V (823–811) spared Syria and Palestine any further Assyrian intervention, for the time being. Many states in the region no doubt took the opportunity to cast off all trappings of Assyrian sovereignty. Kar-Shalmaneser on the Euphrates now became in effect the Assyrians' western boundary. But when Shamshi-Adad's son and successor Adad-nirari III (810–783) mounted the throne, Assyria once more looked westwards, again lured by the rewards to be won by asserting its sovereignty over the lands between the Euphrates and the Mediterranean. In 805, Adad-nirari embarked on his first of a series of expeditions across the Euphrates.[11]

Reports reaching the western lands that a new Assyrian invasion was in the making prompted nine of the northern rulers to form another alliance. Their leader was one of the most powerful local rulers of the age—Attar-shumki, chief of the large Aramaean kingdom Arpad (Bit-Agusi). Adad-nirari's campaign was allegedly triggered by an appeal from one of his loyal subjects, Suppiluliuma, king of Kummuh. The latter complained that his neighbour Halparuntiya, king of Gurgum, was trying to seize a slice of his territory. This provided a good excuse for a fresh reassertion of Assyrian authority in the region, and Adad-nirari set off for the Euphrates. But when he crossed the river, he was confronted by a large allied army, under the command of Attar-shumki. The opposing forces clashed outside Paqarhubunu, on the west bank of the upper Euphrates. Victory was claimed by Adad-nirari, who ordered that a stele recording his success be set up on the boundary between Kummuh and Gurgum. The stele survives today. But Adad-nirari failed to break up the enemy coalition. For at least the next ten years it resisted his attempts to destroy it.

8th century BC

Adad-nirari's western campaigns included one to Damascus, which ended with the local kingdom's submission to him. But Damascus remained a major participant in Syro-Palestinian affairs, illustrated by the leading role played by its king Bar-Hadad II (son and successor of Hazael) in a coalition army that laid siege to the northern Hamathite city Hatarikka (c.800). Hamath was then ruled by a king called Zakur. The coalition included a number of states of northern Syria and south-eastern Anatolia, including Adanawa, Patin, Sam'al, Gurgum, Malatya, Tabal, and probably Arpad under Attar-shumki's leadership. We do not know why these states became hostile to Hamath. Perhaps the kingdom had refused to join them in their resistance to Assyria, and now came under attack from them by way of reprisal. When Zakur marched north to meet the enemy, they blockaded him in Hatarikka. With divine support, he claims, he fought his way out of the city and defeated his enemies. One suspects that Assyrian back-up played no small part in his success.

Despite the coalition's defeat, Damascus and Arpad remained powerful forces in their region, and significant problems for the Assyrians in the west for years to come, particularly during a period of reduced Assyrian authority there in the reigns of Adad-nirari's first three successors. These were Shalmaneser IV, Ashur-dan III, and Ashur-nirari V (in total, 782–746), who limited their activities across the Euphrates to a small number of modest military operations. That served to encourage anti-Assyrian activity in the region. Perhaps already in Adad-nirari's reign, Bar-Hadad had marched upon Assyria's loyal subject Kummuh, during one of his campaigns in the north, and dug up the boundary-stone erected by Adad-nirari on the kingdom's frontier. This must have been a severe humiliation to the Assyrians. The monument that proclaimed Adad-nirari's victory over the anti-Assyrian alliance was now in the hands of one of the vanquished alliance-leaders! Bar-Hadad carried his prize to Damascus in triumph. And in Damascus it remained until it was retrieved in 773—when Damascus fell victim to an attack by Shamshi-ilu, Assyria's commander-in-chief. Shamshi-ilu uprooted the stone and took it back to Kummuh. There it was firmly replanted in its original location.

The Damascus campaign may have gone some way to restoring Assyrian authority in the lands west of the Euphrates. But this authority remained fragile, and was soon put to the test by another power which vied with

Assyria for supremacy over the region—Urartu. Already in the early years of the 8th century, this eastern Anatolian kingdom had established its presence firmly in the west. Around 796, the Urartian king Minua had crossed the Euphrates and imposed tributary status upon the Neo-Hittite kingdom Malatya. His successor Argishti I reasserted this status, around 784, as did Argishti's successor Sarduri II around 760. Kummuh also became subject to Urartu when Sarduri II attacked it and forced the submission of its king in 750 or later. Arpad too had territorial interests west of the Euphrates, well beyond its own borders. Though their ambitions may ultimately have been conflicting ones, the two kingdoms Urartu and Arpad were, for a time, apparently prepared to join forces to rid themselves of their common enemy—Assyria.

Matters came to a head in 754 when the Assyrian king Ashur-nirari V conducted a campaign against Arpad, and Sarduri II joined the conflict on Arpad's side. According to Urartian records, the allies inflicted a devastating defeat on their opponents. They may indeed have won the day, but the consequences for Assyria were probably not as severe or as long-lasting as is sometimes supposed. In fact, some time after the conflict, Ashur-nirari ended hostilities with Arpad by diplomatic means, drawing up with its current king Mati'ilu a treaty of alliance which precluded him from forming alliances with any other states—including Urartu.[12] But Mati'ilu proved an unreliable ally, and probably soon after Ashur-nirari's death in 746, he roused the northern Syrian and south-eastern Anatolian states to rebellion once more against Assyrian rule, with the support of Assyria's most formidable enemy, Urartu.

The closing jaws

It might all have gone very badly for Assyria, were it not for the timely appearance on the scene, in 745, of a man who was to prove one of the most powerful, capable, and ruthless of all Assyrian monarchs—Tiglath-pileser III.[13] Almost certainly an interloper of non-royal blood, Tiglath-pileser usurped his way onto the throne at a time when his kingdom had been weakened by political instability and was facing increasing threats from its enemies abroad. The greatest danger came from the east. Urartu had now consolidated its hold upon a number of territories west of the Euphrates, and upon other territories to which the Assyrians laid claim, as well as menacing the Assyrian homeland itself. Prompt and comprehensive action against it was

Figure 12. Tiglath-pileser III

essential. But first Tiglath-pileser had to turn his attention to another eastern menace, a rebellious land called Namri on the western fringes of the
Zagros mountains. Namri had a long history of hostility to Assyria, and
resistance to Assyrian overlordship had reached the point, by the beginning
of Tiglath-pileser's reign, where it could no longer be tolerated. In a brutal
retaliatory campaign, Tiglath-pileser reasserted Assyrian control over it and
other recalcitrant states in the region, leaving him free, in 743, to muster his
forces for a resolution of the problems across the Euphrates.

Confronting him there was an alliance led jointly by Mati'ilu, king of
Arpad, and Sarduri II, king of Urartu. Other alliance members included the
Neo-Hittite kingdoms Malatya, Gurgum, and Kummuh. The armies clashed
in the land of Kummuh. Battle honours went decisively to Tiglath-pileser,

and Sarduri was forced to cut his losses and retreat to his homeland. There, he would live to fight the Assyrians another day. Which was small consolation for his alliance partners, now highly vulnerable to Assyrian retribution. But to the Neo-Hittite kings among them Tiglath-pileser was disposed to be merciful. He reinstated all of them on their thrones as his tributaries, accepting their pledges of loyalty for the future. It may well be that at least two of them, the rulers of Kummuh and Malatya, had fought on the alliance side against their will, as enforced subjects of Urartu following the Urartian conquest of them some years earlier. Tiglath-pileser may have taken this into account in his lenient treatment of them.

But Arpad was a different matter. Its king Mati'ilu, a former treaty-partner of Tiglath-pileser's predecessor Ashur-nirari V, had broken his oath of allegiance and openly supported Assyria's arch-enemy. He had now to pay the price for his treachery. Tiglath-pileser succeeded in laying waste much of his land. But Arpad's strongly fortified capital remained intact, and Mati'ilu took refuge there. Its capture was vital to Assyrian interests. Placing it under heavy siege, Tiglath-pileser resolved not to withdraw before the city had fallen to him. It took him three years to accomplish this. Regrettably, the section of the king's Annals which must have given details of the siege and the city's final capitulation is missing. No doubt it would have told us what happened to Mati'ilu. His fate remains unknown. He may have fled the city before its fall and taken refuge in the mountains, as other refugees from Assyrian authority had done. Or he may have been captured and deported to Assyria or executed. In any case, Tiglath-pileser had new plans for his kingdom. It became the first of the western states to be brought directly under Assyrian control, by being converted into an Assyrian province, with the name Arpad. No longer was it a semi-autonomous state with tributary status. An Assyrian governor was installed in the province, and very likely a large part of its population was deported and replaced by settlers from other parts of Tiglath-pileser's empire.

Thus began what was to become a regular practice during the rest of Tiglath-pileser's reign and that of his second successor Sargon II. Around 738, Tiglath-pileser made a list of all the western rulers who were subject to him, in Syria, Palestine, and south-eastern Anatolia. Over the next three decades, the states they ruled as tributaries were absorbed one by one into the Assyrian provincial system, becoming provinces on their own, or components of other provinces.[14] In many cases, the catalyst for their conversion was an uprising by a local ruler who broke his allegiance to Assyria, or a coup by a usurper who unseated a king loyal to Assyria. In the newly created provinces, Assyrian governors directly answerable to the Great King were installed in newly built royal residences. And substantial population exchanges frequently took place. Large numbers of the inhabitants of a kingdom, often including their royal family, were deported to other parts of the Assyrian-controlled world, their places taken by thousands of forced immigrants transplanted from elsewhere in the realm. After removal from their former homelands, the new settlers would, it was hoped, adapt to a new life as subjects of the Great King more readily than the brutalized former occupants of the regions. At least that was probably the theory. As it happened, many of the uprooted populations did quickly adapt to and identify with their new homelands—and were ready to defend them, under the leadership of whatever local king called them to arms against an outside aggressor, Assyrian or otherwise.

Before concluding this episode in our story of Syria, we should tie up a couple of loose ends. First of all, the unfinished business with Urartu's king Sarduri. Eight years after defeating Sarduri at Kummuh, Tiglath-pileser decided it was time for a final reckoning with the Urartian on his own territory. So he conducted a campaign into Urartu, advancing all the way to its capital Tushpa, near the south-eastern shore of Lake Van. Sarduri was ready to meet the challenge, and massed his troops outside Tushpa to do battle. In the engagement that followed, Tiglath-pileser was victorious, so Assyrian records tell us, but his forces failed to take the city, into which presumably Sarduri managed to withdraw with most of his troops. That is exactly what Ahuni and other besieged enemies of the Assyrians had done on earlier occasions. Capturing a heavily fortified city was no easy task, even for a large well-trained army. The best Tiglath-pileser could do was to erect a statue of himself outside Tushpa's walls to commemorate his victory before returning home. No doubt the statue was torn down as soon as the Assyrians departed.

There was also the ongoing Damascus problem. Within a year of his Urartian venture, Tiglath-pileser received word of a serious new crisis developing in the Syro-Palestinian region. Damascus was at the centre of this crisis. Its king, Rasyan, had assembled another anti-Assyrian coalition, whose members included Israel (then ruled by Pekah), Tyre, and Philistia, and some Arab tribes. But Judah's king Ahaz refused to join them, and when the Damascene and Israelite kings attacked his land, he requested assistance from Tiglath-pileser, boosting his appeal with the offer of a huge gift of gold and silver from the treasury of the temple in Jerusalem—for Jerusalem, with Ahaz inside it, held out against the invaders' attacks (2 Kings 16:5–10). With or without Ahaz's inducement, Tiglath-pileser returned to the Syro-Palestinian region for a fresh campaign in 734. Ahaz had the satisfaction of seeing his enemies confounded and his kingdom made secure. But if he had expected any reward from Tiglath-pileser for his loyalty or his bribe to him, or even a show of gratitude, he was sadly mistaken. According to 2 Chronicles 28:16–18, the Assyrian king on his arrival dealt brusqely with him, giving him 'trouble instead of help'. What precisely is meant by these words is unclear. In the biblical context, the point is made that Ahaz was punished by the Almighty for his string of evil acts, which included the sacrifice of his son in accordance with Canaanite practices and his appeal to the Assyrians rather than to God in his present predicament.

After a short, successful campaign against Philistia, Tiglath-pileser was ready the following year (733) to march upon Rasyan's kingdom, Damascus. Once there, he met and defeated Rasyan's army in open battle, but—the story has a familiar ring to it—Rasyan escaped the battlefield and found refuge in his capital. Despite mounting a forty-five-day siege upon the city, Tiglath-pileser failed to breach its walls. He had to content himself with destroying the city's surrounding orchards and gardens. But the following year, he was back, and laid siege to the capital once more. This time successfully. Damascus fell, its king Rasyan was captured and executed, and his kingdom incorporated into the Assyrian provincial system. That left only Rasyan's main coalition-partner Pekah, king of Israel, to be dealt with. And that was done easily enough. According to 2 Kings 15:30, Pekah was assassinated by a man called Hoshea, who seized his throne and became, with Tiglath-pileser's support, what was to be Israel's last king (c.732–724).

The last members of the pack

The five-year reign of Shalmaneser V (726–722) has left us with little information, beyond what seems to have been the chief event of it, the capture and destruction of Samaria at the end of the reign.[15] But despite the report in 2 Kings 17:6, 24 of a massive population exchange programme imposed by the Assyrians on the country, the spirit of resistance in Samaria still burned strong, a legacy which the new Assyrian king, Sargon (721–705), inherited from his predecessor. In the year of his accession (722), a number of states in the Syro-Palestinian region sought to exploit what they saw as the instability of the Assyrian regime in this changeover period by rising up in rebellion once more, under the banner of Yaubidi, the current ruler of Hamath.[16] Arpad joined him—as did Damascus. Tiglath-pileser had incorporated Damascus into the Assyrian provincial system in 732. The land now sought to regain its independence.

Sargon marched his troops into Syria along the Orontes valley to confront the rebel coalition forces at a site where Assyrians and rebels had famously clashed in the past—Qarqar on the Orontes. The rebels were crushed, yet again, and their leader Yaubidi captured and flayed alive. His capital Hamath city was put to the torch, his kingdom converted into an Assyrian province (720). Samaria too fell, once more. With the seizure of its capital, the kingdom of Israel was at an end. One of Sargon's eunuch officials was appointed to govern the land. A graphic (though not historically credited) Old Testament source reports the fate of several members of the coalition, in the words it attributes to the field-commander of Sargon's son and successor Sennacherib. This was during Sennacherib's siege of Jerusalem in 691. Demanding the surrender of the city, the commander 'stood and called out in Hebrew: "Hear the word of the great king, the king of Assyria! This is what the king says: 'Make peace with me and come out to me. . . . Do not listen to Hezekiah (the Judaean king), for he is misleading you when he says, "the Lord will deliver us." Has the god of any nation ever delivered his land from the hand of the king of Assyria? Where are the gods of Hamath and Arpad? Where are the gods of Sepharvaim, Hena, and Illah? Have they rescued Samaria from my hand? Who of all the gods of these countries has been able to save his land from me? How then can the Lord deliver Jerusalem from my hand?"' (2 Kings 18:28–35).

By the end of Sargon's reign (705), most of the cities, states, and kingdoms west of the Euphrates had been absorbed within the Assyrian provincial system, generally in response to developments within them that ran counter to Assyrian interests. Thus Carchemish became a province ruled by an Assyrian governor in 717 when its last ruler Pisiri was deposed by Sargon for allegedly plotting with the Phrygian king Mita (Greek Midas). Hamath, as we have noted, was 'provincialized' in 720 when its last king Yaubidi was executed after leading a rebellion against Assyria. Kummuh was annexed in 708 when its last king Muwattalli was accused of plotting with the Urartian king Argishti II. A clear prompt for imposing direct rule over the tributary states, particularly rebellious or recalcitrant ones, was the quite reasonable fear that they would otherwise align themselves with foreign powers hostile to Assyria. We have already seen that happening in the pact made between

Urartu and Arpad prior to Tiglath-pileser III's reign. Urartu remained a threat to Assyria, not only because of the danger it posed to Assyria's eastern territories, but also because of its territorial ambitions in the west, which inevitably involved what Assyria claimed as its subject states. Thus too in Sargon's reign, as we have just seen. Muwattalli was not the only one of Assyria's subject kings to be accused, probably with good reason, of plotting with Urartu.

7th century BC

By the end of the 8th century, all the kingdoms we call Neo-Hittite had disappeared into the Assyrian provincial system. But anti-Assyrian resistance continued to smoulder, in Syria and Palestine as well as in other parts of the Assyrian-controlled world. Several of the former Neo-Hittite kingdoms in southern Anatolia sought to regain their independence during the following century, and the spirit of resistance remained strong in some of the main Phoenician cities. Sidon, which rose up constantly against its Assyrian overlords, was the target of a number of campaigns by later Assyrian kings, including Sennacherib and Esarhaddon.[17] It was the latter who finally destroyed the city, capturing and beheading its king, Abdi-milkutti, and deporting a large part of its population. None the less, Sidon quickly revived and regained its prosperity and its independence, only to be subjected once more, after the fall of Assyria, to the Babylonian king Nebuchadnezzar. Esarhaddon was also responsible for crushing a coalition of rebel forces led by Baal, ruler of the island-city Tyre. He subsequently drew up with Baal a treaty giving back to him the various territories which Tyre had formerly controlled. But the Tyrian king once more rose up against Assyria in the reign of Esarhaddon's successor Ashurbanipal (668–630/27). Tyre's resistance ended when the Assyrians starved the city into submission by cutting off its food supplies from the mainland.

By the late 7th century, Assyrian history had run its course. The final blow was delivered by a coalition formed between Nabopolassar, king of Babylonia, and the Medes (from western Iran). In 615, the Medes invaded the Assyrian homeland, and in the following year captured the city of Ashur. Then in 612, the royal city of Nineveh, now the last great surviving remnant of the Assyrian empire, was placed under siege by an alliance of Babylonian and Median forces. Three months later, it was captured by Nabopolassar.

With its fall, the Assyrians' long lease of power in western Asia was effectively finished, for the backbone of their power had been broken. By year's end, all the chief cities of the Assyrian homeland had been destroyed.

But the Syrian and Palestinian 'beneficiaries' of this had little cause or time for rejoicing. It soon became clear that the death of the Assyrian empire simply paved the way for the imposition of a new and equally brutal overlord upon them.

8

From Nebuchadnezzar to Alexander

The Neo-Babylonian Empire[1]
Late 7th century BC

The prelude to Nebuchadnezzar's reign

As the Assyrian empire expired under its last king Ashur-uballit II (612–610), two years after the fall of Nineveh, the Neo-Babylonian empire, founded by Nineveh's destroyer Nabopolassar, was rising rapidly to take its place. Seizing his kingdom's throne in 626, and initially working in partnership with the king of Media to eliminate Assyria, Nabopolassar established an empire that was to hold sway over much of the Near East for almost ninety years (until 539). Compared with many of its imperial predecessors and successors, the empire which it ruled, from its royal capital Babylon, was short-lived. But in its brief lifespan, the royal line imposed its sovereignty upon a wide array of subject lands, from the south-eastern corner of Anatolia through Syria, Palestine, and parts of Arabia to the Peninsula of Sinai, and through Mesopotamia eastwards across the Tigris into western Iran.

For Syria and Palestine, the fall of Assyria and the rise of Babylonia simply meant an exchange of overlords. And not just a Babylonian for an Assyrian one. There was another major contestant for control over the lands between the Euphrates and the Great Sea. In the year 610, Egypt's throne was occupied by a new pharaoh, Necho II, third ruler of the Twenty-Sixth (so-called Saite) Dynasty, who had plans to rebuild Egypt's once mighty empire and reclaim its former subject lands in Syria and Palestine. In the year after his accession, the pharaoh launched a major expedition into the lands to the north of his kingdom. The professed aim of this expedition was to assist his ally Ashur-uballit. After Nineveh's fall, the Assyrian had taken final refuge in the northern Mesopotamian city Harran, and set up his court there; but he abandoned the place when news came that Babylonian and Median forces were fast approaching. Harran was thus left to the mercy of the enemy who thoroughly pillaged it.[2] The following year, Necho arrived with his army to help Ashur-uballit regain the city.

On the way, he was confronted at Megiddo by an army led by the Judaean king Josiah (2 Kings 23:29). Megiddo was located in northern Palestine, at the western end of the Jezreel Valley, at a major intersection on the Via Maris.[3] We do not know what Josiah's motives were in taking on the Egyptian army. Maybe he was trying to stop Necho from bringing assistance to Ashur-uballit, and thus help ensure that Assyria would not rise again. Maybe he simply wanted to preserve his independence against any aggressor. In any case, he was defeated and killed. And Necho proceeded on his way, having won by military force dominance over the whole of southern Syria and Palestine. The route through Syria into northern Mesopotamia now lay clear before him.

But his rescue mission proved abortive. Assyria was beyond saving. And when Ashur-uballit and Necho failed to retake Harran, they ensured that the last nail was firmly hammered into the coffin of the now well and truly dead empire. Necho could hardly have doubted that the Assyrian cause was hopeless, long before he reached his destination. But what concerned him more than Assyria's fate was the prospect of Babylon now emerging as a serious contender for filling the power vacuum west of the Euphrates left by his ally's fall. He wanted to stake his own claim to the slaughtered wolf's old hunting grounds, and his intervention in the region ostensibly on Assyria's behalf paved the way for a reassertion of Egyptian authority in the Syro-Palestinian lands.

In line with this intention, he set up a regional headquarters at Riblah as he retraced his campaign trail through Syria and Palestine on his way home. Located on the Orontes river in the land of Hamath, Riblah occupied an important strategic position on the route between Egypt and northern Syria and Mesopotamia. While he was in the city, Necho summoned the man appointed king of Judah by his countrymen after the death of Josiah. This was Josiah's son Jehoahaz. The meeting was not a happy one. Necho took an instant dislike to the new king, deposed him, chained him up, and despatched him to Egypt, where he died. His reign had lasted but three months. In his place, Necho installed his rather more amenable younger brother Jehoiakim.[4] To make absolutely clear that Judah was now subject to Egypt, the pharaoh imposed upon its new ruler a tribute of 100 talents of silver and a talent of gold, collected by taxes imposed upon the people of Judah.[5] Jehoiakim occupied his kingdom's throne for eleven years (609–598). But by no means all of them as vassal of Egypt.

For the present, with southern Syria and Palestine apparently firmly under his control, Necho returned to Egypt. He would be back four years later (605).

A new contest for Syria and Palestine

That brings us to the defining figure of the age, Nebuchadnezzar II. Already as crown prince Nebuchadnezzar had become a battle-hardened veteran as his father's comrade-in-arms. And in 605, the year that culminated in his accession, his father gave him command of the entire Babylonian army, for a campaign across the Euphrates to Carchemish.[6] The city was to be used as a base for Babylonian military operations against the Egyptians. For it was now time to determine, by force of arms, who would rule Assyria's former subject territories west of the Euphrates. Egypt had moved quickly to claim possession of these territories once they had been freed of their Assyrian overlord. Babylon now challenged this claim, and Carchemish provided the setting for a contest to resolve it. On an open space outside the city's walls, the two armies met in battle. The result was a triumph for Nebuchadnezzar. Babylonian records state that the entire Egyptian army was wiped out; the remnants of it that did manage to escape the field were overtaken by their pursuers and captured.[7] According to the Babylonian account, not a single member of Necho's army returned to Egypt—obviously an exaggeration, for we know that the pharaoh himself survived the conflict and got safely home (and he can hardly have done so on his own), living to fight another day. But for the time being at least, the question of sovereignty over the western lands had been resolved. For the victor's reputation ensured, particularly after his destruction of the Egyptian army, that these lands accepted their new subjection virtually without resistance.

There was a further victim of the Babylonian–Egyptian showdown—Carchemish itself. In the aftermath of the battle, this, one of the greatest cities in Syria's history, was abandoned. It remained derelict until its partial reoccupation in the Hellenistic period, with a new name, Europos.

While Nebuchadnezzar was busy with his western operations, he received word that his father had died (8 May 605). According to the Jewish historian

Josephus, he quickly set in order the affairs of Egypt and other countries, arranged the transportation of Jewish, Phoenician, Syrian, and Egyptian prisoners to Babylonia, along with the spoils of battle and the bulk of the army, and then returned to the royal capital Babylon,[8] where he was crowned king on 1 June. All this he accomplished within twenty-four days of his father's death. From the very beginning of his reign, one of his priorities was to consolidate and maintain his sovereignty over the lands west of the Euphrates. For these lands were resource-rich and many occupied strategically important positions. No major power could claim supremacy in the Near Eastern world without undisputed control over the kingdoms and cities that lay between the Euphrates and the Mediterranean. And that is what Nebuchadnezzar achieved in his first regnal year when 'all the kings of Hatti came into his presence, and he received their vast tribute'.[9] Hatti in this context must refer to the rulers of the lands of Syria and Palestine. Nebuchadnezzar had now completed his seizure of these lands from Egypt. For the next ten years, he made regular tours of inspection of them—'marching about victoriously' through his realm, as the Babylonian Chronicle puts it—to ensure that his subject kings remained submissive to him. But there was one who did not. Jehoiakim, king of Judah and former vassal of the pharaoh Necho, was initially among the rulers who paid homage to Nebuchadnezzar. After three years, he changed his mind and rebelled (2 Kings 24:1). We shall come back to him.

There was the further matter of Egypt's continuing interests in the region, for Necho still had his eyes firmly set on his former territories there. Indeed, Nebuchadnezzar's tours of the western lands were as much concerned with keeping Egypt out of them as with ensuring their continuing good behaviour. Babylonian garrisons stationed in these lands were reinforced in 601 when news reached Babylon that Necho was mustering an army for a fresh invasion. Nebuchadnezzar led his own army south to confront him before he reached Babylonian-controlled territory. The armies met to the south-west of the city of Pelusium, at the north-eastern end of the Egyptian Delta on the route from Egypt to Gaza. Both sustained heavy casualties. Nebuchadnezzar was forced to return home, suspending operations the following year to rebuild and retrain his forces. Necho may have managed to advance as far as and capture Gaza.[10] But neither he nor any later members of his dynasty ever succeeded in re-establishing Egyptian sovereignty over the Syro-Palestinian region.

600–539 BC

The fall of Jerusalem[11]

Nevertheless, the Judaean king Jehoiakim believed that the Egyptians had got the better of the conflict, and chose this time to break his allegiance to Babylon. Three years of obedient vassalhood were now at an end. Nebuchadnezzar could not let the defector go unpunished; to do so would send a very bad message to Babylon's other vassal states, and might put at risk all of Nebuchadnezzar's holdings west of the Euphrates. The threat was of course intensified by the ongoing Egyptian menace. Action was essential. But an effective strategy had to be carefully planned. Nebuchadnezzar once more led his forces into Syria, and established a base at Riblah on the Orontes river, where Necho had set up his regional headquarters eight years earlier. As we shall see, Riblah was to provide a grim setting for the fate of a later king of Judah. Nebuchadnezzar's initial response to Jehoiakim's defection had been to incite attacks against his kingdom by invaders from the neighbouring Aramaean, Moabite, and Ammonite tribal states (2 Kings 24:2). But Jehoiakim stayed firmly seated on his throne and the sovereignty of his kingdom remained intact for several more years—until Nebuchadnezzar was ready to mount a full-scale campaign against him.

This came in the year 597 when Nebuchadnezzar himself marched into Judah and placed Jerusalem under siege. By now there was a new king on its throne. Three months earlier Jehoiakim had died, apparently of natural causes. Though the prophet Jeremiah had prophesied an undignified end for his corpse ('He will have the burial of a donkey—dragged away and thrown outside the gates of Jerusalem': Jer. 22:19), Jehoiakim appears to have been accorded a traditional interment and 'rested with his fathers' (2 Kings 24:6). He was succeeded by his eighteen-year-old son Jehoiachin (2 Kings 24:8) who had but three months on his throne before Nebuchadnezzar was at his gates. Realizing that resistance was useless, the young king surrendered himself to the Babylonian, along with his wives, servants, princes, and officers (2 Kings 24:12)—thus fulfilling one of Jeremiah's prophecies (Jer. 22:24–30). The prisoners were deported to Babylon, along with 10,000 soldiers, officers, craftsmen, and smiths, leaving only the poorest people in the land (2 Kings 24:14, 16). Treasures from the temple in Jerusalem were among the spoils taken by the invader back to Babylon (2 Chron. 36:10).

Jehoiachin's confinement in Babylon was a long though, in the end, not an arduous one. Our biblical sources tell us (2 Kings 25:27–30; Jer. 52:31–4) that in his thirty-seventh year of exile (561), he was released from prison by Nebuchadnezzar's successor Evil-Merodach (= Amel-Marduk), who raised him to a status higher than that of any other kings then in Babylon, and gave him a place of honour at the royal table. Jehoiachin's submission to the Babylonian king appears to have saved Judah from the severest destruction. Thus the scholar D. J. Wiseman observes, who goes on to note that Judah's subordination to Babylonia marked a watershed in its affairs; henceforth, 'it was destined to be dominated by foreign powers, with but a few years' respite, for the next fourteen centuries'.[12]

But for the moment let us go back to Nebuchadnezzar's dealings with Jerusalem. After removing Jehoiachin from its throne, the Babylonian had installed upon it a puppet ruler called Zedekiah (2 Kings 24:17). For more than eight years, Zedekiah remained faithful to his overlord. Then, in his ninth year (2 Kings 24:20–5:1; Jer. 39:1) and despite the warnings of Jeremiah, he rebelled. Nebuchadnezzar was furious. Without delay, he led another full-scale Babylonian expedition against Judah, laid waste the country, encamped his army beneath Jerusalem's walls, and placed the city under siege. Zedekiah's days—and his city's—were very clearly numbered. He had but one hope left. Egypt! An urgent appeal for assistance was sent to Egypt. It met with a positive response when the pharaoh Apries despatched an expeditionary force to Judah to divert the besiegers (Jer. 37:5–11). For a time, the new arrivals drew off the Babylonians. But Jerusalem's respite was brief. Under their king's personal command, the Babylonians engaged and defeated the Egyptians and drove them out of Syria and Judah.[13] With that problem dealt with, Nebuchadnezzar returned to his assault upon Jerusalem.

The siege lasted, according to Old Testament sources, until the ninth day of the fourth month of Zedekiah's eleventh year (586), when the city's defences were finally breached (2 Kings 25:2–3; Jer. 39:2). By this time, Jerusalem had allegedly been reduced to starvation. So says 2 Kings 25, which further reports that though the Babylonian forces had surrounded the city, Zedekiah managed to escape with his entire army between the two rows of encircling walls. But the Babylonians pursued and caught up with them in the plains of Jericho. Zedekiah was separated from his army, now scattered in flight, and captured. He was taken to Riblah and brought before Nebuchadnezzar. Infuriated by his appointee's rebellion and sustained resistance when his city was placed under siege, the Babylonian pronounced a severe punishment. Zedekiah's sons were dragged before their father and executed.

xxj·roy· Et de ledification du temple iulques
a ceste chetuoilou or· cccc·z·lxx·ans et· vj·
mois et·x·iours· Et de lillue du pueple hors de
egypte iulqs a ceste chetuoilo or· cy·z·lxy·ans
et·vj·mois et·x·iours· Et si auoit eu/ el teple
me lj·xv·louuerais prestres lu aps lautre des
le primer qui ot a nom ladoth iulqs au derre
uer qui ot a no ceraues li prero iosedech· le ql
caraue nabugodonolor ocist· De lamour de

Figure 13. Zedekiah brought in chains before Nebuchadnezzar (from Petrus
Comestor's 'Bible Historiale' 1670, Pitts Theological Library, Emory University)

After witnessing their slaughter, Zedekiah had his eyes put out, and was bound in chains and taken to Babylon. In the following month, Nebuchadnezzar despatched the commander of his imperial guard to Jerusalem, with orders to destroy the city. Jerusalem's temple, palace, every other important building within it, and all its houses were put to the torch. All survivors of the siege and final destruction of Jerusalem were deported to Babylonia, along with the rest of the kingdom's population, 'leaving behind only the poorest people of the land to work the vineyards and fields' (2 Kings 25:12). Thus began the period of the Israelite 'exile', lasting almost fifty years.

Following Jerusalem's destruction, Nebuchadnezzar turned his attention to one last major centre of resistance in Syria. This was the island-city Tyre, which had persistently rejected Babylonian sovereignty. Nebuchadnezzar placed it under siege. For thirteen years the city held out,[14] and even then Nebuchadnezzar failed to take it by force. In the end, no doubt worn out by the length of the assault and despairing of a successful outcome, Tyre submitted of its own accord, and Babylonian officials were installed in the city. Sidon too came under Babylonian rule, as did the regions called Pirindu and Hume in the south-east of the Anatolian peninsula (Classical Cilicia). Nebuchadnezzar may also have conducted a campaign into Egypt, though we have only biblical authority for this (Jer. 43:8–13).

In the years following his death, the empire which Nebuchadnezzar had built remained relatively stable for some years to come, despite a series of power struggles for the royal succession. But in 539, when the last of the Neo-Babylonian kings Nabonidus occupied the throne, the empire fell, weak and divided, to a new power emerging in the east, the kingdom of Persia. The ruler of this kingdom was a man called Cyrus II. We know him better as Cyrus the Great. Syria was soon to get a new overlord.

538–330 BC

The First Persian (Achaemenid) Empire

From his homeland in the region of Persis, south-western Iran, Cyrus mounted a rebellion against his overlord Astyages, king of Media, defeated him in a hard-fought military campaign, and took over his kingdom. He became the founder of what is known as the Achaemenid dynasty, so called after Achaemenes, allegedly a family ancestor.[15] Cyrus and his successors

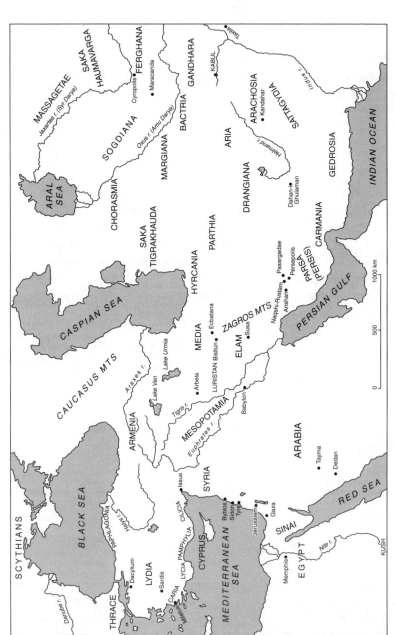

Map 6. The Persian Empire

held sway over the first of three great empires that arose in Iran during the period covered by our story. At its height in the reign of Darius I (522–486), the Achaemenid empire stretched from Thrace and the Aegean coast of Asia Minor in the west across Mesopotamia and Iran to the Indus river in the east, and southwards through Syria and Palestine across the top of the Peninsula of Sinai to the land of the Nile.

By 538, Cyrus had become master of Syria and Palestine. The imposition of his authority over the region was generally accomplished without bloodshed. No doubt this was due largely to the new overlord's policy of peace and tolerance throughout his empire, a policy to which for the most part he adhered. In this way he cultivated the goodwill of his future subject peoples, and ensured that his annexation of their territories was by and large without resistance. There were of course exceptions. One of these, apparently, was the city of Gaza on Palestine's southern coastal plain. It was taken by the Persians only after a siege, according to the Greek historian Polybius, who claims that the rest of the towns in the region had been terrified into submission.[16] But generally speaking, the Persian administration seems to have been accepted with little opposition in most of its subject lands.

The liberation of the Jews[17]

Certainly one group of people welcomed Persian in place of Babylonian overlordship. For it was at the time of his occupation of Babylonia that Cyrus issued a decree permitting the Jews to return to their homeland and rebuild their Temple in Jerusalem (Ezra 1:1–4, 6:2–5). Not surprisingly, Cyrus receives an extremely good press in the Bible, as the 'Anointed of God', the one chosen for the liberation of the Israelite people from their Babylonian bondage. These people were now free to go home. But we can be sure that not all of them greeted the prospect with unallayed delight. The Babylon of Nebuchadnezzar was the largest, most sophisticated city in the world. It was a great centre of learning and culture, a thriving metropolis of commerce, industry, and the arts. At the time of Cyrus' 'liberation', the exile had lasted almost fifty years. Those brought from Judah after the destruction of Jerusalem in 586 were now old men and women, or dead. For the great majority of the exiles, Babylon was their home, the only home they had ever known. How enthusiastically did they receive the news that they could now 'go home'—to a much more primitive, much more inhospitable environment, with the prospect of rebuilding from scratch a city that had lain in ruins for half a century? Would they really have been excited by this prospect? What they needed was an incentive so powerful, so inspiring that they would be prepared to give up their adoptive country to begin afresh in the land of their forefathers. The story of the *Exodus* may have provided just such an incentive. It was one which paralleled closely their own history—a people held in bondage in a foreign land, finally liberated and assured of a new beginning in the land of their great patriarch Abraham, where *they* would be the masters. No doubt some of the younger Jews in particular still needed a good deal of persuading to uproot themselves, and we know that a relatively large Jewish community remained in Babylon, and very likely prospered there under the new Persian administration.

How to manage an empire

In general, the policy of the Achaemenid kings was to rule the Syrian and Palestinian regions as lightly as possible. They were more concerned with conquest, military organization, and administration on a broad scale than with interfering in the local practices and traditions of their subject peoples. And it was particularly important for them to win the support of the populations in the Syria-Palestine region whose control was vital to their interests. For through this region major roads were built connecting the widespread parts of the Persian empire—across Mesopotamia and Syria to the Anatolian peninsula and south into the land of the Nile. It was along these roads that the Persians' famous postal and communication system operated. The road-system linked up with the cities along the Syrian and Palestinian coast. These cities were fortified and became an integral part of the Achaemenid empire's commercial network for its overseas mercantile ventures and for its military operations by sea. Phoenician vessels played an important role in these operations, notably in the Achaemenid empire's wars in the early 5th century against the Greeks. Aramaic was the most widely spoken language of Syria and other parts of the Near Eastern world at the time of the Persian conquests. It was adopted by the Persian administration as the lingua franca of the empire, a profoundly sensible policy which contributed much to the empire's cohesiveness. But local languages continued to be spoken in certain regions, like Phoenician in a number of the Levantine coastal cities.

From the time of Cyrus' foundation of the empire, the various components of it were organized into administrative regions called satrapies (from the ancient Persian word *khshathrapavan*—'protector of the realm'). Initially, Syria was joined with Babylonia as a single satrapy. But under the extensive new administrative arrangements made by Darius I for the empire, which consisted of up to twenty-three satrapies, Syria became a province on its own, the fifth satrapy, called *Ebirnari* in Babylonian, or *'Abr Nahra* in Aramaic, meaning '(the satrapy) beyond the river (Euphrates)'. Damascus was most likely its capital, the headquarters where the local governor or satrap resided. Strabo calls it 'the most famous of the cities in that part of the world in the time of the Persian empire'. It became the headquarters of the Persian forces in Syria, and also, according to Arrian, the place where the last Persian king, Darius III, stored his treasures before confronting Alexander in the battle of Issus. Josephus states that here Cyrus' son and successor Cambyses died on his way home from his Egyptian campaign.[18] For this campaign, Cambyses *may* have received support from Eshmunazar, the current king of Sidon.[19] This city too has been suggested as the capital of the satrapy. There was apparently a satrapal residence on the island of Arwad as well.

Though the satraps themselves were royal appointees, the cities and small states of Syria, like Byblos, Sidon, and Tyre, continued to function as semi-autonomous units, conducting their own administrative activities, performing their own religious practices, and pursuing their own commercial enterprises. Occasionally, they even set up their own colonies in various Mediterranean locations, sometimes with Persian support. Thus the city of Citium on the south-east coast of Cyprus was ruled by a line of Phoenician kings in the 5th and 4th centuries BC, following Darius I's crushing of the five-year Ionian revolt (499–494).[20] Up till then, Citium may have been ruled by a line of Greek kings, the last of whom participated in the anti-Persian uprising. With Persian support, Phoenician trade and commerce flourished. Undoubtedly, the Achaemenid kings found this greatly to their advantage, not least because they had at their disposal the Phoenician navy. More generally, overlordship of Syria brought much profit to Persia, through the development of the region's maritime trade and agricultural wealth, and through the access it gained to the region's rich timber-bearing tracts. The golden goose was bountiful. But its master was wise enough not to make excessive demands upon it. The annual tribute imposed upon the satrapal administration in Syria was a relatively modest one—350 talents of silver, according to the Greek historian Herodotus, compared with Egypt's 700.[21] Restraint in this and other ways ensured a reasonably high level of loyalty among the satrapy's inhabitants to their Achaemenid rulers.

336–323 BC

Alexander the Great

In 336 BC, Philip II, ruler of the northern Greek kingdom Macedonia, was assassinated. He was succeeded by his 20-year-old son Alexander. Within a short space of time, the new Macedonian king had reasserted his father's authority over mainland Greece, using both force and diplomacy, and obliterating the city of Thebes in the process. But that was just for starters. Alexander had his sights set on a much more formidable challenge: the conquest of the Persian empire. He was now ready to embark upon it. Leaving a large force in Macedonia to maintain his authority there, under the immediate control of the viceroy Antipater, he set sail for the coast of Asia Minor[22] with 50,000 troops (not a large number for the Persian enterprise, and perhaps even fewer). The Persian emperor Darius III, destined to be the last of the Achaemenid rulers, was his ultimate target. At the Granicus river in north-west Asia Minor, the first clash between Macedonian and Persian forces took place (334). It resulted in a resounding victory for Alexander, paving the way for his march of conquest, via Sardis, to and along the western and south-western coast of Asia Minor, and from there inland to Gordium in Phrygia. From Gordium, Alexander proceeded east to Ancyra (Ankara), which he subjected, and then headed south to Syria.[23]

The conquest of Syria

In the summer of 333, Alexander descended through a pass in the Taurus mountains into Cilicia, on the south-eastern coast of Asia Minor. There he became the hero of the people of Tarsus when he sent a cavalry contingent to rescue the city from destruction by the Persian satrap. But he had no time to bask in local gratitude. His first concern was to proceed with all possible haste down the Syrian coast to seize from Persia its Phoenician harbour cities. These cities provided the bulk of the Persian navy. While their ports remained under Achaemenid control, Persia still ruled the seas. And while it did, Alexander's land victories could have but limited long-term effect. Persia had to be eliminated as a sea power as well as a land one. For this reason, an invasion of Syria and the seizure of its coastal cities was an urgent priority for the Macedonian. But Darius, determined to stop him, led his army west to confront him before he could penetrate Syrian territory. In November

Map 7. Sites on Alexander's route as far as Babylon

Figure 14. Darius prepares to flee the battlefield of Issus ('Alexander mosaic')

333, the forces of the two kings met, this time on Syria's north-western frontier near the city of Issus, located just west of the Amanus range. In the narrow plain outside the city, the contest took place. Details of it are hazy, but one of the factors that seem to have won the day for Alexander was a devastating Macedonian cavalry charge against the Persian infantry's flank and centre. The Macedonian's victory was decisive. His vanquished opponent managed to survive the encounter, fleeing the battlefield with most of his army. But he was forced to abandon to the conqueror his family and a great deal of his treasure and war equipment.[24]

By this victory, Alexander had fulfilled one of his major objectives— the liberation of the Asia Minor Greeks from subjection to Persia. But so long as the Phoenician port cities, and thus the bulk of the navy, remained under Persian control, Darius could continue to harass Greek settlements in the Aegean area and along the Mediterranean coastlands. That was unacceptable to Alexander. But at this point, Darius made a number of attempts to negotiate a peaceful settlement with the Macedonian, with offers of various financial inducements and territorial concessions.[25] To no avail. Alexander had no intention of making peace on any terms. His first objective now was to impose his sovereignty upon the Syrian cities, hitherto subject to Persian rule, particularly the Phoenician ones along the coast. Darius abandoned his diplomatic initiatives and began rebuilding his military forces on a massive scale, while Alexander proceeded down the coast.

As it happened, most of the cities through which he passed apparently welcomed him, putting at his disposal their port facilities and their ships. He was thus able to re-establish communications by sea with his homeland and with other parts of the Greek world. But Tyre remained a stumbling-block. When he came within sight of the city in 332 and demanded its surrender, the Tyrians refused, feeling secure in their water-girt fortress, and stuck defiantly to their Persian allegiance. Undeterred, Alexander made preparations for a siege. To begin with, his intended victims were not greatly concerned. After all, they were on an island, and Nebuchadnezzar had failed to breach their defences even after a thirteen-year siege. But Alexander made much shorter work of it. As the Tyrians watched with increasing apprehension, he built a causeway across to them, drafting into service a work-force consisting of the entire population of the neighbouring cities. With the assistance also of naval resources supplied by other Phoenician cities and by Cyprus, he finally took Tyre by assault. The Greek historian Diodorus Siculus tells us that seven thousand of the city's inhabitants were slaughtered during the fighting, and that of the survivors, the women and children were sold into slavery, and the young men (no fewer than two thousand) crucified.[26]

In carrying out these atrocities, Alexander had the support of Tyre's bitter rival Sidon. Twenty years earlier, Sidon had rebelled, along with other Phoenician cities, against the Persian king Artaxerxes III, under the leadership of its ruler Tennes. But as Persian retaliation became imminent, Tennes lost his nerve and betrayed his city to Artaxerxes, to save his own skin. The city's position was now desperate. In a last-ditch attempt to save it, five hundred of Sidon's leading citizens approached Artaxerxes, as suppliants bearing olive branches. They were slaughtered without mercy. Tennes too was executed when Artaxerxes decided he had no further use for him. He then put the entire city, and all within it, to the torch.[27] Nevertheless, Sidon managed to rise from its ashes in time to support Alexander in his siege and conquest of Tyre. Though still not fully recovered from its sack by the Persians, the resurrected city welcomed the opportunity to gain ascendancy over its rival, by sharing in the Macedonian conquest of it.

There were better times ahead for both cities. Following the Macedonian's departure, each was to enter a new era of growth and development, prospering under Seleucid rule, and in the Roman imperial period ranking among the most important commercial centres along the eastern Mediterranean coast.

To Egypt and back

That was in the future. For now, Alexander set his sights on the conquest of Egypt. On his way, he encountered another stumbling block—the city of Gaza. Stubbornly refusing to submit to the invader, Gaza held out against him for two months before it finally fell. Alexander was angered by its defiance, and as part of his revenge inflicted a brutal punishment on its Persian governor. This was a fat eunuch called Batis, who had refused to acknowledge his conqueror, even after his city's fall. Alexander's response to this extraordinary display of courage—or stupidity—was to hitch the unfortunate man's feet to a chariot and drag him alive around Gaza's walls, in a grotesque re-enactment of Achilles' treatment of Hector's body.[28] That done, the Macedonian moved on to Egypt.

His Egyptian campaign, and his alleged mystical experience during a pilgrimage to the oasis of Siwah in the Libyan desert (332/1), where he was hailed by the priests as the son of the god Zeus-Ammon, is a topic for another occasion.[29] Let us just say that this episode has been seen as a pivotal point in Alexander's career (albeit one of his own contrivance). For henceforth he openly proclaimed his status as a living god, whose destiny—as 'confirmed' by the oracle at Siwah—was to conquer the whole world; the disparate peoples of this world, Europeans and Asians alike, would be united into a single empire beneath his rule. A self-obsessed megalomaniac Alexander may have been, but his aspirations were also, we can be fairly sure, underpinned by calculated political and strategic reasoning. And they did in fact have a number of tangible and lasting outcomes. One of the most notable of these was their author's founding of Alexandria in the Delta. This was only one of many Alexandrias established by the Macedonian and his successors. But it was by far the most important of them. It was later to become the second city of the Roman empire—and shall be making a number of appearances in our tale.

The spring of 331 saw Alexander back in Tyre. He paused there for a time before proceeding to the Euphrates, where he joined his main army in preparation for a final showdown with Darius. His role in Syria's story is now at an end. Marching his troops into northern Mesopotamia, Alexander encountered Darius and his army at a small town called Gaugamela, between the Tigris and the Great Zab rivers. The Macedonian's decisive victory in the contest, in the summer of 331, effectively ended the reign of Darius (he was assassinated by one of his officers the following year), and with it the Persian empire. But Alexander had yet more lands to conquer.[30] With

Darius disposed of, he now marched eastwards through Iran, where he looted and burned the Persian royal capital Persepolis (in 330), and then through Afghanistan into north-western India (327) before his troops mutinied and compelled him to turn back. In 323, he arrived in Babylon. Here he succumbed to a fever, and died at the age of thirty-two.

Few would dispute that Alexander was one of the greatest warrior-kings in the history of the ancient world—at least in terms of his military achievements—and thus one of the most ruthless butchers of all time. But was this all his blood-soaked progress through the Achaemenid realm amounted to? Scholars now generally take a cynical view of his enterprises: 'The only constant in Alexander's world', Richard Miles comments, 'was himself. He had created a world in which he was the centre of everything, a system that depended on his supposedly godlike genius. Without him the whole thing would fall apart. And that is what almost happened after a further seven years of increasingly aimless conquest for conquest's sake that had taken him into Afghanistan and then on to what is now Pakistan.'[31] Undoubtedly there is much truth in this. But irrespective of whether Alexander's conquests were impelled primarily by his own monstrous egocentricity, they paved the way, intentionally or not, for the great city-building projects and the great commercial and cultural achievements of the following centuries, even if at the outset the whole thing almost fell apart. Greek became widely adopted as a common language in the regions he had conquered, and a uniform coinage was introduced and spread throughout them. Scientific expeditions were despatched to all parts of the known world, and scientific institutions were set up in a number of its major cities, leading to significant advances in many fields of knowledge, from medicine to astronomy. Trade and commerce flourished on a scale unprecedented in the Near East—with a number of Syrian cities becoming focal points of an extensive international trading network.

Much of this came to pass in the era following Alexander's death—the so-called Hellenistic age—despite its unpromising beginnings, for the Macedonian's fragile empire started to break apart soon after his death as his successors fell to dividing up and squabbling over its spoils. Supremacy in the new world order was the prize many of them would so eagerly seek, so often perishing in the pursuit of it.

PART III

Syria Under Seleucid Rule

9

The Rise of the Seleucid Empire[1]

323–281 BC

The contenders for the succession[2]

Alexander's unexpected death in Babylon in 323 might well have precipitated the disintegration of his far-flung realm, built so rapidly within a few years of his first setting foot on Asian soil. The Macedonian royal dynasty was on the verge of extinction, with no one in the direct line of succession but an illegitimate half-witted half-brother, and Alexander's as yet unborn son by the Bactrian princess Roxanne. The dead king's only feasible successor was one of his generals—the so-called Diadochoi, or 'heirs'—who were themselves likely to tear the fledgling empire apart in their rival bids to gain control of it. But leadership tensions were defused, for the time being, when a meeting held in Babylon by most of Alexander's top brass reached an agreement on how the empire would henceforth be ruled.[3] Antipater, Alexander's chief representative in Europe, and Craterus, his highest-ranking military officer, were given joint command of Macedon and the rest of mainland Greece. Perdiccas, another of Alexander's high-ranking officers, was appointed Chiliarch; this title literally meant 'Commander of a Thousand', but in effect it made its holder the regent of the whole empire, and also custodian of Alexander's unborn son Alexander IV and his half-brother Philip Arrhidaeus. Other generals of the dead king were allocated rule over the regions organized as satrapies under the previous Persian administration: thus in the western half of Alexander's domains, Egypt went to Ptolemy, Antigonus got Greater Phrygia (along with Lycia and Pamphylia), Leonnatus was awarded Hellespontine Phrygia,[4] Cappadocia and Paphlagonia

Map 8. Initial western allocations to Alexander's heirs

were assigned to Eumenes, Lydia to Menander,[5] Thrace to Lysimachus, and Syria to Laomedon.

To begin with, these new arrangements looked like working—or at least averted an immediate crisis. But Perdiccas was anxious about his long-term prospects. He saw that his new position was but a temporary and insecure one, and so he sought to bolster and entrench it by plots and intrigues, which brought down upon him the wrath of the European commanders Antipater and Craterus, as well as Antigonus in Asia Minor. All declared war on him, and he further built up hostility to himself by invading Egypt, suspecting (quite rightly as it turned out) that its new ruler Ptolemy was planning to establish an entirely independent kingdom in the land of the Nile. The whole matter was resolved when the troops he took to Egypt mutinied and assassinated him (321), with the blessing and probably the active support of his alienated fellow-heirs.

That brings us to Syria. It seems, at least on the face of things, that Alexander's remaining heirs were initially quite sincere in their professed desire to keep the empire together. It was with this intention that a second top-level meeting was held, in 320, at a town called Triparadeisos in northern Syria, probably on the Orontes river. The meeting was chaired by the venerable Antipater, very likely the least self-seeking and the most loyal of Alexander's successors. And here, in Triparadeisos, a new agreement was reached,[6] one that was to affect profoundly the future course of the history of both eastern and western worlds. Antipater was proclaimed the new regent of the empire and custodian over the two Macedonian princes, and confirmed as ruler of Macedon.[7] Ptolemy retained his post as ruler of Egypt and Antigonus was confirmed as ruler of Phrygia. But there was some reshuffling of other gubernatorial appointments, and an important addition was made to the league of satrapal appointees. One of Alexander's most steadfast comrades-in-arms was a Macedonian officer called Seleucus, son of Antiochus. He had been among Alexander's military commanders in campaigns ranging from Asia Minor through Persia, Bactria, Sogdiana, and India. This was to be of significance in his later career. More recently, he had supported those who had taken up arms against Perdiccas and participated in the latter's murder. In the Triparadeisos settlement, he was rewarded for his services with the satrapy of Babylonia—an appointment that was to play a key role in his future career and the careers of his dynastic successors.[8]

The conference thus appeared to bring new stability to the alliance of heirs, reaffirming as it did the unity of Alexander's empire. But that did not last long. In 319, shortly after his return to Europe, Antipater died. His passing brought to the fore Phrygia's formidable ruler Antigonus, nicknamed Monophthalmus, the 'One-Eyed' (the other one had been lost in battle). At his disposal was a 60,000-strong army, and a massive treasure chest, inherited from Alexander, of over 25,000 talents of gold and silver, supplemented by income from his subordinate satraps amounting to 10,000 talents a year. With these resources, the One-Eyed easily outmatched any of his 'colleagues' in wealth and military muscle. And initially it looked as though he would use his resources on his allies' behalf. This he demonstrated by the military operations which took him into Central Asia, in pursuit of Eumenes, who had fallen foul of his fellow-heirs and gone to the east, joining up there with the satraps of the eastern provinces. Antigonus eventually caught up with him and fought two battles against him in western Iran, at Paraetacene in 317 and Gabiene the following year. Both engagements ended inconclusively. None the less, Eumenes was given up to his opponent by a regiment of his own men, and executed.

With his supremacy secured over a large swathe of Central Asian territory, as far east as the Hindu Kush, Antigonus decided it was time to return to the west. On his way, he visited Babylon, where Seleucus had his headquarters. Seleucus welcomed him into the city with great pomp and lavish hospitality. But relations between the two soured when Antigonus suddenly demanded an audit of his host's accounts.[9] Seleucus refused. His guest had no authority, he protested, to make such a demand. The dispute continued for some days, becoming increasingly bitter. But Seleucus well knew that in the end he would get the worse of it, and that by defying the One-Eyed he was putting himself in considerable danger. Cyclops had already given ample demonstration of his ruthlessness in disposing of anyone who opposed him. Better not to risk a further demonstration. Instead, Seleucus secretly took to his heels, and sought refuge with his old comrade-in-arms Ptolemy in Egypt.

Appian tells us that Antigonus now asserted his personal control over the whole of Mesopotamia and all the peoples from the Medians to the Hellespont. All were regarded as members of his personal fiefdom. Inevitably this blatant display of autocracy, barely disguised beneath One-Eyed's claim that he sought merely to reunify Alexander's empire, provoked confrontation with the other heirs. An anti-Antigonus alliance was formed. Prominent among its leaders were Cassander of Macedon, Lysimachus of Thrace, and Ptolemy of Egypt. The last of these was ably supported by Seleucus, to whom Ptolemy had given command of an Egyptian fleet, for operations in the Aegean and on the island of Cyprus. Antigonus decided to meet the alliance's forces first of all in the north, by invading Thrace. But he opened up a second front by sending his son Demetrius at the head of a large army to Syria and Palestine, then under Ptolemy's control. Demetrius' remit was to conquer Ptolemy's forces there and to seize the region for his father. The mission ended in failure. One-Eyed's son was decisively defeated by Ptolemy at a battle near Gaza in Palestine in 312.[10]

Seleucus had made a significant contribution to the victory, and as a reward for his services sought Ptolemy's assistance in regaining his Babylonian satrapy. His host obliged by giving him a force of a thousand men. At the head of these, Seleucus set off for Mesopotamia. Small though his numbers were, he felt confident of success in his bid to regain his former seat.

The satrap appointed by Antigonus in his place had made himself unpopular by treating his subjects harshly, and had in any case been killed while fighting for Demetrius at Gaza. So it was with high hopes that Seleucus led his thousand across the Euphrates into Mesopotamia. He marched to Babylon via Carrhae, where Macedonian veterans from Alexander's campaigns who had been settled in the region were persuaded, or compelled, to join his ranks.[11] And so, like Cyrus many years earlier, Seleucus proceeded to Babylon and entered it in triumph, warmly welcomed by the local populace (312–311). But he had no time to rest on his laurels, for his hold upon the region was immediately threatened by the satraps in Media and Susiana in western Iran. These too were appointees of Antigonus. Prompt and decisive action by Seleucus was essential to eliminate the threat. And eliminate it he did when he led his forces across the Tigris for a series of military operations which brought Media and Susiana along with other Iranian lands firmly under his control. He was now master of both Mesopotamia and Iran (or at least a large part of these), an achievement which he believed warranted a status equal to that of the other heirs of Alexander, including his comrade-in-arms and former protector Ptolemy. All this he pointed out in a letter he wrote to his new peers.[12]

Seleucus in the ascendant

While Seleucus was occupied with his Iranian operations, Antigonus' son Demetrius made an unsuccessful attempt to win back Babylon for his father, who had by this time re-established himself in Syria and Palestine and was preparing to invade Egypt. He did manage to reach the city and loot it during its current ruler's absence. But that was as far as he got before the time limit his father imposed for completing the assignment ran out. Mission unaccomplished, he was obliged to go back to Syria.[13] On Seleucus' return to Babylon, the popular mood turned against the last remnants of the Antigonus-loyalists still ensconced in the city. To save their skins, they sought refuge in the citadel. But they were quickly flushed out when Seleucus stormed the place, and in the process freed all his friends and slaves imprisoned there by Antigonus when he (Seleucus) had fled to Egypt.[14] Yet Antigonus was far from done with Seleucus and the east. His son's unfinished operation served merely as a prelude to further conflicts between himself and Seleucus for control of Babylonia. Seleucus could not call upon Ptolemy's support in these contests, for Ptolemy and his allies Lysimachus and

Cassander had concluded a peace with Antigonus in 311, which acknowledged the latter as supreme ruler in Asia. That left Seleucus on his own to
sort out with One-Eyed the matter of sovereignty over the lands east of the
Euphrates. Several years of warfare followed, in the course of which Antigonus plundered Babylonia relentlessly in his quest for ultimate victory. Ironically, the ruined and impoverished state in which he left much of the
country[15] helped paved the way for his ultimate defeat. For by assuming
the role of an enemy invader who destroyed all that stood in his way, he
ensured that the Babylonians swung their support firmly behind Seleucus.
With their unequivocal backing, Seleucus finally emerged victorious, in
308, after three years of intense and bitter conflict. Antigonus went back to
the west, where he still wielded enormous power and influence. The final
reckoning was yet to come.

But that was in the future. Now, with Babylonia and western Iran firmly
within his grasp, Seleucus set about consolidating and expanding his control in the east with campaigns of conquest in what were called the 'Upper
Satrapies'. These included Media, and beyond it Sogdiana, located in the
regions of modern Uzbekistan and Kazakhstan, and Bactria in eastern
Afghanistan. There were still more worlds to conquer. Seleucus now mustered his troops for a campaign across the Indus river into the lands of
India and Pakistan. This brought him into conflict with his most formidable adversary yet—Chandragupta (in Greek Sandracottus), head of the
royal Indian dynasty called Mauryas, and thus sovereign over a great empire
whose lands covered almost the entire Indo-Pakistan sub-continent. We
have no details of the military confrontation that took place between the
two kings, but Chandragupta, with his massive army, which included a
large contingent of elephants, clearly got the better of it. Seleucus was left
in no doubt that it would be wise to come to terms with this man. And
indeed Chandragupta was willing to make peace. A treaty of alliance
between the two was drawn up, much to Chandragupta's advantage, it
seems. By its terms, Seleucus was obliged to cede to his treaty-partner a
great chunk of his eastern territories, mostly in the region of Afghanistan.
But thereby he ensured the security, at least against a Mauryan-led invasion, of his remaining territories west of the Indus. In accordance with the
terms of the treaty, Chandragupta handed over to Seleucus an enormous
herd of war elephants (allegedly 500 of them!), and the bond between the
pair was consolidated by a marriage-alliance (its nature is undisclosed in
our sources).[16]

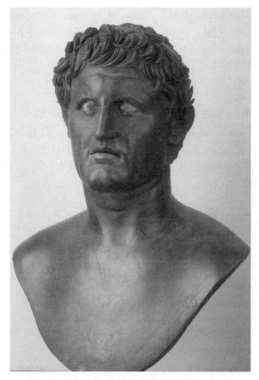

Figure 15. Seleucus I 'the Conqueror'

So ended Seleucus' eastern campaign, a military operation that had extended its leader's sway from the western fringes of Mesopotamia eastwards through Iran and deep into the lands of Central Asia. In the process, Seleucus laid the foundations of one of the greatest empires the Near Eastern world had ever seen, or indeed was to see. Beginning with the end of the eastern campaign in 305, this empire was to last for almost a quarter of a millennium, up until its disappearance, after a long decline, in the first decades of the 1st century BC. At its greatest extent, the Seleucid realm stretched through almost all the lands that had first belonged to the Persian empire and had then been conquered by Alexander the Great. Not without justification Seleucus was accorded the epithet Nicator, 'Conqueror'.[17]

One of the Conqueror's first projects, after declaring himself ruler of his newly created empire, was to establish for himself a new royal capital,

Seleuceia, on the Tigris river.[18] It was to be one of nine cities so named. Occupying an excellent strategic position on a route which linked Iran with Syria and Anatolia via Mesopotamia, Seleuceia rapidly became one of the great commercial centres of the Near Eastern world. It also became a major centre for the spread of Greek civilization eastwards. For it was planned primarily as a Greek city, with an admixture of Jews, Syrians, and other population groups in its citizen body. The city continued to develop and prosper through the Hellenistic and Roman periods. According to Pliny the Elder, its population had reached 600,000 by the end of the 1st century AD,[19] making it one of the largest metropolises of the Roman imperial world.

While it was still in its infancy, its founder had his empire substantially enlarged, thanks mainly to the elimination of his arch-enemy Antigonus. The peace which Antigonus had made with his fellow-heirs in 311 was always a fragile one. It was clear that One-Eyed would never be content with anything less than complete control over the whole of the world won by Alexander. An ultimate and decisive showdown with those who were supposed to be his partners in power loomed ever closer. It came finally in 301, when Seleucus joined forces with Lysimachus, Cassander, and Ptolemy for a fight-to-the-death with Antigonus near the small town of Ipsus in the heartland of Antigonus' kingdom, Phrygia. With a combined infantry force of 65,000 troops, not much short of Antigonus' 75,000, and with superior numbers of cavalry and infantry, the allies won the day. Antigonus was killed in the conflict. His son Demetrius survived and fled the battlefield, with the small surviving remnant of his father's army. He would go on to fight other battles, in other places.[20]

In the wake of their victory, the allied leaders divided among themselves the territorial spoils of conquest. Seleucus did extremely well out of it. In addition to Babylonia and the lands to the east in Iran and Central Asia, he was awarded the economically and strategically rich prizes of Coele Syria[21] and Phoenicia. Though he subsequently ceded these to Ptolemy (who was already occupying them, as he had on several earlier occasions), he gained northern Syria for himself and was later to win possession of large areas of eastern and central Anatolia, including the regions of Armenia, southern Cappadocia, and Commagene. Immediately after the battle of Ipsus, he marched to his newly acquired territories in Syria to claim them and establish his authority there. It is within this context that he founded, in 300, another Seleuceia, this one at the mouth of the Orontes, where there was an excellent harbour, and called it Seleuceia in Pieria.

But this Seleuceia was to be eclipsed by another new city built by Seleucus—on the Orontes thirty kilometres upstream from its mouth and a day's journey away. Work on the city commenced in April 300, one month after the founding of Seleuceia. Seleucus called it Antioch, after his father Antiochus. Reflecting the king's instinct for sites with great potential, Antioch was located in an agriculturally rich area, and thus provided an excellent complement to Seleuceia on the coast, which served as its port.[22] It was also well placed strategically, at the junction of several major routes which linked Anatolia with Syria and the Levantine coast, and to the east with the lands beyond the Euphrates. Seleucus may have had a further motive in choosing Antioch's site. Just eight kilometres to the north of it lay another new city, Antigoneia, built in 307 by his arch-enemy Antigonus, and populated by Antigonus with 5,300 Greek and Macedonian settlers. It was thus the first Greek settlement in Syria. But because it was Antigonus' creation, Seleucus considered its ongoing existence intolerable. And one of his first acts on reaching Syria was to evacuate its population and obliterate all trace of it. Shortly afterwards, work began on Antioch, and Antigoneia's population was resettled there.[23] Henceforth, the development of Antioch proceeded apace, with its original population of Greeks and Macedonians and other Greeks transplanted from Antigoneia being expanded by influxes of Jewish settlers, Aramaeans, and native Syrian population groups.

In its early years, however, Antioch was a mere subsidiary to Seleuceia in Pieria, which served in effect as the Seleucid kingdom's first western capital. But there was a serious problem with the port city's status as a royal seat. Its coastal location and its excellent harbour made it a highly attractive target for what became, for much of its history, the Seleucid empire's greatest rival—the Egyptian-based kingdom of the Ptolemies. Indeed on several occasions, Seleuceia fell to Ptolemaic control. Its vulnerability to enemy occupation was almost certainly one of the reasons Seleucus' son and successor Antiochus I decided to shift his residence to Antioch.[24] But knowing that Seleuceia was dear to his father's heart, Antiochus buried him in the city, perhaps in fulfilment of the dead man's wishes. He built a temple on the site of his father's tomb, and established there a cult in his honour.

But that was after Seleucus' body was shipped home. And we have not yet reached that point in our narrative. We have more to say about Seleucus first.

Seleucus I's later years

A particular highlight of the king's later years was the intensive building programme in which he engaged throughout his subject territories. Many new cities arose during the early period of the Seleucid dynasty, thirty-four of which bore the name of its founder or members of his immediate family: there were allegedly sixteen Antiochs (named after the king's father), five Laodiceias (named after his mother), nine Seleuceias, three Apameias, and one Stratoniceia (the last four cities named after the king's two wives), and many other cities with Greek names.[25] Though quite a few of these were actually built by his successors, Seleucus himself clearly deserves the credit for establishing throughout his empire a programme of constructing new settlements which, thanks to his more enterprising successors, ensured the growth and development of the empire for many generations to come. And the empire's founder can certainly be credited with a number of its new cities, most notably in Syria the group known as the tetrapolis: Seleuceia in Pieria at the mouth of the Orontes, Antioch 30 km upstream from it, Apameia on the Orontes' middle course, and Laodiceia which lay on the coast.[26] These cities above all ensured the continuing prosperity of Syria as one of the great hubs of the international trade network.

Yet Seleucus' plans encompassed much more than a building programme. The construction of the new cities was merely one aspect of a policy which the king now began implementing on a grand scale: the colonization of his new world with Greeks, who settled both in the recently-founded and the long-established cities of the empire, and helped ensure the spread of the Greek language and Greek culture to all parts of the Seleucid realm. But there was another important dimension to Seleucus' policy. Its inclusiveness. Traditional customs and beliefs were to be preserved and respected in the cities and regions where they were practised; indigenous peoples were to be granted citizenship alongside Greeks in both the new and the old foundations; and non-Greek communities were to be recipients of benefactions and patronage from their Seleucid rulers, their religious rites, beliefs, and sanctuaries protected and honoured. Many years earlier, Seleucus may already have dreamed of the empire over which he would one day hold sway, an empire made up of peoples of different cultures and races united beneath his rule. His marriage in 324, in Susa, to a Bactrian woman of noble birth called Apame may well have helped create such a dream. He would one day found several cities called Apameia, in honour of his wife and to symbolize what he hoped would be the peaceful coexistence of the cultures and races who inhabited the lands over which he ruled. The marriage had been instigated by Alexander; it was but one of a number of such unions, with eastern women of noble birth, that Alexander bestowed (or imposed) upon his high-ranking officers, in emulation of his own marriage to the Bactrian princess Roxanne (327) and his marriages now (324) in Susa to two Persian princesses.[27] To be sure, military and political pragmatism may well have determined many of Seleucus' actions. But this in itself is not incompatible with the notion that at least some of these actions reflected, or paved the way for, policies that were genuinely motivated by a broadly based political and cultural ideology.

Seleucus had won himself a vast empire in the east. But his territorial ambitions were not yet satisfied, and from Syria he launched a campaign to the north-west, into Asia Minor. This brought him into conflict with his former ally Lysimachus. The showdown took place in 281 at Corupedium, a plain in Lydia, north of Magnesia on the Hermus river. Lysimachus was defeated and killed.[28] Seleucus was now the supreme ruler of virtually the entire Near Eastern world. But he wanted more, it seems. For instead of consolidating what he had won, he went further west, to his homeland Macedonia. If we can so judge from a fragmentary Babylonian chronicle, his intention was to conquer Macedonia, 'his land', and thus add it to his already huge empire.[29] Was, then, his ultimate objective to re-create Alexander's empire in its entirety? Seleucus may simply have wanted to see his homeland again, although his military expedition into it suggests rather more than this.

But he never left Macedonia alive. While there, he was approached in an unguarded moment and stabbed to death by one Ptolemy Ceraunus—'The Thunderbolt'—son of his benefactor and ally Ptolemy I Soter, ruler of Egypt.[30] Excluded from the succession in Egypt, Thunderbolt sought a kingdom for himself elsewhere, and decided that his ancestral homeland Macedonia would suit quite well. With Seleucus out of the way, he was free to occupy the Macedonian throne. And so he did, becoming sovereign lord of Macedonia and Thrace. But not for long. Within a year of his accession, he was dead, the victim of an invasion by Galatian forces from the north.

281–261 BC

The Succession of the Saviour (Antiochus I)

What now of the Seleucid empire? With the sudden death of its overlord in a remote land that lay beyond the westernmost fringes of his conquered territories, the great imperial domain might well have fallen apart there and then. That it did not was due largely to good management rather than good luck. The succession itself proved quite straightforward, and Seleucus' throne passed without challenge to his son Antiochus I (so named after his grandfather). The Conqueror himself had made sure of this. Heeding well the lessons to be learnt from the succession disputes that followed Alexander's death, he had planned carefully for what would happen after his own. The main thing was to ensure that his successor was up and running at the earliest possible opportunity. Already in 292, twelve years before his assassination, Seleucus had appointed his son first as crown prince, in Babylonia, and then as co-regent, in effect bestowing upon him rulership of all the eastern satrapies of the empire, with the royal capital Seleuceia on the Tigris as his base.

Antiochus exercised full authority as king in the territories assigned to him, and was provided with the military forces to back up his authority in expeditions into the eastern satrapies. That he was half-Iranian, son of Seleucus by the Bactrian princess Apame, may have made him more acceptable in the east, though his mother had probably died before her son's elevation. In any case, Seleucus had married again in the 290s, this time Stratonice, the daughter of Antigonus' son Demetrius. We met Demetrius earlier, on his abortive campaigns in Syria and Mesopotamia and on the battlefield at Ipsus, where his father had been defeated and killed. Demetrius had survived the conflict, and might still prove a force to be reckoned with, especially if he succeeded in resurrecting his father's ambitions. Better to play it safe, Seleucus reasoned, and make an ally of this man rather than have him as an enemy. And so he married his daughter. It was obviously a carefully thought-out political arrangement (on which the prospect of a looming conflict with Egypt may have had no small influence). So too was Seleucus' subsequent decision to pass Stratonice on to his son Antiochus. Demetrius' daughter once more became a bride—this time her stepson's. Seleucus thus ensured that his marriage alliance with Demetrius continued beyond his own reign into his son's, presumably with the object of securing Demetrius' support not only for his new son-in-law's succession, but also against any threat the new king faced from the land of the Nile.

But none of these arrangements succeeded in preventing outbreaks of serious unrest in a number of the Seleucid domains. Syria seems to have been a major centre of this unrest (though far from the only one). Reports of Seleucus' death may have prompted the recently established cities in the region to rise in revolt.[31] Why they did so remains unclear. Most likely, Egypt's new ruler Ptolemy II Philadelphus was involved. After succeeding to his father's throne in 282 (following a three-year co-regency), Philadelphus moved quickly to re-establish Ptolemaic rule in Syria, and appears to have paved the way for this by persuading factions in the Syrian cities to rebel against their new Seleucid overlord. The new Ptolemy's ambitions actually went far beyond Syria, as he sought to expand his empire's territories by conquests in the eastern Mediterranean and the Aegean lands, including the coastal cities of Asia Minor formerly under Lysimachus' control. But it was his intervention in Syria that brought him into direct conflict with Antiochus. This conflict (to which we shall return) became known as the First Syrian War. It was but the prelude to a series of 'Syrian wars', to be fought over many years by the chief representatives of the Seleucid and Ptolemaic dynasties.

War with Egypt was not the only military issue confronting Antiochus when he became sole ruler. One of his most pressing post-accession tasks was to reassert Seleucid control over the territories in Asia Minor won from Lysimachus by his father in the battle of Corupedium. A number of Lysimachus' subject states and cities had no wish merely to exchange one overlord for another, and saw their ruler's defeat and death as an opportunity to regain their independence. There was the question, too, of what to do about those Asia Minor states that had never been subject to Lysimachus—and were firmly resolved to maintain their independence against Seleucid rule.

Notable in this category were the kingdoms of Bithynia and Pontus. They couldn't simply be left to their own resources. Bithynia's king Nicomedes made that quite clear when he sought to exploit anti-Seleucid spirit in the region by organizing a powerful coalition of Asia Minor states to resist Antiochus—at the same time that Ptolemy II was making serious inroads into the territories claimed by Antiochus along the coast. What made the Nicomedes-led coalition seemingly more dangerous was the inclusion in it of large groups of Celtic warriors from the north. These were Galatians. They had done a deal with Nicomedes: in return for their military support, the Bithynian had given them permission to settle in Asia Minor. In fact that proved to be a very bad blunder. But it worked to Antiochus' advantage. The Celtic hordes had run amok when they entered the Anatolian peninsula; groups of them attacked and plundered cities wherever they went, or else extorted huge payments from them—as the price for *not* attacking and plundering them. And that enabled Antiochus to take on the role of champion of the terrorized cities. He amassed a large army to confront the marauders, and won the day with what proved to be his decisive weapon—a herd of enormous, armoured elephants. Never before had the Celtic warriors encountered such monsters, and they broke up in terror as the beasts charged them. In what became known as the Battle of the Elephants (275), Antiochus' victory was complete.[32] The Celts were forced to retreat to a region within the Halys river basin, the former Hittite homeland, where they remained quiescent, relatively speaking, for some time to come.

Antiochus' success won him grateful support from the Greek cities of Asia Minor—he was henceforth known as Soter, 'The Saviour'—and Seleucid power became firmly entrenched in the Anatolian peninsula. Pontus and Bithynia retained their independence, but elsewhere Antiochus consolidated his authority over large parts of the region. From this time on, a number of new Seleucid cities appeared, like Hierapolis in Phrygia and Stratoniceia in Caria. In the west, Sardis, once the capital of the Lydian empire and subsequently the headquarters of the Achaemenid empire in the west, now became a third capital of the Seleucid empire, partner to Antioch in Syria and Seleuceia on the Tigris in Babylonia. Antiochus was in fact in Sardis when news reached him that Ptolemy was preparing to restake his claim to the territories in Syria formerly occupied by his father. That led to the First Syrian War.[33] We do not know how long or how extensive this war was, but by the end of the 270s, terms of peace had been concluded: Coele Syria remained subject to Ptolemy, but the territories Antiochus had won in Asia Minor, along with those in the east over which his father had established his authority, were now confirmed as Seleucid possessions.

With the stability of the Seleucid world thus reasonably assured, Antiochus continued apace his father's building programme, particularly the foundation or refoundation of cities throughout the empire. To populate his cities with Greek inhabitants, he also continued the substantial colonizing programme initiated by his father. In this way, those parts of Syria that were subject to the first two Seleucid kings took on an increasingly Greek character under their rule, particularly with the settlement of some 50,000 or more soldier-colonists in their cities. But the Seleucid-driven hellenization of Syria was by no means all-pervasive. Like his father, Antiochus respected and protected the customs and beliefs of the non-Greek inhabitants of his cities. And many of these cities were allowed a reasonably high degree of independence, not only in the maintenance of their traditional ways and beliefs, but also in the conduct of their political affairs and commercial activities. Seleucid despotism was relatively benevolent, at least to begin with.

But the Ptolemies also had an active interest in, and control over, parts of Syria—Coele Syria and Phoenicia—and maintained this interest and control through the first half of the Hellenistic period. That proved unfortunate for the stability of the region as a whole. For despite the peace accord of the 270s, disputes over the division of Syria's territories provoked an ongoing series of Syrian wars between Seleucid and Ptolemaic rulers, without any conclusive outcome until the Ptolemies were finally expelled from the region in 198 BC by Antiochus III—'the Great'.

261–225 BC

The family squabbles begin[34]

After a long and distinguished reign, Antiochus I died in 261—where and in what circumstances remain unknown—and was succeeded by his son and co-regent Antiochus II. Intent on making a name for himself at the earliest possible opportunity, the new king took up the contest against his father's old antagonist Ptolemy II by trying to wrest southern Syria, Palestine, and Phoenicia from his grasp. This brought about the Second Syrian War (260–253). It ended in failure for Antiochus. He did have more success in holding on to his father's territories in Asia Minor, and in fact seized from Ptolemy a number of Greek cities along Asia Minor's western and southern coasts. But he was unable to stop the continuing development of Pergamum on the western coast as a powerful independent kingdom. Pergamum had initially been subject to Seleucus I, but its king Eumenes I had established its independence with a resounding military victory over Antiochus I near Sardis in 262. We shall be hearing more of Pergamum.

Around this time, a series of intra-dynastic squabbles broke out between rival branches of the Seleucid royal family over the matter of the succession.

These contests were to erupt from time to time throughout the rest of the dynasty's history, and eventually contributed to its demise. The trouble began when Ptolemy offered to Antiochus his daughter Berenice in marriage. It was, on the surface, an attractive proposition for both sides. The houses of the Seleucids and the Ptolemies would once more be united! All conflict between them over Syria and Asia Minor would be at an end! But there was a complication. Antiochus was already married to someone else. This was a woman called Laodice, his half-sister or cousin, and thus already a member of the Seleucid family. Without such an obstacle, a marriage union linking the houses of Seleucus and Ptolemy might be looked on favourably by other members of the Seleucid royal court. But to set aside one of their own for a marriage with the enemy was well-nigh unthinkable! Even if Laodice were childless. The further complication was that she had two sons and at least two daughters by her husband. Which immediately set up a potential conflict for the succession if the new marriage went ahead and produced children. What is more, Laodice was no shrinking violet. She was a strong-willed woman with a robust bunch of supporters ready to stand by her should she seek revenge and reinstatement. For the moment, however, she decided to bide her time, and took herself and her two sons off to Ephesus, where she also had a strong and sympathetic following. That left Antiochus free to marry Berenice.

The newly-weds installed themselves in Antioch, and Berenice duly produced a son and new heir (another Antiochus) for her husband. That's where the trouble really began. The question now was, who was Antiochus' rightful successor? Laodice's offspring or Berenice's? Antiochus thought about the matter and apparently opted for the former, when for reasons unknown to us he left Berenice in Antioch and went to live with Laodice in Ephesus. But not for long. He died shortly after rejoining her—poisoned by her, some suspect. This was in 246, the same year his father-in-law Ptolemy II died. It was perhaps Ptolemy's death that prompted Antiochus to discard Berenice and resume his marriage with Laodice. But despite outward appearances, Laodice may not have been so easily won over. Still smarting from her earlier rejection, she may well have used the reunion as a convenient opportunity to dispose of her inconstant spouse forever.

Wasting no time after his death, Laodice's supporters proclaimed his eldest son Seleucus II Callinicus ('Gloriously Victorious') the new emperor. Berenice, still in Antioch, realized that she and the infant Antiochus were now in grave danger. In a desperate attempt to regain the ascendancy,

Berenice's supporters declared *her* son the new emperor. A face-off between the two queens and their followers seemed inevitable. Berenice at least had the advantage of actually being in Syria at the time, in its chief city Antioch. But this was not enough to protect her against her rival's followers, and her situation became precarious. Her only hope lay in support from the new ruler of Egypt, her brother Ptolemy III Euergetes ('the Benefactor'), son of Ptolemy II. On receiving news of his sister's predicament, Benefactor hastily mustered an army and marched to the rescue. Berenice had fled to her palace in Daphne, near Antioch, in a last bid to hold out until her brother's arrival. But he came too late. Berenice had by this time been driven from her final stronghold, and she and baby Antiochus put to the sword.[35] The grief-stricken brother placed Antioch under siege. Syria was in a state of uproar. Laodice and the newly proclaimed Seleucid emperor were still in Asia Minor, and the empire was virtually leaderless. With no hope of relief, the besieged Antioch surrendered to Benefactor and threw itself on his mercy. To no avail. So enraged was the Ptolemy by his sister's murder that he let his troops loose upon the city.

This was an opening episode in the so-called Third Syrian War (246–241). Following his capture of Antioch, Benefactor stationed troops in a number of Syria's cities, re-established Ptolemaic control over coastal areas in Asia Minor, then marched into Mesopotamia and occupied Babylon. It might well have seemed that the end of the Seleucid era was at hand, and that Ptolemy Benefactor would be the new overlord of the Near Eastern world. But he was unable to sustain his conquests. Reports of an uprising in Egypt reached him while he was in Babylon, and he was forced to abandon his eastern campaign and return home, leaving a few garrisons in the city.

Among his Syrian conquests was the city Seleuceia in Pieria at the mouth of the Orontes. It fell to him in 246. Still of considerable importance because of its strategic location, the city was to remain under Ptolemaic control for the next quarter of a century. (It was finally regained for the Seleucids in 219, by Antiochus the Great.)

Otherwise, it looked as if the new Seleucid king Seleucus II—'Gloriously Victorious'—had been let off the hook. With Ptolemy back in Egypt and the rival claimant to his throne eliminated, along with his Egyptian mother, Seleucus had but to reclaim what he and his own mother believed was his rightful inheritance. But that was easier said than done—particularly because of all the uncertainty over the succession. It was essential for the new king to demonstrate—unambiguously—that he had established his authority over the empire he had inherited, not only by reasserting this authority in Mesopotamia, but also by evicting Ptolemy's remaining forces from Seleucid territory in Syria. For all this he required an army. He had yet to rally sufficient troops to build one, and needed money to hire mercenaries.

That's where his mother came in. Laodice was an extremely wealthy woman, thanks to various land-grants and other endowments bestowed upon her by her husband. And so Gloriously Victorious approached her, cap in hand. She agreed to give him what he asked for, but there were strings attached. He was to appoint his younger brother, Antiochus Hierax ('the Hawk'), as his co-regent and ruler of Asia Minor, where he would be a king in his own right. Hawk would rule from his capital Sardis, Gloriously Victorious from Antioch. That was the condition Laodice imposed upon her elder son before she opened her purse. Gloriously Victorious was desperate to secure funding for his military ventures, and so he agreed. But grudgingly. No love was lost between the two brothers, especially as their mother clearly favoured the younger. Yet it was in their mutual interests to cooperate, particularly when it came to resolving issues with the Ptolemy. Plans were made by the brothers for a joint campaign to Egypt against Ptolemy. They never actually met to discuss the operation, leaving it to their representatives to sort out the details. This in itself did not bode well for the enterprise. But it never took place, partly because Ptolemy, getting wind of it, decided it was better to go for a non-military resolution of his differences with the Seleucids and proposed a ten-year peace.[36] Which was accepted.

That left Hawk and Gloriously Victorious free to fight each other.[37] The conflict was apparently sparked off by their mother, who now proclaimed to one and all that Hawk, the younger son and favourite, was the true heir to the Seleucid throne. Gloriously Victorious was outraged by the news. In prompt response to it, he marched across the Taurus and headed straight for Sardis, determined to eliminate his brother, along with his mother, and re-establish himself as sole ruler of the empire. He did in fact defeat Hawk's forces in battle, but Sardis held out against him and his brother remained safe and unsubdued. In fact, events took a turn very much for the worse for Gloriously Victorious when the pair's brother-in-law, Mithridates II, king of Pontus, threw his support behind Hawk, and brought with him into the conflict the dreaded Galatians who were still infesting the countryside. The forces clashed near Ancyra (modern Ankara). Unlike his grandfather Antiochus I, Gloriously Victorious had no elephants to launch against the enemy, and Hawk's army reinforced with Galatians won a decisive victory over the 'real' Seleucid king. Gloriously Victorious was forced to flee for his life back to Syria. That gave the Galatians the opportunity to indulge in another orgy of looting and destruction in the countryside where the victory had been won. They demanded huge tributes as the price of their mercy—just as they had done in Antiochus I's days.

But they overreached themselves when they extended their tribute demands to the rapidly developing kingdom of Pergamum near the Aegean coast. The kingdom was then ruled by the dynamic Attalus I, after whom the Pergamene dynasty was named (a dynasty which held sway until its last king, Attalus III, bequeathed his kingdom to Rome on his death in 133 BC).[38] Attalus rejected the Galatians' demand and defeated them in battle. This brought him into conflict with Hawk, who had maintained his partnership with the brigand-warriors. Hostilities between Hawk and Attalus lasted three years (230–228). In the end, Attalus was victorious. Indeed, so resounding was his success against the Hawk that the vanquished Seleucid was driven from Asia Minor, and all Seleucid territory north of the Taurus fell under Pergamene authority—for the time being. That left Hawk without a kingdom, or for that matter a home, and he spent the next year attempting to take over his brother's realm. He tried to drum up support for himself in Syria and invaded Mesopotamia with what forces he could muster. But he failed in his bid to re-establish himself in the east, and spent the last brief period of his life (227–226) as an exile in search of a kingdom and a home. Finally he sought refuge in Thrace, which at that time was under Ptolemaic control. Here he was arrested and imprisoned. He managed to escape his guards, but the freedom he gained was abruptly terminated when he fell in with a band of Galatian raiders who slaughtered him.[39]

Gloriously Victorious was thus finally rid of his brother and bitter rival for domination of the Seleucid world. But he had other serious problems to contend with. Asia Minor north of the Taurus was lost to Seleucid control with the Pergamene victory over his brother. Equally serious was the situation in the north-eastern part of the Seleucid realm. From around 230 BC, a new power was developing in the east. Twenty years earlier, large nomadic groups from the grasslands of central Asia had settled in north-eastern Iran, to the south-east of the Caspian Sea. These were the Parthians, who under a royal dynasty founded by a man called Arsaces (regn. 247–217) rebelled against Seleucid rule and began carving out an empire of their own, from Seleucid territories. By the early 230s, in the region of modern Afghanistan, a rebel Greek leader called Diodotus was seeking to convert Bactria, the easternmost of the Seleucid possessions, into an independent kingdom. Gloriously Victorious thus had little choice but to spend most of his reign on the battlefield, in his efforts to stabilize his empire and defend it against its many enemies, including the reigning Ptolemy, the newly emerging Parthian kingdom in the east, and the territorially aggressive Pergamene king in the west. There was also the king's civil war with his brother (and for that matter his mother), which had almost certainly contributed to the loss of much of Asia Minor to Pergamum. All this, coupled with the breakaway of Bactria and uprisings in Babylon and other Mesopotamian centres, might well have put an end—yet again—to the Seleucid empire. But any fears, or hopes, for its imminent demise were premature. The empire was soon to enter its most illustrious phase.

Not quite yet, though. Gloriously Victorious left the world's stage in an inglorious finale. He died after falling off his horse.[40] And his mother Laodice? Though rumour had it that she was murdered on the orders of Ptolemy III, the actual circumstances of her death remain unknown. She simply slips quietly from our view.

10

The Seleucid Empire
in its Prime

(Late 3rd–mid 2nd centuries BC)

225–204 BC

The early years of Antiochus III

Seleucus II Callinicus, fourth ruler of the Seleucid empire, was succeeded by his son, who was enthroned in 225 as Seleucus III Soter ('Saviour'); he was nicknamed Ceraunus, 'Thunderbolt', because of his violent temper. Thunderbolt's brief reign was notable only for a campaign which he conducted into Asia Minor, where he sought to regain the Seleucid territories lost to the Pergamene king Attalus I. He failed to do so. After several inconclusive engagements with Attalus' forces, he probably abandoned the venture and started to head back home. But while still in Anatolia, he was assassinated by two of his comrades-in-arms, perhaps disgruntled by the campaign's failure. This happened in the third year of his reign (223). Thunderbolt had left no direct heirs, nor had he sorted out any of the empire's problems. But an immediate crisis was averted when his uncle Achaeus assumed command of the army, executed the assassins, and declared a resumption of the campaign against Attalus.[1] Delighted by the news, the Seleucid troops urged their new leader to proclaim himself emperor. Achaeus must have been sorely tempted, as later events were indeed to demonstrate. But he turned down the army's offer, declaring that the deceased's emperor's younger brother, another Antiochus, was the rightful heir to the throne. This new Antiochus was a mere stripling at the time. But he was not without experience. At the age of seventeen, he had been sent by Thunderbolt to Seleuceia on the Tigris, to take command of the eastern part of the Seleucid empire. And that is where he was on his brother's death.

Under no illusions about the empire's fragile state, Antiochus promptly made a number of appointments which he believed would help re-establish and maintain its stability.[2] He entrusted to Achaeus control of all Seleucid territories in Asia Minor, with Sardis in the west as his base. He assigned responsibility for the eastern provinces to two men on whose loyalty he believed he could count, Molon, satrap of Media, and Molon's brother Alexander, satrap of Persia. But by far the most powerful of his appointees was a man called Hermeias, a Carian from western Asia Minor. Based in Antioch, Hermeias had already been made civil head of the Seleucid admin-istration by Seleucus III before his departure on his Asia Minor campaign. This gave the man a taste for high authority, which he sought to establish on a more permanent basis by eliminating through plots and intrigues all those he saw as potential rivals. But his ambitions had to be put on hold when the young Antiochus returned to Antioch to confirm and consolidate his position as his brother's successor, ascending the Seleucid throne as Antiochus III—to much popular acclaim. Hermeias was not well pleased with the way things were turning out, and saw his power slipping from his grasp. None the less, he continued to hold authority as vizier or chief min-ister in the new regime, and initially exercised much influence over the young king. In a number of respects, he was the most formidable individual in the whole empire, and one of the most dangerous—a man whose enmity was to be feared.

According to Polybius, Hermeias persuaded Antiochus to reopen hostili-ties with the Ptolemaic regime, by invading Coele Syria, which had been ceded by the first Seleucus to Ptolemy I and was still in Ptolemaic hands. Polybius tells us that Hermeias had used a forged letter to induce Antiochus to take this action; the letter, which he claimed was written by the king's uncle Achaeus, reported that the new Ptolemy, the fourth of that name, called Philopator ('Father-Lover'), had urged Achaeus to seize for himself the Seleucid throne, promising him ships and money in support. Antiochus was taken in by this piece of duplicity. Believing the letter to be genuine, he prepared to invade Coele Syria, with the object of reasserting Seleucid rule over it, knowing that war with Ptolemy would inevitably follow. In this way, says Polybius, Hermeias sought to involve his king in wars on every front so that he could continue to exercise his present authority and secure for him-self immunity from punishment;[3] for he had been ruthless in the exercise of his authority, and had made many enemies who would not hesitate to seek revenge if he fell from the king's favour. The best thing he could do, he reasoned, was to keep the king fully occupied in foreign military ventures, leaving the conduct of the administration in his vizier's hands.

But Antiochus had another matter to attend to before taking on the Ptolemaic regime. He was at the time near a city called Seleuceia (yet another city so called), on a crossing of the Euphrates (it was a fortress settlement in Osrhoene near Samosata, modern Samsat),[4] and here he met a delegation from Mithridates II, king of Pontus. The delegation was entrusted with the task of delivering to Antiochus his promised bride, another Laodice, this one Mithridates' daughter. The princess was received by her bridegroom with all due ceremony, and the marriage took place on the spot with much pomp and splendour. Thence Antiochus escorted the bride to Antioch, where he proclaimed her queen of the Seleucid realm.[5] It may seem odd that Antiochus should meet and wed his princess in this small fortified settlement rather than arrange for the Pontic delegation to bring her to Syria's chief city for the wedding. For some reason, he considered it more prudent to have the ceremony conducted in what was apparently a remote and secure location before returning to Antioch and installing his new queen on the throne.

Rebels and traitors

That done, he returned to his preparations for a campaign in southern Syria. But as the campaign was getting under way, alarming news came from the east: Molon, the satrap of Media, had revolted against Seleucid rule (220), much as Parthia and Bactria had already done, and was carving out an empire for himself in the region. In this he had at least the moral support of his brother Alexander, satrap of Persia. Antiochus was ready to abandon his Syrian campaign and march against him to restore order and reassert his authority over the rebels. But Hermeias talked him out of it, arguing that it was the business of generals to fight rebels, whereas the king himself should fight against other kings.[6] What ulterior motives Hermeias may have had for seeking to persuade Antiochus not to abandon his campaign against the Ptolemy are unknown to us. At all events, he did prevail upon him, and arranged for the command of an expedition against Molon to be assigned to one Xenoetas, the Achaean.

Xenoetas' expedition ended disastrously. Molon inflicted a crushing defeat on him, advanced upon and captured the eastern Seleucid capital Seleuceia on the Tigris, and then seized the Upper Satrapies and established his control over the whole of Babylonia to the shoreline of the Persian Gulf.[7] He proclaimed himself king of all the conquered lands. The situation for the Seleucid regime was dire. With virtually the whole of his eastern empire lost to him, Antiochus abandoned his Syrian expedition and threw his full resources into a campaign of recovery in the east, which he led in person. It was the first major test of the king's military abilities. The opposing forces confronted each other for battle at a site called Apollonia, across the Tigris from Babylonian territory. Antiochus won decisively, his victory paving the way for the restoration of Seleucid sovereignty over all the eastern provinces seized by Molon. Knowing that he could expect no mercy from his conqueror, the vanquished enemy leader committed suicide; he thus spared himself the horrors of the torture that awaited him if taken alive. It was not enough to satisfy Antiochus. After plundering the enemy's camp, he ordered that Molon's body be crucified in the most conspicuous place in Media—as a warning to all others who dared defy his authority. The corpse was hung on a cross at the foot of the Zagros range. When he received news of his brother's defeat and death, Molon's brother and co-rebel Alexander also took his own life.[8]

Antiochus then set about the task of reasserting his control over the eastern provinces. Pragmatic considerations induced him to act with mildness. And so, after rebuking the rebel troops at length for their conduct, he told them they were pardoned. Similar clemency was shown by the king in his dealings with the rebels in the neighbouring satrapies. But Hermeias wanted to take a tougher line, particularly against Seleuceia on the Tigris for its failure to hold out against Molon. A harsh fine, the exile of its leading officials, and the torture of many of its citizens by mutilation, the sword, or the rack were the punishments he began meting out. He was fully engaged in these activities when, allegedly with much difficulty, the king either talked him round, or overrode him, substantially reducing the penalty imposed on the city to a relatively modest fine and sparing its populace any further reprisals. Again reasons of diplomacy or sheer pragmatism made this a much more prudent course of action.

Hermeias could not have been well pleased at his orders being countermanded in this way, even by his king. But he had to tread carefully now. The king had firmly established his leadership credentials with his subjects, proving himself a warrior-emperor in the best traditions of his illustrious predecessors. And in the euphoria of his success against the rebels, he now sought to overawe and intimidate the rulers of the lands that lay beyond his authority. This was to prevent their supplying any form of assistance, including armed forces, to any of his subjects who later rose up against him. A particular target was Artabazanes, king of the land called Atropatene (modern Azerbaijan), which bordered on Media. Antiochus considered Artabazanes the most important and most energetic of the rulers independent of his control, and thus made preparations to invade his land. To begin with, Hermeias tried to talk him out of the enterprise, which would take his troops deep into Iranian territory with all its attendant risks. He urged him instead to return to Syria, to resume there his operations against Ptolemy. But then he had a change of heart—prompted by a message that Laodice had borne her husband a son. This was not good news for Hermeias, for he feared that the new arrival would ultimately weaken his influence with Antiochus. On the other hand, if his sovereign did proceed with the Atropatene mission and he managed to contrive his death during it, blaming it on enemy action, his own position would be considerably strengthened, as regent for the infant prince and thus as master, for an indefinite period, of the Seleucid realm. And so Hermeias gave his support to the campaign. But things did not go according to plan—at least not according to Hermeias' plan. The Atropatene campaign ended successfully, with little or no bloodshed. Polybius tells us that as Antiochus launched his attack upon the kingdom, its ruler Artabazanes, now an old man, was terror-stricken and made peace with him.[9]

Not long after, Hermeias met his end—thanks to an initiative taken by one of the king's close friends, a physician called Apollophanes. Dr Apollophanes had become deeply concerned at the vizier's unchecked, arbitrary exercise of power, and rightly feared that he posed a serious threat to the king's life (as well as his own). So when he found a suitable opportunity for a secret audience with Antiochus, he laid bare all his concerns about the royal counsellor, reminding the king of the fate that had befallen his brother Seleucus. By speaking to Antiochus in this way, Apollophanes was taking a considerable risk, for he knew that Hermeias had, at least until recently, exercised great influence over the king. But he suspected that Antiochus now thought differently about the man—and was relieved to find he was right. Antiochus thanked him for what he said, and confessed that he too had come to dislike and suspect his vizier.

But how were they to rid themselves of him? He had undoubtedly fortified himself against such an eventuality, with a loyal body of supporters whose own vested interests would ensure that they defended him to the

end. A way had to be found to get Hermeias on his own, without his mind-
ers and without arousing his suspicions. A plan was eventually agreed. Hermeias was persuaded to accompany the king on one of his early morning
walks—this one much earlier than usual—and when the group that escorted
them reached an isolated spot well away from the royal camp, the king dis-
creetly withdrew, leaving his supporters to fall upon the unsuspecting Hermeias with their daggers. 'So perished Hermeias,' Polybius tells us, 'meeting
with a punishment by no means adequate to his crimes.'[10] Antiochus then
set out for home, and to a hero's welcome throughout his domains, due at
least as much to his elimination of Hermeias as to his accomplishments on
the battlefield. For Hermeias had been widely feared and detested by the
king's subjects. His family too became victims of their hatred. They were
residing in the city of Apameia at the time the news came of his assassination. Their end was swift and brutal. The vizier's wife was hauled out and
stoned to death by the women of the city, his sons by the city's boys.

Once back in Antioch, and after dismissing his troops for the winter,
Antiochus had another serious problem to deal with. It concerned Uncle
Achaeus and his activities in Asia Minor. We recall that Achaeus had initially
refused to accept the emperorship when his troops offered it to him after the
death of Seleucus III, and had endorsed Seleucus' brother Antiochus as the
rightful heir to the throne. But he subsequently changed his mind. Deciding
now that he did want to be emperor, he chose to make his play while his
nephew was far away in the east, preoccupied with both the Molon revolt
and subsequently his campaign against Artabazanes. Antiochus would be too
busy with these operations to counter any move made by his uncle from the
west, or better still, might be killed in the course of them. Or so Achaeus
hoped. It is possible that he really had been in communication with his
nephew's declared enemy Ptolemy IV (even if the letter allegedly written by
Achaeus about Ptolemy *was* a forgery), and had negotiated some arrangement with him should his venture succeed. At all events, he set out from his
capital Sardis at the head of a large army, with the secret object of invading
Syria and making himself master of the Seleucid empire.

When he reached Laodiceia in Phrygia, he put on the royal diadem, and
for the first time ventured to take the title of king (220). Then he led his
army southwards towards Lycaonia. And it seems that now, for the first time,
his troops realized what the true purpose of the campaign was—to go all
the way to Syria in order to depose Antiochus and make their commander,
the king's uncle, emperor in his place. But Achaeus had seriously misread his

troops' allegiance. They remained firmly loyal to Antiochus, 'their original and natural king', and Achaeus suddenly found himself with a mutiny on his hands. To save his skin, he protested that he had no intention of overthrowing their beloved king, but was bent merely on wreaking havoc on enemy territories in Asia Minor. Achaeus was nothing if not a persuasive orator. He managed to convince his troops that this was in fact his intention all along, sweetening his words by declaring that they would all now turn back and head home, plundering the neighbouring country of Pisidia on the way. The rich spoils of the land would be shared by everyone. Thus laden with goodwill for their leader, and plenty of booty, Achaeus' troops returned home—and Achaeus retained his post, for the time being.[11]

Antiochus had been kept fully informed of his uncle's activities, including his alleged dealings with Ptolemy. After returning to Antioch, he sent him messages detailing his offences and deploring them. A stronger response might well have been warranted. Antiochus must have realized that by failing to take more robust action against his renegade relative, he was simply putting off the inevitable, a final test of strength between the two of them on the field of battle. But for the moment, the king had his sights firmly set on another objective—the recovery of southern Syria and Palestine from Ptolemaic rule. The contest with Ptolemy IV came to a head in 217 at a site near the city called Raphia in southern Palestine.[12] Ptolemy put into the field a total of 70,000 infantry, 6,000 cavalry, and 73 war elephants. Antiochus' forces were fewer in number, 62,000 infantry and 5,000 horse, but he had 103 elephants. Most of these beasts survived the conflict, but made little difference to it, for battle-honours went decisively to Ptolemy. Antiochus was forced to accept defeat after losing 10,000 of his infantry and 300 of his cavalry, and returned with his surviving troops to Antioch, beaten and humiliated. He had no option but to acknowledge Ptolemy's hold over the contested territories, and sent envoys to him, including his nephew Antipater, to make terms of peace. Thus ended the Fourth Syrian War. Ptolemy was only too pleased to oblige, delighted at his unexpected success. In any case, he was rather too much inclined to peace because of his indolent and depraved way of life, according to Polybius.[13] Antiochus was of a different stamp. He had by no means abandoned his ambitions of wresting back the southern territories from Ptolemaic control, and would one day return to fulfil this ambition. That is what his forefathers would have wanted.

In the meantime, his readiness to make peace with Ptolemy was due partly to his unfinished business with Uncle Achaeus. He was very conscious of the risks of venturing on any further operations in the east, and these were clearly on his agenda, while Achaeus remained at large in the west and free to pursue his ambitions for sovereignty of the Seleucid world. The problem needed resolving once and for all. So in the summer of 216, Antiochus embarked on a campaign against Achaeus, marching from his Syrian base across the Taurus into Asia Minor. Details are scant, but we know that eventually Antiochus' forces prevailed, and by 214 had occupied Sardis, the western Seleucid capital and Achaeus' base. For a time, Achaeus held out with a small band of followers in the capital's citadel. But this last stronghold fell after a siege, and Achaeus was captured while attempting to escape (213). Bound hand and foot, he was brought before the emperor. Antiochus burst into tears when he saw the condition to which his uncle, ruler of all the Seleucid realm 'on this side of the Taurus', had been reduced.[14] But he was a traitor and a rebel and had to suffer a punishment to fit his crime. A council was convened to decide on the most appropriate form of this punishment. Many suggestions were made. The final decision was 'to lop off in the first place the unhappy prince's extremities, and then, after cutting off his head and sewing it up in an ass's skin, to crucify his body.'[15]

Antiochus 'the Great'

That left Antiochus free to turn his attention eastwards once more. The famous series of campaigns on which he now embarked, from 212 to 205/4 BC, are known as the king's *anabasis* or 'ascent'.[16] They began with Antiochus' assertion of his control over the lands of Commagene and Armenia in eastern Anatolia, after which he marched his troops across Mesopotamia and the Iranian plateau deep into central Asia. Seleucid authority was reimposed over all the countries through which he passed, including the rebel lands Parthia, Bactria, and Gandhara. The king had now reached the frontier-territories of India. Here, he reaffirmed the links which his great-grandfather Seleucus I had established with the Mauryan ruler Chandragupta, by renewing the old Seleucid alliance with the current Indian king Sophagasenus. This provided an appropriate finale to Antiochus' eastern enterprises. It was now time for him to return home. On the way, he decided to attack and plunder the wealthy Arab city of Gerrha on the Persian Gulf (in the northeast of modern Saudi Arabia). But before the attack began, the Gerrhaeans sent a delegation to him, begging him 'not to abolish the gifts of perpetual peace and freedom that the gods had bestowed upon them'.[17] Their plea proved persuasive, especially when they sweetened it with a substantial bribe: 500 talents of silver topped up with spices from the Persian Gulf, consisting of 1,000 talents of frankincense and 200 of stacte (oil of myrrh or cinnamon). Such a gift was worth a king's mercy. Antiochus left the city intact and set sail from the Gulf along the Tigris for his royal capital Seleuceia.

His *anabasis* restored to Seleucid control virtually all the territories won by Seleucus I, and in recognition of his achievement, he was called Megas, 'the Great'. 'He put his kingdom in a position of safety,' comments Polybius, 'overawing all subject to him by his courage and industry. It was this expedition, in fact, which made him appear worthy of his throne, not only to the inhabitants of Asia, but to those of Europe likewise.'[18] Modern scholars have rather mixed views on what Antiochus actually accomplished by his *anabasis*. One sees real substance in his achievement, with the firm re-imposition of Seleucid control over formerly held Seleucid territories, and perhaps new territories added, another sees it as something of a mirage, with the eastern lands quickly settling back down to doing their own thing after Antiochus and his army left.[19]

204–196 BC

In any case, Antiochus was not yet done. In 204, he conducted a campaign into Asia Minor where he won back, by diplomacy, perhaps, rather than by force, a number of territories from the control of the Pergamene king Attalus I, including the Ionian city of Teos, near the Aegean coast. Then in 202 he turned his attention to his unfinished business in Syria, where he sought to recover the territories lost by him to Ptolemy IV in the battle of Raphia. The time for restaking his claim to these lands was opportune. Word had reached him that the Ptolemy had recently been murdered, leaving his throne to his five-year-old son, Ptolemy V Epiphanes, and the management of his kingdom in the hands of a couple of unscrupulous rogues.[20] The situation was ripe for exploitation. During the next five years, between 202 and 198, in the so-called Fifth Syrian War, Antiochus established his control firmly over all the contested territories, strategically valuable and economically rich, in Coele Syria, Phoenicia, and coastal Palestine. His most significant victory came in the year 200, when he defeated Ptolemy V's forces in a battle near the city of Panion, gateway to southern Palestine, and thus gained

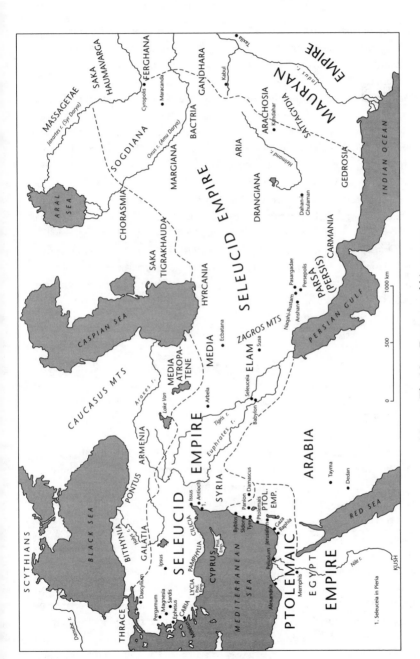

Map 9. The Near Eastern world in 200 BC

1. Seleucia in Pieria

control of the Palestinian coast down to Gaza, on Palestine's southern coastal plain. By 198, Antiochus' conquests in the region were complete.[21] He was still not done. The crushing defeats of Ptolemy's armies had so weakened Ptolemaic military power that he could move with ease to his next military objective, the capture of the last of Ptolemy's overseas possessions, in Asia Minor. Attacks by land and sea brought Ptolemaic-controlled cities in southern and south-western Asia Minor—in Pamphylia, Lycia, and Caria—under Seleucid sovereignty. Ephesus on the Aegean coast became the western Seleucid capital.

196–187 BC

In conflict with Rome [22]

These successes were perhaps all too easily achieved. For Antiochus was spurred by them to extend his conquests even further afield. In the spring of 196, he conducted a campaign into Thrace, a region in Europe over which the Seleucids had claimed sovereignty since the reign of Seleucus I. But they had never been able to enforce their claim. Antiochus was now doing so.

Inevitably, his operations on the European mainland added further heat to a simmering issue with Rome, which had but recently withdrawn its forces from Greece and declared that all Greek cities should be free. The Seleucid intrusion into Europe was seen as ultimately threatening that freedom. Indeed, Antiochus had already given credence to the threat by subjugating the Greek cities of Asia Minor, not only those formerly subject to Ptolemaic control, but the previously independent ones as well. The European Greek cities could well be next. But Antiochus had no wish, yet, for a confrontation with Rome. So he entered into negotiations with it via a number of diplomatic missions. Initially, the Romans demanded that he relinquish his claim to all Greek cities over which he had asserted his control, both in Europe and in Asia Minor, including the cities won from Ptolemy. They subsequently modified their demands: they would be content if the Seleucid simply kept out of Europe. Four years of negotiations, from 196 to 193, failed to produce an outcome satisfactory to Antiochus. And so he launched a campaign into mainland Greek territory—in effect, declaring war on Rome. In taking this step, he may have been emboldened by his establishment of peaceful relations with Egypt during the same year, consolidated by a marriage alliance between his daughter Cleopatra I and Ptolemy V, now in his teens.

Antiochus' conflicts with Rome continued from 192 to 189. In 191, his army was routed at Thermopylae (almost three hundred years after the massacre of Leonidas' Spartan contingent there) by the forces of the Roman consul Manius Acilius Glabrio, and the Seleucid was compelled to abandon his operations on the Greek mainland. But it was in western Asia Minor that the war reached its climax, in a final showdown at the site of Magnesia ad Sipylum in Lydia, probably in December 190 or January 189. Here the Romans, under the command of Lucius Cornelius Scipio, reinforced by an army led by the Pergamene king Eumenes II, inflicted a massive defeat on Antiochus' forces. This single engagement was to affect profoundly the future course of the Seleucid empire, and ultimately the future of the entire Near Eastern world. By the terms of a treaty drawn up the following year between the two protagonists at the city of Apameia (formerly Celaenae) in southern Phrygia, Antiochus was obliged to pay a huge war indemnity, and to give up most of his possessions in Asia Minor.[23] These were henceforth apportioned by Rome between Eumenes, Rome's ally at Magnesia, and Rhodes. Other terms imposed upon Antiochus included a substantial reduction in the size of his war fleet, and the provision of twenty hostages of high status, amongst whom was the king's third son Antiochus (later Antiochus IV).

Rome's victory at Magnesia is often considered a turning point in the history of the Seleucid world. The empire had but recently reached its peak with Antiochus' conquests in Asia Minor. It had now overreached itself, and its territories were significantly reduced by the terms of the peace settlement. Even so, the realm over which Antiochus continued to hold sway remained a vast one. He retained large parts of southern Asia Minor, including Pamphylia and Cilicia, and his imperial holdings through Syria, Mesopotamia, Iran, and central Asia were still intact. The Seleucid empire continued to be one of the greatest the world had ever seen. Its overlord's victories, and his achievements in general, far outshone the Magnesia disaster.

But Antiochus' life ended abruptly and ignominiously. Not long after Magnesia, he was once more in the east, campaigning in his 'Upper Satrapies'. While doing so, he came to the city called Elymais (modern Kuzistan in south-western Iran), where he outraged the local populace by pillaging the temple of Bel. This ill-considered and probably impulsive act of sacrilege proved fatal to him; he died from injuries sustained in the uprising which it sparked off (July 187).[24]

187–164 BC

The reign of the God Made Manifest (Antiochus IV)

Antiochus had four sons by his wife Laodice. Two of them in succession followed him upon the Seleucid throne—Seleucus IV Philopator ('Father-Lover', 187–175) and Antiochus IV Epiphanes ('(The God) Made Manifest', 175–164). Seleucus had in fact been made his father's co-regent in 189, after the battle of Magnesia, and became sole ruler in 187 after his father's death. His thirteen-year reign seems to have been an undistinguished though conscientious one. He may not have had the scope, or the drive, to make it anything more—the harsh war indemnity (1,200 talents a year) which Rome imposed upon his father as part of the terms of peace in itself severely limited his ability to fund fresh military ventures of his own. He seems to have held faithfully to the treaty imposed by the Romans upon his father at Apameia after the battle of Magnesia. But meeting his payments on the war indemnity proved at times a task beyond him, and in one of his attempts to raise them, he sent his chief minister Heliodorus to Jerusalem, to extract

Figure 16. Antiochus IV Epiphanes

funds from the Temple's treasury. As the story is told in 2 Maccabees 3, divine intervention ensured that the treasury remained untouched by the Seleucid forces, and Heliodorus experienced a religious conversion and returned empty-handed to his king. Some time after this, he contrived the king's assassination in a palace conspiracy.[25] His motive is unknown. Was it in any way linked with the Jerusalem episode? Or were other factors involved?

Seleucus' sudden demise raised questions about the succession. The rightful heir was the deceased's first-born son Demetrius.[26] But the succession was not straightforward. As part of the Apameia deal, Rome had demanded that Antiochus (III) send twenty high-status Seleucid hostages to Rome, for indefinite detention there as a pledge that the terms of the treaty would be honoured. One of the hostages was his younger son Antiochus, later to become Antiochus IV.[27] But some time before 178/7, Seleucus sent his son Demetrius to Rome as a goodwill gesture, and in exchange for his brother Antiochus. Rome agreed to the swap, and Antiochus was thus free to return to Syria.[28] There is no evidence that Rome played any part in the decision to replace the one royal hostage with the other, though it was no doubt quite pleased with the arrangement. Antiochus' enforced stay in the imperial capital had acculturated him to Roman ways as well as Greek ones, and he could be relied upon to promote these back in his homeland. Indeed, from Rome's point of view, the installation of Antiochus on the Seleucid throne might not be a bad thing.

But at the time of his release, there was no question of his becoming emperor. Nor can we imagine that Seleucus would have initiated his brother's return, had he any thought that he coveted his throne. Antiochus himself apparently had no ambitions for kingly power, at least not to begin with. Being in no hurry to return to Syria after his release, he looked forward to a long and leisurely trip back to his homeland. On his way, he visited Athens, a city which as a man of culture and sophistication he found very conducive to his tastes (he was later to become a generous benefactor of it). Indeed his stay in Athens may have become a lengthy one. But then he received news of his brother's assassination. Abandoning his banqueting couch, his female companions, and his symposiastic friends, he hurried home, perhaps now with his sights set firmly on the royal throne. He had a powerful supporter in the Pergamene king Eumenes II, who put an armed force at his disposal to ensure his safe journey back to Syria. And there can be little doubt that Pergamene military muscle facilitated his installation as the new Seleucid

king Antiochus IV Epiphanes.[29] Actually, the precise circumstances of Antiochus' accession are somewhat mysterious—because of what we *don't* hear.
There is no record of any opposition to his enthronement. Heliodorus, his
predecessor's assassin, disappears from the scene (and is heard of no more);
so too does Seleucus' youngest son, yet another Antiochus and still a child,
and there is certainly no thought of Demetrius, the rightful heir, being
released from Rome to become the new Seleucid ruler. This makes it tempt-
ing to suspect that Rome had some hand in Antiochus' succession. But we
have no evidence of this, despite various conspiracy theories. The only
external assistance Antiochus is likely to have received is from Eumenes,
who may well have seen future benefits to be derived from forging close
bonds with the Seleucid kingdom, particularly now that it was ruled by a
man who, in part at least, owed his elevation to him.

In any case, from Rome's point of view Antiochus was a fairly safe bet.
An affable *bon vivant* and cultural sophisticate of a somewhat eccentric dis-
position,[30] he would be unlikely to disturb the status quo in that part of the
Near Eastern world where Rome had a direct interest. Indeed, as emperor,
he turned out a good deal better than many might have suspected. In the
early years of his reign, he did all that could be expected of him, meeting
payments to Rome on the war indemnity and acting as benefactor to a
number of Greek cities by the gifts he bestowed upon them; and while he
ensured that he remained on good terms with Rome, he focused on
strengthening and consolidating what was still a huge Seleucid empire,
extending from Cilicia through Syria eastwards into central Asia. Stability
and continuity were dominant themes in Antiochus' empire.

But problems were developing with Egypt. The Ptolemaic regime there
had never accepted its loss of Coele Syria and Palestine, and the reigning
Ptolemy V, whose army had forfeited the territories to Antiochus III in the
battle of Panion in 200, was bent on getting these territories back. His death
in 181 put paid to his plans, and for a while there was peace between the
Seleucid and Ptolemaic families. This was during the first five years of the
reign of Ptolemy V's son and successor Ptolemy VI Philometor ('Mother-
Lover', 180–145), who had come to the throne as a child and reigned jointly
with his mother Cleopatra I. We have already met this Cleopatra. The first
of *seven* Cleopatras (we shall meet the last and most famous of them in
Chapter 13), she was the daughter of Antiochus III and thus the sister of
Antiochus IV. The family relationship may have been largely responsible for
the peace that prevailed between the two regimes during her lifetime. But

on her death in 176, in the year before Antiochus' succession, her son began building up his forces for a fresh invasion of Syria, calculating that the Seleucid regime was at that point weak enough to ensure the success of such a venture. He was no doubt all the more encouraged by the untimely violent death of Seleucus IV and the questionable succession of his brother.

News of the preparation of an invasion force must have reached Antiochus soon after he mounted his throne. The prospect was an alarming one. Antiochus sent a delegation to Rome to lodge a protest about Ptolemaic aggression, but with no confidence of a positive response. In the meantime, he made his own preparations to meet the threat, mustering an army and leading it to the very borders of Egypt. His prompt action proved timely. For when an Egyptian army set out for Syria in November 170, it found itself confronted by a stronger Seleucid force within Egypt's own borders.[31] The allegedly fun-loving Seleucid king was now ready to demonstrate his worth as a war-leader. A showdown, which thus began the Sixth Syrian War,[32] took place on Egyptian soil not far from the city of Pelusium at the easternmost mouth of the Nile river. It was a key strategic location for the invasion of Egypt, figuring, for example, in the invasions of the Achaemenid king Artaxerxes III and subsequently Alexander the Great. Antiochus' crushing defeat of the Ptolemaic army, followed up by his occupation of Pelusium, paved the way for further expeditions into Egypt during 169 and 168. Their aim was to incorporate both Egypt and the island of Cyprus into the Seleucid realm.

What made things easier for Antiochus was that at this time the Ptolemaic regime was split (from 170 to 164) between two rulers, Ptolemy VI Philometor and his younger brother Ptolemy VIII Euergetes.[33] The former ruled at Memphis, the latter at Alexandria. A third person, the brothers' sister Cleopatra II, formed with them a royal triumvirate. Initially, the brothers were divided against each other, with Cleopatra supporting the younger. But after Antiochus' 169 invasion of Egypt, and his departure from there when he failed to take Alexandria by siege, they joined forces—for they knew the Seleucids would be back. At the time of Antiochus' first Egyptian enterprise, in 170, delegations had been sent to Rome by both Euergetes and Antiochus, the former requesting help against the Seleucids, the latter protesting that he was in Egypt merely to support the throne-rights of his older nephew Philometor. Now, after his departure from Egypt in 169, and in the knowledge that he would return, the Ptolemaic triumvirate sent another appeal to Rome for assistance. Up until that point, the Romans had been heavily involved in a war with Macedonia (the Third Macedonian War) and could give little thought to sending a military force south of the Mediterranean to sort out the problems there. None the less, Rome did keep a watchful eye on what was happening in the region, for it had no wish to see any of the Hellenistic rulers becoming too powerful by seizing control of his neighbour's territories. For that reason, it viewed Antiochus' intrusions into Egypt with no little concern. The appeal from Egypt's royal siblings catalyzed it into action.

In response to their appeal, the Roman senate despatched to Egypt a three-man delegation, headed by Gaius Popilius Laenas, with Alexandria as its final destination. The delegation's brief was to deliver an ultimatum to Antiochus. But before doing that, it was to go to the Aegean island of Delos, and wait there for further instructions. This detour would give Rome time to complete its war with Macedonia before committing itself to major military operations in other places. The end of the Macedonian war came on 22 June 168, when the Roman commander Aemilius Paullus inflicted a decisive defeat on the enemy, led by Perseus, at the battle of Pydna. Rome's military resources were now freed up for use elsewhere. Word was sent to the delegation in Delos to continue with its mission. Without delay, it proceeded to Alexandria. Just outside the city, Antiochus had encamped his army after marching it from Memphis, where it had received a warm welcome. Already by this time Cyprus, formerly a Ptolemaic possession, was under Antiochus' control; a naval victory by his forces off the island's coast had won the submission of its governor. Egypt too now seemed Antiochus' for the taking.

But then the delegation from Rome turned up. Antiochus met its members in a village called Eleusis on Alexandria's outskirts. Hoping to set a positive tone for the meeting, he extended his hand in friendship to them. Their leader Popilius refused to take it. Instead, he placed a copy of the senate's ultimatum in it. The document was blunt and to the point. Antiochus must without delay withdraw all his forces from Egypt. Refusal would immediately bring upon him the full military might of Rome. This was no idle threat. Now that they had finished their war with Macedonia, the Romans could have moved in great force and with considerable speed against the emperor. Antiochus asked for time to consult with his advisers. Popilius' reply was curt. The matter was not negotiable. Stepping close to the emperor, Popilius drew a circle in the sand around his feet. 'You will not put one foot outside this circle', he declared, 'until you have given your answer.' Antiochus was left with no choice. He had to accept the ultimatum.

Utterly humiliated, he led his army out of Egypt, back to Syria. This marked the end of the Sixth Syrian War. Shortly after, the Seleucid fleet was ordered out of the waters of Cyprus.[34]

But it was not all loss, not by any means. The Seleucid had in fact established his credentials as a great warrior-king by his military successes in Egypt, he had acquired rich spoils from his victories, and he had won the contest with the Ptolemies for control over southern Syria and Palestine. This last had been his chief objective in his war with the Ptolemaic regime. And that objective had been achieved. For obvious propaganda reasons, Antiochus put a positive spin on the whole Egyptian episode, proclaiming it a great success. And it needed to be celebrated in a fitting way. The emperor had heard of the festivities that Aemilius Paullus had staged, including a triumph and games, to celebrate his victory in the Macedonian war. Antiochus decided he would surpass these in magnificence with festivities of his own (166/5). Daphne near Antioch was to be their venue, and embassies and sacred missions were sent out to cities near and far to announce them. People from all over the Greek world flocked to Antioch for the occasion.

Proceedings began with an enormous procession, headed by a parade of 46,000 infantry, 5,000 of whom were armed in the Roman fashion and clad in breastplates of chain-armour, and 10,000 cavalry. Thirty-six war elephants brought up the rear of the parade, and these were followed by a vast array of other participants, and trophies for display—800 young men wearing gold crowns, 1,000 cattle, 800 ivory tusks, innumerable statues of the gods, some gilded and draped in garments embroidered with gold, 600 of the king's slaves bearing articles of gold plate, 200 women who sprinkled the crowd with perfumes from golden urns, followed by 80 women seated on litters with golden feet and 500 in litters with silver feet, all richly dressed. The programme for the games included gladiatorial shows and beast-fights and lasted thirty days. Polybius describes in detail the splendour and spectacle of the occasion, with the emperor figuring prominently throughout the festivities. But his description ends on a sour note: 'All the above display and outlay was provided for by the robberies Antiochus had committed in Egypt when he treacherously attacked King Philometor while yet a child, and partly by contributions from his friends. He had also sacrilegiously despoiled most of the temples.'[35]

By all this ostentation, the historian Erich Gruen comments, Antiochus was making a public statement that the Seleucid incursion into Egypt had brought victory, not failure.[36] There is no doubt that the emperor was keen to rebuild his reputation as a great ruler, but in a way that was consistent with Seleucid policy from the reign of Seleucus I onwards. This policy is well summed up by Davis and Kraay: 'Seleucus Nicator had known that for his empire to endure it must have a strong Graeco-Macedonian population, settled in cities strategically placed along the main trade routes and boundaries. He and his son Antiochus I had devoted much energy and wealth to the building and peopling of these cities, but since their time there had been much intermarriage with the local peoples, while the Seleucid expulsion from Asia Minor west of the Taurus had greatly reduced the flow of settlers.'[37]

It was thus for practical reasons, underpinned by his own strong philhellenic convictions, that Antiochus set about strengthening Greek customs and institutions in many cities where these elements were becoming diluted, reasserting the Greekness of these cities by the building or rebuilding of temples to the Greek gods, and by the institution of other typically Greek elements, like theatres and gymnasia. The spread of the Greek language to the point where it became the lingua franca of the world ruled by the Seleucids provides a signal example of the success of the promotion of hellenic culture by Antiochus and his predecessors in large parts of their realm. At the same time, the Seleucids seldom interfered with the customs and institutions of the indigenous peoples of the lands they governed, and sometimes bestowed generous grants upon them. It was all helpful in reconciling these widely diverse peoples to their rule, and above all in establishing a modus vivendi between them and the Greek settlers in their regions. By and large, the Seleucid world was one whose peoples were free to conduct their affairs and practise their customs as they wished, often in a time-honoured way.

This policy of freedom and tolerance was generally sincerely applied. But it has to be offset by an episode that figures large in the accounts of Antiochus IV's reign, and leaves a dark shadow upon it—the Jewish uprising commonly known as the Maccabean rebellion. We shall take this up in the next chapter.

Otherwise, there is one final episode to be dealt with in Antiochus' career. In the spring of 165, the emperor set off from Antioch with 40,000 troops on a series of campaigns to be conducted in his eastern territories. These are known as his *anabasis*, in emulation of the one on which his father Antiochus III had embarked almost half a century earlier. The son's new eastern enterprise would establish beyond doubt that the Seleucid empire was still a mighty one, and that its present ruler's grip upon it remained as firm as his father's had been. Things went well, to begin with. Antiochus first marched into Armenia and reimposed Seleucid sovereignty over its ruler Artaxias. Formerly a vassal of Antiochus III, Artaxias had declared his independence after the Seleucid defeat in the battle of Magnesia. The current Antiochus had now brought him to heel (though we have no information as to whether there was an actual battle), and then marched eastwards into Iran. In 164, he fell ill and died during his operations in the region. We know little of what he achieved there.[38]

By and large, Antiochus IV Epiphanes' reign was a highly successful one. His ambition to extend Seleucid control over Egypt came close to fulfilment, and may well have been achieved if Rome had not so promptly brought its war with Macedonia to an end. He had reasserted Seleucid control over the disputed territories of southern Syria and Palestine. And he had come back from his Egyptian campaigns heavily laden with the spoils of victory. Seleucid coffers were well filled during his reign, enabling him to fund his lavish celebrations at Daphne and to provide generous benefactions to Greek cities in both the Near Eastern and the Aegean worlds, consistent with his promotion of philhellenism through the Seleucid empire and its neighbours. Antiochus IV may indeed be accounted one of the most successful of the Seleucid kings, well deserving to be ranked alongside his illustrious predecessors Seleucus I, Antiochus I, and Antiochus III.

I I

The Maccabean Rebellion

Early 2nd century BC

All the people of the nation shall govern themselves in accordance with their ancestral laws, and the senate, the priests, the scribes of the Temple and the Temple singers shall be exempted from the poll tax, the crown tax and the salt tax.[1]

A policy of tolerance

Antiochus III's victory over Ptolemy V at Panion in 200 BC won back for the Seleucids control of southern Syria and Palestine. Including Judaea. In keeping with his policy of tolerance of local customs and traditions, Antiochus issued 'a charter of rights' for the Jewish people, in a letter he sent to Ptolemy, son of Thraseas, the administrator of Coele Syria and Phoenicia. This still surviving document speaks of the warm reception Antiochus and his troops had received from the Jews when they entered Judaea, and of their assistance in expelling the Egyptian garrison occupying Jerusalem's citadel. Antiochus was seen as Judaea's liberator from Ptolemaic rule—which had become deeply unpopular, particularly, it seems, because of Ptolemy IV's attempts to impose Greek cults upon the land.

In acknowledging the Jewish people's support, Antiochus declared: 'We thought it right on our part to repay them for these services and to restore their city which had been destroyed by the accidents of war, and to re-people it by bringing back to it those who have been scattered abroad.' The letter goes on to list a number of benefits to be bestowed upon the Jewish people, including, because of their piety, 'an allowance for sacrifices consisting of sacrificial animals, wine, olive oil and frankincense, to the value of 20,000 silver pieces', and grants to be made to enable 'the work on the Temple to be completed together with the stoas (i.e. porticoes) and anything else which needs to be built'. Most notable was Antiochus' restoration of the Jews' right 'to govern themselves in accordance with their ancestral laws'. He also proclaimed that those who had been abducted from the city and reduced to slave status were to be freed and their property returned to them. Then, to emphasize the respect to be accorded the sacred rites of the Jews, he issued a proclamation 'throughout the whole kingdom'[2] in the following terms: 'No foreigner shall be allowed to enter the precinct of the Temple which is forbidden to the Jews, except for those who are accustomed to doing so after purifying themselves in accordance with ancestral custom. Nor shall anyone bring into the city the flesh of horses, mules, wild or tame asses, leopards, foxes, and hares, and generally of any of the animals forbidden to the Jews.... Only the sacrificial animals used by their ancestors, necessary for a propitious sacrifice to God, shall they be allowed to use. Whoever transgresses any of these rules shall pay the priests a fine of 3,000 drachmas of silver.'

171–167 BC

Antiochus thus declared the right of the Jewish people to live under their own laws, beliefs, customs, and traditions, an enlightened policy which ensured that for the rest of his reign Seleucid–Jewish relations remained highly positive. But under his second successor Antiochus IV Epiphanes, these relations took a turn very much for the worse. This was partly due to the imposition of what was known as *hellenismos*. By the early years of Epiphanes' reign, a group of Jews, primarily from the elite elements of Jewish society and including some members of the temple priesthood, began a movement to turn Jerusalem into a Greek city, by introducing Greek customs and institutions. Their leader was a certain Jason, who acquired the office of high priest in Jerusalem by means of a substantial bribe to Antiochus. And it was in this capacity that he, along with his supporters, obtained Antiochus' consent to set aside the concessions granted by his father, Antiochus III. Their intention in doing this was to convert the Jewish people to a Greek or 'hellenic' way of life—called *hellenismos* in the second book of Maccabees (4:10)—for example, by building a Greek gymnasium at the foot of the citadel and encouraging the most athletic of the city's young men to use it, wearing Greek hats called *petasoi*.

Epiphanes' volte-face

Antiochus Epiphanes himself eventually sought to impose *hellenismos* upon the Jews. But not for some years. To begin with, he was popular with his Jewish subjects, as demonstrated by the hearty welcome he received on his first visit to Jerusalem around 171, when he was ushered into the city by Jason and a cheering, torch-bearing crowd (2 Macc. 4:21–2). Three years later, Jason was out of office and on the run. This happened after he had sent one of his subordinates, Menelaos, to Antiochus with funds to renew his bribe. Menelaos took the opportunity to outbid his master with a bigger bribe and was duly appointed high priest in his place (2 Macc. 4:23–6). Fearing for his safety, the deposed Jason fled Jerusalem and took refuge in the land of Ammon (in modern Transjordan). That left Menelaos free to exercise, for a time, unchallenged authority over the city, which he did in the manner of a despot, displaying, according to 2 Macc. 4:25, 'the temper of a cruel tyrant and the rage of a savage wild beast'. Hostility within the city rapidly mounted against him. Matters came to a head during Antiochus' third expedition to Egypt in 168, when, we recall, the king received an ultimatum from Rome and was forced into an ignominious withdrawal from the country. In Jerusalem, rumours that Antiochus had been killed in Egypt prompted an outbreak of civil war, between the followers of Menelaos and those of his former boss Jason. The latter had returned from his place of exile, and launched an attack on the city with a thousand men (thus 2 Macc. 5:5–10). Caught unawares, Menelaos took refuge in the citadel, and Jason carried out a mass slaughter of his supporters. But the ex-high priest failed to consolidate his hold upon the city and was forced to flee once more, from city to city before ending up in Egypt where he died a lonely death.

Antiochus was still smarting from his humiliation in Egypt, and concerned about the effect this might have on his authority in his own lands, when he received news of the turmoil in Jerusalem. He reacted furiously. What this news indicated, he believed, was not a war between opposing Jewish factions, but a general Jewish uprising against his rule. So on his way back from Egypt, he attacked Jerusalem, took it by storm, and ordered his troops to carry out mass slaughter.[3] Within the space of three days '80,000 were destroyed, 40,000 in hand-to-hand fighting; and as many were sold into slavery as were slain' (2 Macc. 5:11–16). Then, after plundering the temple, with Menelaos as his guide, he put Jerusalem and Judaea under the authority of Seleucid governors. But he was not yet finished with the city.

2 Macc. 5:24–6 reports that he subsequently sent his military commander
Apollonius there, with orders to carry out a further massacre of the city's
remaining adult males, and the enslavement of its women and boys. Even
allowing for some exaggeration in the scale of the atrocities presented to us
in the Maccabees text, we can have no doubt that the devastation which
Antiochus inflicted upon Jerusalem was substantial.

None the less, Antiochus was still not satisfied that Judaea had been fully
reconciled to his authority. He feared that its inhabitants' strong sense of their
ethnos, their national identity and way of life, might lead to fresh uprisings
against him in their efforts to preserve it. And so, 'the king sent letters by messenger to Jerusalem and the cities of Judah that they should follow customs
alien to their land, banish holocausts, sacrifices and libations from the sanctuary and profane the sabbaths and festivals, defile the sanctuary and the holy
men, build altars and sacred enclosures and idols' temples, sacrifice pigs and
unclean animals, leave their sons uncircumcised, and defile themselves with
every kind of impurity and abomination, so as to forget the Law and change
all their ordinances. Anyone who did not conform to the king's edict would
be punished with death' (1 Macc. 1:44–50).[4] This proclamation was in effect
a comprehensive attack on the whole Jewish way of life (*ioudaïsmos* in 2 Macc.
2:21). It involved a ban on traditional Jewish religious and social customs and
beliefs, and the imposition of Greek customs and traditions in their place. In
accordance with this policy, Antiochus issued a command that sacrifice was to
be made to the Greek gods in all Judaean cities and villages, and appointed
inspectors to ensure that this command was carried out (1 Macc. 1:51). And
thus, on the 15th day of Kislev (November/December), 167, a day that lives in
infamy in Jewish records, a pagan altar was set up on the altar of the Temple at
Jerusalem; ten days later, the first sacrifice was made to Zeus there. This is
what is referred to, in the book of Daniel, as the 'abomination that makes
desolate' (Dan. 11:31; 12:11; see also 1 Macc. 1:54; 2 Macc. 6:1–5). It sparked off
what is commonly known as the Maccabean rebellion.

166–142 BC

The rebellion and its aftermath

From what has already been said in this chapter, and from what is to follow,
it will be obvious that our reconstruction of this period of Jewish history is

based heavily on the first two (of the four) books of Maccabees, part of the biblical Septuagint.[5] In using these books as our central texts, we should take note of the important reservation expressed by the scholars Sherwin-White and Kuhrt. The books, they say, are 'extremely hard to analyse because of their highly emotive, biased, and even, at times, fictitious character. They reflect a later perception of the revolt against Seleucid rule as a "Holy War" in which Israel stood alone against the massed hostile forces of the Macedonian and Greek world. They have therefore become a manifesto for the evolving history of Jewish orthodoxy and the definition of Judaism and Jewish identity—all of which has an importance quite divorced from the realities of the fairly small-scale local upheaval that the revolt really was.'[6] You will need to keep this reservation in mind while reading accounts of both the rebellion itself and the events leading up to it.

The uprising is associated particularly with a man called Judas Maccabeus, who with a small group of companions, including his father and brothers, escaped Apollonius' massacre in Jerusalem and fled into the wilderness. There, Judas 'kept himself and his companions alive in the mountains as wild animals do; they continued to live on what grew wild, so that they might not share in

Figure 17. *The Maccabees*, painting by Wojciech Stattler (1842)

the defilement' (2 Macc. 5:27). Judas and his family finally settled in a village called Modein (1 Macc. 2:1), which lay about 40 km north-west of Jerusalem. His epithet 'Maccabaeus', which probably means 'hammer', became the defining name of the Jewish rebellion that was soon to erupt. It was applied to Judas' followers in general, and to himself, his father Mattathias, and his four brothers in particular. Mattathias quickly became the leader of his village. And it was to him that Antiochus' officers came, following the 'abomination decree'. Noting his honoured position in the community, they tried to persuade him to obey the king's command, for they were confident that if he apostasized, others in the community would follow. An altar was set up where Mattathias was urged to make sacrifice. But the old man was defiant. He declared that he and his sons and brothers would live by the covenant of their fathers, and refused to obey the king's orders. It was a stand-off—until one of his fellow-villagers meekly came before the altar, and sacrificed upon it in accordance with the king's orders. This drove Mattathias into a rage. He killed the offender along with the officer who was attempting to persuade them to sacrifice, and tore down the altar. Then he urged all those who remained loyal to their faith to follow him, and he fled with his sons and followers to the hills, in preparation for a guerrilla war against the king's forces. Thus began the Maccabean rebellion (166/5) (1 Macc. 2:15–48).

Mattathias was given little time to lead his band of guerrillas, for within a year of the rebellion's beginning he fell ill and died. Leadership now passed to his third son, Judas Maccabaeus (1 Macc. 2:49–3:1). This provided a good opportunity, so Samaria's Seleucid governor Apollonius believed, to bring the uprising to an end. So he set out with a military force to confront the rebels under their new leader. At a place called Gophna, the opposing sides met. It was a disastrous encounter for the Seleucids. The Maccabeans won a resounding victory, which left Apollonius dead on the battlefield and Judas in possession of his sword; he used it in battle for the rest of his life (1 Macc. 3:10–12). There were further confrontations between the Maccabean and the Seleucid forces.[7] They had something of a David–Goliath air about them, as the Jewish leader's small warrior band trounced the more powerful and better equipped Seleucid armies led by the general Lysias. Judas' successes were many, but his crowning achievement was his victory over a Seleucid army at Beth-zur (a settlement in the hill country of Judah, southern Palestine, 30 km south-west of Jerusalem). This victory allegedly claimed 5,000 Seleucid lives (1 Macc. 4:34),[8] and paved the way for Judas' march upon and occupation of Jerusalem. His finest moment came with his rededication of the Temple in Jerusalem on the 25th day of Kislev in the year 164.[9]

This year was also the last of Antiochus' life. We recall that he died while on campaign in the east. His son and successor, Antiochus V, was only a nine-year-old child at the time, and the management of the affairs of state fell to his father's trusted military commander and friend Lysias. A final resolution of the Jewish question was among those matters that needed the new regime's urgent attention. Already shortly before his death Antiochus IV had taken the first step towards a reconciliation with the Jewish people by proclaiming an amnesty for them and declaring that they would now be free once more 'to enjoy their own food and laws' (2 Macc. 11:27–32). Lysias went further by issuing, in the boy-king's name, what was in effect a proclamation reversing Antiochus IV's 'abomination decree'. Of course for diplomatic reasons, it was important to attribute this new pronouncement to the new king himself. Thus it was expressed in the form of a command issued by His Majesty to his chief minister: 'King Antiochus (V) to his brother Lysias, greeting. Now that our royal father has gone to join the gods, we desire that our subjects be undisturbed in the conduct of their own affairs. We have learnt that the Jews do not consent to adopt Greek ways, as our father wished, but prefer their own mode of life and request that they be allowed to observe their own laws. We choose, therefore, that this nation like the rest should be left undisturbed, and decree that their temple be restored to them and that they shall regulate their lives in accordance with their ancestral customs. Have the goodness, therefore, to inform them of this and ratify it, so that, knowing what our intentions are, they may settle down confidently and quietly to manage their own affairs' (2 Macc. 11:22–6).[10] This was a pragmatic response to a fait accompli, since Judas had already established control over Jerusalem and was already in the process of restoring traditional customs and practices. At this very unstable time in the Seleucid monarchy's history, the regent Lysias had no wish to prolong hostilities with the Jewish state. There were other priorities and concerns, most notably the threat of pretenders to the Seleucid throne.

None the less Judas continued hostilities with the Seleucid forces, for his ultimate aim was to establish the Jewish state's independence of Seleucid rule. In February/March 161, he won a major victory over the army of the Seleucid general Nicanor at Adasa, north of Jerusalem. But his career and his life were now almost at an end. Later, in the same year, in autumn, he was defeated and killed in the battle of Eleasa by a vastly larger Seleucid army

led by the commander Bacchides. His brothers Jonathan and Simon managed to retrieve his body from the battlefield and took him back to Modein
for burial. Jewish resistance to Seleucid rule continued, with leadership of
the Maccabean resistance movement now assumed by Jonathan, the youngest of Mattathias' five sons.[11] But under Jonathan's leadership, relations with
the Seleucid monarchy shifted from the military to the diplomatic arena.
Which generated problems of its own! Inevitably Jonathan was drawn into
the struggles within the Seleucid dynasty for the royal succession. His support of Alexander Balas against Demetrius won him recognition by Balas as
the Jewish leader, but a few years later he fell victim to the Seleucid pretender Diodotus Tryphon, who initially formed an alliance with him, but
then had him captured and murdered (143 or 142). (We shall come back to
all this in the next chapter.) Leadership of the Jews was now in the hands of
Mattathias' last surviving son, Simon.

142–early 1st century AD

It is from this year until 63 BC, when Judaea was absorbed into the Roman
provincial administration, that the Jewish state is said to have been ruled by
the Hasmonean dynasty. According to Josephus, the dynasty derived its
name from a man called Hashmon, the great-grandfather of Judas Maccabaeus' father Mattathias. But the dynasty effectively began with Mattathias
himself and secured its primacy in the Jewish state, where its members ruled
as high priests, initially through the military victories of Mattathias' son
Judas and Judas' recovery of Jerusalem. While remaining under Seleucid
control, the Hasmoneans exploited divisions within the Seleucid royal family to expand their territories, and finally gained independence for their
state following the death of Antiochus VII (129 BC). Though it lost its autonomy in 63 BC, the dynasty itself was still recognized in the time of Herod the
Great (37–4 BC), and survived until the early years of the Christian era.

12

The Decline and Fall of the Seleucids

164–150 BC

The return of Demetrius

Antiochus Epiphanes' death in 164 while on his eastern campaign sparked off the first of a series of succession crises which bedevilled the Seleucid dynasty for the rest of its existence, and played no small part in the destabilization, contraction, and ultimate disappearance of the empire over which it held sway. The dead king had been duly succeeded by his son Antiochus V. But this latest Antiochus was a mere child, whose occupancy of the throne, despite the efforts of his minder Lysias, was precarious in the extreme. All the more so since there was another contender for the purple, with a very good claim upon it. This was Demetrius, the eldest son of Seleucus IV and nephew of Epiphanes. Sent to Rome by his father as a hostage when he was eleven years old, Demetrius was now twenty-three, and believed that Rome would support his bid for kingship once it had received news of Epiphanes' death. In an impassioned plea to the senate, Demetrius begged permission to return home and become king, arguing that he had more right to the throne than his uncle's children. For good measure, he declared that Rome was his fatherland, and that the senators were like fathers to him, since he had come to Rome as a child, and their sons like brothers. That would make clear his intention of remaining loyal to Rome once he was back home. The good senators were deeply moved by what he said. But they were not persuaded. Not because they doubted that Demetrius would make a good king. They rather feared that he *would*. Rome's interests would be better served, they reasoned, if the Seleucid kingdom *lacked* a firm and able ruler capable of giving it strength and unity. Better to keep Demetrius in custody, despite his professions of loyalty, and support the accession of his young cousin; that would help keep the empire weak and unstable. So they sent their representatives to Antioch to make sure that Antiochus V remained on his throne. While in the region, they were instructed to burn the king's decked warships and hamstring his elephants. That would help ensure that Seleucid military power remained permanently crippled.[1]

Rome's 'divide and destabilize' policy paid off; unwittingly, it made Demetrius its first beneficiary. Bereft of support from Rome in his bid to get back his father's throne, Demetrius decided to take matters into his own hands. With the help of Polybius (who was a fellow-hostage at Rome and one of his circle of friends), he secretly left Rome and boarded a ship bound for the Phoenician coast.[2] News of his return quickly prompted an uprising against the current regime, and the seizure of the child-king and his unpopular regent Lysias. Both were executed on the orders of Demetrius, who now installed himself on the throne in Antioch.[3] But almost immediately he was confronted with a serious challenge to his sovereignty. In the east, a man called Timarchus had been appointed by Antiochus IV as governor of the eastern provinces. Declaring that Demetrius was a usurper who could not claim his loyalty, Timarchus now broke away from Seleucid rule and proclaimed himself king of Media. He did so with the approval of Rome, still smarting from Demetrius' escape and harbouring deep suspicions about his intentions now that he had assumed his kingdom's throne. Timarchus assembled his army for an invasion of Syria (161 or 160). He was met on the Euphrates, not far from Babylon, by a Syrian army led by Demetrius, and was defeated and killed.[4] From this episode, Demetrius acquired the title Soter—'Saviour'. His sovereignty over the Seleucid empire was now undisputed—at least in Asia.

There was still the matter of a settlement with Rome. Alarmed by developments in Syria—which had gone quite counter to their plans—the Senate sent a delegation there on a fact-finding mission. By the time the delegation arrived, Demetrius was firmly seated upon his throne. But in a spirit of reconciliation, he warmly received and entertained his former host's representatives, then sent them home with an assurance that he would remain Rome's true friend. With that assurance, the senate would have to be content. For the time being.

As his reign progressed, Demetrius became increasingly unpopular among his own subjects, despite their initial support for him. The contrast with the affable Antiochus IV Epiphanes was striking. Demetrius was a gloomy man, lacking his predecessor's warmth and charm, and not disposed to the public entertainments and displays that Antiochus customarily put on. On the contrary, he seems to have become something of a recluse, 'being much given to drink and tipsy for the greater part of the day', according to Polybius.[5] Fresh tensions with Egypt also developed during his reign, and in the west the Pergamene king Attalus was distinctly hostile to him—not surprisingly, given the close relations that had existed between Antiochus IV and the Pergamene court. In Pergamum's view, Demetrius was an inter-loper. And indeed it was the Pergamene court that sparked a new crisis in the Seleucid succession. For from its circles there emerged a pretender to the Seleucid throne, a good-looking young man of humble origins called Balas, who bore a striking resemblance to Antiochus IV's son, the child-king crowned as Antiochus V and executed by Demetrius. Claiming to be another son of Antiochus IV, this personable, handsome young man was enthusiasti-cally proclaimed at Pergamum (after being brought there from his home-town Smyrna) the rightful Seleucid king.[6] He was so acknowledged by both Rome and Egypt—and given the name Alexander. With Pergamene, Ptolemaic, and Roman support, Alexander Balas put together a military force with which he entered Syria in 150, from his base in a city called Ptolemais on the southern coast of Asia Minor, and did battle with and defeated Demetrius, who was killed in the conflict (150). Thus Alexander Balas became the next ruler of the Seleucid empire.[7]

150–129 BC

The reigns of the impostor, the conqueror, the usurper, and the pious one

Balas' accession was warmly received by the Syrians, and for a time the young emperor was highly popular with his subjects. As he was with the Jews, to whom he granted a greater measure of political and religious inde-pendence than had any of his predecessors. He had already won over from Demetrius their ruler Jonathan Maccabaeus, by promising him the office of Jewish high priest, and sending him a purple robe and golden crown. More importantly on the international scene, Balas strengthened his kingdom's relations with Egypt, by marrying Cleopatra Thea ('Cleopatra the Divine'), daughter of Ptolemy VI Philometor.[8] But Balas was a man of little substance. He quickly proved himself a weak and ineffective ruler, caring little for the affairs of state and plunging himself into a life of idleness and dissipation. That suited Ptolemy very well. Right from the beginning, Balas was scarcely more than a puppet in the hands of his father-in-law, whose influence over the Seleucid regime ensured that Ptolemaic interests always prevailed in whatever dealings he had with Syria. It was but a matter of time, and little time at that, before Balas' subjects began turning against him, and unrest became widespread throughout the kingdom. During this troubled period, the Jewish nation came close to establishing its independence, and the satraps of Media and Susiana broke free from Seleucid rule.

For Balas, the writing was clearly on the wall. His tenure of power had almost run its course. It effectively ended in 147 when a second Demetrius, son and namesake of his predecessor-but-one, came by ship to Syria with a band of mercenaries. Many regarded the newly arrived Demetrius as the true heir to the Seleucid throne, and his mere presence back in Syria[9] turned hostility to Balas into outright revolt. Abandoned by his troops and allies (except for the Jews), Balas fled across the Taurus mountains into Cilicia. In this same period, Ptolemy VI entered Syria from the south, occupying and garrisoning Palestine and the Phoenician cities on his way. He had marched into Syria initially (so we are led to believe) in support of his son-in-law against Demetrius. But when he reached Palestine, he switched his support, along with his daughter Cleopatra, to Demetrius, whom he now installed in Antioch as the new Seleucid emperor—in effect, his vassal.[10] But Balas had not yet given up. From his place of refuge, he gathered his own band of mercenaries and returned to Syria, resolved to fight it out with his enemies and regain his throne. It was a courageous but doomed enterprise. In the showdown with Ptolemy and Demetrius that followed, the battle of Antioch (fought in 145 and also known as the battle of the Oenoparus river), Balas' troops were decisively defeated, and their leader forced to flee once more for his life, taking refuge with the ruler of one of the Arab Nabataean tribes.[11] But victory for the Ptolemaic forces came at a heavy cost. Ptolemy Philometor, their commander-in-chief, sustained a fatal wound in the conflict. He was, however, granted one last moment of satisfaction before he expired—the sight of his former son-in-law's head. This was per favour of the Arab chieftain Zabdiel with whom Balas had sought refuge. Seeking to ingratiate himself with Balas' enemies, Zabdiel had decapitated his guest, and sent the lopped-off member to the dying

Ptolemy as proof. Demetrius II, now the undisputed ruler of the Seleucid world, adopted the title Nicator, 'Conqueror', to celebrate his final victory over Balas—a victory for which Ptolemy clearly deserves the credit, and for which he paid with his life.

Despite the support he had received from Ptolemy, Demetrius had no intention of maintaining his alliance with Egypt after his father-in-law's death, and promptly reneged on his agreement to cede southern Syria and Palestine to Ptolemaic control. This brash new leader of the Seleucid world was a mere youth on his accession, barely midway through his teens. But tender years were not matched by tender behaviour. With the backing of the mercenary force that had helped him secure his throne, Demetrius ruthlessly enforced his rule over his subjects.[12] The mercenaries, mainly Cretans, were let loose on the countryside, looting and pillaging at will and committing the most brutal atrocities. Hostility towards the new emperor rapidly spread. Inevitably, an opposition force rose against him and his supporters, including his thuggish hired troops. It was commanded by a man called Diodotus, who proclaimed Alexander Balas' two-year-old son Antiochus (son also of Cleopatra Thea) the rightful king, and enthroned him as Antiochus VI in Antioch after an anti-Demetrius riot broke out there. This plunged the Seleucid state into armed conflict between the two opposing Seleucid regimes—Demetrius II on the one side and Diodotus on the other, acting as regent for Antiochus.[13] Antioch and its hinterland were firmly in the camp of the infant king, as also the island-city Arad (Aradus, Arwad), and the coastal cities Orthosia, Byblos, Beirut, Ptolemais, and Dora. Further, Diodotus secured an alliance with the Jewish leader Jonathan Maccabaeus. The coastal cities of Seleuceia, Laodiceia, Sidon, and Tyre maintained their loyalty to Demetrius, as did the governors of the provinces of Mesopotamia and Babylonia.

For several years the civil war continued without a conclusive outcome. But in 142, Diodotus revealed his true intentions by setting aside his protégé Antiochus and assuming the imperial throne himself, with the name Diodotus Tryphon Autokrator (142–139/8). (Antiochus remained alive and probably in seclusion until his usurper executed him several years later.[14]) It was around the time of his coup that Tryphon, as we shall now call him, decided to dispense with the support of Jonathan Maccabaeus, and had him captured and murdered. This turned out to be a serious mistake. The position of Jewish high priest was now assumed by Jonathan's brother Simon, who had the backing of Demetrius and secured with his support the independence of the Jewish capital Jerusalem (an independence which Rome subsequently acknowledged). Simon could prove a useful ally for Demetrius in his contest with Tryphon.[15] But the stalemate continued between the opposing Seleucid factions. And the empire continued to fall apart. In the east, the Parthians under their king Mithridates I took full advantage of the warring Seleucids to extend their control over the Seleucid empire's Iranian and Mesopotamian territories. In an attempt to stem the Parthian tide, Demetrius took time out from his contest with Tryphon to march eastwards into Mesopotamia and Iran where he waged a series of campaigns, apparently with no small success, against Mithridates. Yet it all came to an inglorious end when, through either ill fortune or ill-planning, he fell into the hands of the Parthians and was taken off to Hyrcania (a region located south of the Caspian Sea).[16] He spent the next ten years there in Parthian captivity. (But we are not yet finished with Demetrius.) That effectively left Tryphon, in 140, in sole command of the Seleucid empire.

And that paved the way for the entry into our story of the next 'genuine' Seleucid king—Demetrius' younger brother Antiochus VII (139/8–129). Generally accounted one of the most successful of the Seleucid rulers, and easily the best of the tail-enders, Antiochus had been sent as a child by his family to live in Side on Asia Minor's southern coast (hence his later epithet 'Sidetes'). It was a wise decision, for it kept him out of harm's way until such time as he could take up his family's cause against the arch-enemy Tryphon.[17] Which is what he eventually did. But he had other matters to attend to first. One of these was to become the third husband of Cleopatra Thea. Her second husband, his brother Demetrius, was still alive at the time, in captivity in Parthia. But there were compelling reasons for the new marriage, above all the need to enhance Sidetes' status as the legitimate ruling Seleucid while Demetrius' future was still uncertain. Cleopatra also had a personal motive for consenting to, if not actually pressing for, the marriage—jealousy when she heard that Demetrius had married the Parthian king's daughter Rhodoguna.[18] Far from suffering in captivity, it seems that Demetrius lived in considerable comfort and style as the Parthians' prisoner, with various fringe benefits bestowed upon him, including Princess Rhodoguna. And so, partly out of spite, Cleopatra married his brother. She would one day take more drastic revenge on husband no. 2. But for the moment, with the additional authority of his marriage to the current Seleucid queen, daughter of Ptolemy VI, Antiochus was able to turn his attention to the matter of Tryphon. Within a year of his accession, probably in 138, he hunted his enemy down, cornered him in Antioch, and defeated him. Tryphon took his own life.

Antiochus apparently had Jewish support in his action against Tryphon. Even so, the Jews remained rebellious, and to reimpose his authority over them, he invaded Judaea and laid siege to Jerusalem. The city fell to him. But unlike many of its other conquerors, Antiochus was disposed to be merciful in his treatment of it, and thus acquired the title Eusebes, 'the Pious One'.[19] He was now ready to take on the east, eager to revive the glories of the old Seleucid empire—at least as far as they *could* be revived. Almost sixty years earlier, his great namesake Antiochus III had lost to Rome a substantial part of his territories in Asia Minor following the battle of Magnesia. And Rome's hold on what was once the western part of the Seleucid empire had tightened and expanded in 133 when the last Pergamene ruler, Attalus III, bequeathed his kingdom to the Roman people. The west was irretrievably lost. But there was still the eastern world. And it was on this world that the new Antiochus now set his sights. In 131, with Syria and Palestine firmly under his control, he set out with a large army for a campaign in the east, to take on the might of the Parthian empire, then ruled by Phraates II.

The Pious One had also a personal mission to fulfil—the rescue of his brother Demetrius II, who had now been in Parthian captivity for ten years. Things went well, to begin with. Antiochus had a number of successes against the Parthian forces he encountered on his eastwards march, recapturing from them Babylonia and the former Seleucid eastern capital Seleuceia on the Tigris (130). On his entry into Babylon, he assumed the title 'Great King'.[20] And from Babylonia he moved into Iran, where he seized Susa and Susiana. He was now approaching the heartland of the Parthian empire. In Media, he set up his winter quarters, with high hopes of successfully completing his campaign the following year. But his plans went awry when the cities where he had quartered a number of his troops rose up in revolt. Hastily mustering what forces he could, he set out to rescue his beleaguered men. But this brought him into head-on conflict with the main Parthian army, under Phraates' personal command. In the battle that followed, Antiochus was killed and his army destroyed (129).[21]

Thus ended the reign of the last of the Seleucid kings who might have helped save the empire from its continuing decline. As a final mark of respect for his adversary, Phraates encased his body in a silver casket and sent it back to Syria for burial.[22] Antiochus' aspirations were high and his abilities not inconsiderable. But his ill-fated eastern campaign and sudden death deprived him of the opportunity to revive his kingdom's fortunes. His was the last attempt by any Seleucid king to regain the empire's eastern provinces. They were forever lost to the Seleucids. At this time too, the Jewish nation established its independence from Seleucid rule.

129–64 BC

The Divine Cleopatra takes centre stage

Before moving on from Antiochus, we should retrace our steps a little. We have observed that the king's elder brother Demetrius II had been held at the Parthian court, since his capture ten years earlier, and treated extremely well there. Despite this, he seems not to have been happy with his confinement, or won over to the Parthian side, and made several unsuccessful attempts to escape. The Parthians kept him safe and secure throughout this period, in the belief that one day he might prove politically useful to them. After all, Demetrius could still claim to be the rightful Seleucid king, and the knowledge that he was still alive could well have had a destabilizing effect on his empire. At an appropriate time, Parthia might turn this to its advantage. Phraates believed that that time had come when news reached him that Demetrius' brother Antiochus had arrived in Media, wintering his troops there in preparation for a spring offensive against Parthia. And so while Antiochus was in the east, he sent Demetrius to Syria with an armed escort, to reclaim the throne from which he had never actually been deposed. As it turned out, his plan of action proved unnecessary. The news of Antiochus' defeat and death meant that Demetrius had no need to bother with a coup, and got his throne back by default—along with his wife Cleopatra the Divine, from whom he had never actually been unmarried.

For a second time, Demetrius II Nicator ruled the Seleucid world (129–125). But he soon became as unpopular as he had been the first time round. Ten years of confinement in the Parthian court had in no way mellowed him or improved his fitness for kingship. The resumption of his harsh rule quickly roused the hostility of his subjects, at a time when the kingdom's resources were low, after the severe losses of troops in Media during Antiochus' campaign; the royal treasury too had been seriously depleted. Nevertheless, and in spite of the need to consolidate what was left of the empire, Demetrius made ready for a campaign into Egypt, setting out on it in 127.

He had got as far as the fortress settlement Pelusium (where, we recall, Antiochus IV had inflicted a crushing defeat on the Ptolemaic forces), when he was confronted by a much larger army, led by Ptolemy VIII Euergetes. And just at this time, he received news of trouble back home. Northern Syria had risen in revolt against him, under the banner of a new pretender to the throne, another Alexander, this one nicknamed Zabinas—the 'Bought One' (an indication that he was of slave origin). Antioch had gone over to him, along with the inland cities of Syria. But Seleuceia in Pieria had remained loyal to Demetrius, as did a number of other coastal cities. The shrunken Seleucid kingdom was thus again split between two leaders—the occupant of the throne and the pretender to it. It seems that the latter had been backed, indeed put up, by the Ptolemy, who supplied him with an Egyptian armed force, expressly with the intention of destabilizing Demetrius' regime. His action had the immediate effect of forcing Demetrius to abandon his Egyptian campaign and hurry back home to deal with the rebels.

The next two years (126–125) were taken up with conflicts between the two contestants for the throne, until a final showdown took place near Damascus. Demetrius was trounced, and fled to the city of Ptolemais on the Phoenician coast.[23] He could be assured of a safe refuge there, so he believed, because he had left the city in the capable hands of his wife. But a shock was in store for him. When he arrived at Ptolemais, the divine Cleopatra (who had by no means forgotten Princess Rhodoguna) refused him access, probably to the city and certainly to herself. In desperation, the locked out husband took ship and sailed for Tyre, hoping to find sanctuary in a temple there. But as soon as he stepped ashore, he was arrested, tortured, and executed[24]—all no doubt on the orders of his wife.

Which left the grieving widow in charge of the Seleucid kingdom. With long first-hand experience of the politics and intrigues and power-plays of the Seleucid court, and with her husband Demetrius now eliminated, Cleopatra decided to occupy the throne herself. There was of course still the matter of Alexander Zabinas' rival regime to be dealt with, and that was to take another three years. But Cleopatra's credentials for ruling what was left of the Seleucid empire could scarcely be denied. Except that she was a woman. Not that she herself saw this as a drawback. If anything, it simply made her all the more determined to maintain her grasp on royal power, using whatever means were necessary. This she demonstrated, in 125, when her own son Seleucus (V) claimed the throne as his father's rightful successor;

she resolved the matter by shooting an arrow through him.[25] But she was aware that her subjects did not take kindly to the notion of having a woman as their sole ruler, whatever her merits may have been. So in the same year, she decided it would be politic to associate with herself, as co-regent, another of her sons, the teenage Antiochus (VIII), known as Grypus, 'Hook-Nose' (joint reign 125–121).

The ugly young prince has been described as 'little more than another hunting, drinking, and fighting man, intent on his pleasures, with little thought for the kingdom'.[26] But if this description fairly represents the prince,[27] his image of degeneracy and decadence was perhaps a deliberately cultivated one; he may simply have been doing his best to live down to the standards of his more dissolute predecessors, and was probably not as bad as he tried to make out. He did in fact succeed in putting paid to the activities of Alexander Zabinas. Alexander was defeated in a battle between the two, a conflict instigated and militarily backed by Ptolemy VIII, and fled to Antioch for refuge. But while there, he committed an act of sacrilege in the temple of Zeus, when he ordered the removal of golden statues of Victory and Zeus from it (he was short of cash and his troops were now demanding payment), and was forced by the outraged Antiochenes to take to his heels again. Deserted by his supporters, he fell into the hands of robbers, and was delivered up to Hook-Nose (no doubt for a considerable reward), who executed him forthwith.[28] Not long after, relations between mother and son

Figure 18. Antiochus VIII Grypus ('Hook-Nose')

deteriorated. Fearing that her son's successes were undermining her status, Cleopatra decided that Hook-Nose was getting too big for his boots, and that she and the kingdom would now be better off without him. So one day, on his return from taking exercise in the country, she offered him refreshment, a cup of poisoned brew she had mixed for him herself. But Hook-Nose had been forewarned. As his mother held the cup out to him, he insisted that she drink from it before he did. At first, she refused. But finally, after repeated demands from her son, who told her of his suspicions and was now giving her the opportunity to prove them wrong, she gave in, swallowed some of the concoction, hoped for the best, and promptly expired.[29]

Surprisingly, given the world of intrigue and plots that were a normal part of life in the rapidly decaying Seleucid court, Hook-Nose managed to hold on to his throne for a further twenty-five years (121–96), up to the time he was murdered by his military commander. But his territory had been much reduced when a half-brother wrested part of it from him. By the time of his death, the once mighty and far-reaching Seleucid empire had been reduced to a mere fragment of Syrian territory, covering a number of coastal cities and the area around Antioch on the Orontes. Further squabbles over the last scraps of the Seleucid kingdom occupied much of the reigns of Hook-Nose's seven successors,[30] until the last of them, Antiochus XIII, was unceremoniously cast aside by Pompey the Great.

PART IV

Syria Under Roman Rule

13

The Coming of the Romans

64–31 BC

Syria joins the Roman world

In the year 64 BC, Syria became a province of Rome. Several years earlier, the Roman commander Pompey had been wintering with his troops in Cilicia (67–66 BC), after his spectacular success in eradicating the scourge of piracy from the Mediterranean and Black Seas. The People of Rome now assigned him a fresh task—to bring about a settlement of the political and military affairs of the eastern lands. Thus he embarked on a series of campaigns which took him far into these lands, through much of the Near Eastern world as the Romans knew it. First he sorted out, by a combination of force and intimidation, the troublesome kingdoms of Pontus and Armenia in northern and eastern Anatolia. Then he turned his attention to Syria. His task there was effortlessly accomplished. Entering Syria's chief city Antioch without resistance, he swept aside the last feeble vestige of the Seleucid empire, and declared Syria a Roman province. Antioch became the administrative centre of the new province, and under Roman rule the third city of the empire, surpassed only by Rome itself and Alexandria. Indeed, several Roman emperors were to use it as their main place of residence. Thus without fighting, Appian informs us, 'the Romans came into possession of Cilicia and both inland Syria and Coele Syria, Phoenicia, Palestine and all the other countries bearing the Syrian name from the Euphrates to Egypt and the sea'.[1]

By and large the Syrian world was receptive to Roman rule, for its new overlord held out hopes of greater political and economic stability than the Seleucid regime had provided, especially in the last decades of its existence. And the sense of a new era of peace and stability was reinforced by Pompey himself in his dealings with the peoples and kingdoms of the region, with

Map 10. Syria in its Roman Near Eastern context

the emphasis he placed on diplomatic rather than military resolutions of outstanding issues. Thus in his settlement of Syrian affairs, he did not pursue operations against the Nabataeans who had invaded Syria during the final years of the Seleucid kingdom and briefly occupied Damascus. For many decades, they were allowed to retain their independent status. (We shall have occasion to refer several times to the Nabataeans in the course of this chapter, so this might be a good moment to refer you to the brief account of these people in the chapter that follows.)

With Judaea Pompey took a firmer stand. Under the line of independent Hasmonean kings, from the death of the Seleucid ruler Antiochus VII in 129, Jewish territory was greatly expanded, allegedly to the former limits of the kingdom of David and Solomon, and including such territories as Idumaea (the Greek name for Edom) in southern Palestine and

Figure 19. Pompey the Great

Ituraea, a region occupied by a bedouin Arab people, the Ituraeans, in the Biqa' valley in Lebanon. When Pompey arrived in Syria, the Hasmonean kingdom had been destabilized by leadership rivalries between two brothers, John Hyrcanus (II) and Aristoboulus (II). The brothers referred their dispute to Pompey, who decided in favour of John, the older and less effective of the two. But in 63, Pompey occupied Jerusalem, stripped John of his royal title—henceforth, he could only call himself High Priest—and greatly reduced the size of Judaea, depriving it of much of the territory it had recently acquired; he left it with only Galilee, Idumaea, and a slice of Transjordania's borderland.[2] The territories taken from it were incorporated into the new Roman province of Syria, which at this point extended southwards from the frontier of the kingdom of Commagene (whose ruler had submitted to Pompey and become one of Rome's client kings[3]) through Judaea to parts of Arabia. Like Commagene, a number of the incorporated lands retained their own rulers who enjoyed a harmonious relationship with Rome and, under Rome's patronage and protection, a fairly high degree of autonomy.

At the same time, Rome stamped its presence firmly upon its newly acquired eastern territories, in Syria as well in Asia Minor, by the spread throughout the region of many aspects of its culture and civilization. And of course with Romanization came all the material appurtenances of Roman life—baths, theatres, stadiums, and the like. Under Roman rule, hundreds of towns and cities were built from scratch, or refounded on the sites of earlier settlements, beginning with a rebuilding programme undertaken by Pompey in both Asia Minor and Syria. Populating these new settlements with time-expired soldiers from Rome's armies (as well as with local peoples) was a policy particularly associated with the man who became Pompey's arch-enemy, Julius Caesar, and subsequently with Caesar's nephew, the emperor Augustus. The settlement of retired soldiers as colonists of the eastern cities served a dual purpose: it fulfilled a promise to the veterans to provide them with land-grants as payment for their years of service, and it contributed to the process of Romanization in the lands where they were located.

The cities both old and new were connected by a much upgraded road network, major features of which were the north–south Via Maris ('The Way of the Sea') which linked Egypt with Palestine and coastal Syria, the Via Nova Traiana, the former King's Highway which linked the Gulf of 'Aqaba to Damascus, and a west–east route that connected Damascus with the Euphrates via Palmyra. The new roads joined together both big and small settlements, and in the open countryside enabled the growth of many new farmsteads. These afforded a livelihood to large numbers of veterans and other settlers, and added significantly to the provisioning of the region, as well as producing large surpluses of grain and wine for overseas export. So too with the development of these routes of communication, Syria became a major centre for the conveyance of luxury items from the East, from China, India, and Transoxiana, to the western Roman world. For the Roman satirist Juvenal, the Orontes river, with its distinct whiff of Oriental decadence, was the symbol of all this eastern exotica that was polluting the Roman way of life. 'The dregs of Orontes have (now) been flushed into Father Tiber', he laments.[4]

Enter the Parthians

Pompey's establishment of Syria as a Roman province marked the final stage in his mission to sort out the affairs of the Near Eastern world, a mission intended primarily to consolidate and protect Roman interests in the region. On his return to Rome, he was awarded a splendid triumph for his achievement. The move into Syria had been a natural extension of Rome's Asia Minor interests. But Rome could not stop there. Inevitably, it was drawn further and further eastwards as it sought effective buffers against enemies and potential enemies who threatened its frontiers. That raised a big question. Just how far east should Rome go? Where should it set its frontiers? After Pompey's settlement, much of the region commonly identified as Syria in its broadest sense (see p. 5) still lay outside Roman control, as also the neighbouring land now called Transjordan, where the Nabataean kingdom held sway. Besides, it was only in the north-east that the Roman province reached the Euphrates river. A great deal of non-Roman territory lay between the river and the province's eastern boundaries. How long would Rome be content to stay within these boundaries, following the momentum generated by Pompey's successes? How long would it allow the wealthy Nabataean kingdom to remain independent—merely as a client kingdom? There was also a major defence consideration, involving Rome's most formidable potential enemy in the east—the kingdom of Parthia.

Parthia and Rome were now, effectively, neighbours with only the Euphrates and an expanse of desert separating them. But the East was big enough for both. There was ample scope for them to reach a peaceful settlement on how far each could extend its territories without intruding upon the other. Even so, their relationship was marked by intermittent conflicts until the fall of the Parthian dynasty almost three centuries later (AD 224). Not that it started out that way. Indeed, Rome's first official contact with Parthia, which took place in 96 between Sulla, the Roman governor in Cilicia, and the Parthian king Mithridates II (not to be confused with any of the Pontic kings so named), paved the way for ongoing diplomatic relations between the two powers. The relationship never developed to the point where an actual alliance was formed. But for the time being it remained a relatively positive one. In 66, two other major rulers in the region, Mithridates VI of Pontus and Tigranes II of Armenia, became embroiled in conflict with Rome and sought support from the current Parthian ruler Phraates III. Phraates refused, not because he favoured Rome, but simply because he had no intention of taking sides with any of the protagonists. So too he rejected overtures by the Roman commanders Lucullus and (subsequently)

Pompey. Phraates wanted no alliance with Rome. He wanted no quarrel with it either.

But the Parthians had little choice in the matter when the Roman commander Marcus Crassus, appointed governor of Syria in 53, used his position to provoke a war with them. He probably did so in the hope of winning military honours (by taking possession of Mesopotamia, or at least the northern part of it) prestigious enough to rank him as a war-leader alongside his former political colleagues, Caesar and Pompey. Parthia was at that time ruled by a king called Orodes II. The showdown came at Carrhae (formerly Harran) in north-western Mesopotamia. On the site of what became one of the most infamous events in Roman history, Crassus' 35,000-strong army was outmanoeuvred and routed by a contingent of 10,000 Parthian cavalry and mounted archers. In abject humiliation, the survivors of the disaster forced their commander to surrender and give up their prized military standards. Soon after, Crassus was killed in an altercation with a Parthian officer.[5] One final indignity awaited him. The story goes that the Armenian king Artavasdes, erstwhile enemy of the Parthians and supporter of Rome, was visiting Orodes after the battle to draw up with him an anti-Roman alliance. During his stay at the Parthian court, Orodes entertained him with a performance of Euripides' play *Bacchae*. A real human head was used as a stage prop in this performance. It belonged to Crassus.[6]

The Parthian victory at Carrhae had potentially serious, more far-reaching consequences for Rome's developing influence and interests in the Near Eastern world. At particular threat was the newly established province of Syria. Two years after Carrhae, in 51 BC, the Parthian king sent his son Pakores (Pacorus) to occupy it. Which he did, but only briefly before being driven out by the Roman commander Cassius (the later tyrannicide). Orodes also sought to destabilize the province and threaten the Roman presence in the entire region by encouraging the local rulers to declare their opposition to Rome. Similar encouragement was given to the territories established as Rome's client kingdoms, like Commagene, which bordered Syria to the north, and Judaea (or what was left of Judaea after Pompey's reorganization and dismemberment of it), which lay to its south. Orodes may also have made overtures to the Nabataeans, as well as to Palmyra, the desert city located between Damascus and the Euphrates. But the Parthian's ambitions west of the Euphrates were soon to receive a much greater boost—from Rome itself.

In the year 44 BC, Julius Caesar was assassinated, and Rome was plunged into yet another civil war.[7] Inevitably, Syria and Rome's other eastern pos-sesssions were drawn into the conflict, particularly when the assassins Brutus and Cassius sought to win Orodes over to their cause.[8] In the winter of 43/2, Cassius sent a representative, Labienus, to Parthia to try to secure Parthian support against the assassins' opponents, the triumviral gang of Antony, Octavian, and Lepidus. Orodes' response was positive. But he had his own agenda; he was only too willing to exploit the war's divisive impact on Rome's military power, and the opportunity it provided for him to launch an invasion, once more, into Roman territory across the Euphrates. His best chance came with news that the assassins' forces had been destroyed by Antony and Octavian in 42 at Philippi in northern Greece.

Their debacle had left Labienus high and dry in Parthia. But Orodes had a further use for him. Aware that his position was no longer tenable in Rome, and confident that he would remain firmly attached to Parthia, Orodes appointed him joint commander, along with his (Orodes') son Pakores, of an expedition across the Euphrates with the prime object of conquering Syria, and holding on to it. The enterprise was conspicuously successful. The Syrian governor Lucius Decidius Saxa, Mark Antony's appointee, was defeated and killed by the invaders. Many of the Roman troops stationed in Syria had served under Brutus and Cassius, and now swung their support behind Labienus, enabling him with Pakores, his partner-in-arms, to win control in 40 BC over the entire Syrian province, except for a few coastal cities. Palestine, still under the control of Hyrcanus II, also fell to Pakores. The High Priest was replaced by his nephew Antigonus, Orodes' protégé, who added to his uncle's misfortunes by cutting his ears off—to ensure that he would never become High Priest again.[9] Labienus followed up his success in Syria with further campaigns in Asia Minor. They resulted in Rome's loss of control over much of the region to the Parthians—thanks largely to Labienus, once the representative of the tyran-nicides, now the agent of the Parthian king.

Antony's abortive eastern ventures

It is at this point that Mark Antony enters the eastern scene in person. With the defeat of the tyrannicides at Philippi, the Roman world rapidly divided once more, this time between the forces of the victors at Philippi, Antony and Octavian. Antony set his sights on regaining the lost eastern provinces

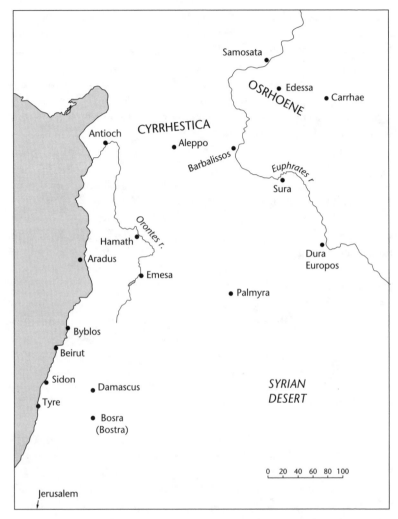

Map 11. Syrian and north-western Mesopotamian cities in the Roman imperial period

at the earliest opportunity. An army which he despatched to Asia Minor under the command of one Ventidius forced the retreat of Labienus from the region, captured the renegade in the process, and re-established Roman control over Asia Minor. Subsequently, Ventidius confronted and defeated the army of Pakores, the two sides clashing in a region of northern Syria called Cyrrhestica, which lay between the plain of Antioch and the Euphrates (38 BC). Pakores himself was lured into a trap set for him by Ventidius and killed. The Roman victory resulted in the expulsion of the Parthians from Syria, and effectively paved the way for Antony's arrival there. Ventidius returned to Rome in triumph—and was awarded one for services rendered in the East. Among other things, he was seen to have avenged the ghost of Crassus—though the Roman standards captured in the Carrhae debacle had yet to be recovered.[10]

The restoration of Roman control over Syria was followed up by action against the kingdom of Judaea. Its throne was at that time occupied by Antigonus (40–37 BC), the Parthian-appointed successor of Hyrcanus II. Now that Syria was back under its authority, Rome's next step was to get rid of Antigonus. The Senate appointed one of his ministers, a twenty-five-year-old youth called Herod, as king of the Jews (he had won the favour of both Antony and Octavian on a visit to Rome in 40 BC). There was but one proviso. Herod had to give substance to his title himself, by capturing Jerusalem from Antigonus in order to assume the throne of Judaea. This he succeeded in doing, with the support of one of Antony's lieutenants.[11] At Herod's request, Antigonus was executed by the Romans. But Herod retained his links with the Hasmonean family by marrying Mariamne, granddaughter of Hyrcanus (she was but one of Herod's ten wives). Henceforth, from 37 until his death in 4 BC, Herod retained his throne as King of the Jews, a reign which was distinguished as much by its flamboyance as by the king's unswerving loyalty to his Roman overlords.[12]

With affairs in Syria and Palestine now satisfactorily settled, Antony turned his attention further eastwards, for a final reckoning with Parthia.[13] In 36 BC, he set out for the Iranian kingdom with a 70,000-strong army, made up of cavalry and light infantry. One of the reasons for moving against Rome's arch-enemy at this time was news that in Parthia a new king, Phraates IV, had replaced his long-reigning father Orodes II, and that the kingdom had suffered some degree of destabilization with the change of regime. Orodes appears to have freely abdicated his throne in favour of his son. But Phraates had him murdered all the same, just in case he changed his mind. Phraates also executed his thirty brothers, his eldest son, and a number of Parthia's leading families, to make his kingship even more secure. The situation was ripe for exploiting, so Antony believed. Reinforced by 13,000 troops from the Armenian king Artavasdes through whose territory he passed on his campaign route, and another 17,000 troops from Rome's other

client kingdoms, he was ready for all-out war with Parthia. (Artavasdes fluc-
tuated between Parthia and Rome in his loyalties, but as Antony's army
approached his kingdom, he thought it best to throw in his lot with the
Romans.) Penetrating deep into enemy territory, Antony laid siege to the
royal Parthian city Phraaspa in Media Atropatene (modern Azerbaijan).

Here things began to go horribly wrong. The strong fortifications of the
city easily resisted Antony's attempts to breach them, partly because the
Romans were without their 300 waggonloads of siege equipment and weapons. Antony had decided to proceed ahead of the siege train, thus leaving it
exposed to enemy attack and seizure by a Parthian detachment as it was
travelling through Armenia. Further, a Parthian attack on the rear of Antony's
troops destroyed two of his legions, leaving the Roman commander with no
choice but to abandon the siege and retreat with the rest of his army back
through Atropatene and Armenia in harsh winter conditions. Antony lost
some 22,000 troops in the process. There was also a score to settle with
Artavasdes. The Armenian king had apparently deserted the Romans as the
tide turned against them and was held responsible by Antony for the loss of
his siege train. But revenge would have to wait. For the moment, it was all
Antony could do to secure Artavasdes' cooperation in getting his troops out
of Armenia. Funds sent to him by his Ptolemaic paramour Cleopatra (the
seventh, last, and most famous of that name) enabled him to pay off his army
and join her in Alexandria.

In a bid to salvage Roman honour, and most importantly his own, and
eager to claim some success in the region he had been forced to abandon,
Antony resumed operations in the north-east two years later, in 34, beginning with Armenia. He achieved some measure of satisfaction from this new
enterprise, by overrunning and annexing Armenia, deposing Artavasdes and
taking him prisoner along with his family. This was in retaliation for what
he saw as Artavasdes' betrayal of him two years before. Artavasdes and his
family were packed off to the tender mercies of Cleopatra in Egypt, where
the king, his wife, and two of his sons were tortured and executed. In the
following year, Antony once more marched eastwards, to Media Atropatene,
heartened no doubt by news that the country's vassal ruler, formerly an ally
of Phraates, had turned against him. With Armenia firmly under his control
and Media Atropatene on his side, the time now seemed opportune for
Antony to mount a successful invasion of the Parthian heartland.

But he got no further than Atropatene's borders. Disturbing reports had
reached him of developments in the west—above all, the looming conflict

with Octavian—and he was forced to cut short his campaign and return home. His new northern venture had thus achieved virtually nothing. But that did not stop him from celebrating a military triumph in Alexandria for his victory over Armenia. With Cleopatra, he now divided up virtually the whole of the Near Eastern world among their three children. These apportionments were the so-called 'Donations of Alexandria'. They included Roman provinces and the lands of both foreign and client kings—Armenia, Parthia, Media, Syria, and Cilicia, along with Cyrenaica and Libya in Africa. But before any of these arrangements could be put into effect, Antony's and Cleopatra's forces met Octavian's in a final naval battle, in 31 BC, at Actium on the coast of mainland Greece. The engagement ended in Octavian's decisive victory, and shortly after, the losers' deaths by their own hands. With Cleopatra's suicide, the long line of Ptolemaic rulers, which began with the accession of Ptolemy I in 305, was at an end.

27 BC–early 1st century AD

Augustus' dealings with the East

In 27 BC, Octavian was formally acknowledged, under the name Augustus, as the supreme ruler of the Roman world. He was in effect Rome's first emperor, though the actual title he assumed was deliberately a much less imposing one—*princeps*, meaning 'first citizen'. One of the important matters with which he had to deal on assuming imperial authority was Rome's unfinished business with Armenia and Parthia. Antony's removal of the Armenian king Artavasdes had provoked a backlash against Rome. For Artavasdes' son Artaxias now seized the Armenian throne (which Antony had reserved for Cleopatra's son) and massacred all the Romans in his kingdom. And revenge against Parthia for the Carrhae disaster was still high on Rome's list of priorities. But Augustus bided his time. Armenia and Parthia could be kept on hold until a suitable opportunity arose for action.

That came in 20 BC. Taking advantage of political instability in Armenia and attempts by rival factions to secure its throne, Augustus sent his stepson Tiberius there, with instructions to install Rome's preferred candidate, Tigranes III (who up till then had lived many years in Rome), in the kingship in place of his brother Artaxias; the latter was disposed of by assassination. From Armenia, Tiberius was well placed to mount an invasion of Parthia and thus avenge, finally, the Carrhae debacle thirty-three years earlier. But conquest proved unnnecessary, for the Parthian king Phraates IV had no wish to take on the Romans at this time, distracted as he was by a war with a pretender to his throne. Negotiations conducted between Tiberius, on his stepfather's behalf, and Phraates resulted in all Roman prisoners held in Parthian custody being handed over to Tiberius. Most importantly, the Roman standards captured at Carrhae were returned, together with those seized from Antony during his abortive Parthian campaign in 36. This act of peace was regarded, at least at the time, as an event of the greatest significance. Rome had now reached an accord with its most powerful and most dangerous enemy in the East. Twenty-one years later, in 1 AD, the peace was formalized by a ceremony on a small island in the Euphrates.[14] The participants in this ceremony were a Roman delegation led by Gaius Caesar, grandson of Augustus, and a Parthian one led by the Parthian king himself, Phraates V, son, murderer, and successor of Antony's opponent Phraates IV. The armies of both parties kept watch over the proceedings from opposite river-banks, no doubt ready to intervene at the slightest hint of treachery by the other side. But everything went smoothly. The Euphrates now became the official boundary between the two empires.[15]

With this Augustus was satisfied. He could claim the 'conquest' of Armenia and the resolution of the Parthian affair by diplomatic means. His dealings with Armenia (whose loyalties continued to fluctuate) and Parthia fell well short of a more permanent and robust solution to the problems Rome faced in the east. But in the short term the emperor had consolidated Rome's hold on its eastern territories with relatively little military effort or cost, and could genuinely claim to have begun an era of peace in a region which had for centuries been wracked by constant warfare both within and between the kingdoms and city-states of their ages. This had applied most recently to Syria, which had been drawn into the contest between Octavian and Antony in the last phase of Rome's civil wars. Syria now became one of Rome's most important provinces, governed in the emperor's name by the emperor's own appointee. And by an incremental process, Rome extended its rule over a number of Syrian cities and small principalities that had hitherto enjoyed a largely autonomous status. City-states like Emesa on the Orontes and the island-state of Aradus (which we earlier met as Bronze and Iron Age Arwad) now came directly under Roman administration. Overall, the Augustan period was one of peace, stability, and consolidation. Augustan policy determined that there would be no further territorial expansion—and indeed there was none of any significance until the reign of Trajan, early in the 2nd century. In the intervening years, Rome generally remained on peaceful terms with its eastern neighbours, though Armenia remained problematic, and the peace with Parthia was at best spasmodic.

This brings us to one of the most difficult problems the Romans faced in the east: the establishment of frontiers that were practicable to defend.

1st century AD

Rome strengthens its grasp

The province of Syria as created by Pompey stretched to the Euphrates in the north-east, and Augustus had reached agreement with the Parthians that the Euphrates would mark the boundary between their empires. That was all very well. But as the Classicist Richard Stoneman comments: 'Rome never felt safe with an armed nation directly on its frontiers. Instead they produced what Freya Stark has called the policy of the "weak periphery", the "theory that only the sea or an unarmed nation must exist on her borders." To achieve this, Rome had a policy of establishing client kingdoms, or in the now preferred terminology, "friendly kings". Rather than garrison a volatile border, Rome relied on the use of buffer states under kings who could be relied on to favour Roman interests.'[16] During the 1st century AD, however, a number of the client kingdoms and semi-autonomous states were converted or absorbed into Roman provinces. And the following two centuries witnessed a series of extensions of the Romans' direct rule in the Near East.

The process began effectively in the region of Judaea, to Syria's south. After Herod's son and successor Archelaus fell out of favour with Augustus and was deposed and banished by him in AD 6, Judaea was made into a separate Roman province. But relations between the Roman authorities and the predominantly Jewish population of the region were often fraught with tension, over a range of issues of both a religious and a secular nature. Matters came to a head in the year 66 when the Jews broke out in rebellion against their overlords, beginning the so-called Great Jewish Revolt or First Jewish War.[17] The local Roman military garrison was taken completely by surprise by the uprising, and forced to flee from Jerusalem. With them went the Roman officials stationed in the city, and the local king Agrippa II, last of the Herodian line of rulers; Agrippa had failed to stop the revolt and now openly declared his support for Rome. Things went from bad to worse for the Romans when an army led against the rebels by Syria's governor Cestius Gallus was ambushed and defeated in a battle at Beth-Horon, which lay north-west of Jerusalem.

A much more determined effort was needed to restore Judaea to Roman control, and at the same time to provide the rest of the region with an object lesson in the consequences of defying Roman authority. The battle-hardened commander Vespasian was assigned the task, at the head of four Roman legions. He began by invading the Galilee region, and from there marched to Jerusalem, crushing all rebel resistance as he proceeded. But Jerusalem itself had a temporary reprieve when severe political turmoil back in Rome led to the suspension of operations in the east—turmoil resulting from the assassination of the emperor Nero in 68. From the notorious 'year of the four emperors' that followed, Vespasian emerged victorious, winning widespread support for himself as the new emperor and returning to Rome the following year. The unfinished Jewish business he assigned to his son Titus, who fulfilled his commission with alacrity. Jerusalem was placed under siege, captured, and destroyed two years after Nero's assassination. During the sack of the city, the great temple was stripped of all its possessions and reduced to ruins. Thus ended the Second Temple period.

Figure 20. The plunder of Jerusalem, Arch of Titus, Rome

The rape of city and temple can still be seen, graphically illustrated on Titus' celebratory arch (erected by his brother and successor Domitian) to the south-east of the forum in Rome.

Much of our information about the Jewish War comes to us from the pen of the historian Josephus, a Jewish soldier and statesman who witnessed the fall of the Judaean capital, and subsequently became a firm friend of Vespasian and his family.[18] The Judaean king Agrippa, who had supported Vespasian and Titus in their war with his fellow-countrymen, was restored by the Romans to his throne after Titus' victory. But he subsequently went to Rome, where he lived under imperial patronage until his death around 93.

In the aftermath of the Jewish episode, Vespasian set about further changes in the east.[19] In 72, Commagene was incorporated into the province of Syria, thus extending Syria's north-eastern border along the Euphrates from Sura northwards to above Samosata. Further to the north, Lesser Armenia[20] and with it Cappadocia (which had been annexed under the emperor Tiberius in AD 17) were placed under the authority of the governor of Galatia. The result of these extensions was that direct Roman authority now reached the northernmost limits of the Upper Euphrates, along its right bank, and beyond it the south-eastern shores of the Black Sea. Later, in 106, Trajan annexed the Nabataean kingdom and converted it into the province of Arabia, with Bosra (now Nova Trajana Bostra) as its capital.[21] Then, sometime between 107 and 113, he established the new province of Cappadocia with Pontus, a union which lasted until the reign of Diocletian at the end of the following century.[22]

But the emperor remained uneasy about his Euphrates frontier. To be sure, by incorporating the territories west of the Euphrates into provinces, Rome had achieved greater authority over the region than it had through the client kingdom system. But the Euphrates was an easily fordable river, and certainly not in itself an effective line of defence against invasion by enemy powers to the east of it. Of considerable strategic importance in this respect was the kingdom of Greater Armenia, which extended east of the Euphrates to the Caspian Sea, where it shared a frontier with Media Atropatene and bordered upon Parthia. It became the subject of what has been called a tug-of-war between Rome and Parthia, and 'generally managed to maintain a balance, remaining Parthian in sympathy while professing friendship to Rome'.[23] That the kingdom would at least remain benevolently neutral, and thus serve as a buffer for Roman territory against Parthian attack, was no doubt Rome's fond hope. But its loyalties were unpredictable. At any time, it might well take sides with Parthia, either voluntarily, if this served its own interests, or compulsorily, if Parthia sought once more to invade the territories west of the Euphrates that were now part of the Roman world.

2nd century AD

Trajan strikes east [24]

Trajan decided that a more aggressive policy was called for. Particularly after Greater Armenia's throne had been seized in 113 by a member of the Parthian royal family. The following year, he took action. Setting aside the policy of Augustus, which established the Euphrates as the limit of Roman rule, he led his forces across the river into Armenia, where he deposed the Parthian interloper and proclaimed Armenia a Roman province. Over the next two years, the emperor's campaigns carried Roman arms through northern Mesopotamia, now also declared a Roman province, to the Tigris. To begin with at least, the main objective of these campaigns may have been to ensure Roman control over the Euphrates region by establishing an extensive buffer zone beyond it. But Trajan's eastwards progress took him deep into Parthian territory, and finally to the city of Ctesiphon on the Tigris, winter capital of the Parthian king Chosroes. His operations against the Parthians were no longer merely pre-emptive, if indeed they ever had been. At the approach of the Roman army, Chosroes fled his capital, leaving the invader as master of his kingdom. The emperor installed Chosroes' son on his father's throne, as Rome's puppet.

In military terms, Trajan's trans-Euphrates enterprises may be accounted spectacularly successful, and the emperor marked their completion with a triumphal voyage down the Tigris to the Persian Gulf. It was all very grand, but very short-lived. For by his eastern campaigns (115–16) Trajan had stretched Rome's resources too far. News of uprisings in the recently captured territories and a major rebellion in Judaea, along with security concerns about other frontier regions of the empire, forced the emperor to turn back. We are told that shortly after he began his return journey, he visited the ruins of Babylon; here, allegedly in the very room where Alexander the Great died, the emperor offered sacrifice to the dead man's memory. Like his famous predecessor, Trajan had been forced to abandon his great enterprise while there were yet more lands to conquer. At least in his opinion. In fact, the conquests he did achieve had no lasting consequences—in the short term. His successor Hadrian (117–38) relinquished all the trans-Euphrates territories over which he had claimed control, and brought the Roman frontier back to the river.

What really prompted Trajan's trans-Euphrates military operations? Cassius Dio believed that the emperor was motivated primarily by a desire to win great military renown for himself, particularly in emulation of Alexander; his ventures were by and large exercises in self-aggrandizement.[25] Of course, even if this were true, Trajan could be accused of doing no more than upholding a tradition of royal ideology that went back through the Hellenistic and Iron Age monarchies to the Near East's Bronze Age rulers. To be a Great King one had to prove oneself a great warrior, matching and even surpassing the achievements of one's predecessors. There may well have been something of this in Trajan. But it would be unfair to charge him with making it the sole, or indeed the overriding, motive for his campaigns. Commercial and economic considerations very likely figured large in his thinking as he planned the campaigns. The acquisition of control over important trade-routes from the Far East may well have been among the emperor's chief objectives. Along these routes many valuable commodities and other trade-items passed westwards, including a wide range of the exotic goods destined for the Roman world.

But almost certainly the emperor's prime motive for his enterprises beyond the Euphrates was a strategic one, to do with his concerns about the weakness and porosity of Rome's eastern frontier. South of the small stretch of Roman territory along the Euphrates which marked the north-eastern border of the province of Syria, the rest of Rome's Syrian possessions were separated from the river by a large expanse of desert. It was extremely difficult, indeed virtually impossible, to patrol the entire region on the west side of the Euphrates. To ensure its security, Trajan believed that Rome needed substantial buffer territory beyond the river, and to acquire this meant invading Mesopotamia and reopening hostilities with Parthia. Yet as Stoneman points out, 'The area was too great to be successfully consolidated with existing manpower, and Rome did not hold it long. Even with Roman garrisons present, Parthian troops could move to the Euphrates much more easily than Rome could march to it eastward across hostile desert.'[26]

None the less, Trajan's eastern enterprises had a number of significant consequences, some of which were only to become evident in later years. His successor Hadrian pulled the Roman frontier back to the Euphrates.

But despite this, Trajan had created an important, long-term precedent. The Euphrates would no longer be considered the ultimate territorial limit of Rome's power. Trajan had demonstrated that a Roman army could success-fully campaign well beyond it, at least as far as the western borders of Iran, and defeat the Parthians on their own territory. Later emperors would be inspired by this precedent and follow in his footsteps. Further, Trajan's reign marked the beginning of a re-orientation of the Roman world, politically, culturally, and commercially. Rome would remain the chief focus of this world for many decades to come. But Antioch became a major secondary focus, and on occasions a primary one, the first occasion when Trajan resided there for a period of three years. During that time Antioch was in effect the empire's administrative capital. Later on, a number of emperors and pre-tenders laid claim to the imperial title in the city, reinforcing its de facto status as the empire's alternative capital. 'The eventual transformation of Rome into an oriental empire had begun.'[27]

Hadrian's re-establishment of the Roman frontier along the Euphrates meant that Syria again became vulnerable to enemy incursions from the east. The development of a road system to ensure, among other things, rapid movement of reinforcements to areas threatened by attack, and the con-struction of a number of fortresses in the frontier region, eventually pro-vided the province with reasonable defence against enemies from the east. On the frontier itself, built on a rock plateau on the west bank of the Euphrates, the fortress-city Dura Europos played an important part in Rome's eastern defence system, but only from the mid 2nd century AD when it came under Roman control.[28] Founded *c.*300 BC as a military col-ony by the Seleucid king Seleucus I, it enjoyed a semi-independent status for most of its existence under a loose form of Parthian overlordship. It had for a brief time become subject to Rome during Trajan's reign, in 116, in the context of the emperor's eastern campaigns. But shortly after his death it reverted to Parthian sovereignty, coming once more under Roman control in 165, during the reign of Marcus Aurelius. We shall have more to say about it in Chapter 16.

The Jews in revolt once more

Before moving on to the next part of our story, we should mention another important episode in Jewish history. This one, belonging to Hadrian's reign, reflects rather less well on the emperor than many of his other actions and policies. To provide context, we need to go back to the final years of his predecessor. During Trajan's last three years on the throne (115–17), the flame of Jewish rebellion had once more been ignited when Jewish communities in Mesopotamia set about massacring the garrisons which Trajan had stationed there in the course of his trans-Euphrates campaigns. One of the main triggers for the uprisings was, almost certainly, the fear that traditional Jewish practices and beliefs were being forcibly replaced by western ones. From Mesopotamia the rebellion had spread to communities elsewhere in the Jewish diaspora, notably at Alexandria in Egypt, Cyrenaica in Libya, and on the island of Cyprus. Trajan's lieutenants had brutally suppressed the uprisings, but only after the rebels had slaughtered large numbers of gentiles.

Trajan had died shortly after. A new regime brought the Jews new hope. And indeed, soon after his accession, Hadrian had sought to assure those who lived in Alexandria that their traditions would be fully respected and preserved. But Hadrian was a man with a mission—to confer, and if necessary to impose, the benefits of Roman civilization upon the eastern world that lay within Rome's sway. And he gave demonstration of this in 131 when he established on the site of Jerusalem a new Roman colony called Aelia Capitolina. Within it, he ordered the construction of a temple to Jupiter Capitolinus—on the site where the revered Second Temple of Jerusalem had stood (before the Romans had destroyed it six decades earlier). This blatant act of cultural and ethnic insensitivity[29] had predictable consequences. Under the leadership of a messiah-like figure called Bar Kochba, 'Son of the Star', the Palestinian Jews (to whom the uprising seems to have been confined) rose up in revolt.[30] For almost four years (131–4), their conflict with Rome continued—and not without its successes for the rebels. For a time an independent Jewish state was established. For a time, the rebels took their toll on the Romans in a series of sieges and small sorties. But it could not last. Under the command of a man called Gaius Iulius Severus, brought especially from Britain to lead the operation, Rome's forces reduced the rebel communities one by one, often starving them into submission, until the whole of Judaea had been subjected once more to the Roman yoke. The Romans themselves suffered heavy casualties as they fought to restore order. And this no doubt intensifed the savagery of their reprisals, which were comprehensive and devastating. Judaea's towns and villages were systematically put to the torch, and thousands of their inhabitants massacred or enslaved. Their places were taken by large influxes of non-Jewish

peoples imported from neighbouring lands.[31] The very identity of the Jews'
homeland was now to be obliterated. The land once called Judaea was given
a new name: Syria Palestina. Those of the Jewish population who survived
were henceforth forbidden to set foot in their sacred city, under pain of
death. Bereft of their identity, forbidden to practise their ancestral customs,
the Jews faced continuing decline, if not extinction.

But their fortunes took a turn for the better in the reign of Hadrian's
successor Antoninus Pius. Antoninus allowed the persecuted people to
revive and maintain their religious beliefs and customs and to practise their
traditional forms of worship. 'A *modus vivendi* between Jews and Romans
was at last established, and the Jews, though henceforth a stateless and home-
less people, were unimpeded in the exercise of their religion—a concession
that enabled them to maintain themselves as a separate nation.'[32]

14

Nabataean Excursus

The Nabataeans are a sensible people, and are so much inclined to acquire possessions that they publicly fine anyone who has diminished his possessions and also confer honours on anyone who has increased them.

(Strabo 16.4.26)

Especially 2nd century BC–2nd century AD

In the period when the rulers of the Persian Achaemenid empire dominated the Near Eastern world, from Central Asia in the east to the Aegean coast of Anatolia in the west, large groups of nomadic herdsmen and merchants from the deserts of north-eastern Arabia began moving into the semi-arid regions of Syria and the Levant. Some of the Arab wanderers finally settled in southern Jordan, in what was once the homeland of the Edomite and Moabite peoples.[1] The Nabataeans, as they were called, achieved fame and wealth during the Hellenistic and Roman periods as one of the great trading peoples of the Near East. At its peak, the kingdom which they built controlled an extensive span of territories, stretching from southern Syria and Transjordan in the north to the peninsula of Sinai in the south. Continuing links with their original homeland in Arabia gave the Nabataeans access to the Persian Gulf, and to the regions lying beyond— indeed as far beyond as Han Dynasty China. Rose-red Petra, an 'exceedingly well governed city' according to Strabo,[2] became the chief base of their international trading operations.[3]

Petra was the hub of routes which led in many directions from the city and on which many Nabataean settlements were established, throughout Edom and Moab and extending to Bosra, the second great Nabataean city, and to Damascus, captured by the Nabataeans in the 1st century BC.[4]

From Damascus, Nabataean merchandise was transported to the Mediterranean coast, for transhipment to lands across the Mediterranean. Like Palmyra (as we shall see), the Nabataean kingdom had its own military forces, which no doubt it used, as Palmyra did, both to protect its stations along its trading routes and to defend its homeland cities. Petra served as a processing and repackaging centre for many of the raw products acquired by the Nabataeans in their trading enterprises. Here oils and balms and incenses were converted into medicinal and cosmetic products before they were sold on to the Nabataeans' international customers. Beginning with a highly profitable trade in frankincense and myrrh, acquired from Arabia, the Nabataeans rapidly diversified their merchandise into a wide range of exotic and luxury products—spices and incenses of many kinds, ivory, sugar, a glittering array of precious and semi-precious gems, and a curious assortment of strange creatures from far-off lands. There was a never-ending supply of buyers for everything on offer, especially among wealthy clientele in the Greek and Roman as well as the Near Eastern worlds.

Scholars have generally concluded that the Nabataeans' spoken language was a form of Arabic. But from their inscriptions, it is clear that they used Aramaic for their written language—understandably so, since Aramaic was the international lingua franca of the day.[5] Some 4,000 Nabataean inscriptions, in Aramaic, have been discovered, widely distributed throughout the Mediterranean region as well as parts of the Near Eastern world.[6] Combined with literary sources, the inscriptions enable us to reconstruct a virtually complete list of Nabataean kings, beginning with Aretas I, who apparently founded the royal line about 170 BC, and ending with the reign of Rabbel II (70–106), whose death provided the emperor Trajan with the opportunity of absorbing the Nabataean kingdom into his newly created province Arabia.

Throughout the Roman period, up to this point, the Nabataean kingdom had enjoyed a fair degree of autonomy from Rome, as did its commercial 'twin' Palmyra. In the years following Pompey's creation of the province of Syria in 64 BC, Nabataea was brought within the Roman fold by becoming a Roman client state, which effectively left it free to manage its own political and economic affairs, while acknowledging Rome as its overlord. It was an arrangement that must have suited both Rome and Nabataea, and perhaps gave the latter some guarantee of protection, if such were needed, from the Parthian Empire which loomed large across the Euphrates. Relations between the kingdom and Rome remained close during the first century of the Roman empire, and indeed it is said that Nabataea reached its peak in the empire's early decades when its throne was occupied by a fourth king called Aretas (9 BC–AD 40). A number of the trappings of Greek (more precisely Hellenistic) and Roman culture were adopted by the Nabataean kings.

Petra and Bosra

Let us say a few more words about Petra. Its name is in itself highly evocative, for it immediately brings to mind one of the world's most spectacular ancient monuments—the Khazneh. Commonly known as the 'Treasury', this splendid two-storeyed Corinthian-columned façade cut from the living rock bursts suddenly upon us as we pass through the city's traditional entrance, a narrow rock cleft called the Siq. The structure was probably created by the Nabataean king Aretas IV in the early 1st century AD. But its nature and purpose remain a mystery. All we can be sure of is that it is not a treasure house of the Nabataean kings, as its common nickname might lead us to believe. Perhaps it is a temple, dedicated to an unidentified god or gods—at least that is what some scholars suggest. Others think that it is a tomb, built on a very grand scale. But this is simply guesswork. For all its fame, we do not know what the 'Treasury' actually was. Nor is it the city's only puzzling feature. Petra's other remains have also generated much debate about their nature and purpose. In many respects, Petra is an enigma. But that is something else we must leave for discussion in another place at another time.

Located some 80 km south of the Dead Sea, in a basin called in Arabic the Wadi Musa ('Valley of Moses'), Petra was, according to Arab tradition, the place where Moses struck a rock and water gushed forth. Here too, in Arab tradition, Moses' brother Aaron was buried. Petra is a Greek name meaning 'rock'. Diodorus informs us that the name came from a particular rock where the Nabataeans took refuge when Antigonus the One-Eyed attacked their settlement in 312 BC.[7] Josephus tells us that in their own language the Nabataeans called their city Rekem, after its alleged founder.[8] The native name is confirmed by a Nabataean inscription in which the city is called Raqmu. Though there are traces of earlier sporadic occupation, Petra was not properly settled, to judge from archaeological evidence, until the early Hellenistic period. This means it must have been a very young

Figure 21. Petra, the Khazneh (commonly known as the 'Treasury')

settlement when Antigonus attacked it—but wealthy enough even then to attract the Macedonian predator's attention.

The site offered several obvious natural advantages, sufficient to induce a group of semi-nomadic Arab desert merchants to establish their chief city there. The 'Valley of Moses' lies in the midst of towering mountain ridges, rising to the east and the west of it. These provided its inhabitants with excellent natural fortifications, later supplemented by built walls which protected the city from access by enemies who sought to invade it from the north or the south. But of crucial importance to the establishment and continuation of the settlement was an abundant natural supply of water, which came from two perennial springs. Excavations have demonstrated that the Nabataeans at Petra developed a high level of skills in managing the local water resources, by building a system of dams, cisterns, and channels which enabled them to control their water supply in times of flooding and to conserve it in times of drought. Their hydrological skills were above all a key to Petra's success as the centre of a great desert kingdom and a highly prosperous focus of Near Eastern trade. It became in effect a man-made oasis city—like Palmyra. And strategically, it was well located at the hub of major international trade routes that passed through the desert from the Persian Gulf in the east to Gaza on the southern coast of Palestine in the west, and from Bosra and Damascus in the north to the Gulf of 'Aqaba and the Red Sea in the south.

Politically and commercially, Petra remained the dominant centre of the Nabataean civilization throughout the Hellenistic period, and for 170 years during the period of Roman overlordship throughout the region. Then in 106, Trajan established the Province of Arabia and made Bosra its capital. Whatever the reasons for this development, the effect of it was to shift both the political and the commercial centre of gravity of the Nabataean world northwards, to Bosra, called Bostra by the Romans (probably simply for ease of pronunciation).[9] But henceforth the major beneficiary of this development was the kingdom of Palmyra, 235 km north-east of Damascus, on a new major route which connected the Euphrates with the ports of north-western Syria, Antioch in particular. With this greater focus on Antioch, now effectively the third city of the Roman empire, it is understandable that the major commercial routes from which Rome gained much advantage should be shifted well north of Petra. Thanks to the new importance bestowed upon Bosra by the Romans, particularly Trajan, who renamed the city Nova Trajana Bostra, the new Nabataean capital developed as an impressive urban centre from the early 2nd century AD onwards. A Roman legion was stationed here, the Third Legion Cyrenaica, and the city replaced Petra as the hub of a southern network of roads. The most notable of these was the famous Via Nova Traiana, a great highway, probably built shortly after AD 106, made secure by Roman forts dotted along it, which connected Damascus with the Gulf of ʿAqaba.

15

The Syrian Emperors[1]

Get along with each other, enrich the troops, and disregard everyone else.

(A dying emperor's advice to his sons)

AD 193–211

Septimius Severus becomes emperor

During the second half of the second century, Syria enjoyed increasing prosperity as goods from the east flowed through it to meet the ever-more voracious demands of the markets of the west. The affluence of Syrian society becomes particularly evident in what was effectively a new era in Roman history, the so-called Severan period (AD 193–235). It began with the accession of a man who founded a new royal dynasty and became one of Rome's most distinguished emperors: Lucius Septimius Severus. Septimius had four dynastic successors, all of whom were of Syrian origin. Himself a north African of Phoenician ancestry (he was born in Lepcis Magna in Libya), the new emperor had formerly been governor of Pannonia Superior in the Danube region, where he had emerged the eventual winner in a power struggle for the imperial purple in the year 193. He was proclaimed emperor by his troops at the Danubian settlement Carnuntum on 9 April, twelve days after the assassination of his predecessor-but-one Pertinax, and thereupon proceeded to Rome to demand formal recognition of his status. Sixteen legions stationed in the Rhine and Danube regions were ready to back his demand.

There was a minor complication. A wealthy senator called Didius Julianus had already been proclaimed emperor. The title had been awarded him by the praetorian guard, after they had murdered Pertinax. The assassins followed up their act by holding an auction for the empire's now vacant top job. Didius was the highest bidder—and that is how he came to be emperor. Already occupying the imperial palace in Rome when news came of Septimius' approach, the senator-turned-emperor tried to buy off his rival with the offer of a co-emperorship, and probably a substantial cash payment to go with it. But this time his money didn't work. As Septimius drew ever closer to Rome, the Senate, no doubt quaking in its sandals, deposed and executed Didius. That was on 1 June. Didius' reign had lasted all of nine weeks. Nine days later, Septimius entered Rome unopposed, and was hailed as the new emperor. One of his first acts thereafter was to disband the praetorian guard.[2]

There was a further obstacle to be cleared. The Roman army in Syria had already taken it upon itself to appoint Syria's governor Pescennius Niger to the purple, two months before Septimius' entry into Rome. Once more Antioch, where the declaration was made, appeared to have achieved the status of an imperial capital, providing yet another illustration of what the Roman historian Tacitus was pleased to call 'the secret of empire' (*arcanum imperii*): emperors could be made elsewhere than at Rome. Thus he wrote in his account of the power struggles after Nero's death (AD 68).[3] In the following centuries, the truth of this maxim was to be demonstrated over and over again. Nor was there anything particularly secretive about many of the contests for the imperial purple that erupted throughout the empire in these centuries. On this occasion, Niger had strong support in the east, both from Rome's own subjects, and from foreign rulers including the king of Parthia, who officially recognized him as emperor. He also had the backing of the plebeian elements at Rome.

Buoyed by all this support, he decided to make a bid for the entire empire. Within a brief space of time, he won possession of the whole of Asia Minor and was preparing to cross the Bosporus into Europe when Septimius' forces confronted him, inflicted severe defeats upon his army at Nicaea and Cyzicus in northern Asia Minor, and forced him to abandon all his newly achieved conquests. But he was not quite finished off. There was one more battle to be fought. It took place at Issus, the site just west of the Amanus range made famous by Alexander the Great's victory there over the Persian king Darius in 333 BC. At Issus too, 527 years later, Niger was conclusively defeated.[4] The vanquished emperor managed to escape the field on horseback and get back to Antioch, which he found in a state of deep mourning because of all the battle casualties. Many of its inhabitants were preparing to abandon their city. So the fugitive took to his heels once more. But he got no further than the city's outskirts before Septimius' pursuing cavalry caught up with him, flushed him out of his hiding place, and removed his head from his shoulders.

The new dynasty is established

Septimius introduced a new blood strain into the Roman emperorship. As a young officer, he had served in the Roman army in Syria, and consolidated his ties with the province by marrying the daughter of a high priest of Emesa (modern Homs), a city on the Orontes river. Her name was Julia Domna. The marriage took place in 187, six years before Septimius became emperor. Many have perceived Julia as the real power behind her husband's throne, becoming to Septimius what Livia had been to Augustus, or indeed a latter-day Semiramis.[5] What is beyond doubt is that she became one of the most influential women in Roman history, as a politician, as the progenitor of a line of Syrian kings, and as a pervasive matriarchal presence within her own family. She was in fact the first of three women within the Severan family to exercise a powerful influence over those who actually held the reins of sovereignty. We shall discuss all three below.

Within a few years of his elevation to royal power, Septimius embarked in 197 on the greatest enterprise of his career—the conquest of Parthian-controlled Mesopotamia.[6] Two years earlier, in 195, he had conducted a punitive expedition across the Euphrates. It was directed against the Parthian king Vologeses V for his offer of assistance to Niger (nothing actually came of the offer), and Abgar IX, ruler of the western Mesopotamian kingdom Osrhoene, for renouncing his allegiance to Rome. The expedition resulted in Osrhoene being converted into a Roman province, and Vologeses coming to terms with Septimius in a peace settlement. But Vologeses soon broke the peace and attempted to regain his lost Mesopotamian territories. That was

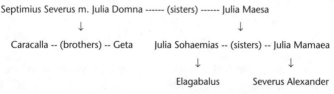

Figure 22. The Severan line of succession

the prompt for Septimius' full-scale invasion of Parthian territory to the banks of the Tigris. In the footsteps of Trajan, he advanced upon, attacked, captured, and sacked the Parthian capital Ctesiphon, securing all the territory of northern Mesopotamia that lay between the two rivers. This time there would be no retreat like the one forced upon Trajan. Mesopotamia would now become a permanent province of Rome, with Nisibis (modern Nusaybin) its capital. It was a significant achievement. By his eastern conquests, the emperor had paved the way for a substantial growth in the spread of Roman civilization through the cities of eastern Syria[7] and across the Euphrates into Mesopotamia. But his time in the East was almost done. Upon completing his administrative arrangements in Syria, he left Antioch, in 202, called in on Egypt, and then returned to Rome. Here he was hailed as Parthicus Maximus, the conqueror of the Parthians, and his achievements celebrated on an arch set up in his honour and still to be seen in the Roman forum. This marked the peak period in the Severan dynasty's history, and indeed the last high period in Roman history until the reign of Diocletian. But Septimius was not immortal. Would later members of his dynasty maintain what he had achieved?

AD 211–217

Alexander redivivus

The emperor died in Eburacum (York) while he was campaigning in Britain in 211, his death due possibly to complications associated with a disease from which he chronically suffered—gout. He had taken his family with him on his campaign, including his two sons. The younger son was called Septimius Geta. The older one, Marcus Aurelius Antoninus, is better known to us by his nickname Caracalla (the name of a long tunic worn by the Gauls). To both of them the dying emperor bequeathed rulership of the Roman world, plus the advice that they should be on good terms with each other, enrich the soldiers, and show contempt for everyone else.[8] Septimius well knew that his sons bitterly hated each other, and he may have taken them with him to Britain in the hope that the rigours of campaigning in the deep north would impose some discipline upon them, and force them to cooperate. But Caracalla had a different and simpler way of resolving his differences with his brother. After their father's death, he had him murdered, and imposed upon him a *damnatio memoriae*, removing all trace of his existence and making it an offence even to speak his name. That was back in

Figure 23. Septimius Severus, Julia Domna, and Caracalla (Geta has been erased); Tondo from Djemila (Algeria), probably AD 199

Rome, where the brothers had returned after their father's death, abandoning their conquests north of Hadrian's wall. Thus Caracalla became sole ruler of the Roman world, winning the support of the troops with a substantial pay rise, and with lavish and ultimately financially crippling further donatives throughout his reign. At least he fulfilled that part of his father's dying wishes.

But he had aspirations far beyond anything his father could have envisaged. A year after conducting military operations in Germany and Pannonia, he departed for the lands of the East. In these lands, he would conduct a grand campaign in the manner of Alexander the Great—as Alexander born anew![9] In his earlier incarnation's footsteps, he advanced through Asia Minor to Syria, and then marched into Egypt (215). Here he had a score to settle with the inhabitants of Alexandria, who had mocked him after his accession as sole emperor. The alleged offenders were rounded up and massacred in their thousands. That done, Caracalla marched back through Syria into Armenia, which he converted into a Roman province after deposing its vassal king Vologeses (216). And from there he turned his attention to the kingdom of Parthia. He would subjugate not merely a part of it as his father and Trajan had done. The whole of the Parthian realm would fall to him,

just as the Achaemenid empire had when he was Alexander. That was Caracalla's grand plan.

And just as Alexander had married a daughter of his now dead enemy
Darius III to symbolize the new union between eastern and western worlds,
so too Caracalla appeared to seek by diplomatic means a merging of the
Roman and Parthian empires—by marrying a daughter of the Parthian king
Artabanus IV. There are two versions of what happened next. According to
Cassius Dio, Artabanus rejected the marriage proposal and Caracalla resumed
his offensive, conducting a raid into Media.[10] Herodian gives us a more
detailed and more lurid version of events: Caracalla continued to press his
suit, despite initial refusals from the Parthian, and finally won him over by
his eloquence and his gifts. But it was a trick. When the Parthian guests had
assembled for the wedding on the plain outside one of Artabanus' palace-
cities and were in high celebratory mood, decked out in all their finery and
well into their cups, Caracalla suddenly gave his troops the signal to set
upon them. Wholesale slaughter followed. Artabanus himself escaped the
carnage, but only just. He was snatched up by his bodyguard in the nick of
time and spirited away on horseback. Caracalla followed up his act of treachery by marching the length and breadth of Parthian territory, until his soldiers were exhausted from looting and plundering, and then returned to
Mesopotamia.[11]

Either on his way back from his pillaging expedition (the Parthian campaign was no more than that) or at the beginning of preparations for a
resumption of it the following year, the emperor was assassinated on 8 April
217, near Carrhae, a site infamous in Roman history for the rout there of
Crassus' forces more than 250 years earlier. He fell victim to a plot hatched
by a group of his officers, led by the praetorian prefect Opellius Macrinus.
The assassination took place while Caracalla was making a pilgrimage with
a small cavalry escort to the temple of Selene, which lay a few kilometres
from the town. On the way, the emperor was caught short with a severe
stomach-ache. He called a halt to the progress, dismounted his horse, and
retired a brief distance to relieve himself, while the rest of his group dis-
creetly turned their backs and walked the other way. One of Macrinus'
henchmen, Martialis, seized the moment to rush upon the emperor, pre-
tending he had received a call from him for assistance, caught him with his
pants down (quite literally), and stabbed him to death.[12]

Macrinus now had himself accepted as emperor, by both the army and
the Senate, and resumed without delay his predecessor's campaign against

Artabanus. But he lost two battles to the Parthians and was forced to withdraw from Mesopotamia, leaving him no choice but to negotiate a settlement with the Parthian king. That severely undermined his credibility in
the eyes of his troops, who were further angered when he cut their pay
(no doubt a necessary measure to counter his predecessor's overly generous donatives to them), and by his refusal to allow the European legions
stationed in Syria to return home. With the army now turning against
him, and with powerful supporters of the Severan family eager to eliminate him, it was clear that Macrinus was not destined to wear the imperial
purple for long.

The other Severans

At this point we can return to Septimius Severus' widow Julia Domna.
Through most of her husband's reign, this formidable, politically astute
woman had played a highly influential role in imperial affairs, her broadly
based popularity among the empire's subjects reflected in her titles 'mother
of the (military) camp' and 'mother of the Senate and the fatherland'. Almost
certainly her popularity with the troops arose from her practice of accompanying her husband on his military campaigns, just like Semiramis' historical prototype Sammu-ramat, who had gone with her son Adad-nirari III on
his expeditions west of the Euphrates. She also cultivated the elite intellectual and artistic elements of Roman society, forming around herself a circle
of sophisticates—philosophers, historians, doctors, and lawyers. Yet in the
process of winning herself widespread popular support, Domna had also
accumulated a crop of enemies who accused her of various offences, including treason and adultery. No doubt some of these accusations reached the
emperor, and it is possible that his consort fell out of favour with him for a
time. But if so (and for whatever reasons), she had regained her influence in
time to accompany her husband and their sons Caracalla and Geta on the
British campaign in 208–11.

   After Severus' death and Caracalla's accession, she maintained her influence in the empire's affairs (despite her ultimately futile attempts to save the
life of Geta, murdered on his brother's orders and apparently dying in her
arms). She had returned to her homeland Syria when Caracalla undertook
his eastern campaigns, and was very likely a driving force behind many of
his policies and enterprises, including, probably, his famous decree of 212
which conferred citizenship upon all free members of the empire. Then

came news of her son's assassination and the accession of the man who had brought it about. Julia Domna knew that her own days were nearing their end. And not simply because of Macrinus. The matriarch of the Severan dynasty had but a short time to live anyhow. She had breast cancer, now in its final stages. Unwilling to prolong her sufferings or become a victim of Macrinus, she took her own life by self-starvation.[13]

AD 218–222

But the family to which she belonged was far from finished. Julia Domna had a sister, Julia Maesa, who proved just as formidable a figure in the Severan dynasty. This second Julia, whom we shall henceforth call Maesa, was determined to restore the imperial throne to its rightful line of occupants, by having one of her grandsons installed upon it. She went about this by involving herself in a plot to get rid of Macrinus, and by offering to spread her wealth, which was considerable, among the local militia in return for their support. This they readily granted. Maesa's grandson was a young man originally called Bassianus, after his maternal great-grandfather. His mother was Maesa's daughter Julia Sohaemias. Up to this point, the youth had lived quietly, as a priest of the sun god Elah-Gabal (Elagabalus), chief deity of Emesa.[14] That suddenly changed in May 218, when he found himself proclaimed emperor by the local troops, and the nominal leader of an army which marched to Antioch for a final showdown with Macrinus. The battle took place on 8 June. It was a contest barely worthy of the name. Already deserted by most of his troops, Macrinus was soundly defeated and fled the field, later to be captured and executed in Cappadocia. The Severan dynasty had once more become the ruling family of the Roman world, and Bassianus was confirmed as emperor. Many of the troops who supported him must still have retained strong loyalties to the memory of his second cousin Caracalla, for on his assumption of the purple, Bassianus took on Caracalla's formal name. He was thus the second emperor to be called Marcus Aurelius Antoninus. In fact, he was now proclaimed Caracalla's son.[15] And so, at the tender age of sixteen (or less), Marcus Aurelius Antoninus II became ruler of the Roman world. He was known in Rome as Elagabalus, an additional name which he adopted in honour of his god (and by which later ages best remember him).[16]

Our ancient sources are united in attributing to Elagabalus just one positive quality—his extraordinary good looks.[17] But the negative side of the man was yet to emerge. The day following Macrinus' defeat, the new emperor entered Antioch and remained there for several months before beginning his progress across Asia Minor and thence to Italy. He arrived in Rome in July or August 219. It had been five years since a reigning emperor had been seen in Rome,[18] and for this reason in particular, Elagabalus' prompt journey to the capital was a wise move—at least in theory. Initially, there seems to have been no opposition or challenges to his appointment, by the Senate or the people of Rome, or by the armies stationed elsewhere throughout the Roman world. This may have been due largely to the fact that he was of the family of Septimius Severus, who was still highly esteemed in the empire.

But the goodwill extended to the new man on his arrival soon evaporated, particularly because of his aggressive attempts to make his god the supreme deity of the Roman world. Repugnance at the cult itself was intensified by the wild orgiastic rites apparently associated with it, at least in the way it was practised by Elagabalus. Combined with this, the reports of the emperor's scandalous private life, his injudicious divorces, and his unsuitable appointments of persons to high office in exchange for cash quickly made him extremely unpopular with his subjects, and his position a very precarious one. Said also to be fond of playing practical jokes, he was apparently in the habit of placing his dinner guests on inflated cushions, which were contrived to deflate suddenly, sending their unsuspecting accumbents sprawling under the tables. Admittedly, this story comes from the *Historia Augusta*.[19] But if in fact the worst the emperor's victims lost was their dignity, they had little enough to complain about. There were many of Elagabalus' subjects who lost a great deal more.[20]

His grandmother Julia Maesa saw the mounting anger of the Roman people. But she was aware that the Severan family remained popular, despite its black sheep. So she persuaded Elagabalus to adopt his cousin, her other grandson, originally called Gessius Alexianus Bassianus, and confer upon him the title Caesar—in effect appointing him junior co-emperor. Upon his adoption, the new Caesar was known as Marcus Aurelius Alexander Caesar. Since he was born around 209, he was barely in his teens at the time, possibly younger. History may well have played out differently if Elagabalus had stuck to the arrangement. It seems indeed to have been a popular one with the people and, importantly, with the troops. But perhaps the adoptee was proving too popular, and Elagabalus decided to unadopt him. That proved a fatal mistake. His grandmother Maesa now switched her support to her younger grandson, as did the household troops who lynched the emperor, along with his mother Sohaemias, mutilated their bodies by dragging them through the streets of the capital, and then tossed them into the sewers that ran down to the river. How prescient the Roman poet Juvenal had been when more than a century earlier he wrote of the dregs of the Orontes being flushed into Father Tiber![21]

These were the circumstances in which the new emperor came to power in March 222. Significantly, he was called the 'son of the deified Antoninus'—that is to say, 'the son of Caracalla'—a sure sign that Caracalla was still well favoured in the Roman world, despite the unremitting efforts of our sources to blacken his name and his career. He also took on his accession the name Severus after the founder of his royal dynasty, and is commonly known by two names—Severus Alexander. Born at Arqa (Classical Arka) on the coast of what is now Lebanon, Alexander became like his cousin a member of the priesthood at Emesa. But he was far too young to have attained high office in the cult before he was summoned to Rome.

Both ancient sources and modern scholars have dealt positively with Alexander, generally considering him 'one of the wisest and most moderate emperors of the chaotic third century'.[22] Edward Gibbon called his reign 'exemplary'. As we shall see, this lavish praise needs some qualification. But there is no doubt that in both his personal attributes and behaviour and his conduct of the empire's affairs, Alexander contrasted strikingly with his cousin and predecessor. For this no small credit is due to the two most important women in his life. Throughout his reign, which began when he was a mere thirteen-year-old, he was heavily influenced, if not dominated, by these matriarchal figures, first his grandmother Maesa, and after her death around 226 his mother Mamaea until the end of his reign in 235. Mamaea was accorded the title Augusta and, like her aunt Domna, that of 'mother of the Senate and the fatherland'. She was arguably the most powerful of the Severan female triad (Julia Domna, Maesa, and herself), for she was virtually co-emperor throughout the last nine years of her son's reign. In recognition of her role, her son conferred upon her the title *consors imperii*—'partner in the empire'. To Edward Gibbon, Mamaea was even more exemplary in her virtues than Domna. And to her was due, he believed, much of the credit for what Alexander's reign achieved.

More sober assessments of her career still allow that the major role she played in Roman affairs worked by and large for the good of the empire. Her son collaborated closely with her in restoring the prestige of the Senate and bolstering the state's civil and judicial authorities, partly in an attempt, it seems, to counter the military anarchy that had all too often dictated the course of the empire's history. Under their joint rule, a variety of state-sponsored benefits were provided for the Roman populace. In addition to the usual handouts and entertainments, these included a range of goods and services which were the products of trades and industries operating under imperial supervision. Overall, this last Severan regime managed to secure and maintain a reasonably high level of stability throughout the empire for much of its existence, and for a time there appears to have been a reduction in the number of military uprisings that had so disfigured Roman imperial history through much of the preceding century.

But as we shall see, things were to get a good deal worse in Alexander's final years. And to compound the empire's internal problems, a new power was soon to burst upon the Near Eastern scene, one that was to affect the Near Eastern world profoundly for the rest of our story.

16

The Crisis Years

On one of the most impressive rock monuments at Naqsh-i-Rustam near the ruins of the once great Achaemenid capital Persepolis, an eastern king is depicted, mounted on a horse with a sword by his side. He is an imposing figure, his fierce visage adorned with a beard and curled flowing locks of hair surmounted by a huge globular crown. Before him are two submissive figures, one kneeling and offering him homage, the other standing with his wrists bound above his head. The two men so humiliatingly portrayed are Roman emperors. The man on horseback is their conqueror, the great Shapur I, 'King of Kings', ruler of the Sasanian empire. Two separate events are shown in this scene. In the first, dating to 244, the new emperor called 'Philip the Arab' is depicted, allegedly having been forced into a degrading peace settlement with the Sasanian and now acknowledging his status as Shapur's tributary by kneeling before him. There is a neat irony in the timing of this, as we shall see. The second event, dating to the year 260, depicts the capture of the emperor Valerian. That was even more devastating than the first event. In the view of many commentators, it represents the lowest depth to which the Roman empire sank in the 350 years of its history between Augustus' accession as its first emperor in 27 BC and Constantine the Great's dedication of his new city Constantinople in AD 330.

AD 222–238

The Sasanians

From 247 BC until AD 224, the greatest power in the east and Rome's most formidable rival had been the kingdom of Parthia. Then in 224, the Parthian regime was overthrown and a new empire created in Iran. This was under the leadership of a king called Ardashir I, founder of the Sasanian

Figure 24. Shapur I and the submission of Philip and Valerian

empire, so named after Ardashir's supposed ancestor Sasan. According to one Sasanian foundation tradition, Sasan was descended from the Achaemenid rulers whose empire was destroyed by Alexander the Great. This, the Sasanians believed, sharply distinguished them from their predecessors: unlike the Parthians who came in from outside, the Sasanians had originated in the very heart of Persia, the Achaemenid homeland in south-western Iran; and the emergent Sasanian kings had Achaemenid royal blood in their veins. That at least was their claim. It may have been no more than propagandistic invention. There was certainly nothing new about the founder of a new dynasty seeking to legitimize his regime by declaring blood-links with an earlier ruling line. But whatever their origins, the Sasanians from the very beginnings of their history, from a base in south-western Iran and in the manner of their Achaemenid forerunners, rapidly extended their sway over much of the eastern half of the Near Eastern world, where they remained a major political and military force till the Arab conquest of Mesopotamia and Iran in 651. Their great ambition was to resurrect the power and the glory of the Achaemenid empire. Inevitably, this led to repeated conflict with Rome and later Byzantium. The rise of the Sasanian kingdom had far graver implications for the Roman world than its Parthian predecessor. And it would prove far less amenable to peace, cooperation, and compromise.

Severus Alexander was in Rome when he received word of the coup in Iran and the usurper's rapid invasion and occupation of Roman territories in Mesopotamia. The news came in a series of despatches conveyed to him by his governors in Syria and Mesopotamia. They warned that Syria too was under threat. And not only Syria. Ardashir's sights were set firmly on the acquisition of the whole of western Asia, up to the borders of the Aegean Sea. At least that is what Herodian tells us: 'Artaxerxes (i.e. Ardashir)[1] wished to recover for the Persian empire the mainland facing Europe, separated from it by the Aegean Sea and the Propontic Gulf, and the region called Asia. Believing these regions to be his by inheritance, he declared that all the countries in that area, including Ionia and Caria, had been ruled by Persian governors, from the rule of Cyrus, who first made the Median empire Persian, and ending with Darius, the last of the Persian monarchs, whose kingdom Alexander the Macedonian had destroyed. He asserted that it was therefore proper for him to recover for the Persians the kingdom which they formerly possessed.'[2]

Scholars doubt whether Ardashir ever did plan to extend his frontiers to the westernmost limits of the empire established by Cyrus the Great.[3] But there is no doubt that the new Iranian kingdom under its aggressive founder posed a substantial threat to Rome's eastern territories. Alexander was well aware of the threat, and took action to meet it without delay. Summoning the best of his troops from Italy and the Roman provinces, he mustered them in Rome and announced to them the great enterprise that lay ahead. It was a stirring speech, if we can accept Herodian's version of it. The emperor made clear to the assembled multitude the determination of the enemy they were soon to face, an enemy who had treated all attempts at negotiation with disdain. He would have to be fought to the bitter end. It would be all or nothing: 'The Persian Artaxerxes (Ardashir) has slain his master Artabanus. And the Parthian empire is now Persian. Despising our arms and contemptuous of the Roman reputation, Artaxerxes is attempting to overrun and destroy our imperial possessions. I first endeavoured by letter and persuasion to check his mad greed and his lust for the property of others. But the king, with barbarian arrogance, is unwilling to remain within his own boundaries, and challenges us to battle. Let us not hesitate to accept his challenge!'[4] The speech was met with rousing cheers from the troops. They supported the war, enthusiastically and wholeheartedly, particularly when the emperor bestowed a lavish bonus upon them as an incentive.

Alexander now made preparations for his return to the East, at the head of a large campaign force. Reaching Antioch without delay, he strengthened his army there with a huge reinforcement of local troops, and used the city as a base for training his troops for warfare in the harsh conditions they would soon encounter. But while all this was going on, he tried once more to negotiate a peace with Ardashir, through the agency of a diplomatic mission which, he hoped, might persuade or intimidate the Sasanian into accepting a settlement. Ardashir would have none of it. In response to the Roman initiative, he selected from his cavalry four hundred very tall horsemen, decked them out in fine clothes and gold ornaments, and sent them to Alexander, with the expectation that the emperor would be overawed by their splendour. (Presumably this was a piece of one-upmanship, intended to show up the Roman envoys' meaner physical appearance and more modest apparel.) The horsemen brought their king's own terms of peace. But nothing significant had changed: the Romans had to withdraw from Syria and Asia Minor, and cede all these territories to the Sasanians. This was totally unacceptable, and Alexander continued to make ready for war.

The Severan dynasty's final years

The year was 231. With all preparations complete, the emperor was ready for Ardashir. His strategy was to divide his huge forces into three armies, for a three-pronged invasion of Iran through Armenia, northern Mesopotamia, and Babylonia. As far as we can judge from Herodian's somewhat vague and confusing account of the invasion,[5] the emperor's overall plan seems to have been this: after subjugating the enemy regions through which they separately passed, the three armies were to rendezvous for a final massed attack on the heartland of Ardashir's kingdom. The emperor was to take personal command of the 'central army', which was to advance into the enemy's territory through northern Mesopotamia. That was apparently the plan. But if so, it went badly wrong. It seems that the emperor after setting out on the campaign suddenly lost his nerve and failed even to enter Sasanian territory. Maybe, suggests Herodian, his mother Julia Mamaea talked him out of it, fearing for his life. In any case, it was this failure of nerve, Herodian tells us, that led to the destruction of the southern army, which without the backing of the other two armies was attacked, trapped, and slaughtered by Ardashir's forces.

Already weakened by illness, the emperor was plunged into deep depression when news of the disaster reached him.[6] Not that he won much sympathy. On the contrary, what was left of his armed forces furiously denounced him for not carrying through his original plans. He was held directly responsible for the disaster that befell the southern army, which was now but a shattered remnant of its former self. There was of course still the northern army, the one that had invaded Armenia. At this point, it was still intact. Alexander was now eager to return to the relative security of Antioch, and for his northern army to do the same. He sent orders to its commanders to withdraw there immediately. That was not so easily done. Though the army had apparently entered Armenia with little opposition, getting back again to Antioch proved disastrous. Severe winter conditions and the harsh mountain environment almost wiped the entire army out. Only a handful of survivors reached Antioch alive.

All of this comes to us from Herodian. If we accept his account at face value, it is hard to see how Alexander could have survived such a debacle, for which he himself was allegedly responsible, given the readiness with which Roman troops had on many other occasions disposed of an emperor who fell out of favour with them. But not only did he survive, and apparently win over the troops with another lavish donative, but after he and his forces were revived by the congenial cool air of Antioch, he made ready for a fresh assault on the Sasanians should they once more show signs of aggression. In fact, the Sasanians had now gone rather quiet. We are told by Herodian that far from following up on his apparent success against Alexander's southern army and the disastrous retreat of the northern army, Ardashir had disbanded his own forces, sending each soldier back to the country whence he had come. It seems that his troops too had suffered heavy casualties in their conflicts with the Romans. But this only emerges at the end of Herodian's account of the contest, and appears to contradict the earlier impression he had given of a comprehensive Sasanian victory: 'Since the total number of troops which fell on both sides was virtually identical, the surviving barbarians appeared to have won, but by superior numbers, not by superior power. It is no little proof of how much the barbarians suffered that for three or four years after this they remained quiet and did not take up arms.'[7] Alexander was understandably delighted when news that the Sasanians had ceased hostilities was brought to him at Antioch. He could now devote himself to the pleasures the city had on offer (whatever they may have been). And he capped it all off when he returned to Rome in 233 and celebrated his 'conquest' of the Persians with a magnificent triumph. An extraordinary piece of chutzpah, we might think. But let's not be too cynical. It does seem that the emperor's eastern operations had been rather more successful than Herodian's account might initially lead us to believe. Fergus Millar notes that in 232 the Romans were able to build a road leading from Singara towards Carrhae, which means that by this time nearly all Roman Mesopotamia, if lost, must have been regained.[8]

But Alexander had little time to enjoy his military successes, questionable though his claim to them may have been. During his absence in the East, a Germanic people called the Alamanni had become aggressive, making incursions into Roman territory in Upper Germany and Raetia. In 234, Alexander mounted an expedition to the region to resolve the problems there, and spent the winter of 234–5 in Germany in preparation for the campaign the following season. On this campaign too he was accompanied by his mother. But his days were now almost at an end. Growing insubordination among his troops, with whom his perceived betrayal of his army in Mesopotamia may still have rankled, and who were perhaps resentful of his mother's influence (she remained a highly visible presence) prompted one of the troops to lead a mutiny against him outside the city now called Mainz. Alexander and his mother were killed in their tent, along with many of their friends and favourites. The mutineers' leader Maximinus was a Thracian of peasant origin who had risen to equestrian status before the massacre. An enormous bearded giant reputed to consume up to forty pounds of meat and eight gallons of wine a day, Maximinus was acclaimed Rome's new emperor. He managed to survive in that role for the next four years (235–8).

Herodian ends his account of Alexander's reign with a very positive assessment of the man, indeed rather too positive, some might argue. According to Herodian, the emperor's fourteen-year lease of power was, 'as far as his subjects were concerned, without fault or bloodshed. Murder, cruelty, and injustice were not part of his nature; his inclination was towards humane and benevolent behaviour. Indeed, his reign would have been notable for its complete success, but for the blame he incurred through his mother's faults of avarice and meanness.'[9] This moralistic appraisal of the emperor's personal qualities passes over the significant shortcomings of his reign, particularly in the military arena. But there is no doubt that on a purely personal level Alexander shone by comparison with many of those who occupied the throne before and after him. Of course, that's not saying very much.

His assassination marked the end of the Severan dynasty's lease of imperial power. This major era in Roman history had its share of substantial successes, offset by some notable failures and the bizarre excesses of some of its members, as well as being distinguished by the fact that for a period of more than four decades, the Roman emperorship lay in the hands of a Phoenician-Syrian family. Another feature of it is the high prominence of three of the family's female members—the three Julias: Domna, Maesa, and Mamaea. Maximinus abruptly put an end to it all. His accession marked the beginning of a fifty-year period commonly referred to as 'The Crisis Years'—from the Thracian peasant's seizure of power in 235 to the troops' proclamation of Diocletian as emperor in 284. This half-century saw, and saw off, at least eighteen generally recognized emperors, and far more if one counts the numerous usurpers of the period. Nearly all met violent deaths after short reigns.[10]

AD 238–258

The *Res Gestae* of the 'Divine Shapur'

In the same period, the Sasanian empire reached one of the highest peaks in its development. Though it never achieved its founder's alleged ambition—expansion to the westernmost limits of the former Achaemenid empire—it none the less remained a significant threat to all of Rome's eastern territories. For a brief time there seems to have been an accommodation between Rome and Ardashir, which kept Sasanian-controlled territory to the east of the Euphrates. Perhaps some credit for this is due to Severus Alexander. In any case, a *modus vivendi* was established between the two empires which continued after Alexander's death through the reigns of his first five successors, Maximinus, the co-emperors Gordians I and II (father and son), and the co-emperors Balbinus and Pupienus. Not that there was anything particularly impressive about this since the reigns of these men lasted in total a mere four years; all five of them died violently in 238, the last four almost immediately after their accession.

Following their deaths, relations between Rome and the Sasanian kingdom took a turn very much for the worse. This happened in the reign of Alexander's sixth successor, Gordian III (238–44), a grandson of the first Gordian, foisted on the Senate by the praetorian guard after they had murdered his predecessors Balbinus and Pupienus. The change in relations with the Sasanian kingdom came about with the accession of a new Sasanian ruler—Shapur I, son, co-regent, and successor of Ardashir. Shapur's long occupancy of his throne (from 239/40 to 271/2) began when Ardashir abdicated in favour of him, though the new king waited until his father died, in 241 or 242, before proclaiming himself emperor. The new regime meant new policies. Shapur very quickly made it clear that he had no intention of maintaining any sort of modus vivendi with Rome. At the earliest opportunity, he ordered the occupation of the Roman-controlled city of Hatra in northern Mesopotamia (about 80 km south of modern Mosul) and other outlying settlements of the Roman empire. It was but a matter of time before he carried his standards further westwards.

Gordian III, one of the better emperors of this 'crisis period', took prompt and decisive action, launching a counter-offensive across the Euphrates in 243. But his campaign ended disastrously the following year when, according to the Sasanian account, Shapur's forces defeated and destroyed what was left of his army in a showdown at Misiche in northern Mesopotamia. Shapur claimed that the emperor himself was killed in the battle. According to our Roman sources, he survived it, only to be assassinated shortly after by the man who assumed the emperorship in his place, his praetorian prefect Marcus Iulius Philippus (regn. 244–9).[11] The new emperor was of Arab origin, from the region of Shahba in southern Syria, south-east of Damascus. He is commonly known as 'Philip the Arab' ('an Arab by birth and consequently a robber by profession' is how Edward Gibbon describes him). Once again, a Syrian became ruler of the Roman world. Philip's first priority was to come to terms with the Sasanian conqueror. And so he did. Theoretically, he concluded a peace treaty with Shapur. But according to Shapur, he paid him an enormous bribe for the release of himself and his army and became the Sasanian's tributary. It is in fact Philip the Arab who is depicted kneeling before Shapur on the Naqsh-i-Rustam monument referred to at the beginning of this chapter. A clear gesture of submission, *if* it represents the truth, not one of a treaty-partner! But whatever the nature of the peace settlement, it enabled Philip to return unscathed to Rome, just in time to preside over a great celebration—the thousand-year anniversary of the founding of Rome (247–8). Rome had indeed managed a thousand-year Reich of sorts, though the circumstances of the celebration and the reason Philip was able to conduct it in person were hardly inspiring ones.

The great monument at Naqsh-i-Rustam on which Philip's submission to Shapur is depicted (along with the submission of the other Roman emperor shown there, to whom we shall shortly come) is inscribed with a famous trilingual text—in Parthian, middle Persian, and Greek. Shapur used these languages to record his victories over the armies of the west and his expeditions west of Mesopotamia. Modern scholars refer to his account as the *Res Gestae Divi Saporis*—'the achievements of the Divine Shapur'—by way of a sardonic comparison with the famous inscription of Augustus, the *Res Gestae Divi Augusti*.[12] Shapur's monument provides details of three victorious campaigns against the Romans. The first—to which we have already referred—included the defeat and destruction of Gordian III's army in the battle of Misiche, so alleged, and the subsequent submission of Gordian's successor Philip. The second had even more devastating consequences for the Romans and their eastern territories, according to Shapur's version of events. Shapur claims that his campaign was sparked off by the Roman emperor referred to simply as Caesar, who 'lied again and did wrong to Armenia'. The events that follow in the text are not recorded in any of our surviving Classical sources, and the precise date of their occurrence is uncertain. But it is likely they are to be assigned to the year 252, and the emperor in question is probably the short-lived Trebonianus Gallus (251–3).[13] It was at all events clear to Shapur that the time was ripe for him to begin to fulfil what his royal line *may* have believed to be its destiny, the subjugation of the whole of the Near Eastern world, to the shores of the Aegean and the Propontis. The old Achaemenid empire would thus be restored.

And here we must rely entirely on Shapur's own words for a reconstruction of what happened. He claims first of all to have confronted and destroyed a 60,000-strong Roman army at the site of Barbalissos. This was a city on the Euphrates, upstream of its confluence with the Balih river. Then follows a list of forts and border towns captured, ravaged, and burnt by Shapur's forces. A total of thirty-seven conquered forts, towns, and cities are included in the list. Though the overall geographical picture of Shapur's campaign is confused and confusing, what does seem clear is that the Sasanian advance was aimed on this occasion at Syria, not at Roman Mesopotamia,[14] and that the progress up the Euphrates marked the first stage of this advance, beginning with Shapur's conquest of Sura, and then Barbalissos. Shapur's forces appear to have swept all before them in their progress through Syria, including the greatest city of the land, Antioch, and a number of cities in northern Syria and Commagene. One group of Sasanian forces also moved south along the Orontes valley, capturing cities in the region, including Hama (Hamath/'Chamath').

Significantly, no mention is made of the important city Emesa on the Orontes' east bank. The likelihood is that the Sasanians did attack it, but were resisted—successfully. So we are told by John Malalas, a sixth-century citizen of Antioch who wrote what was purportedly a history of the world—his eighteen-book *Chronographia*.[15] In dealing with the Sasanian campaign, Malalas relates that a man of Emesa called Sampsigeramus, priest of the goddess Aphrodite, gathered together an army of sling-bearing peasants to fight against the Sasanians. But the priest made a show of seeking a diplomatic resolution of the matter. His request to Shapur for a one-to-one meeting was granted by the Sasanian king, who ordered his troops to hold their fire and seated himself on a high platform for the occasion. This made him an easy target for an assassin, and he was promptly picked off by one of Sampsigeramus' slingers. On news of his death, pandemonium broke out among the Sasanian forces. Believing that the Romans were coming for them, they took to flight, abandoning all their booty, with Sampsigeramus and his slingers in hot pursuit.[16] Millar points out that since Shapur did not die during the campaign the story must be at least partly legend.[17] But there may be some truth in it—at least as far as a successful defence of Emesa is concerned. The very fact that Shapur makes no mention of the city in his advance through Syria quite possibly indicates that his forces suffered an embarrassing reverse there. He would hardly have put that in his *Res Gestae*. In any case, the consequences of the Persian invasion of Syria during Shapur's 'second' campaign seem not to have been profound or long-lasting. As Millar notes, the minting of imperial coins began again at Antioch in 253/254, and the new emperor Valerian must have arrived in Syria during 254, since on 18 January 255 he wrote a letter from Antioch to the city of Philadelphia in Lydia.[18] But we do not know the circumstances of Rome's reassertion of its authority in Syria following Shapur's invasion.

The Valerian disaster

It is to the emperor Valerian that we must now turn in discussing the last of the three campaigns recorded by Shapur at Naqsh-i-Rustam. An elderly man (in his sixties at the time of his appointment to the purple in 253), he had achieved imperial office through election by his troops, who had murdered his predecessor after a reign of less than a year. Upon marching to

Rome, Valerian was accepted by all as the new emperor, along with his son Gallienus as co-emperor. The choice was seen to be a good one. 'In proclaiming Valerian emperor', the historians Cary and Scullard write, 'the troops blundered upon a man of integrity who won the confidence of the senate and restored some measure of discipline in the military forces.'[19] Father and son were both accorded the imperial title 'Augustus'. By mutual agreement, it seems, there was a decision that the empire, with its vast problems in both Europe and Asia, should be split between them, Gallienus taking on the task of defending the west, Valerian that of re-establishing and maintaining control in the east.

In 254, within a year of his appointment, Valerian set out for the east. The aggression of the Sasanians under Shapur, and the total inability of his predecessors to do anything about it, meant that Syria in particular, and probably Asia Minor as well, was at serious risk of being swallowed up in Shapur's empire. But there was a further problem in the east—new raids by the Goths, who were irrupting into Asia Minor via the western and eastern coastlands of the Black Sea. Valerian had taken up residence in Antioch before the end of 254. Once more the city assumed the role of a Roman imperial capital. And here, or more generally in the Near East, the emperor was to remain almost continuously for the next five years—up to his fateful encounter with Shapur. Part of this time may well have been spent in overseeing some rebuilding of the city, which no doubt had suffered devastation in the Sasanian invasion.[20] But his mere presence in Syria did nothing to deter Shapur from continuing his inroads into Roman territory.

In the course of his enterprises, Shapur attacked the fortress-city of Dura Europos, which, as we noted in Chapter 13, occupied a strategically valuable position on a plateau overlooking the Euphrates. Fluctuating in the pre-Sasanian period between Parthian and Roman control, Dura was garrisoned by Roman troops in the last years of Septimius Severus' reign (209–11), and further reinforced by his successors in the 220s to 230s against the newly emerging Sasanian menace. Ultimately to no avail. An obvious target of Sasanian aggression, the fortress-settlement suffered a first attack by Ardashir in 239, which it withstood, and a more sustained one by Shapur who placed it under siege in 253/254. Shapur's assault upon it began in Valerian's accession year and may have been one of the (probably many) triggers for the emperor's march to the east. He reached the city in 255, but he could do nothing to save it from its attackers. Despite its heroic defence, Dura fell to Shapur in 256 and was largely destroyed and then abandoned.

This provides our lead-in to the showdown, or supposed showdown, between Valerian and Shapur, and its disastrous outcome for the Roman emperor. Valerian is the wrist-bound figure who stands before Shapur on the Naqsh-i-Rustam monument. The stage for the confrontation was set when Shapur was laying siege to the cities of Carrhae and Urhai (Edessa, modern Urfa) in northern Mesopotamia. His action against these cities prompted Valerian to march to their rescue, at the head of a 70,000-strong army gathered from all parts of his empire. But he proved no match for his adversary. In a great battle fought beyond Carrhae and Edessa, the Sasanian won a resounding victory, capturing the entire Roman army and deporting it to his homeland in Persia, along with its emperor-commander and substantial quantities of booty. All this Shapur tells us in his *Res Gestae*. He gives us no details of the battle itself. But there is a record of it in the epic poem the *Shahnameh* written by the 10th–11th century Persian poet Firdausi; here we are informed that 10,000 of Valerian's forces were slain in the conflict and 1,600 taken prisoner.[21]

A rather different version of events is provided by the 5th–6th century Greek historian Zosimus, generally regarded as our most reliable ancient source for this period. According to Zosimus, Valerian, his army greatly reduced by plague, did not confront Shapur in battle but tried to buy him off, sending him envoys with an appeal to conclude hostilities, and a large gift of money as an inducement. Shapur refused to deal with the envoys and sent them back empty-handed. He insisted that he would discuss terms of peace with none but the emperor himself, who should come to him for this purpose. And that is what Valerian foolishly did, taking with him only a small escort. On his arrival, he was seized by the enemy and ended his days as a slave in Persis, to the great disgrace of the Roman empire.[22] Whether Valerian fell to the enemy in battle or by such an act of treachery, Shapur claims that in the aftermath of his victory he swept westwards, burning, sacking, and pillaging the Roman provinces of Syria, Cilicia, and Cappadocia.

Valerian's capture was a disaster of the gravest proportions for the Roman empire. It was bad enough for a Roman army commanded by its emperor to be defeated in battle. Worse if the defeated emperor was himself killed in the engagement (as happened on a number of occasions). But worst of all was for an emperor not merely to lose a battle but to be seized and held prisoner by his enemy. And Valerian remained his enemy's prisoner until his death. This humiliation was in itself bound to have a serious destabilizing effect on the empire, particularly when fuelled by rumours of the indignities to which the captive emperor was allegedly subjected. The most lurid of

Figure 25. Valerian humiliated, sketch by Hans Holbein the Younger

these rumours are reported by the 3rd–4th century Christian writer Lactantius, who tells us that the emperor was used by Shapur as a footstool for mounting his horse and his carriage, and degraded in various other ways up to the time of his death; even then the humiliation continued, when the corpse's skin was stripped off, dyed vermilion, stuffed with straw, and put on display in one of the local temples.[23] But whether Valerian suffered gross degradation in captivity and death, or was more graciously treated by his captors, the very fact of his captivity, and his subjects' inability to do anything about it, served as a powerful propaganda weapon for the Sasanian king, and a great fillip to the ambitions of Rome's enemies elsewhere. As we have noted, his capture is commonly seen, by both ancient and modern writers, as the very lowest point which the Roman empire's fortunes reached in its history, before the beginning of the Byzantine era in AD 330.

To be sure, it had not left the Roman world entirely leaderless. Valerian's son and co-emperor Gallienus still occupied the imperial throne, as the head of the 'western' empire. But that was very small consolation when it came to ensuring the maintenance of Rome's vital interests in the east. Gallienus had problems enough of his own to contend with in the west, including a secessionist movement by the Gauls in 258 and the establishment of a breakaway 'Gallic empire',[24] a series of major Gothic incursions across the Danube and into the Balkans, and a rash of pretenders to the throne (perhaps not surprising in the circumstances), spurred on by the emperor's considerable unpopularity with the senatorial class. To top it all off, it seems that a virulent plague had broken out in many of the empire's cities.

None of this was helped by the emperor's reputation for debauchery and loose living. He was a man 'born for his belly and his pleasures', according to the *Historia Augusta*.[25] Let us emphasize once more that the *HA* is dodgy as a source of reliable historical information. But it does seem to reflect a wide-spread ancient perception of Gallienus' behaviour. And not just an ancient one. Writing many centuries later, Edward Gibbon is hardly less censorious. In conceding that the emperor was not without his talents, albeit misdirected ones, he comments: 'In every art that he attempted his lively genius enabled him to succeed; and as his genius was destitute of judgement, he attempted every art except the important ones of war and government. He was a master of several curious but useless sciences, a ready orator and elegant poet, a skilful gardener, an excellent cook, and most contemptible prince.' In fact, Gallienus was probably a much better emperor than either Gibbon or our ancient sources would have us believe. He certainly faced enormous challenges in his attempts to re-establish Roman authority in the west, in a period when both the western and the eastern Roman worlds were rapidly disintegrating, and seems to have been not altogether unsuccessful in dealing with these.

Importantly for our story, the massive problems of the west meant that he could do little else but leave the east to its own resources. Here too there were secessionist movements under way, in Syria in particular, spurred on no doubt by the successes of the Sasanian king whose removal of Valerian had laid Rome's eastern territories open to him.

But then, remarkably, a champion of Rome's interests in the east suddenly emerged, radically transforming the balance of power in the region.

PART V

The Rise and Fall
of Palmyra

17

From Desert Oasis to Royal Capital: The Story of Palmyra

Palmyra, for a while, stood forth the rival of Rome; but the competition was fatal, and ages of prosperity were sacrificed to a moment of glory.

(Edward Gibbon)

The story of Palmyra's rise and fall is one of the most extraordinary episodes in the history of the ancient Near Eastern world, and indeed of the ancient world in general. It is a story which belongs primarily within the context of the Roman empire and unfolds over a period of almost three centuries. But this is no more than a fraction of Palmyra's long lifespan. The history of the site where Palmyra was built, some 235 km north-east of Damascus, extends over almost 3,000 years and perhaps more, from at least the end of the third millennium BC until the early Islamic era (7th–8th centuries AD). Popularly known as the *Bride of the Desert*, Palmyra was explored by a succession of visitors from the 17th century AD onwards, and has been extensively excavated since 1924. Its oasis-location in the Syrian desert midway between the Euphrates and the coastlands of Syria made it a natural focus for the caravan trade which brought the goods and products of a remote eastern world, from as far afield as Indonesia, China, and India, to the lands of the Mediterranean.

The name 'Palmyra', by which the city was known in Classical texts, was inspired by the groves of palm trees which no doubt adorned the site throughout its existence. But Palmyra was originally called Tadmor. We first come across this earlier name, whose etymology remains unknown, in letters written by Assyrian merchants in the 19th century BC. It subsequently resurfaces in texts from the Late Bronze Age city of Emar on the Euphrates.

And the Assyrian king Tiglath-pileser I tells us that at the time of his campaigns in Syria, in the late 12th and early 11th centuries BC, Tadmor belonged
to the country called Amurru.[1] There is also a tradition that appears to give
Tadmor an important biblical association. In 2 Chronicles 8:4, we are told
that King Solomon 'built up Tadmor in the desert'. The 6th-century AD
chronicler John Malalas took this to be a reference to the city later known
as Palmyra, and believed that the city was also the site of David's duel with
Goliath.[2] So too the rather more astute and more scholarly Josephus believed
that Palmyra was founded by Solomon.[3] But almost certainly 'Tadmor' here
should be read 'Tamar', as in 1 Kings 9:18, which reports that Solomon built
a city called Tamar in the wilderness, in the land of Judah. Attractive though
it may be to associate Tadmor with King Solomon, the great builder-king
of Israelite tradition, the association is one we must discard. Apart from anything else, Solomon belongs to the 10th century BC, much too early, as we
shall see, to be linked with any known building activity at Palmyra.

Late 2nd century BC—1st century AD

Under Roman patronage

For many centuries, indeed from its earliest appearances in our texts, Tad-
mor/Palmyra seems to have played an important role in the history of
regional and international Near Eastern trade. But before the Romans
appear on the scene, practically all our information about the site comes
from written sources. Apart from some Bronze Age ceramic ware and a few
other meagre remains, we have almost no material evidence of any settlement at all at Palmyra before the Hellenistic period. Finally, in the late 2nd
century BC (the late Hellenistic period), more substantial evidence does
emerge—in the form of remains of building activity on the site. From this
period, the earliest phases of temples subsequently rebuilt in the Roman era
have come to light—temples dedicated to the goddess Allat and the god
Baal-Shamin, and perhaps also a forerunner of the great Temple of Bel.

But it was in the first two centuries of the Roman imperial period that
Palmyra experienced its greatest development, in company with a number
of other commercial centres of international trade. 'The first two centuries
AD', Richard Frye comments, 'was an age of commerce and the oasis states
of the Fertile Crescent flourished as never before. This was the time of the

"caravan cities" of Petra, Palmyra, Hatra, and the commercially oriented kingdoms of Adiabene or Hadyabh, Characene, Elymais, Gerrha on the western shore of the Gulf, and other trading emporia.'[4] In contrast to most of these caravan cities, Palmyra had, at least by the time of Roman intervention in the Near East, built its own army. This is understandable, given its vulnerable position in the middle of the desert, and its apparent lack of substantial fortifications. As we shall see, Palmyra's military forces were to figure significantly in the history of its relations with Rome and the two post-Achaemenid Iranian empires, the Sasanian in particular.

Palmyra began to develop as an urban centre in the 1st century BC. We have no indication of organized settled occupation before this time. Indeed, our evidence even then for its existence as a city is fairly slight and indirect. It comes from the Greek historian Appian, writing two hundred years later.[5] Appian tells us that Mark Antony despatched a force of cavalrymen to the settlement in 41 BC, to attack and plunder it and thereby enrich themselves. But the Palmyrenes had been forewarned that the Romans were coming. So they abandoned their city, carrying all their possessions with them, and withdrew to the Euphrates. Across the river, they took up a defensive position, and threatened to use their expert bowmen to destroy anyone who approached them. (The Euphrates was actually 200 km away, not close by as Appian seems to think.) Thus when Antony's horsemen reached the city, eager for plunder, they found not a soul within it, and absolutely nothing worth looting. And so with empty saddle-bags, heavy hearts, and no doubt sand-filled lungs, they returned to their home base without catching even the barest glimpse of the enemy they were sent to despoil.

If this episode is correctly reported by Appian, we can conclude from it first that Palmyra had a settled population by the middle of the 1st century BC; secondly, that if it did have walls or fortifications of any kind at this time, its inhabitants were not confident that these would protect them against attack, even by a lone cavalry contingent; hence their decision to move to a more suitable defensive position, where they could rely on their archery forces to deter or ward off any assault upon them—leaving nothing behind in their city worth looting. This story reinforces the notion that Palmyra had not yet developed into much more than a well-watered encampment for caravaneers. But it may well have served at that time as the centre of a large Arab tribal organization, whose leaders could command a significant fighting force when needed. Indeed, we learn from the Greek historian Polybius that already in the late 3rd century BC a Palmyrene tribal chief called

Zabdibel contributed 10,000 Arab troops to the army of Antiochus III in his showdown with Ptolemy IV at Raphia (217).[6] We might also mention here that some of the tower tombs which were erected in the desert outside Palmyra (see below) date back to the 2nd century BC. These in themselves mark the settlement as an important centre of the Arab world, well before we have significant material evidence for its existence.

By the early decades of the Roman empire, the material transformation of Palmyra had begun, and in the following three centuries the city developed progressively, with its rich cultural mix, into one of the most distinctive centres of urban civilization in the ancient Near East. This was largely due to Roman influence and Roman patronage. Palmyra benefited greatly from its association with Rome, and indeed enjoyed a highly privileged status in the Roman imperial period. Pompey left it independent when he established the province of Syria in 64 BC, and it retained this independence, despite Mark Antony's attempt to subdue it in 41 BC, until the early years of the emperor Tiberius (AD 14–37), when it 'probably paid tribute and should then be seen as part of the empire'[7] in the context of a mission to the east by the emperor's nephew Germanicus (AD 18–19). Even so, Roman control over Palmyra was no more than nominal. Roman military units were later stationed there, but the city was allowed considerable freedom in the management of its own affairs and in the development and expansion of its commercial enterprises.

2nd–3rd centuries AD

A great boost to the city's fortunes came in AD 106 when Petra, capital of the Nabataean kingdom, was annexed along with the rest of the kingdom by the emperor Trajan. In this year, Trajan created the Roman province of Arabia with its capital located in the Nabataean city Bosra (Roman Bostra). Though Petra still remained a significant centre of Nabataean culture, the commercial centre of gravity within the region now shifted to Palmyra. The archaeologist Warwick Ball comments that 'with the collapse of Nabataean control of the trade routes at the end of the 1st century AD, Palmyra's unique geographical position gave it a major advantage. The trading routes moved further north, a move dictated as much by the increasing importance of Antioch as by the decline of trade controlled by Petra.'[8] Palmyra thus became the eastern hub of international trading operations. Inscriptional and archaeological evidence from the first decades of the 2nd century AD informs us of the enormous range of goods that passed through the city—slaves, salt, dried foods, purple cloth, perfumes, prostitutes (from an inscription on a stele of AD 137), silk, jade, muslin, spices, ebony, incense, ivory, precious stones, and glass.[9] Palmyra's centrality in the Near Eastern trading network, and the oft-quoted insatiable demand in the Roman world for the goods which passed through the city as they were conveyed from east to west contributed substantially to the enormous wealth of the city and its merchant class.

Already in the 1st century AD, some of the great building projects that were to become defining features of Palmyra's urban landscape had been undertaken and were rapidly transforming the city's appearance. This century saw the construction of the first temples for which Palmyra became renowned, and is still renowned today—above all, the magnificent Temple of the god Bel, one of the oldest deities in the Semitic pantheon, followed by the Temple of Baalshamin, the Lord of Heaven, and the Temple of the Babylonian god Nabu. Funds may originally have been provided by Rome to start the building programme off. But the city's monumental projects were financed mostly by the Palmyrenes themselves, sometimes by wealthy individual citizens. In 129, just as the city was approaching the peak of its development, it received a visit from the emperor Hadrian, during the course of one of his imperial grand tours. Hadrian was deeply impressed by what he saw, and to commemorate his visit—the entire cost of which was borne by a wealthy Palmyrene merchant called Male Agrippa, probably the city's richest and most generous benefactor—he renamed the city Hadriane Palmyra. Ten years later, Agrippa opened his coffers again (as he probably did on many occasions) to finance the rebuilding of the Temple of Bel. With its imposing set of Corinthian columns, this, the greatest of Palmyra's religious structures, well exemplifies the pervasive effects of Graeco-Roman influence on Palmyrene culture. Indeed, to outward appearances, Palmyra displayed many elements of a Graeco-Roman city. But in fact, the distinctive Palmyrene culture arose from a blend of these elements with indigenous ones, the latter reflected in sculptural representations of a number of Palmyrene deities and cult ceremonials. More about this below.

A blend of cultures

In the reign of Septimius Severus, the city entered a new stage in its relationship with Rome when it was elevated to the status of a Roman *colonia*, the highest civic status that could be accorded a city of the empire; in effect, its inhabitants now enjoyed full Roman citizenship rights.[10] The city's administrative structure was *apparently* organized along Greek lines, with the institution of an assembly called by the Greek term *demos*, and a deliberative council by the Greek term *boule*. Greek and Latin nomenclature was widely used alongside Palmyrene terms. But Arabic was the most frequently heard language in the city's streets and thoroughfares. Probably at least half, and perhaps a good deal more, of the city's population was of Arabic origin. We learn this from their own names and from the names of a number of their deities, as well as from what we know of their cults and rituals. No doubt their ancestry could be traced back to nomadic desert wanderers, reflected in their continuing social organization along tribal lines, who finally adopted a settled way of existence and developed skills and wealth as caravaneers. But the language most frequently appearing in the city's written records was Aramaic, the international lingua franca of the Near Eastern world from the Achaemenid era through the periods of the Seleucid and Roman empires. The language we call Palmyrene is a local version of Aramaic, with some Arabic terms and expressions blended in. (Otherwise, there is no trace of the written Arabic language in Palmyra.) Some 3,000 inscriptions in the Palmyrene language have come to light in the city, the earliest dating to 44 BC, and the latest to AD 272. But Palmyrene inscriptions have a much wider distribution. Some are found as far east as the Euphrates, and others, to the west, in Numidia, Dacia, and Britain in the far north. No doubt their appearance in these regions indicates the presence of Palmyrene units in Roman military garrisons stationed there.[11]

The Greek language also appears fairly frequently in Palmyra, and is partnered with Palmyrene in a number of bilingual inscriptions. There is little doubt that many of the wealthier elements of the city's population spoke both Greek and Palmyrene, for very good commercial as well as diplomatic reasons. Given the Palmyrenes' active involvement in international trade, it was essential that the practitioners of this trade had fluency in both languages. Greek as well as Aramaic was widely used throughout the Near Eastern world, from the Seleucid era onwards. Latin is very much less in evidence at Palmyra, even after the city had become fully incorporated into the Roman administrative system. There are some trilingual inscriptions, in Palmyrene, Greek, and Latin, but these are exceptional. At least in this relatively remote part of the Roman-controlled world, a knowledge of the overlord's official language was not an essential prerequisite for advancing and prospering under Roman imperial rule—provided one could speak Greek and Aramaic.

Beneath its overlay of Graeco-Roman culture, Palmyra had many features that were reflective of Near Eastern cultural elements and traditions. Thus the towering Corinthian porticoes of the great Temple of Bel enclose an inner sanctuary whose design and layout show a blend of both Semitic and Graeco-Roman elements. At each end of the sanctuary, there is an enclosed shrine. The northern and more elaborately decorated one probably housed images of Palmyra's holy, and wholly Semitic, trinity: Bel, Palmyra's divine patron, and his colleagues Yarhibol and Aglibol, sun and moon gods respectively. The southern shrine may have been dedicated to Bel on his own, and may once have contained a portable image of the god, to be taken out and displayed in the processions which appear to have been a regular feature of Palmyra's religious life. Massive Corinthian columns also provide the city with what is today its most distinctive feature—the Grand Colonnade, built in the 2nd century AD, and marking out Palmyra's main street, the 'Cardo Maximus' in Roman terms. The sheer monumentality of the colonnade

Figure 26. The Grand Colonnade, Palmyra

suggests that it was used as a sacred Processional Way and not—or not only—as simply a main thoroughfare. It also served as a market arcade, with numerous shops and booths displaying their wares, their owners' names and trades inscribed on the doors above. Indeed this *may* indicate that the Grand Colonnade was nothing more than a grand oriental bazaar. The notion of customers haggling over items displayed for sale in a row of shopkeepers' booths within the majestic setting of the great Corinthian colonnade is an attractive one, with a distinct Oriental feel about, as anyone knows who has visited the Covered Market in Istanbul and the great souks of the Eastern world. Of course, the Colonnade could have been used for a number of purposes including religious processions, and no doubt for the parades of dignitaries and emissaries from Rome and Parthia and elsewhere visiting the city. Multifunctionality is by no means an uncommon feature of the Near Eastern world's architectural culture.

We do not know whether the Greek and Roman terms for officials and the offices they held genuinely reflect the adoption of Graeco-Roman political and administrative institutions. Or, if so, to what extent. Probably these terms too were part of an overlay beneath which native traditions long pre-dating the Roman period persisted. Tribal organization may have continued to play a major role in the Roman-era city. Stoneman notes that we know the names of at least thirty tribes of Palmyra, including seventeen major ones, many of which bear names clearly representing their dedication to a particular god.[12] Much of the organization and funding of the city's trading enterprises may have been the responsibility of tribes rather than individual merchants, as indeed the funding of most of the city's great construction enterprises was likely to have been. A building now known as the Tariff Court, because of an inscribed stone found there, dating to AD 137 and bearing the text of a decree which sets out tariff arrangements, was probably the place where caravaneers were required to pay customs dues or taxes on the goods they had acquired for trading purposes.

Some rationalization or simplification of the tribal organization may have occurred by the time the city reached the peak of its development in the 2nd century AD, but the tribal tradition probably remained strong. The building located just behind the Severan-period theatre and commonly identified as a senate house may in fact have served as a venue for 'a gathering of tribal elders or chiefs'[13] rather than as one where meetings were conducted in the manner of a provincial Roman Senate. It was a small structure built on Graeco-Roman lines with a peristyle court and a chamber with apse at one end and rows of seating around it. We should again remember that the Palmyrenes were allowed considerable freedom in the way they conducted their affairs. The theatre itself (never completed) may not have been used for theatrical performances in the traditional Classical sense, despite its convenional Classical features. Stoneman suggests that it was used perhaps less for dramatic performances than for public announcements, political meetings and speeches, and displays of oratory.[14]

One thing certain is that Palmyra prospered and flourished under Roman rule, particularly from the time it superseded Petra in 106 as the most important trading centre in the Near East. In material terms, the city's affluence at this time is reflected in its major rebuilding programme, which saw the restoration of old monumental buildings and the construction or reconstruction of its temples. By now Palmyra had become a markedly cosmopolitan city, its streets thronged with persons, especially those involved in commercial activities, of many different countries, including Syrians from various cities, Aramaeans, Jews, Parthians, Babylonians, Persians, and traders and entrepreneurs from the western world. The city's pervasively cosmopolitan character is displayed in the eclecticism and syncretism of its cults, with a pantheon of more than sixty deities. But this cosmopolitanism never obscured Palmyra's Arabic origins and traditions, as illustrated by the military garb in which many of its gods were dressed and in depictions of some of them riding horses and camels.[15]

We have stressed that Palmyra's wealth derived essentially from its oasis location in the middle of Syria and from the skill and enterprise of its inhabitants in establishing and maintaining international trade-routes which linked the Far East with the Mediterranean world. These routes extended from China, Trans-Oxiana, and India to the cities of coastal Syria, and thence to the western world. Silks and spices were among the wealth-generating exotic items that figured prominently in the trade. Palmyrenes were very 'hands on' in their conduct of these international ventures, avoiding wherever possible the use of foreign agents or middlemen on the routes along which their merchandise was transported. Thus we find colonies or outposts of Palmyrenes themselves at various strategic places on these routes. There were also enclaves of Palmyrene merchants or their representatives at Babylon, and further afield at Coptos in Egypt and Merv in modern Turkmenistan. And Palmyrene merchants regularly sailed the Red Sea in their commercial activities. This was a matter of no small importance, as we shall see when we turn finally to the story of Zenobia.

The power and wealth of Palmyra

All this raises the question of how much territory Palmyra actually controlled. Traditionally, the former oasis encampment probably served as the centre of a group of tribal lands controlled by a confederation of sheikhs. But as Palmyra came within the Roman orbit and as its own urban character developed, the territories over which it had immediate control must have been more clearly defined. A boundary marker found at Khirbet el-Bilaas, 75 km north-west of Palmyra, indicates the limits of Palmyrene territory to the north-west.[16] To the east and north-east, its territory seems to have reached the Euphrates, if we can so judge from Appian's account of the Palmyrene expedition of Mark Antony's cavalry. And to the south-west, a boundary marker at Qasr el-Hair al-Gharbi, 60 km south-west of Palmyra, marked a point on Palmyra's border with the territory controlled by Emesa, which lay 90 km to the north-west.[17] Thus the city itself was merely the nucleus of a much larger state covering some thousands of square kilometres. It was very largely from this catchment area that Palmyra must have drawn its substantial military forces, needed for both the protection of the metropolis and its trade-routes and merchant enterprises. Caravans laden with a wealth of exotic items were attractive targets for desert brigands and larger predatory forces. A significant part of Palmyra's military resources must have been deployed on escort duty to safeguard these precious cargoes and their carriers.

Perhaps the greatest threat to Palmyra's safe conduct of its merchant operations was posed by a rival confederation of Arab tribes called the Tanukh—aggressive, warlike groups whose predatory activities and territorial ambitions brought them into head-on conflict with the Palmyrenes. Additionally there were the Great Kingdoms of the east to deal with. First the Parthians. Though Palmyra's political orientation was clearly to the western world, and indeed it had become an integral and formal part of this world during the 1st century AD, its position on the edge of Roman territory and its relative proximity to Parthian territory gave it a distinctiveness which both Rome and Parthia acknowledged and respected. Rome did so by the special status it accorded the city, and the various benefactions it bestowed upon it. Parthia accepted the city's pro-Roman orientation and left it virtually unmolested throughout the period when Parthian and Palmyrene history coincided, even at times when relations between Rome and Parthia became overtly hostile. This generally happy state of affairs, from which Parthia also benefited, ensured the continuance of Palmyrene trade free from interference by the Iranian-based kingdom. The Sasanian successors of Parthia would not prove so obliging.

By and large, however, Palmyra conducted its international enterprises without serious intervention from outside forces. These enterprises not only generated enormous wealth for its leading citizens, but must also have had a substantial flow-on effect to its inhabitants lower down the socio-economic scale. All alike could participate in the city's cosmopolitan lifestyle and in the pomp and circumstance of its public ceremonies. But most of what we know about Palmyrene society has to do with the city's commercial and social elite, their families, and their apparently luxurious manner of living. And much of our information comes from their burial places. These are located in the necropolises beyond the walls, especially the Valley of the Tombs west of the city. The tombs are of two basic types—those above ground, consisting of house, temple, and tower tombs, and the below-ground burial places we call hypogaea, of which there are many hundreds. The tower tombs in particular (two are depicted on the cover) tell us much about the life and society of their occupants, for each was a family tomb, often several storeys high. Some of them contained hundreds of bodies— families of the very extended type. Painted scenes and sculptures of those laid to rest within them provide us with a wealth of detail about their lives and lifestyles, with banqueting assigned a prominent role. The tower tombs are the most remarkable index of the prosperity of individual Palmyrenes, Stoneman comments. But the impression their occupants have left us, he says, is a disturbing one; their portraits, male and female alike, are of haughty people who stare out at us with an unsettling self-assurance, indeed an arrogance.[18]

Haughtiness, self-assurance, arrogance? Were these among the qualities that raised the Palmyrenes to great heights, and then helped precipitate their downfall? In Palmyra's story we may have some of the classic ingredients of a *hubris–nemesis* morality tale.

18

Syria's 'King of Kings': The Life and Death of Odenathus

Around 250, several years before Valerian's appointment to the purple, a citizen of Palmyra called Udaynath makes his first appearance in Syria's story. Udaynath is his Arabic name (Uday in modern Arabic). We know him better by his Roman one, Septimius Odenathus. By the year in question, Odenathus' family seems to have won considerable prominence in Palmyrene society, much to the benefit of his own standing in this society. Both he and his son Septimius Hairanes (Hairan, Classical Herodianus) achieved senatorial rank in 251. And both were endowed with the Greek title '*exarchos* of the Palmyrenes', and the Palmyrene one, RŠ TDMWR, 'head of Tadmor'.[1] If Odenathus was born around 220 as commonly supposed, then his son Hairanes was still only a boy at the time he became a senator. But we do not know what precisely the rare terms *exarchos* and Palmyrene RŠ mean; *exarchos* could be used in the Roman imperial period to describe a priesthood, and RŠ could simply mean 'leading citizen'.[2] There is, however, no doubt that Odenathus' family enjoyed at this time an important status in Palmyra, if not a pre-eminent one. Quite possibly, it was a relative newcomer to the city, perhaps having joined a westward movement of Arab tribal groups into Syria at the time of the Parthian empire's collapse. This had happened a quarter of a century before Odenathus first appears in our records.

Then nothing more is heard of him for the next few years, until the capture of Valerian in 260.[3] It may well be that Odenathus used the intervening period to build his authority in Palmyra—and at the same time Palmyra's military strength, probably reinforcing it by alliances with desert tribal groups as he became increasingly concerned at the mounting Sasanian threat to his city's prosperity, and indeed to its very existence. When Valerian fell, it was time for action. Perhaps after an unsuccessful attempt to reach a diplomatic settlement with the Sasanian king Shapur (we shall return to this below), Odenathus resolved to confront the Sasanian forces in the full flush of their victory over the Romans, now seemingly powerless to defend their eastern territories.

The Sasanian Goliath confronted

From our literary sources, we can piece together a stirring tale of great derring-do—the tale of an upstart Arab leader from a merchant city in the midst of Syria's wastelands who took on the mighty warlord of the Sasanians, still exulting in his humiliation of Rome, by confronting his forces head-on in battle. It was a challenge of the greatest audacity, bound to end in disaster. That is how it must have seemed. Yet—if we accept our sources at face value—this latter-day David of the desert achieved a stunning victory. Mustering an army of Syrian peasants,[4] he welded them into a formidable fighting force which secured Syria against the invaders, attacked the Sasanians as they headed back to the Euphrates, and drove them out of Mesopotamia, recapturing the important Roman frontier cities Carrhae and Nisibis. Odenathus' ragtag army pursued Shapur's forces as they retreated all the way to the Sasanian capital Ctesiphon, plundering their baggage train and even capturing the king's harem.[5] Ctesiphon itself was placed under siege. It may have held firm against capture, but the countryside around it was ravaged and destroyed by its attackers.

Odenathus was not yet done. Returning to Syria, he marched upon the city of Emesa, where a pretender to the imperial throne, Quietus, had taken up residence. He assembled his armed hordes outside Emesa's walls, and demanded the city's surrender. According to one version of events, the demand was refused,[6] and the city had to be taken by force. But another version informs us that Quietus' supporters, deciding that self-preservation was the smartest option, executed the pretender, threw his body over the walls to prove it, and then surrendered to Odenathus.[7] Either way, the siege of Emesa came to an end, and Odenathus entered the city in triumph. All this was accomplished, apparently, within the space of a couple of years (260–1). Valerian still remained in captivity, but Odenathus had won back for Rome all its eastern territories, and eliminated at least for the foreseeable future the Sasanian menace. As a further warning to Shapur to keep out of Roman affairs, he *may* have conducted a second expedition down the Tigris several years later (267?). Everything was done apparently in the name of Gallienus, emperor of Rome.

When news reached Rome of the Palmyrene's spectacular successes in the east, Gallienus must have been overjoyed—initially at least. It was in effect *his* victory over the Sasanian enemy, albeit carried out by a local representative on his behalf, and *his* was the triumph he celebrated in Rome in 263 to mark the victory, displaying in the triumphal procession the prisoners, Sasanian satraps, whom Odenathus had respectfully(?) sent him.[8] Great honours were bestowed upon the Palmyrene. One of our sources claims that 'he was made emperor over almost the whole East',[9] in another, he is accorded the title *dux Orientis* 'Commander of the East'. So too, scholars have concluded that he may have borne a title like 'Restorer of the East'. We shall question below whether these titles were actually bestowed, and if so, by whom, and what precisely they meant. In the flush of his success, Odenathus may now have called himself 'King of Kings', thus equating himself with the greatest monarchs of the Near Eastern world, dating back to the rulers of the Achaemenid empire. He may also have conferred this title upon his son Hairanes, perhaps as an explicit statement of dynastic succession.

But it is time for us to do a reality check. There has been much scholarly harrumphing about almost every detail of the above story, since most of it is based on literary sources whose historical reliability is highly suspect. Especially the *Historia Augusta*! It is of course patently absurd to suggest that Odenathus fought the Sasanian army with no more than a band of Syrian peasants (even if they were armed with more than staves and pitchforks). Admittedly, the notion that this actually happened is an appealing one, exemplifying as it does a theme commonly found in folklore—uprisings by peasant militias whose courage and just causes carry them to victory, against apparently insuperable odds, over oppressive regimes, evil overlords, and rapacious enemy invaders. History and literature are dotted with episodes of this kind. We should not, however, entirely discard our current story, which is repeated in a number of our ancient sources. For one thing, we know very little about the forces upon which a Palmyrene military leader could call, and it is quite possible that to strengthen his army, Odenathus did in fact recruit widely among the Syrian peasantry. But his army must also have included a significant number of Roman troops who had survived the Sasanian onslaught and were still stationed in Syria, and also troops which the Palmyrene leader was able to recruit from alliances he had made with desert sheikhs. But very likely the backbone of Odenathus' army was provided by his own Palmyrene soldiery, including a contingent of Palmyra's famed mounted archers. We should not underestimate the strength of the merchant city's military forces. Palmyra must long have had a highly trained and substantial militia, drawn from a large catchment area, for defending its far-reaching trade routes and widespread trading outposts. We have already noted the likelihood that a Palmyrene tribal chief provided Antiochus III with a contingent of 10,000 troops in his confrontation with Ptolemy IV at Raphia in 217 BC.

None the less, questions have been raised about how comprehensive Odenathus' campaign against the Sasanians really was. A sceptical view is that it was no more than a minor affair, essentially an exercise in propaganda that greatly exaggerated the reality.[10] There is also some doubt about the claim that Odenathus recovered the cities of Nisibis and Carrhae in Mesopotamia, allegedly seized by Shapur. We do not know when their initial capture took place, and Millar seems not entirely convinced that it ever happened.[11] On the other hand, there is no doubt that after Odenathus' operations, whatever their nature, the Sasanians did not reappear in Rome's eastern provinces for some years to come, and all lost territory was restored to Roman authority. While there may be reasons unknown to us for Shapur's sudden withdrawal of his forces back to their homeland after his substantial victories (perhaps there were internal political problems that required his immediate attention), we should not detract too much from Odenathus' achievement. Undoubtedly, he brought much needed stability to the eastern Roman world, at least to that part of it between the eastern Mediterranean coast and the Euphrates, and may well have saved it from total disintegration after Valerian's capture. But if in fact there had been no Odenathus to oppose them, would the Sasanians have consolidated their hold upon the region and made it part of their empire? That remains open to question—particularly if, as our sources suggest, it was only when the Sasanians were actually withdrawing from their western operations that Odenathus attacked them.

In whose interests?

In any case, we have further questions: In what capacity was Odenathus acting when he took on the Sasanians? Did he do so primarily in his own and his city's interests? Was he forced to take action when it became clear that Rome could no longer afford him any protection against the invader? In contrast to their Parthian predecessors, the Sasanians if given the opportunity were not likely to tolerate the continuing commercial monopoly Palmyra had enjoyed under Roman patronage in the Near Eastern world. And if Shapur had the chance, he would most likely have taken the city and its kingdom into his own orbit, even if he spared it the ravages to which he had subjected other cities belonging to Rome. Odenathus may well have believed that in defence of Palmyra's continuing *quasi*-independence, indeed its very survival, he had no option but to take up arms against the enemy. Particularly if the story is true that he had first tried unsuccessfully to buy peace with Shapur, as Philip the Arab had done.

According to this story, he sent Shapur a large camel-train laden with rare and valuable merchandise in an attempt to win him over. Shapur scornfully rejected the gifts, ordering that they be cast into the Euphrates, and demanded that the sender appear in person before him, falling prostrate at his throne with his hands bound in chains. So the story goes. On the assumption that it is true,[12] does Odenathus' initiative reflect an attempt to secure his city's safety and independence by doing a separate deal with the enemy? Or was he acting on behalf of Rome? The latter was how it was seen in the Roman world. Indeed, Odenathus may have been assigned a formal role as Rome's chief representative in the East. Particularly if he had held the appointment of governor of Syria Phoenice at that time, an appointment that Valerian would have conferred.[13] For what they are worth, a couple of our literary sources might indirectly support the inscriptional evidence for such an appointment. They inform us that Odenathus' activities in the East, both his operations against Shapur and the pretender Quietus, were ordered by Gallienus.[14] And that is the most likely scenario. But Odenathus clearly had an eye to his own interests as well. Alaric Watson comments: 'By making himself the indispensable ally of Rome while steadfastly championing Palmyrene interests in the region, Odenathus thus skilfully exploited the situation in the east to his own personal advantage.'[15]

There is much debate about the titles allegedly accorded to Odenathus in the wake of his Sasanian victory and the elimination of the pretender Quietus. The list of these titles, which crop up in various sources, is impressive: *Dux Romanorum, Corrector Totius Orientis, Imperator Totius Orientis, Augustus*, and *King of Kings*. Were all of these—or indeed any of them—officially bestowed upon Odenathus by the emperor Gallienus? The first, meaning 'Commander of the Romans', quite possibly was. The title was later borne by Odenathus' son Vaballathus after his father's death. It may well have been granted first to Odenathus in recognition of his role as commander-in-chief of the combined army of Romans and Palmyrenes and other Syrians against Shapur's forces.[16] We have no direct evidence that the second title, *Corrector Totius Orientis*, 'Regulator/Restorer of the whole East', was conferred upon Odenathus, at least during his lifetime. Most scholars think that it probably was, on the basis of its supposed Palmyrene equivalent on an inscribed statue set up posthumously for Odenathus by his generals Zabdas and Zabbai in 271.[17] There is a question too of what precisely is meant by the term *Oriens* in these contexts. Its application here is probably a fairly restricted one, covering at most the region of Syria in its broadest sense.[18]

As for the third title, *Imperator Totius Orientis*, 'Emperor of the whole East', the *Historia Augusta* is alone in claiming that it was bestowed on Odenathus. That in itself is enough to make us doubt the claim.[19] As too the claim made by the *Historia Augusta* that the title *Augustus* was conferred upon Odenathus by Gallienus after his alleged victory over the Sasanians.[20] That would in effect have made Odenathus Gallienus' co-emperor. Even if the emperor did accord some titles of distinction to the Palmyrene for his achievements in the east, the possibility that he went so far as to appoint him his partner in the purple can be safely dismissed. Finally there is the title *King of Kings*. Again, we have no evidence that Odenathus himself used this title in his lifetime, either of himself or of his son Hairanes. It is first attested in the posthumous inscription referred to above, dedicated to Odenathus in 271 by his generals.[21] Would their living leader have dared proclaim himself in such a seemingly provocative way, while he was still, at least nominally, a subject of the Roman emperor? Perhaps he did, and did so without causing a stir in Rome. Some scholars believe that the title's sheer exoticness, so remote from anything in the official Roman titulary, and so absurdly pretentious from a western point of view, was unlikely to ruffle any important feathers in the western world.[22]

Murder most foul?

In 267 or 268, Odenathus' life ended abruptly and suspiciously, leaving us with an intriguing unsolved murder mystery. There are a number of suspects, but none of them stands out conspicuously from the rest. We cannot even be sure *where* Odenathus met his end. One of our sources, Syncellus, claims that he was killed in Pontus in Asia Minor, just as he was about to attack the Goths who had invaded the region. In this version, he was treacherously murdered by his namesake, another Odenathus; whether or not this otherwise unknown man was related to the king and what his actual motive was are not revealed by our source. Another commentator, Zosimus, generally considered the most reliable of all those who deal with the Palmyra episode, tells us that Odenathus was killed by conspirators in Emesa, while he was residing there and celebrating the birthday of one of his friends. A third source, this time the *Historia Augusta*, claims that the king was despatched by his cousin Maeonius, along with his son Hairanes (here Herodes), out of sheer jealousy; for a brief time Maeonius was mistakenly hailed as emperor, before the troops assassinated him. It was also rumoured, the *HA* tells us, that Maeonius had previously entered into a conspiracy with Odenathus' wife Zenobia, who could not bear that her stepson should be more highly ranked than her own son; but there is no suggestion that Zenobia herself was actually involved in her husband's murder. Another conspiracy theory, presented to us by John of Antioch, implicates the emperor Gallienus; no details are given, but in the unlikely event that Gallienus did arrange for Odenathus' murder, we can only suppose that he acted out of fear that the champion of Rome's interests in the East was starting to acquire a lean and hungry look, and might join the long line of pretenders to his throne.[23] Other possible candidates for Odenathus' assassination include the Sasanian king Shapur (via his agents), clearing the way for another expedition to the west, and the Palmyrenes themselves, or a group of malcontents among them, disgruntled about the way things were turning out in their city under Odenathus' leadership.[24] So we have plenty of suspects, but no famous detective to gather them all together in the drawing room and reveal to us who actually 'done the deed'.

It may, after all, have been a chance thing, sparked off by an act committed in the heat of the moment. That possibility is indicated by another of our ancient sources. Zonaras, a 12th-century Byzantine historian, tells us that Odenathus was killed by his nephew following an argument that blew up between the pair while they were on a hunting expedition.[25] Tempers flared when the nephew struck dead an animal that had leapt out at them; in so doing, he had denied his uncle the right of first strike, the king's royal prerogative. Odenathus was furious and immediately took the young man's horse from him. That made things worse. To be deprived of one's horse was a great insult in that part of the world. The nephew now angrily threatened his uncle, and was promptly clapped in irons. There he remained until the king's eldest son persuaded his father to release him. But the young man had not yet cooled off. Once his fetters were removed, he rushed at his uncle with sword drawn, and slew both king and heir.

Whatever the manner of Odenathus' death, one thing on which all our sources agree is that it was sudden and unexpected. And that might well have had grave political and military consequences for his fledgling kingdom. As it turned out, there were neither. The king's abrupt departure left the way open, without let or hindrance, for the ascendancy of his wife. For a few brief years, Zenobia became one of the most powerful rulers of the ancient world, and within that time one of Rome's most formidable enemies.

19

Zenobia, Queen of the East

The seamless succession

On Odenathus' death, the transition of power in Palmyra, and along with it the territories over which the self-styled(?) 'king of kings' had held sway, was a smooth, seamless one. The royal widow Zenobia now became *de facto* ruler of the Palmyrene world. *De facto* because, to begin with, she acted merely as the regent for her son by Odenathus. His name was Wahballath, 'Gift of (the goddess) Allat'. Roman sources call him Vaballathus, and we shall henceforth use his Roman name. Vaballathus was still a child when his father and his step-brother Hairanes, heir to the Palmyrene throne, were assassinated. Unsurprisingly, suspicion has fallen on Zenobia as the instigator of their deaths, her motive being to secure the succession for her son—rather like a latter-day Livia.[1] But motive though she appears to have had, we have absolutely no grounds for attributing the deaths or the following succession to any maternal plotting. Zenobia's assumption of power was a testimony to her husband's success not only in establishing his supreme rule over his fellow-Palmyrenes, and winning the recognition both of Rome and undoubtedly the desert tribes of the region, but also in gaining recognition of himself as the founder of a royal dynasty. There appears to have been no challenge to the assumption that the dead king's own family would continue to hold supreme power in the kingdom he had established—even though royal dynastic succession was, as far as we know, unprecedented in Palmyra's long history.

But Zenobia herself must be given much of the credit for the easy, unchallenged passage from Odenathus' reign to her own. She had already built herself a formidable reputation throughout the region, in Palmyra and beyond, as a great hunter and warrior, accompanying her husband on his military expeditions and demonstrating those qualities of endurance and courage for which her husband was apparently renowned. Both Classical and Arab sources present her as a powerful, charismatic figure, noted for her great beauty as well as her skills in the hunt and on the field of battle. This has inspired one of the best-known passages in Gibbon's *Decline and Fall*: 'If we except the doubtful achievements of Semiramis, Zenobia is perhaps the only female whose superior genius broke through the servile indolence imposed on her sex by the climate and manners of Asia. She claimed her descent from the Macedonian kings of Egypt, equalled in beauty her ances- tor Cleopatra, and far surpassed that princess in chastity and valour. Zenobia was of dark complexion (for in speaking of a lady these trifles become important). Her teeth were of a pearly whiteness, and her large black eyes sparkled with uncommon fire, tempered by the most attractive sweetness. Her voice was strong and harmonious. Her manly understanding was strengthened and adorned by study. She was not ignorant of the Latin tongue, but possessed in equal perfection the Greek, the Syriac, and the Egyptian languages. She had drawn up for her own use an epitome of oriental history, and familiarly compared the beauties of Homer and Plato under the tuition of the sublime Longinus.' Gibbon goes on in similar vein, and in so doing takes his material entirely from the *Historia Augusta*. Which should immedi- ately sound warning bells. But let's not be too alarmed. Here at least the *HA* ties in reasonably well with what we learn about Zenobia from other sources. Later, we shall talk about the references to Semiramis, Cleopatra, and Longi- nus, and the queen's erudition and linguistic skills.

The most romantic account of the Palmyrene queen's origins comes from Arab tradition, as recorded in the history of the 9th–10th century Arab historian al-Tabari (839–923).[2] In this tradition, the queen's name is al- Zabba' (aka Na'ilah). She was the daughter of an Arab sheikh 'Amr Ibn Zarib, chief of the 'Amlaqi tribe, and sister of a woman called Zabibah, who became her close confidante. A bitter feud had broken out between her father and another Arab sheikh, Jadhimah, leader of an Arab alliance of tribes called the Tanukh. The feud was apparently resolved when the armies of the two sheikhs met in a fierce and final showdown. 'Amr was defeated and killed, and his forces scattered. Laden with the spoils of battle, Jadhimah returned home triumphant. But the final reckoning was yet to come. Al-Zabba' promptly assumed leadership of the 'Amlaqi tribe, and after consolidating her authority over her desert subjects, prepared to exact vengeance on her father's destroyer. She would do so on the field of battle. At least that was her original intention. But she was persuaded by her sister not to risk the uncertainties of war, and so sought revenge by a more duplic-itous path.

She wrote to Jadhima, pleading that she was but a woman with all the weaknesses of her sex, and invited him to come to a meeting with her, so that a partnership between them and an alliance between their kingdoms could be made. Despite the urgent advice of one of his own counsellors, who warned of treachery, Jadhimah accepted the invitation. It was to prove fatal for him. He proceeded to the agreed meeting-place, but once there, he was suddenly cut off from his own troops by the queen's horsemen and brought before her. Sentence of death was pronounced. But his captor dis-played chivalry in the way it was carried out. She respected the belief that it was not seemly for a king to be put to death by decapitation; beheading a person of such exalted status was appropriate only on the field of battle. Al-Zabba' took a more civilized course, and gave Jadhima the most painless exit possible: she plied him with wine until he was pleasantly inebriated, and then ordered that the veins in his arms be opened. As the order was being carried out, she made sure that not a single drop of his blood fell outside the bowl that was gathering it—for she had been told that if this happened, his blood would be avenged. Thus al-Zabba' satisfied her father's spirit, and destroyed her most dangerous enemy.

There is not the slightest trace of any of this tradition in our Greek and Roman sources, or any other sources for that matter. The story told by al-Tabari very likely reflects a conflation of Arab traditions which had to do originally with a number of desert rulers, including queens. Though cer-tainly in the minority, female Arab rulers were far from unknown in the ancient Near Eastern world. The Arab queens Zabibe and Samsi, referred to in Assyrian inscriptions of the 8th century BC, and the Queen of Sheba are but three of the female rulers whose names come to mind. In al-Zabba''s case, the smooth transition between her father's death and her immediate assumption of his tribe's leadership, along with her readiness to lead his forces into battle, indicate that she had already become a seasoned warrior in her father's lifetime, and may well have accompanied him on a number of his military expeditions. Other prominent female members of Near East-ern royal families did likewise. The 9th-century BC Assyrian queen mother Sammu-ramat, historical prototype of Semiramis, accompanied her son Adad-nirari III on his western military campaigns, and much later Julia

Domna shared military expeditions with both her husband Septimius Severus and her son Caracalla, as did Julia Mamaea with her son Severus Alexander, last ruler of the Severan dynasty. Zenobia went further. Not only did she accompany her husband on his expeditions. She actually fought alongside him, so we are told, and won great praise and renown for doing so, further endearing herself to the masses by disdaining the use of a carriage, kitting herself out as a soldier, and riding and drinking with the troops, without ever getting drunk (*sic HA*).

Our non-Arab sources are rather less dramatic than our Arab ones in what they tell us of the desert queen's entry into history. In Palmyrene inscriptions, Zenobia is known as *sptymy'btzby*,[3] which means 'Septimia Bat-Zabbai', that is to say, 'Septimia, daughter of Zabbai'. This is perhaps of some help in determining what Zenobia's family origins were. The name Zabbai might in fact tie in with the tradition recorded by al-Tabari that she was the daughter of an Arab sheikh—or at least a descendant of one, since the inscription could simply mean that she belonged to a family whose ancestral head was Zabbai (thus she would have been Zabbai's descendant, not literally his daughter). A man of this name is also well known from Palmyra as one of Zenobia's two most important commanders during her campaigns in the west. It is just possible that this Zabbai was actually her father. More likely, Zenobia and her commander were members of the same family or clan group whose ancestral titular head was called Zabbai. The Roman name 'Septimia' clearly betokens continuing respect for the emperor Septimius Severus, still remembered as one of Palmyra's greatest patrons. There were no doubt many Palmyrene citizens who had a Septimia or Septimius component in their names. Several pieces of epigraphic evidence suggest that Zenobia's father was called Antiochus, and that has given rise to much speculation as to who this Antiochus might have been. The name was common enough elsewhere in the Near East, going back to the Seleucid period when no fewer than thirteen Seleucid emperors were so called. But it was quite rare in Palmyra.[4]

Anyhow, the sum total of our knowledge of Zenobia's ancestry is very slight and very confused. The likelihood is that she was at least partly of Arab descent, and that one of her recent ancestors was a desert sheikh, in accordance with the tradition preserved by al-Tabari. But by the time of her birth around 241, Zenobia's family was almost certainly a settled part of Palmyra's urban community. It was no doubt a highly distinguished family, of wealthy merchants who had cast off their desert ways and become an important element in the city's affluent elite commercial class, a family who shared in the benefits, political, commercial, and social, that came from Roman patronage. Its status and wealth made Zenobia a fitting consort for the man who had assumed kingship of Palmyra.

And it seems that she sought to enhance her status by identifying with great women leaders of the past, like the legendary Queen of Sheba, and more especially Dido, the legendary princess of Tyre and queen of Carthage. On her husband's death, Zenobia decked herself out in Dido's robes, so the *Historia Augusta* informs us.[5] Sheba and Dido may have served as role models for Zenobia. But most of all, Cleopatra VII, last of the Ptolemies, was her guiding light and inspiration. That she was also her ancestor is a claim we can readily dismiss, despite Gibbon's acceptance of it. Gibbon had mixed views about the comparative qualities of the two women. Zenobia was as beautiful as Cleopatra, so Gibbon says, but she far surpassed her in chastity and valour. Indeed Zenobia seems to have been as renowned for her virtue as for her fighting and hunting qualities—if we go by the *Historia Augusta*. This literary hodgepodge informs us that the queen allowed her husband to have sex with her only once a month, and then only for the purpose of producing an heir. Or as Gibbon decorously puts it: 'She never admitted her husband's embraces but for the sake of posterity. If her hopes were baffled, in the ensuing month she reiterated the experiment.'

Her reputation for chastity may also be reflected in Arab tradition. We have reported al-Tabari's account of her meeting with Jadhimah, and the Tanukh leader's capture and execution. Al-Tabari relates that on Jadhima's arrival, the Arab queen promptly hitched up her robes and exposed to him her pubic hair, which she had plaited. 'O Jadhimah,' she said to her astonished visitor, 'do you see the concern of a bride?' The purpose of her gesture was apparently to demonstrate to her father's destroyer that she had no intention of marrying him. One might wonder why she felt it necessary to make this point (unless she was simply taunting him) since she was about to kill him anyway. But it probably serves to illustrate not only her contempt for her enemy, but more generally, in some unclear way, her pride in her chastity. (The plaiting of her pubic hair perhaps had something to do with this.)

The early regnal years

The first (almost) three years of Zenobia's reign passed peacefully enough. Her installation of her son Vaballathus on the throne of Palmyra as his father's formal successor seems to have been readily accepted by the Palmyrenes. As was her role as regent, since Vaballathus could have been no more than ten years of age at the time. Let us say at this point that Vaballathus never becomes for us more than a shadowy figure, whom we know of almost entirely through the honorifics, attested in inscriptions and coin legends, which were bestowed upon him at his mother's instigation. We can trace through these progressively grander titles the nature of the royal authority which Vaballathus exercised—in theory. In fact, they are more reflective of the authority his mother wielded, supposedly on his behalf, in the years between her assumption of the Palmyrene throne as regent after her husband's death and her later confrontations with the Roman emperor Aurelian. Throughout his mother's career, Vaballathus remained merely a name without substance, and that may well have been as his mother wanted it. We cannot of course altogether rule out the possibility that she would one day have allowed her son to assume actual leadership of his subjects. Perhaps that was her original intention. But as her reputation grew ever greater along with her conquests, she may well have put aside any thought of relinquishing power to her son. We shall never know for sure, for Vaballathus was still a youth, perhaps no more than fifteen, when his mother's career and his own, for what it was worth, were abruptly terminated.

The circumstances which brought this about will be dealt with later in our story. For the present, we must return to the first years of Zenobia's reign. The queen spent these in consolidating her authority within the region where her husband had held sway, which included much of Syria and part of north-western Mesopotamia. But she took care not to provoke Rome. None of the titles she assumed initially for herself and her son was inconsistent with her status, inherited from her husband, as a subject of the Roman emperor and the protector of Rome's interests and provincial territories in the east. At the same time, she must have seen to the strengthening of her kingdom's defences against future threats from the Sasanians. This she would have done by building up her outposts in the border regions,[6] and no doubt also by increasing substantially her military resources, either through direct recruitment of desert tribesmen or through alliances with their leaders which guaranteed reinforcements for her army whenever the need arose. This was in the period between Odenathus' death in 267/268 and 270. One of the main threats to the security of Zenobia's kingdom at this time came from hostile Arab groups like the Tanukh confederation in the Hauran.[7] In the short term, the Sasanian threat was a less pressing one.

Shapur I's reign was nearing its end, and the ageing emperor was more concerned with ensuring stability in his own kingdom and smoothing the way
for the succession of his son Hormizd I than with making a fresh bid to
reassert Sasanian claims in the west.

Things were changing in the western world as well. In the heartland of
the Roman empire, a new regime was installed in 268 when the emperor
Gallienus was assassinated by a group of his officers while he was laying siege
to Milan. A pretender Aureolus was holed up there with his supporters. The
murdered emperor was replaced by another of his officers, Marcus Aurelius
Claudius (III), who promptly disposed of Aureolus and assumed the imperial
purple, winning for himself the support of the Senate and, more importantly,
the troops. As soon as his position was secure, Claudius devoted himself to
driving the Goths out of the Balkans, an enterprise which culminated in his
victory over the enemy at the battle of Naissus in Moesia (a country located
on the lower Danube). For the time being, the Gothic threat in the region
had been significantly reduced; hence the new emperor's epithet 'Gothicus'.[8]
What is important for our story is that his focus on the Gothic problem
meant that Zenobia was left free to pursue her military enterprises and her
ambitions in the east. Which was not at this stage a serious issue for Rome,
for the Palmyrene's activities did not as yet conflict with her professed loyalty
to the emperor, whoever that happened to be.

She also devoted the early period of her reign to activities of a more
peaceful nature—and above all, it seems, to boosting her city's cultural pro-
file. Palmyra may have been a wealthy city with a socially sophisticated elite,
but it lacked cultural sophistication. Impressive though its architectural
achievements were, one might take the uncharitable view that Palmyra
erred on the side of vulgar ostentation. Significantly perhaps, there is not
one surviving structure in the city, let alone a major public building, that can
be attributed to Zenobia's reign. Even the complex, long thought to be her
palace, turns out to be the camp of the later emperor Diocletian. Arguably,
Zenobia's reign has left no tangible remains simply because it was too short
for the queen to engage in any major building activity, especially since after
her first couple of years on the throne she devoted the rest of her career to
military campaigns. But that aside, bricks and stone and mortar probably
aroused no great passion in her. What she was more intent on, in her first
years, was the development of her city as a great cultural centre, with the
royal residence as its focal point. The queen's 'ancestor' Cleopatra VII, her
model and mentor across the centuries, may have provided an important

source of inspiration for this undertaking. Whatever else we might think of Cleopatra, she was apparently a woman of sophistication and learning, an *arbiter elegantiae* who set the standards of good taste for those around her, and not just by writing (as she did) books on hairdressing and cosmetics.

Zenobia sought to create about herself a court that was renowned for its culture and learning, wherein she would be surrounded by 'a glittering salon of poets, rhetoricians, and philosophers'.[9] Palmyra would become the greatest intellectual and cultural centre of the eastern Roman world. Or so she hoped. But it was all something of a pipe-dream. The city would never come close to Alexandria or Antioch in this respect. But the queen did her best to attract the best. Most notably, she hired one of the most prominent Greek philosophers of the age—Cassius Longinus, a native Syrian, probably born in Emesa, who taught philosophy in Athens. Longinus was to become one of Zenobia's closest confidants and advisers, a role for which he was later to pay a heavy price. Edward Gibbon calls him 'the sublime Longinus', probably because his name is associated with a famous philosophical treatise called *On the Sublime*—which he did not write. He was, however, the author of a number of scholarly treatises and commentaries, including several books on Homer, and a commentary on Plato's *Timaeus*. None of his works has survived, but he was judged to be a good scholar, if not much of a philosopher, and was also described as 'a living library and walking museum'.[10] He certainly seems to have been widely known and respected for his scholarship and immense learning. The 'living library' attribute may well have provided Zenobia with one of her chief incentives for hiring him, because one thing conspicuously lacking in Palmyra was books—as Longinus later lamented in a letter to one of his students in Athens; he none the less encouraged the student to come and live in Palmyra because of its excellent climate.

But presumably it was not the city's climate that induced Longinus to spend the remainder of his days in what some might have regarded as a cultural backwater, far removed from the stimulating intellectual life of Athens. Scholars are somewhat cynical about his motives in going to Palmyra. Ball comments that he was not the first to hasten to some well-endowed provincial sinecure simply because the pay and perks were good.[11] Having reached the age of sixty, he might have welcomed the opportunity to spend the rest of his life in comfort and ease—not realizing how little of it would be left to him because of his decision. Another suggestion is that he did not trust the Romans to protect his beloved Athens against an invasion by the

Goths, and so he abandoned the city while the going was good. But it may well be that more visionary motives persuaded him to accept Zenobia's invitation. The queen was looking not merely for a well known scholar- and philosopher-in-residence to grace her literary salons, but someone who would be an intellectual and philosophical mentor to herself and her son, one whose counsels would help catalyze her ambitions and aspirations, by providing an ideological justification for them, and by advising on how best to put them into effect; he would thus play a significant part in shaping Palmyra's future, and indeed the future of the Roman world. That may have been the hired man's vision. Whether or not he actually made any differ- ence to anything that Zenobia subsequently did, he was later held respon- sible, by herself and by others, for 'leading her astray', and he paid the ultimate price.

AD 270–271

Zenobia goes west

It was probably in the spring of 270 that Zenobia embarked on her grand programme of westward military expansion. Her initial venture took her armies into the Roman province of Arabia, and beyond it into the broader region the Romans called Arabia Felix.[12] One of the purposes of the expe- dition was no doubt to carry out a pre-emptive attack on tribal groups of north-eastern Arabia, like the Tanukh confederation, which threatened Palmyrene trading activities in the region, and ultimately Palmyra itself— especially at times when the bulk of the Palmyrene forces were occupied in lands far removed from the capital, as they soon would be. Up to this point, Zenobia could claim to be acting also on Rome's behalf, by securing its territories in the Syrian-Arabian region while the emperor was preoccu- pied with problems in the west. But most importantly, Zenobia was seeking to establish control over the area which gave her forces access to the Red Sea and the Nile Delta. With that accomplished, her next objective lay immediately ahead—Egypt.

Before following her progress into Egypt, let us for a moment turn our attention to what was happening in the west. In the later summer of 270, the emperor Claudius Gothicus died of plague in Pannonia, in the city of Sirmium. Initially, his brother Quintillus seized the imperial mantle, but he was promptly assassinated and replaced by one much more suited to wear it, a highly experienced soldier of humble origins from the Danube region, who had risen through the ranks under Gallienus, and become Master of Horse, virtually the second highest officer in the army, under Claudius: Lucius Domitius Aurelianus. Aurelian was quick to prove himself one of the late empire's most formidable rulers. The time would soon come when he would confront Zenobia's army on the field of battle, and finally the queen herself face to face. But other matters had to be attended to first.

The new emperor's first major objective was to sort out the problems of the west—Germanic invasions of Italy, Vandal invasions of Pannonia, and the ongoing secessionist crisis in Gaul, where a 'Gallic empire' had arisen out of the revolt there in 258. Closer to home, Aurelian also had to put down rebellions by three pretenders to his throne, and disaffection in the Senate and amongst a number of his officers. Within eighteen months, or little more, he had dealt with most of these problems with exemplary efficiency, driving the Germanic hordes out of Italy, and ruthlessly eliminating the would-be usurpers and their followers. To give Rome greater security against invasion, he embarked on what was to be the most conspicuous building project of his career: the provision of the capital with massive new walls. The rebel Gallic empire in the west had still to be dealt with. But that problem was put aside for the time being. Resolution of it would come later. For now, the emperor was ready for the east, and began his march there probably in late 271.

Which brings us back to Zenobia. There is no doubt that the queen had kept herself fully informed of developments in the western world as she set about fulfilling her expansionist ambitions in the east. The several changes of regime in the west and the serious problems with which the succession of emperors had to deal, in Gaul, Germany, and Pannonia as well as in the Roman heartland itself, had distracted imperial attention from the east and given Zenobia virtually a free hand in building her power-base in Syria while she continued to profess her loyalty to Rome. But then she ordered the invasion of Egypt. That brought about a total change of scenario—the beginning of a new phase in Zenobia's expansionist programme, and a dramatic shift in her relations with Rome. For Egypt was at this time directly ruled by Rome, under a governor called Tenagino Probus. Invading it was in effect a declaration of war on Rome itself. There would inevitably be a reckoning, as Zenobia well knew. But she did not shrink from it. Some time in the second half of the year 270, she ordered her general Zabdas to march into Egypt with an invasion force of 70,000 men. Here he was met by a significantly smaller force consisting of some 50,000 Egyptian and Roman troops.[13] But they proved a tough and defiant enemy, inflicting at least two defeats on the invaders and once driving them from their land before the queen's commander finally prevailed. In a last engagement at Babylon, a Roman fortress in the Nile Delta, Probus was taken prisoner. He was executed, or took his own life to avoid it.[14] The way was now clear for Zenobia herself to enter the land of the Nile. She did so in triumph, proclaiming herself Queen of Egypt.

Sound, practical motives may have underpinned her Egyptian enterprise. For her victory there gave her access to the country's abundant sources of wealth, including its rich grain-producing areas, and won her control of the ports on Egypt's Mediterranean coast, and along the Red Sea and the Nile river where Palmyrene sea merchants plied a lucrative trade (when not harassed by pirates). There may also have been an important ideological dimension to Zenobia's campaign. Her rule in the land of the Nile would be an enlightened one; it would nurture a genuine, liberal cosmopolitan environment, with the traditions of all elements of the population respected and preserved in a blending of Arab, Aramaic, Greek, Roman, and native customs and lifestyles and ideals. No doubt the queen used her professed family link with Cleopatra as a means of winning over the minds and hearts of her newly acquired subjects. The link was a spurious one, but her belief in it also added an important personal dimension to her campaign: to seat herself upon the throne once warmed by her greatest role model may well have been the fulfilment of one of Zenobia's most cherished dreams.

But the price she would pay for all of this was potentially a heavy one: it would be but a matter of time before her occupation of Egypt brought down upon her the wrath of Rome. Of this she was fully aware. Even her identification with Cleopatra was provocative, for at the end of her life Cleopatra had become Rome's mortal enemy. Besides, the Palmyrene seizure of Egypt from Rome's governor could be seen as a direct threat to what was vital to Rome—the grain supplies. Egypt had become an essential supplier of basic food to the Roman world, and by attacking it Zenobia struck at Rome's stomach.[15] She had probably chosen her time to occupy Egypt very carefully, calculating that Rome's preoccupation with its problems in Europe would prevent it from taking immediate action against her. And this would give her space, she may well have reasoned, to establish her credentials not as an enemy of Rome but as an equal and worthy partner of it. That

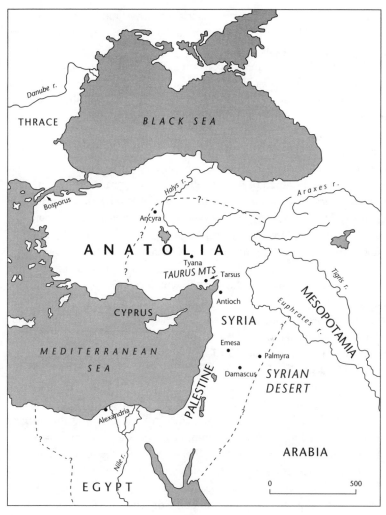

Map 12. Zenobia's 'empire'

is to say, she would try to negotiate a diplomatic settlement with the emperor. In Roman eyes, her invasion and occupation of Egypt must have stretched her credibility beyond all reasonable limits. But she may well have believed that by her conquests of large parts of the eastern world, up to and including Egypt, she had demonstrated her fitness for the broader role which she sought for herself in the Roman imperial structure; and her occupation of the land of the Nile would serve to strengthen her negotiating power with whoever happened to be emperor at the time.

That proved to be Aurelian. As soon as she heard of his elevation, she must have despatched envoys to him with her terms for a settlement. The emperor would surely prefer to embrace a partnership with the Palmyrene regime, which had already give ample demonstration of its military capabilities, albeit at Rome's expense, than to declare himself its enemy. Matters had reached the point where there was really no third option. But Zenobia had no need to wait for his response. As far as she was concerned, she had already acquired peer status with him, in the name of her son. That is reflected in papyrus documents dating to the Palmyrene occupation of Egypt. Aurelian is explicitly acknowledged as emperor in these documents, but his name is followed by that of Vaballathus, accompanied by the titles 'most illustrious king, Consul, Imperator, Strategos (Military Commander) of the Romans'.[16] It was undoubtedly at Zenobia's express command that Vaballathus was so titled in the records, which in effect accorded him the status of co-emperor, without any say from Rome. Of course, behind all this was the queen's own personal agenda. She continued to maintain a façade of acting on her son's behalf until such time as he was old enough to assume power in his own right. But Vaballathus served merely as the front for her own ambitions and aspirations. There was one thing essential to the achievement of these—the emperor's cooperation and approval, even if granted grudgingly in response to a fait accompli. So Zenobia needed to convince him that by launching her campaigns through Syria and Arabia into Egypt she was not rebelling against or attempting to break away from Roman rule. On the contrary, she wanted to ally herself with the leader of the Roman world, as his colleague and as ruler of the eastern half of it.

It was a far from preposterous idea. The splitting of the empire into western and eastern parts, each under an emperor who formed a complementary partnership with his co-emperor, had already been attempted by Valerian when he assigned himself responsibility for the eastern half of the empire, moving there to fight the Sasanians, while he left his son Gallienus in charge of the western half. His capture had created a power-vacuum in the east which Odenathus had to a large extent filled, though not, as far as we know, with a co-emperorship in mind. The division of east and west between two or more emperors would later become for a time a fundamental feature of Roman imperial rule, as demonstrated by the joint regimes of

Diocletian and Maximian. This was the type of arrangement that Zenobia almost certainly envisaged. And her campaigns up to and including Egypt gave proof of her abilities to acquire and control large parts of the eastern Roman world. But that cut no ice with Aurelian. The queen's earlier campaigns in the east might already have given the Romans some cause for concern about what she was getting up to. But her seizure of Rome's breadbasket was completely beyond the pale.[17] As soon as Aurelian had settled affairs in the west, he would deal with her. And in late 271, he set out from Rome to do just that.

AD 271–272

Aurelian retaliates

By this time, Zenobia was already looking for new conquests. Departing Egypt some time during the middle months of 271, she returned to Syria, to begin preparations for a grand new enterprise: the invasion and occupation of Asia Minor. (Significantly, Aurelian's name ceases to appear on Zenobia's and Vaballathus' coin issues.) With barely time to recuperate from their Egyptian venture, the queen's troops were once more on the march. We have little information about the Asia Minor campaign, and no information about what prompted her to undertake it. Perhaps some sort of Alexander-type megalomania drove her on. But whatever her motives may have been,[18] the enterprise proved a dismal failure. Her forces probably managed to get as far as Ancyra (modern Ankara), in north-central Anatolia, but failed to penetrate anywhere west of it before the queen ordered their withdrawal and return to Syria. Asia Minor had proved a step too far, and Zenobia had clearly outstretched her resources in seeking to win control of it, achieving nothing in the process but the alienation of the local populations. Her famed beauty and soldierly reputation meant nothing to them. But there was probably one thing above all that prompted her to abandon Asia Minor: alarming news from the west that Aurelian had rejected any prospect of a diplomatic settlement, and was now marching east at the head of a large army, determined to resolve once and for all Rome's differences with the queen by force of arms.

By April 272, he had crossed the Bosporus into Asia Minor, and then proceeded rapidly across the Anatolian plateau. Everywhere along his campaign route city-gates were eagerly thrown open to him. There was apparently just one city, Tyana in the south-east, that offered any resistance. Why Tyana was the odd one out we cannot be sure, since Zenobia's forces seem to have left the city defenceless. We can only think that some residual and misplaced loyalty to the queen induced its inhabitants to defy the emperor. At all events, Aurelian was infuriated by its stand, so we are told by the *HA*,[19] and declared that once he had taken the city not even a dog would be left alive within it. Tyana fell after a traitor showed the Romans a way through its defences, and its inhabitants awaited in terror the dreadful retribution in store for them. But they were saved by a miracle—in the form of a ghost who suddenly confronted the emperor as he was about to enter his tent. It was the spirit of Apollonius, a famous holy man of Tyana who lived in the 1st century AD and was honoured by a cult after his death. Apollonius appealed to the emperor to show mercy to his fellow-citizens, warning him that he would not survive long if he did not. That was enough for Aurelian. Terrified by the apparition, he quickly issued a new order, that only the traitor was to be put to death. But his troops' blood was up, and they clamoured for the destruction of the entire city, reminding the emperor that he had promised he would not leave even one dog alive in it. Aurelian was a man of his word, and he knew he had to keep it. So he ordered all the city's dogs to be rounded up and slaughtered. This story comes to us, the reader should be reminded, courtesy of the *HA*. We are assured by its author that he has it all on very good authority—indeed on a number of very good authorities!

By one means or another, Rome regained controlled of Egypt during Aurelian's eastern campaign. According to the *HA*, the emperor's military commander Probus (later to become an emperor himself) invaded the country and wrested it back from Palmyrene control.[20] But none of our other sources indicate that military action was required to rid Egypt of its Palmyrene occupiers. The likelihood is that Zenobia had withdrawn all her troops from it for the defence of her territories in Syria, enabling the Romans to re-establish their authority there without opposition. Syria was a different story. The emperor would have to take it by force—and he was ready and eager to do so. From Tyana he proceeded to Tarsus on the Cilician plain, and thence to Issus on the coast, famous as the site of Alexander's victory over Darius III in 333 BC, and Septimius Severus' victory over Pescennius Niger in AD 194. Issus lay on the edge of Syrian territory, and from it Aurelian marched directly to the city where Zenobia and her forces were stationed—Antioch. Near the city, just to its east, was a place called Immae. Here Aurelian's and Zenobia's forces, the latter under the command of the queen's general Zabdas, clashed for the first time.[21]

To begin with, the Palmyrenes appear to have got the better of the contest. But in the end, they were outmanoeuvred and outfought. Resorting to a tactic that would become a standard feature of the battlefield repertoire, Aurelian ordered his troops to flee the field when the heavily armoured Palmyrene cavalry charged them, and then wheel round and attack their pursuers when the heat and the weight of their armour began to take their toll. The tactic proved successful. Casualties among Zabdas' forces were heavy, many trampled to death as they fell beneath their horses. Facing imminent defeat, Zabdas cut his losses and retreated. Zenobia was in Antioch at the time, and Vaballathus was probably with her. It would not be long before Aurelian arrived, with the demand that the city give up its royal occupants. The city could hardly refuse if its survival was at stake. There was but one slim hope for the queen and her party. According to Zosimus, Zabdas hit upon a scheme that would give them, and what survived of their army, the chance to steal out of the city at night, before Aurelian's forces arrived and without rousing the suspicions of the populace. Zabdas 'chose a bearded man who bore some resemblance to the emperor in silhouette, and clothing him in a dress such as Aurelian was accustomed to wear, led him through the city as if he had taken the emperor prisoner. After deceiving the Antiochenes by this ploy, he stole out of the city by night, and took with him Zenobia together with the remainder of the army to Emesa.'[22] Zenobia and her army lived to fight another day.

Antioch now lay open to the emperor. Many of its inhabitants fled in panic as he approached, fearing retribution for their loyalty to Zenobia. But their fears were quickly put to rest when the emperor published edicts urging them to return, with the promise that no one would be punished for supporting the queen. This proved a very effective strategy, for it won the people's goodwill, along with much support from other cities in the region as Aurelian continued his pursuit of Zenobia. The queen had retreated with her forces along the Orontes to Emesa, and prepared to make a second stand there against the emperor. According to Zosimus, she mustered outside the city a force of some 70,000 men for this second test of strength. The size of the Roman army is unknown, but it must have been at least equal to that of the queen, with forces gathered from Mesopotamia, Syria, Phoenicia, and

Palestine to reinforce those who had accompanied the emperor from Europe. The Palestinians were among the fiercest of the troops. Their particular weapons were the club and the stave, which they wielded with lethal effect. Once again, at the beginning of the battle, Aurelian ordered his cavalry to withdraw, aware that the queen's horse had superiority in both skill and numbers. But this time, the Palmyrene cavalry did not let up in their pursuit. Instead, they launched themselves against the enemy's mounted troops and killed them in great numbers. Most of the Roman cavalry force was wiped out. But discipline among the Palmyrenes' ranks was poor. As soon as their cavalry began their attack, the rest of the queen's forces relaxed their vigilance, broke their ranks, and started to disperse. Quick to exploit the situation, Aurelian immediately ordered his infantry to wheel about and throw themselves upon the enemy, now scattered and in disarray. The Palmyrenes suffered an immense slaughter. Those that survived the initial carnage fled in panic, trampling each other in the process and thus making it all the easier for their opponents to hack them to pieces. The field was littered with the corpses of Palmyrenes and their horses. Those who escaped took refuge in Emesa.

Zenobia still had possession of the city. But she was warned to leave it as quickly as possible, for the populace was ill-disposed towards her and would welcome the Romans. She had no choice. If she were to save herself from the enemy, she had to abandon Emesa and flee home to Palmyra, taking with her whatever remnant of her army had survived and remained loyal to her. The treasure she carried with her on her campaigns had to be dumped. It became part of Aurelian's spoils of conquest when he entered the city in triumph, to an enthusiastic reception from its inhabitants.

It was the next stage that was to prove the most challenging and the most hazardous for the emperor. He continued his pursuit of the queen—but now in her own territory. Though her troops had been greatly reduced in numbers, they would henceforth fight the enemy in surroundings they knew well. The Roman forces on the other hand were marching through unfamiliar desert terrain. Its harsh conditions were in themselves an enemy to their progress, made all the worse by the attacks launched by desert brigands against them[23]—probably against their supply train in particular, which was vital to their survival. But Aurelian too must have had his supporters among the local peoples, some of whom had fought on his side in the battle of Emesa. No doubt they included groups from the Tanukh confederation, one of Palmyra's bitterest enemies. Local allies must have provided valuable support for the Romans, both military and logistical, as they drew ever closer to Palmyra.

Zenobia's last stand

Finally, Aurelian reached the queen's capital and immediately placed it under siege. Zenobia remained defiant, her city remained intact, and the siege went on—and on. It was just a matter of holding out long enough, so the queen hoped, for reinforcements to come to the rescue; indeed, the *HA* tells us that she was expecting these any day from Persia.[24] If this claim is credible, it suggests that Zenobia had been in contact with the Sasanian king (Shapur or his son and successor Hormizd I) with a view to forming an alliance against the Romans. But even if there were no prospect of Persian intervention, Palmyra may well have put up fierce resistance to its attackers, for a considerable period of time. The *HA* contains a letter purportedly written by Aurelian which describes the formidable defences the emperor encountered when he invested the city—by way of explaining to his critics why he was taking so long to bring the siege to a successful conclusion. The letter can be dismissed as pure fiction. But quite possibly it does reflect difficulties experienced by the emperor, including a spirited resistance by Zenobia and her subjects, in rounding off his campaign with the capture of Palmyra. For this reason it's worth quoting part of it: 'The Romans are saying that I am merely waging a war with a woman, just as if Zenobia alone and with her own forces only were fighting against me.... It cannot be told what a store of arrows is here, what great preparations for war, what a store of spears or of stones; there is no section of the wall that is not held by two or three engines of war, and their machines can even hurl fire.'[25]

We are given the impression of a well fortified city. In fact, there is no evidence that Palmyra was at this time protected by fortifications of the type we associate with walled cities. (It was only later, in Diocletian's reign, that the city seems to have been provided with substantial walls.) Even so, we need not doubt that Zenobia's troops mounted a highly effective defence by some means or other against the Romans, one that long kept the attackers at bay and began taking its toll upon them. The *HA* goes on to tell us that the emperor, exhausted and frustrated by his lack of success, wrote once more to Zenobia requesting her surrender. He promised that if she complied, she and her children would be spared—though she must give up all her other possessions. Zenobia remained defiant. She rejected the request and the offer, and at the same time announced that help was on its way from Persia. She also took the opportunity to remind Aurelian that she was the descendant of the great and noble Queen of the Nile: 'You demand my surrender as though you were not aware that Cleopatra preferred to die a queen rather than remain alive, however high her rank.'

But there is little doubt that her city began to suffer extreme privations as the besieging army blockaded all supplies to it. Realizing that its fall was inevitable, Zenobia decided on one last ploy: she would secretly abandon her capital and travel with a few companions to the Euphrates, mounted on a female camel (allegedly the swiftest of that kind of animal, much faster than horses); after she had crossed the river, she would be in Persian territory, and would there throw herself on the mercy of the Sasanian king. That would be better than falling into Aurelian's hands, she believed, and her departure would allow her beleaguered city to surrender to the Romans, thus bringing its sufferings to an end. It was a desperate ploy, and it almost came off. Zenobia left Palmyra without being seen by the enemy. But Aurelian had got word of her escape, and sent a detachment of cavalry in pursuit. As she was about to cross the river, they caught up with her. She was taken directly to the emperor.

So we are told by Zosimus,[26] our most reliable source on the story of Zenobia. The story may well be true. More likely to be fiction is the exchange which the *Historia Augusta* reports between the emperor and the queen after her capture: Aurelian asked his prisoner why she had dared show insolence to the emperors of Rome. To which she replied: 'You, I know, are an emperor indeed, for you win victories, but Gallienus and Aureolus and the others I never regarded as emperors.'[27] The conversation is almost certainly an invention, like other episodes of the Aurelian–Zenobia saga narrated by the *HA*. But there has understandably been much speculation on what emperor and queen may have said to each other when they first met, and what the nature of their relationship was henceforth. One suggested scenario is that despite being enemies they formed a kind of mutual admiration society, which provided the basis for a lasting bond between them. This is of course an instance of a common literary topos—and for that reason all the more suspect as far as Zenobia's story goes. In any case, it represents but one end of a spectrum of possible relationships between conqueror and captive. The other is represented by a story (admittedly also suspect) which John Malalas tells. In this Aurelian publicly humiliated the queen by parading her, mounted on a dromedary, through all the lands of the East, perhaps as a sardonic reminder of her failed bid to flee to Persia; he completed her degradation in Antioch, where he displayed her for three days, bound in chains, on a stage he had specially built for the occasion.[28]

Let us return for a moment to Palmyra. As soon as Zenobia's capture became known, the city surrendered to Aurelian without further resistance, and its inhabitants paraded before the emperor, bearing gifts and sacrifices and pleading for mercy. Aurelian was disposed to be merciful. Everyone was spared and allowed to go about their business, except for a select group of the queen's supporters who were taken prisoner. Palmyra itself was left intact. On his departure, the *HA* tells us, the emperor stationed in the city a detachment of 600 archers as a peacekeeping force, under the command of a man called Sandarion.[29] Whether or not he did so, Palmyra appears to have remained free to administer itself as it wished. Its conqueror would soon have cause to regret this.

What happened to Zenobia?

From Palmyra Aurelian returned to Emesa. Zenobia and her supporters were put on trial there.[30] And at this point, the queen's nerve failed her. (In the *Historia Augusta*, her sudden loss of courage is set within the context of an uproar by Aurelian's troops, who demanded her punishment.) When confronted by her accusers, she protested her innocence of all charges. She was but a simple woman, she said, led astray by her advisers—whom she now openly denounced. Among them was Cassius Longinus, who had served the queen faithfully as mentor and confidant. He was found guilty of the charges laid against him and immediately sentenced to death by the emperor. To his fate he calmly resigned himself. 'He bore the sentence with such fortitude', Zosimus tells us, 'that he was a comfort to those who were indignant at his suffering.' Cassius Longinus made a good exit from this world. Indeed, some might have said of him that nothing in his life became him like the ending of it.

AD 273–274

Aurelian then began his return to Europe, taking with him Zenobia and her son Vaballathus and other supporters who had been spared execution. But before he reached Rome, and while he was attending to some problems in the Balkans in the Danube region, urgent news came from Palmyra. A rebellion had broken out there. According to the *Historia Augusta*, the entire 600-strong garrison left behind by Aurelian had been massacred by the locals. Zosimus tells us that the Palmyrenes were encouraging a man called Marcellinus, governor of the province of Mesopotamia, to make a bid for the imperial throne.[31] But Marcellinus remained loyal to the emperor and informed him of the plot. In the meantime, the Palmyrenes decided to appoint one of their own, a man called Antiochus, to the purple. Aurelian acted promptly. He set off for Palmyra without delay, taking whatever troops were immediately at his disposal, and caught the Palmyrenes totally unawares. This time, he supposedly razed the city to the ground (273). But he spared the life of Antiochus, simply dismissing the man. This was not to be seen as an act of mercy. Antiochus was of obscure origins and the emperor didn't want to dignify his bid for power by going to the trouble of punishing him. At least that is what Zosimus tells us.

It should be said that Aurelian's alleged destruction of Palmyra when he attacked the city a second time has left absolutely no trace in the archaeological record. We have no indication that any of the buildings of Palmyra, dating primarily to the first half of the 3rd century, suffered any destruction at this time, or were restored following such destruction. This is but another instance where our literary and our archaeological sources appear to be at odds. But what does seem clear is that Palmyra now slowly ran out of puff. There was certainly some building activity there during Diocletian's reign, in the course of which the city was increased in size to include a large fortified camp where a Roman legion was quartered, and substantial defence works were built. Both measures were designed to protect the city against the ongoing Sasanian menace. But as Roman control of Palmyra became more direct, the city lost its importance as an international trading centre, and continued to exist primarily as 'a strategic asset—a nodal point in a network of strategic roads that secured Rome's eastern frontiers'.[32]

We might mention here a story, admittedly found only in the *Historia Augusta*, of an anti-Roman pro-Zenobia rebellion that broke out in Egypt about the same time as the uprising in Palmyra.[33] The instigator was a man called Firmus, a merchant of Alexandria, who sought to revive what was left of Zenobia's supporters in Egypt by setting himself up as emperor in opposition to Aurelian. Firmus was a swarthy-complexioned, curly-headed giant of a man, with a scarred, bug-eyed face and a huge white hairy torso. He was nicknamed Cyclops. Endowed with a gargantuan appetite and prodigious

Figure 27. *Queen Zenobia's Last Look Upon Palmyra*, painting by Herbert Schmalz

strength, Cyclops gave public demonstrations of both qualities—the former by devouring an entire ostrich at a single sitting, the latter by getting onlookers to pound an anvil on his chest without any ill effect upon him. Thus we are informed by the *HA*, which adds that such things are mere trifles and that we ought to be getting back to more important matters! And so we do when we are told that Aurelian promptly left Thrace for an expedition to Egypt to crush the rebellion, mindful of its possible disruption to Rome's grain supply, and dispose of its leader. The expedition ended with Firmus' defeat, capture, torture, and strangulation. No other ancient source talks of this man, and we may suppose the whole account is fictitious. Except that Zosimus does refer to a victory quickly won by Aurelian over the Alexandrians who were on the point of revolt, after his final subjection of Palmyra.[34] There is no mention of Firmus in Zosimus' account, and no indication that if there were indeed an uprising in Alexandria it spread to the rest of Egypt.

And now we come to the last phase in Zenobia's story. Back in Rome, Palmyra's queen was to be one of the emperor's two star attractions in a spectacular triumphal procession. The triumph was held in the year 274. Its other main attraction was the Gallic chief Tetricus (Zenobia had presumably been held in confinement in Rome after her arrival there until it was time for the triumph). For early in that year, Aurelian had finally crushed the Gallic rebellion and captured Tetricus, its leader. The Gaul was to share top billing with Zenobia in the parade. Together they would serve as living proof that Aurelian had re-established Roman authority over the farthest flung parts of his empire. Several of our sources record the triumph,[35] the most colourful and most detailed of which, not surprisingly, is the *Historia Augusta*. As far as we can trust the details recorded there in particular, and in the ancient sources in general, Zenobia along with Tetricus were paraded before the emperor's chariot. The queen was weighed down with jewels so huge that she struggled under their burden, frequently stumbling and halting. Her feet were bound with golden shackles, her hands with golden fetters, and even upon her neck she wore a chain of gold, the weight of which was borne by a Persian buffoon (Latin *scurra*).[36] This last was perhaps an ironic reminder of the claim that she would not surrender to Aurelian at Palmyra because she was expecting, imminently, support from Persia. Here now was her Persian support, in the form of a Persian *scurra*!

So in the end, what happened to Zenobia? We have a number of different versions of her eventual fate. According to a story reported by Zosimus,[37] she died on the journey to Rome, either because of a disease she contracted or because she starved herself to death; the latter out of grief, presumably, for the loss of her homeland, perhaps after receiving word of Aurelian's alleged destruction of her capital when he returned there to crush the local rebellion. But she was not the only one to die; all her fellow-prisoners, save Vaballathus, perished as well, drowned while crossing the Bosporus. A sad ending to our story, if it's true. But most of our sources concur that Zenobia did actually reach Rome and grace the emperor's triumph there. What then? In one account, she was beheaded on the emperor's orders immediately after the triumph (there was no longer any reason for keeping her alive). Thus we are told by Malalas.[38] But in all other sources, Zenobia lived on after the triumph. One of these tells us that Aurelian presented her with a fine house in Tivoli, near Hadrian's villa, where she lived out her days in comfort and security, with her children and in the manner of a Roman matron.[39] In another account, one of her alleged daughters married the emperor himself. In yet another, Zenobia married a Roman senator.[40] And if we are to believe Eutropius (a 4th-century AD historian) and Jerome (a 4th–5th century historian and theologian), Zenobia's descendants still lived in Rome long after she herself had become no more than a memory.[41]

That brings us to one last tale. It is about a latter-day Zenobia.

In the early 19th century of this era, a titled Englishwoman, Lady Hester Stanhope, niece to Britain's Prime Minister William Pitt the Younger, set forth from her homeland and travelled to the East. Here she adopted Oriental ways. On 20 March 1813, she departed the city of Damascus and travelled to Palmyra, dressed in exotic eastern garb. Already a charismatic figure among the local Arab peoples, she made an extraordinary entry into the city, still magnificent in its decayed ruins. Hundreds escorted her on her progress, the first European woman to enter Palmyra, as she rode along the Grand Colonnade. On the columns that flanked it stood beautiful girls draped in long white diaphanous veils. They leapt down as she passed and danced by her side. Young boys accompanied her, playing music on Arabian instruments, bearded old men recited odes in her honour. For the great queen Zenobia had come back to her people. It was a role Lady Hester relished. Zenobia was her model and inspiration, as Cleopatra had been Zenobia's. And as the procession honouring her halted beneath the city's great monumental arch, the loveliest of the living statues leant down from her pedestal and placed a wreath on her head. An old prophecy had been fulfilled. Zenobia reborn had been crowned Queen of the East.[42]

It is an extravagantly romantic tale, which may well contain some elements of truth. We can be sure the author of the *Historia Augusta* would have been proud of it.

The Last Farewell

Farewell, O Syria, my beautiful province. You belong to an enemy now.
How fair a country it will be for him.

(The emperor Heraclius)

Aurelian's triumphal parade through Rome in 274 marked a fitting climax to the emperor's five-year occupancy of the imperial throne (270–5). The procession's star attractions—Zenobia, queen of Palmyra, and Tetricus, leader of the rebel 'Gallic empire'—were indisputably the most precious jewels in their conqueror's crown. Aurelian now stood high in public favour, and he sought to make the most of this while it lasted. Much of his triumph year he spent in the capital, where he undertook several major projects designed to strengthen and stabilize the empire. There was the matter of the empire's silver coinage, in serious need of reform after four decades of progressive debasement. The emperor resolutely set about the task. Within the religious sphere, he introduced into Rome the cult of the Sun God, Sol Invictus, making it the centre of Roman state religion. It was financed partly with funds acquired from the booty of Palmyra. More generally, Aurelian did much to consolidate and strengthen the empire following decades of disunity and internecine contests for the royal succession. And as a tangible legacy to his reign, he set about strengthening the capital's defences by building an impressive new wall around it. The fortification was completed in the reign of his third successor, Probus (276–82).

Much more Aurelian might have achieved, but his career and his life were abruptly cut short when he fell victim to an in-house conspiracy early in 275 at a place called Caenophrurium near Byzantium. He had reached there in the course of leading an expedition to the east against the Sasanians.

The decade following his assassination was a period of further instability, during which a succession of generally weak and insignificant contenders found their way onto and were removed from the throne, usually in short order. Greater stability came with the accession in 284 of a battle-hardened warrior from the imperial bodyguard called Diocletian, who proved to be one of the most distinguished of the last emperors of the Roman imperial period. His reign ended with his abdication on 1 May 305, following which the ex-emperor spent his last years as a peaceful retiree in the palace he had built for himself at Spalatum (modern Split) in Dalmatia, not far from his birthplace. Among the wearers of the purple, Diocletian had the rare distinction of dying of natural causes, and the unique distinction of quitting his throne voluntarily.

Syria seems not to have been affected, at least to any significant degree, by the power struggles and rapid turnover of emperors that weakened other parts of the empire during the decade between Aurelian's death and Diocletian's accession. By and large its commercial and cultural activities prospered, remote from the political and military turbulence that so often disrupted the orderly conduct of affairs elsewhere in the Roman world. There was always, of course, the threat of further Persian intervention in the region. Sasanian kings had not given up their long-held aspirations of imposing their sovereignty over the lands west of the Euphrates. Yet the threat was greatly diminished when Diocletian secured terms of peace with the Sasanian king Narseh in the treaty of Nisibis (297). This meant substantially increased security for Syria's cities and the lands attached to them. In accordance with the treaty's terms, Rome's eastern frontier was shifted east of the Euphrates, to the Habur river. Diocletian strengthened the frontier areas with a series of fortifications, and rebuilt a number of Syria's strategically important roads, thus greatly facilitating communication-links and rapid movement of troops in the empire's eastern regions. Palmyra became the location of a large Roman camp. All these things contributed much to Syria's sense of stability and well-being during Diocletian's reign, greatly enhancing, through the peaceful conditions thus created, the region's overall prosperity.

But the benefits the Syrians derived from their emperor's eastern policies brought with them a number of changes in the way their affairs were handled. From Diocletian's reign onwards, Syria was closely integrated into the imperial bureaucratic system, particularly after Constantine's refoundation of Byzantium as Constantinople in 324 and his inauguration of his new city in 330. Syria was organized into new administrative districts with an increasing number of imperial officials appointed to govern them on behalf of the emperor. The changed arrangements which these entailed were not always welcomed by the local populaces. They were now more tightly controlled by imperial bureaucrats, and subject to higher taxes, calculated on the basis of census figures and often ruthlessly extracted from those unwilling or unable to afford to pay them. On the other hand, the imperial bureaucracy opened up new opportunities for many local Syrians, who could look forward to flourishing careers as officials On His Majesty's Service in their home districts. By and large, the first centuries of the Byzantine era saw many Syrian cities grow and flourish. Most notable among them was Antioch, the third greatest city of the eastern half of the empire, surpassed only by Constantinople and Alexandria.

There was little perceptible change in the outward appearance of Syria's material civilization as the old Roman world was transformed into what we now call the Byzantine era. In both periods, Syria's cities reflected a strong westward orientation while retaining their richly cosmopolitan character. But there was one fundamental exception: the birth and growth of Christianity. 'To begin with, the Byzantine period was above all an ecclesiastical age: Christianity had all the arrogance and self confidence, not only of a newfound religion, but also of the world's first universal religion. A religion, furthermore, adopted as the official state religion of the world's foremost power of the time, the Romans. This new confidence and continuity applied equally all over the Roman world, but for Syria there was an added dimension. For the east saw the origin of Christianity, both in terms of its birthplace in Palestine, and its formative growth in Damascus and Antioch. After the initial "Romanization" of Syria in the first centuries of Roman rule, the adoption of a Syrian religion by the greatest world power of antiquity, therefore, represented a "Syrianisation" of Rome.'[1]

By the end of the 2nd century, Christianity had already secured a firm hold in a number of parts of Syria, mainly in the large cities and especially Antioch. Over the next two hundred years, and especially in the fourth century, the religion spread to the smaller cities and to the rural areas, dividing at the same time into a number of sects. 'By the time Constantine gave Christianity official recognition after 313, increasingly encouraging it as the state religion, Syria (and particularly Antioch) was already an area of intense Christian activity going back as far as the missions of St Paul in the mid first century. Christianity, with its blending of Jewish and Greek influences, was one more element, albeit a powerful one, in the Syrian melting pot. Before Christianity became part of public life in the fourth century, churches were merely adapted dwelling places, but after the official recognition of Christianity, they took on the scale and form of Roman public buildings.... By the sixth century, Syria was dotted with countless village or monastic churches as well as major pilgrimage centres.'[2]

There was still the Persian question. During the 4th and 5th centuries, brief and sporadic wars had been waged between the armies of the western Roman/Byzantine empire and the eastern Sasanian empire. These were fought outside of and did not directly affect Syria. And in the first half of the 5th century, the emperor Theodosius II (408–50) managed to conclude a 'hundred-year peace' with the Sasanians. This afforded some temporary relief from the conflicts, and thus from the consequent draining of the empire's resources needed to conduct them. But the wars flared up again in the reign of Justinian (527–65), placing a further heavy burden upon imperial resources. And now Syria was directly affected. From 527 onwards, it was frequently attacked by Sasanian armies, its cities and their inhabitants suffering siege, capture, plunder, and massacre by the invaders. Many who survived were carried off as booty to the Persian homeland. In 573, the city of Apameia in the Orontes valley was sacked, and some 290,000 of its population deported.

To compound their misfortunes, the Syrians suffered a succession of natural disasters, including earthquakes, famine, and plagues, which began afflicting their cities and lands in 530 and continued sporadically thereafter. In the same period, the Christian church was being riven by bitter disputes on matters of theological dogma, like the great schism over the question of Monophysitism. But the sky was not about to fall in—at least not just yet. On the contrary, the 6th century witnessed a great surge in building activity in many parts of Syria, both in the large cities and in many small towns and villages. This is reflected in the remains of many churches and monastic establishments of the period—often large and well appointed institutions, even in the villages. All is suggestive of continuing prosperity through the region, despite whatever man and nature and religious squabbles could do to it. But the wealth of the period was unevenly distributed, with affluence in some areas counterbalanced by impoverishment in others where the impact of god- and human-made disasters had proved irreversible. And the Sasanian menace constantly loomed. Increasingly, Justinian and his successors found themselves unable to protect their eastern frontiers against the enemy from Persia. Antioch became one of the victims of their failure. Early in the 7th century, the Sasanian king Chosroes II invaded Syria, seized Antioch, and massacred 90,000 of its inhabitants. The whole of Syria now came under Sasanian control, where it remained until 627.

But constant warfare between Byzantine and Sasanian armies inevitably took its toll on both sides. Ultimately, both powers were weakened beyond recovery. And that paved the way for a new intruder upon the scene, one that rapidly filled the power vacuum conveniently left for it by the debilitating wars of the previous contenders for control of the lands which lay between them. On 8 June in the year 632 the prophet Muhammad died. His political and administrative successor Abu Bakr, leader of the faithful, set a bold new aggressive course for the armies gathered beneath his command, under the banner of the new religion Islam. His sights were fixed upon the conquest of the lands to the north of Arabia. Syria was the first of the northern regions to be invaded by Muslim armies, in 634. Damascus was briefly occupied before the Byzantine army could respond. A showdown took place two years later, in 636, at a place called Yarmuk, near the present border between Jordan and Syria. The Byzantine forces of the emperor Heraclius were routed, and Damascus was again occupied. Yarmuk proved a major turning point in world history: the Islamic peoples were here to stay; a single victory had given them the whole of Syria. 'Farewell, O Syria, my beautiful province,' Heraclius is said to have declared on his defeat. 'You belong to an enemy now. How fair a country it will be for him.'[3]

In 661, Damascus was chosen as the capital of the first Muslim empire. Thus began the Umayyad period of Islamic history. Syria was now not merely a part of the Muslim world. It was the centre of it.

Appendix I: Chronology of Major Events and Periods

regn. = reign(s) of; C = century (thus C17 = 17th cent.); M = millennium

<u>**BC**</u>

Early Bronze Age (*c.*3100–2000 BC)

C27	Beginning(?) of Eblaite line of kings
C24	Ebla dominant in n. Syria; Palace G tablets (Mardikh IIB1 period)
C24	Amorites first attested (Ebla tablets)
C23	Akkadian destruction of Ebla (by Sargon or Naram-Sin)
*c.***2000**	Ebla again destroyed (after partial rebuilding, Mardikh IIB2 period)

Middle Bronze Age (*c.*2000–1600 BC)

*c.***2000–1800**	Ebla's new phase (Mardikh IIIA)
*c.***1810**	Yahdun-Lim occupies throne of Mari
*c.***1800–1600**	Yamhad dominant in n. Syria; Ebla further developed (Mardikh IIIB)
early decades C18	Qatna's involvement in conflicts/alliances of the age
*c.***1792**	Assyrian king Samsi-Addu seizes Mari
*c.***1782**	Samsi-Addu's son Yasmah-Addu installed as viceroy there
*c.***1774**	Zimri-Lim occupies throne of Mari
*c.***1762**	Babylonian king Hammurabi conquers Mari
2nd half C17	Yamhad/Aleppo ruled by Yarim-Lim III
between *c.***1650 and 1620**	Hittite king Hattusili I's Syrian campaigns

Late Bronze Age (*c.* 1600–early C12 BC)

c. **1595**	Hittite king Mursili II conquers Aleppo and Babylon
about this time	Ebla destroyed and largely abandoned
mid C16	Pharaoh Ahmose expels Hyksos from Egypt
by end C16	Emergence of kingdom of Mitanni
early C15	Palestinian and Syrian campaign by pharaoh Tuthmosis I
1st half C15	Westward expansion of Mitannian power by king Parrattarna
same period	Idrimi becomes king of Alalah as Parrattarna's vassal
c. **1457–1433**	Palestinian and Syrian campaigns by Tuthmosis III
later C15	Saushtatar re-establishes Mitannian authority in n. Syria
late C15	Hittite campaigns in Syria under Tudhaliya I/II; Mitanni suppressed
same period	Amenhotep II renews Egyptian campaigns in Syria
same period	Resurgence of Mitanni under Artatama I
1st decade C14	Pact between Artatama and Amenhotep's successor Tuthmosis IV
before mid C14	Hittites, now excluded from Syria, suffer homeland invasions
by *c.* 1350	Invasions repelled, and Suppiluliuma I becomes Hittite king
middle decades C14	Amurrite warlords' enterprises in Egypt's Syrian territories
c. **1345**	Suppiluliuma's 'Great Syrian War' and capture of Mitannian capital
1327	Siege of Carchemish, last Mitannian stronghold; letter from Egypt
1327	Carchemish (and Aleppo at this time?) become Hittite viceregal seats
1326	Suppiluliuma attacks Egypt's Syrian states
late C14–early C13	Hittite campaigns against Syrian rebels in Mursili II's reign
c. **1285**	First Qadesh battle (pharaoh Seti I vs Hittite king Muwattalli II)
1274	Second Qadesh battle (Ramesses II vs Muwattalli)
c. **1267**	Hittite king Urhi-Teshub banished to Syria by usurper Hattusili (III)
1259	Peace treaty between Ramesses and Hattusili III
1246	Marriage alliance between Ramesses and Hattusili
3rd quarter C13	Failed marriage alliance between Hittite vassals Ugarit and Amurru

later, same period	Battle of Nihriya (Hittite Tudhaliya IV vs Assyrian Tukulti-Ninurta)
late C13–early C12	Breakdown of Hittite authority in Syria (and elsewhere)
same period	Sea raids on eastern Mediterranean coastlands; Ugarit etc. destroyed
between 1184 and 1153	Pharaoh Merneptah repels Sea Peoples' incursions

Iron Age (period covered here: C12–end C7 BC; see Ch. 6, n. 3)

mid C12–late C8	Period of the Neo-Hittite kingdoms
late C12–early C11	Assyrian king Tiglath-pileser I's Syrian campaign
C11	Philistine rule in Aleppo?
1099–1069	Reign of Ramesses XI; period of Wenamun story
late C11	Saul establishes united kingdom of Israel (biblical tradition)
by end M2	Aramaeans establish settled communities in Syria etc.
C10	Reigns of David and Solomon (biblical tradition)
934	Beginning of Neo-Assyrian era (accession of Ashur-dan II)
***c.*925**	Pharaoh Sheshonq I's campaign in Syria and Palestine
***c.*870**	Ashurnasirpal II's Syrian campaign
858–824	regn. Shalmaneser III; nineteen trans-Euphrates campaigns
856	Shalmaneser captures Til Barsip, and in 855 its king Ahuni
853, 849, 848, 845	Shalmaneser's campaigns against Syro-Palestinian alliance
between 845 and 841	Hazael seizes throne of Damascus
841	Hazael defeated by Shalmaneser, but subsequently builds small empire
805	Adad-nirari III (810–783) begins Syrian campaigns
***c.*800**	Syrian coalition's siege of Hamathite city Hatarikka
between 782 and 746	Further sporadic Assyrian military operations in Syria
746 or slightly later	Mati'ilu, king of Arpad, leads coalition rebellion against Assyria
738–708	Gradual absorption of Syrian states into Assyrian provincial system
734–732	Tiglath-pileser III's Syro-Palestinian campaigns
732	Fall of Damascus and incorporation as an Assyrian province
720	Hamath-led Syrian coalition defeated by Assyrian king Sargon II

720	End of kingdom of Israel
704–630/27	Further Syrian uprisings, regn. Sennacherib, Esarhaddon, Ashurbanipal
626–539	Neo-Babylonian empire
612	Royal Assyrian city Nineveh captured by Babylonian king Nabopolassar
610	Assyrian empire ends with death of last king Ashur-uballit II

From Nebuchadnezzar to Alexander (609–323 BC)

609	Necho II's first Syrian campaign; appoints Jehoiakim king of Judah
605	Nebuchadnezzar (Babylonian crown prince) defeats Necho at Carchemish
605 (1 June)	Nebuchadnezzar becomes Babylonian king
601	Nebuchadnezzar's confrontation with Necho near Pelusium
597	Jerusalem falls to Nebuchadnezzar; Zedekiah appointed puppet king
597	First deportations to Babylon
586	Zedekiah rebels, Jerusalem destroyed; second deportations
by 572	Nebuchadnezzar completes reassertion of control over Syria–Palestine
539	Babylon falls to the Persian king Cyrus; repatriation of Jews
by 538	Cyrus asserts control over Syria and Palestine
521 or after	Under Darius I, Syria becomes separate Persian satrapy
336	Alexander becomes king of Macedon
333	Alexander defeats Darius III in battle of Issus
333–332	Alexander establishes control over Syria
330	Fall of Persian empire to Alexander
323	Alexander dies in Babylon

Syria Under Seleucid Rule (late C4–64 BC)

320	Conference of Alexander's heirs at Triparadeisos
319	Antigonus gains ascendancy among heirs
312–305	Seleucus I establishes his authority through eastern lands
311 (April)	First official year (in Seleucid tradition) of the Seleucid dynasty
305	First official year of Seleucid I's reign
301	Antigonus killed in battle at Ipsus

300	Seleucus founds Antioch
281	Victory at Corupedium gives Seleucus control of most of Asia Minor
281	Seleucus assassinated in Macedonia, and accession of Antiochus I
275	'Battle of the Elephants'; Antiochus extends control through Asia Minor
*c.***274–271**	First Syrian War (Antiochus I vs Ptolemy II)
262	Pergamum establishes independence from Seleucid kingdom
261–225	Intradynastic conflicts (regn. Antiochus II–Seleucus II)
260–253	Second Syrian War (Antiochus II vs Ptolemy II)
*c.***247**	Arsaces founds Parthian royal dynasty
246–241	Third Syrian War (Seleucus II vs Ptolemy III)
223	Accession of Antiochus III
220	Antiochus' campaigns against eastern rebel rulers and enemies
219–217	Fourth Syrian War (Antiochus III vs Ptolemy IV)
217	Antiochus defeated by Ptolemy IV, battle of Raphia
212–205/4	Antiochus' eastern campaigns (*anabasis*)
202–198	Fifth Syrian War (Antiochus III vs Ptolemy V)
200	Antiochus III defeats Ptolemy V in battle of Panion
196	Antiochus III's Thracian campaign
192–189	Antiochus III's conflicts with Rome
December 190 or January 189	Antiochus III defeated by Rome in battle of Magnesia
175	Antiochus IV Epiphanes succeeds father Seleucus IV
170–168	Sixth Syrian War (Antiochus IV vs Ptolemy VI)
168	Rome compels Antiochus IV to withdraw his forces from Egypt
166/5	Antiochus IV's festivities at Daphne (near Antioch)
166–142	Maccabean rebellion
165	Antiochus' eastern campaign (*anabasis*) and death the following year
162	Demetrius I seizes Seleucid throne
150	Alexander Balas defeats, kills, and succeeds Demetrius I
145	Demetrius II with Ptolemy VI's support defeats and succeeds Balas

145–142	Conflicts with Diodotus Tryphon (who represented Antiochus VI)
142	Tryphon seizes Seleucid throne while Demetrius on eastern campaign
142–63	Hasmonean dynasty rules Judaea
141	Demetrius II captured by Parthian king Mithridates
139/8	Antiochus VII, Demetrius' brother, claims throne; eliminates Tryphon
129	Antiochus VII killed on Parthian campaign
129	Demetrius II resumes Seleucid throne
129–63	Independence of Jewish state
125	Demetrius II assassinated; his wife Cleopatra Thea occupies throne
125–121	Joint rule between Cleopatra and son Antiochus VIII Grypus
121–96	Grypus' sole rule
64	Last Seleucid king Antiochus XIII removed by Pompey

Syria Under Roman Rule (64 BC up to AD 274)

64	Pompey declares Syria a province of Rome
63	Much of Judaea incorporated into Syrian province
53	Roman defeat by Parthians at Carrhae
51	Parthian prince Pakores occupies Syria; driven out by Cassius
41	Abortive attack on Palmyra by Antony's cavalry
40	Pakores (with Roman Labienus) reconquers Syria
38	Pakores defeated and killed by Roman Ventidius in Cyrrhestica
37–4	Rome's appointee Herod rules Jewish state
36, 34, 33	Antony's north-eastern campaigns
31	Antony and Cleopatra defeated at Actium; Ptolemaic dynasty ends
27	Augustus becomes first Roman emperor
20	Rome reaches accord with Parthia

AD

1	Roman–Parthian peace formalized at ceremony on Euphrates
18–19	Palmyra becomes part of Roman empire

66	Outbreak of 'First Jewish War' ('Great Jewish Revolt')
70	Romans, led by Titus, destroy Jerusalem
106	Trajan annexes the Nabataean kingdom
106	Commercial centre of gravity in region shifts from Petra to Palmyra
115–16	Trajan's eastern campaigns
115–17	Widespread Jewish rebellions (regn. Trajan)
129	Hadrian visits Palmyra
131–4	Bar Kochba rebellion (regn. Hadrian)
193–235	Severan dynasty
193	Septimius Severus proclaimed emperor by Danubian troops
195	Septimius' peace settlement with Parthian king Vologeses V
197	Septimius' eastern campaign
early C3	Palmyra's inhabitants granted full Roman citizenship
211	Septimius is succeeded by his sons Caracalla and Geta
212	Murder of Geta on Caracalla's orders
215	Caracalla's campaign though Asia Minor, Syria, and Egypt
216	Caracalla's campaign into Armenia and Parthia
217 (8 April)	Caracalla assassinated
218 (8 June)	His successor Macrinus defeated in battle; replaced by Elagabalus
222	Elagabalus assassinated in Rome; replaced by Severus Alexander
224	Parthian dynasty ends; Sasanian empire begins (founded by Ardashir I)
231	Severus Alexander's Sasanian campaign
235	Alexander assassinated in Germany; replaced by Maximinus
235–84	The Roman empire's so-called 'Crisis Years'
239/40–271/2	Reign of Sasanian king Shapur I
early 250s	Shapur's conquests in Syria
251	Odenathus achieves senatorial rank and pre-eminence in Palmyra
254	Roman emperor Valerian takes up residence in Antioch
256	Shapur's capture and destruction of Dura Europos
260	Shapur defeats and captures Valerian; recaptures Antioch?
260–1	Odenathus confronts Sasanian forces; eliminates pretender Quietus
267	Second Sasanian campaign by Odenathus?

267/8	Assassination of Odenathus
267/8	Odenathus' wife Zenobia succeeds him as regent for son Vaballathus
270	Zenobia embarks on western campaigns, first against Arabian tribes
2nd half 270	Zenobia invades Egypt
mid 271	Zenobia invades Asia Minor
late 271	Aurelian sets out for east
by April 272	Aurelian crosses Bosporus and advances across Asia Minor
mid 272	Aurelian defeats Zenobia's forces in battles near Antioch and Emesa
later 272	Aurelian pursues Zenobia to Palmyra and captures city and queen
273	Zenobia taken as prisoner to Rome
273	Aurelian returns and destroys Palmyra
274	Aurelian celebrates triumph, starring Zenobia and Gallic chief Tetricus

Aftermath (AD 275–661)

275	Assassination of Aurelian
284–305	Reign of Diocletian
297	Diocletian secures peace with Sasanian king Narseh
306–37	Reign of Constantine
313	Christianity officially recognized by Constantine
324	Constantine refounds Byzantium as Constantinople
1st half of C5	Theodosius II concludes a '100-year peace' with the Sasanians
527 onwards	Syria frequently attacked by Sasanians
573	The Orontes city Apamea destroyed; 290,000 of its inhabitants deported
early C7	Antioch seized by Sasanian Chosroes II
early C7–627	All Syria under Sasanian occupation
636	Muslim army defeats Byzantine emperor Heraclius' army at Yarmuk
661	Damascus becomes capital of first Muslim empire

Appendix II: King-Lists

(The lists below provide a chronology of the most important kingdoms and their rulers referred to in this book. *** indicates an interval, occupied by one or more other kings, before or after the reigns of the kings specified.)

Early Bronze Age

Akkad (c.2334–2193)

Sargon	c.2334–2279
***	
Naram-Sin	c.2254–2218
***	

Ur III Dynasty (c.2112–2004)

Middle Bronze Age
(continuing into Late Bronze Age)

Assyria (c.2000–1735)

***	
Samsi-Addu	c.1796–1775
Ishme-Dagan	c.1775–1735

Mari (c.1810–1762)

Yahdun-Lim	c.1810–1794
Sumu-Yamam	c.1793–1792
***	
Yasmah-Addu	c.1782–1775
Zimri-Lim	c.1774–1762

Babylon (c.1894–1595)

***	
Hammurabi	c.1792–1750
***	
Samsu-ditana	c.1625–1595

Yamhad (early 18th–later 17th cent.)

Sumu-epuh	–c.1781

Yarim-Lim I	*c.*1780–1765
★★★	
Yarim-Lim III	2nd half 17th cent.

Hatti (Hittite Kingdom) (early 17th–early 12th cent.)
★★★?

Labarna	–*c.*1650
Hattusili I	*c.*1650–1620
Mursili I	*c.*1620–1590

Late Bronze Age
(continuing into early Iron Age; other chronologies have been proposed)

Hatti (cont.)
★★★

Tudhaliya I/II	late 15th–14th cent.
★★★	
Tudhaliya III	1st half 14th cent.
Suppiluliuma I	*c.*1350–1322
Arnuwanda II	*c.*1322–1321
Mursili II	*c.*1321–1295
Muwattalli II	*c.*1295–1272
Urhi-Teshub	*c.*1272–1267
Hattusili III	*c.*1267–1237
Tudhaliya IV	*c.*1237–1209
★★★	
Suppiluliuma II	*c.*1207–?

Mitanni (16th–14th cent.)
★★★

Parrattarna	1st half 15th cent.
★★★	
Saushtatar	late 15th cent.
Artatama I	15th–14th cent.
★★★	
Tushratta	mid 14th cent.–*c.*1327

Egypt (New Kingdom) (1550–1069)
(The lengths of the reigns are generally precise, but the actual regnal dates are raised or lowered *en bloc* in other proposed New Kingdom chronologies. Overlaps indicate co-regencies.)

Ahmose	1550–1525
★★★	
Tuthmosis I	1504–1492
Tuthmosis II	1492–1479

Tuthmosis III	1479–1425
Hatshepsut	1473–1458
Amenhotep II	1427–1400
Tuthmosis IV	1400–1390
Amenhotep III	1390–1352
Akhenaten (Amenhotep IV)	1352–1336
Smenkhkare	1338–1336
Tutankhamun	1336–1327
Ay	1327–1323
Horemheb	1323–1295
Ramesses I	1295–1294
Seti I	1294–1279
Ramesses II	1279–1213
Merneptah	1213–1203

★★★

Ramesses III	1184–1153

★★★

Ramesses XI	1099–1069

Assyria (Middle Kingdom) (early 14th cent.–935)
★★★

Shalmaneser I	c.1263–1234
Tukulti-Ninurta I	c.1233–1197

★★★

Tiglath-pileser I	c.1114–1076

★★★

Iron Age

Assyria (Neo-Assyrian empire) (934–610)
(The reigns are dated, in accordance with standard convention, from 1st full regnal year.)

Ashur-dan II	934–912

★★★

Ashurnasirpal II	883–859
Shalmaneser III	858–824
Shamshi-Adad V	823–811
Adad-nirari III	810–783
Shalmaneser IV	782–773
Ashur-dan III	772–755
Ashur-nirari V	754–746
Tiglath-pileser III	745–727
Shalmaneser V	726–722
Sargon II	721–705
Sennacherib	704–681

| Esarhaddon | 680–669 |
| Ashurbanipal | 668–630/27 |

★★★

| Ashur-uballit II | 612–610 |

Egypt (3rd Intermediate Period 1069–664)

★★★

| Shoshenq (Sheshonq) I | 945–924 |

★★★

| Osorkon II | 874–850 |

★★★

Israel (1020–724)

(The first three dates depend entirely on biblical chronology.)

Saul	c.1020–1000
David	c.1000–960
Solomon	c.960–920

★★★

| Omri | c.876–869 |
| Ahab | c.869–850 |

★★★

| Jehoram | c.849–842 |

★★★

| Pekah | c.735–732 |
| Hoshea | c.732–724 |

Babylonian and Achaemenid Periods

Neo-Babylonian empire (626–539)

Nabopolassar	626–605
Nebuchadnezzar II	605–562
Amel-Marduk	562–560
(= Evil-Merodach)	

★★★

| Nabonidus | 556–539 |

Achaemenid empire (559–330)

(Bracketed names are not mentioned in this text.)

Cyrus II	559–530
Cambyses	530–522
(Bardiya	522)
Darius I	522–486

★★★

| Artaxerxes III | 359–338 |
| (Artaxerxes IV | 338–336) |

Darius III	336–330

Egypt Late Period (664–332)
★★★

Necho II	610–595

★★★

Apries	589–570

★★★

Hellenistic Period

Seleucid empire (305–64 BC)
(Overlapping dates indicate competing regimes.)

Seleucus I Nicator	305–281
Antiochus I Soter	281–261
Antiochus II Theos	261–246
Seleucus II Callinicus	246–225
Seleucus III Soter	225–223
Antiochus III Megas	223–187
Seleucus IV Philopator	187–175
Antiochus IV Epiphanes	175–164
Antiochus V Eupator	164–162
Demetrius I Soter	162–150
Alexander Balas	150–145
Demetrius II Nicator	145–141
Antiochus VI Epiphanes	145–142
Diodotus Tryphon	142–139/8
Antiochus VII Sidetes	139/8–129
Demetrius II (restored)	129–125
Cleopatra Thea	125
Seleucus V	125
Cleopatra Thea/	
Antiochus VIII Grypus	125–121
Antiochus VIII Grypus	121–96

★★★

Antiochus XIII	69–64

Ptolemaic empire (305–30 BC)

Ptolemy I Soter	305–282
Ptolemy II Philadelphus (co-regent)	285–246
Ptolemy III Euergetes	246–221
Ptolemy IV Philopator	221–205
Ptolemy V Epiphanes	205–180
Ptolemy VI Philometor	180–145

Ptolemy VII Neos Philopator   145
Ptolemy VIII Euergetes   170–116
Ptolemy IX Soter   116–107
★★★

Cleopatra VII Philopator   51–30

Hellenistic–Roman Period

Parthian empire (247 BC–AD 224)

Arsaces I   c.247–217 BC
★★★

Mithridates I   171–139/8
Phraates II   139/8–128
Artabanus I   128–124/3
Mithridates II   124/3–88/7
★★★

Phraates III   71/70–58/7
Orodes II   58/7–38
Phraates IV   38–3/2 BC
Phraates V   2 BC–AD 2
★★★

Chosroes (Osroes)   AD 108/9–127/8
★★★

Vologeses V   191–207/8
★★★

Artabanus IV   213–24

Roman Period

Roman empire (pre-Byzantine era) (27 BC–AD 337)

Augustus   27 BC–AD 14
Tiberius   AD 14–37
★★★

Nero   54–68
★★★

Vespasian   69–79
Titus   79–81
Domitian   81–96
★★★

Trajan   98–117
Hadrian   117–38
Antoninus Pius   138–61
Marcus Aurelius   161–80
★★★

Pertinax   193
Didius Iulianus   193
Septimius Severus   193–211
Caracalla   211–17
Geta (co-regent)   211–12
Macrinus   217–18
Elagabalus   218–22
Severus Alexander   222–35
Maximinus   235–38
Gordian I & II (co-regents)   238
Balbinus & Pupienus   238
(co-regents)
Gordian III   238–44
Philip the Arab   244–9
★★★
Trebonianus   251–3
★★★
Valerian   253–60
Gallienus (co-regent)   253–68
Claudius Gothicus   268–70
Aurelian   270–5
★★★
Numerian   283–4
Diocletian   284–305
Maximian (co-regent)   286–305
★★★
Constantine   306–37

Sasanian empire (AD 247–651)
Ardashir I   224–239/40
Shapur I   239/40–270/2
Hormizd I   270/2–273
★★★
Narseh   293–302
★★★

Appendix III: Literary Sources

Ammianus Marcellinus 4th cent. AD Byzantine historian (Latin), a continuation of the history of Tacitus

Appian 2nd cent. AD Greek historian, *Syrian Wars* (cited as *Syr.*), *Bellum Civile* ('Civil War') cited as (*Bell. Civ.*)

Arrian 2nd cent. AD Greek historian, *Anabasis* (cited as *Anab.*)

Athenaeus 2nd–3rd cent. AD Greek litterateur, *Deipnosophistae* ('The Learned Banquet')

Cassius Dio 2nd–3rd cent. AD Greek historian, *History of Rome*

Curtius (Quintus Curtius Rufus) 1st cent. AD Roman historian, *History of Alexander*

Diodorus Siculus 1st cent. BC Greek historian, *Bibliotheke Historike* ('Library of History')

Eusebius 3rd–4th cent. AD Greek chronicler and biblical scholar, *Ecclesiastical History*

Eutropius 4th cent. AD Byzantine historian (Latin), *Abstract of Roman History*

Firdausi 10th–11th cent. AD Persian epic poet, *Shahnameh*

Herodian 2nd–3rd cent. AD Greek historian, *History of the Roman Empire*

Herodotus 5th cent. BC Greek historian, *Histories*

Historia Augusta—see Scriptores Historiae Augustae

Homer 8th cent. BC Greek epic poet, *Iliad*

Jerome 4th–5th cent. AD Byzantine historian and theologian (Latin), chronicle of world history

John of Antioch 5th cent. AD Byzantine historian and Patriarch of Antioch (Greek), chronicle of world history

John Malalas 6th cent. AD Byzantine chronicler (Greek), chronicle of world history

Josephus 1st cent. AD Jewish historian, *Contra Apionem* ('Against Apion'), *Jewish Antiquities* (cited as *JA*), *Jewish Wars* (cited as *JW*)

Justin 2nd, 3rd, or 4th cent. AD Roman historian, *Epitome* (i.e. abridged version) of the *Historiae Philippicae* ('Philippic Histories') of Pompeius Trogus (cited as *Epit.*)

Juvenal 1st–2nd cent. AD Roman satirist, *Satires*

Lactantius 3rd–4th cent. AD Christian apologist, *De mortibus persecutorum* ('On the Deaths of the Persecuted')

Livy 1st cent. BC–AD Roman historian, *Ab urbe condita libri* ('Books from the Foundation of Rome (onwards)')

Lucian, 2nd cent. AD satirist and litterateur, *Zeuxis*

Petrus Patricius 6th cent. AD Byzantine lawyer, diplomat, and historian, historical works

Pliny the Elder 1st cent. AD Roman encyclopaedist, *Naturalis Historia* (cited as *NH*)

Plutarch 1st–2nd cent. AD Greek philosopher and biographer, *Lives of Alexander, Antony, Crassus, Demetrius*

Polyaenus 2nd cent. AD Greek rhetorician, *Strategemata* ('Stratagems')

Polybius 2nd cent. BC Greek historian, *Histories*

Procopius 6th cent. AD Byzantine historian (Greek), *De bello Persico* ('On the Persian (i.e. Sasanian) War')

Scriptores Historiae Augustae ('Writers of the Augustan History'), a late 4th cent. AD pseudo-historical literary concoction (see Introduction)

Strabo 1st cent. BC–AD Greek geographer, *Geographia*

Syncellus 8th–9th cent. AD Byzantine chronicler (Greek), chronicle of historical events

al-Tabari 9th–10th cent. AD Arab historian, *History of the Prophets and Kings*

Tacitus 1st–2nd cent. AD Roman historian, *Histories*

Velleius Paterculus 1st cent. BC–AD Roman historian, history of Rome

Zonaras 12th cent. AD Byzantine historian (Greek), world history

Zosimus 5th cent. AD Byzantine historian (Greek), *Historia Nova* ('New History'—a Roman history)

Notes

THE TALE TO BE TOLD

1. Readers who know their Shakespeare will understand why I have refrained from quoting the next words.
2. The emperor came to Syria around AD 290 to direct operations against Rome's eastern enemies. During his time there, and also in the years 300–2, he used Syria's leading city Antioch as his place of residence and administrative base (see Millar, 1993: 177–80). He left his mark on the region in a number of ways, e.g. by his administrative reorganization of it, his rebuilding of Syria's road networks, his restoration projects in Antioch and nearby Daphne, and his military installations in Palmyra. I shall say a little more about his involvement in Syrian affairs at the end of the book.
3. A stele (plural stelae) is an upright stone slab or pillar, on whose surface inscriptions and relief sculptures were generally carved.
4. The Old Testament passages cited in this book are translations from the New International Version of the Bible.
5. I have in fact touched on this in a number of chapters, without dealing with it as a discrete topic.
6. Herodotus extends Syrian territory as far south as the borders of Egypt (e.g. 2.116, 3.5).
7. See also Bunnens (2000: 3–12).

CHAPTER I. THE FIRST KINGDOMS

1. Akkermans and Schwartz (2003: 235).
2. 'Cuneiform' is a modern designation for the script used in the Near Eastern world, primarily on clay tablets but also on other writing surfaces, over a period of several millennia. Cuneiform symbols were most commonly produced by pressing into soft clay the triangular ends of reeds cut from the banks of the Mesopotamian and other rivers. The term, meaning 'wedge-shaped', is derived from the Latin word *cuneus*, 'wedge'.
3. Thus Akkermans and Schwartz (2003: 239).
4. See Akkermans and Schwartz (2003: 240–1, with Figs. 8.5, 8.6).

5. For accounts of Ebla's archaeology, language and written sources, society and administration, see Milano (1995), the articles Ebla, Eblaites, and Ebla Texts (by P. Matthiae, G. A. Rendsburg, and A. Archi respectively) in *OEANE* 2: 180–6, and Akkermans and Schwartz (2003: 235–44).

6. For accounts of the Amorites, see Roux (1980: 169–83), Whiting (1995), *OEANE* 1: 107–11 (G. Buccellati), *DCM* 40–2 (N. Ziegler).

7. Transl. E. Chiera, quoted Roux (1980: 166).

8. For accounts of Mari's history and archaeology, see Kupper (1973: 8–14), Kuhrt (1995: 95–8), Margueron (1995a), Akkermans and Schwartz (2003: 262–7), Van de Mieroop (2004: 96–104), Bryce (2009: 450–3).

9. For accounts of Yamhad's history, see Kupper (1973: 14–22), *DCM* 30–3, under **ALEP** (B. Lion).

10. Chavalas (2006: 96–7, transl. F. van Koppen).

11. For Qatna, see Kupper (as n. 9), *DCM* 705–6 (B. Lafont), Bryce (2009: 80).

12. Transl. Oates (1986: 63–4). See Chavalas (2006: 113–20, transl. F. van Koppen) for a selection of other letters to Yasmah-Addu in the Mari archive. A comprehensive edition of the letters unearthed from the palace of Mari has been published by Durand (1998–2002).

13. For the correspondence of his reign, with translations, see Heimpel (2003).

14. It is possible, however, that the pact had already been established before Zimri-Lim's occupation of Mari's throne.

15. Transl. J. Sasson, *CANE* 2: 906.

CHAPTER 2.   THE INTERNATIONAL INTRUDERS

1. Mitanni's capital and heartland lay in the triangular area east of the Euphrates that is now part of modern Syria. In the introduction ('The Tale to be Told', p. 5), I noted that the term 'Syria' when used in an ancient geographical context is commonly limited to the region between the Euphrates and the Mediterranean Sea. On this basis, Mitanni can be included among Syria's international intruders.

2. Further on Alalah and its texts, see Kupper (1973: 30–6), *OEANE* 1: 55–61 (D. L. Stein, E. L. Greenstein), *DCM* 29–30 (B. Lion).

3. On the Bronze Age Hittites in general, see Bryce (2005).

4. For possible links between the Bronze Age Hittites and the biblical Hittites, see Bryce (2012: 64–75).

5. On the site of an abandoned Middle Bronze Age city called Hattus.

6. For a translation (by G. Beckman) of Hattusili's own account of his Syrian campaigns, see Chavalas (2006: 219–22).

7. Though it has been suggested that Alalah was at this time independent of Aleppo, taking advantage of a dynastic dispute in the royal capital.

8. After G. Beckman in Chavalas (2006: 220).

9. This episode is recorded in what is often referred to as Hattusili's Testament, transl. by P. Goedegebuure in Chavalas (2006: 222–7).

10. Transl. by P. Goedegebuure in Chavalas (2006: 230).

11. The text, which has the catalogue number KBo III 57 (vv. 10–15), is listed as no. 11 in E. Laroche's *Catalogue des textes hittites*, Paris: Éditions Klincksieck, 1971.

12. The relevant passages are transl. in Chavalas (2006: 230) (P. Goedegebuure) and *ABC* Chron. 20: 156 = Glassner (2004: 273, no. 41).

13. On the Kassites, see Bryce (2009: 375–6).

14. For accounts of the Hurrians and Mitanni, see Wilhelm (1989, 1995), Van de Mieroop (2004: 142–5).

15. Tuthmosis' campaign to the Euphrates is recorded in the biography of Ahmose, a distinguished military officer who served under Tuthmosis. The biography is transl. by J. K. Hoffmeier in *CS* II: 5–7 (see esp. p. 7, lines 36–9).

16. For transls. of the inscription, see *CANE* 4: 2426 (E. L. Greenstein) and *CS* I: 479–80 (T. Longman III).

17. I have thus taken a different view from those scholars who regard Idrimi's alleged war with Parrattarna as a separate episode subsequent to his period of exile (even if not of seven years' duration); e.g. Podany (2010: 136).

18. For the records of Tuthmosis' Asiatic campaigns, see *CS* II: 7–23 (transl. J. K. Hoffmeier).

19. The exploits of this king have sometimes been divided between two rulers so called. They should probably all be attributed to one man, but to keep the question open, this 'man' is commonly designated as Tudhaliya I/II.

20. The ruler is unnamed in the Hittite text which records this event (see note below), but is presumably either a subordinate of Niqmepa or Niqmepa himself.

21. The Hittite text which records this information (transl. Beck. 93–5) dates more than a century after the events which it reports. The passage of time and the bias of the record cast some doubt on its reliability. For the text and discussion of it, see Bryce (2005: 140–1).

22. For details and source refs. to the events outlined in this paragraph, see Bryce (2005: 145–53).

23. *EA* 17: 30–8.

24. *EA* 41: 7–13, after Moran (1992: 114).

25. Information about this campaign (its actual length is debated) is contained in a treaty which Suppiluliuma later drew up with Shattiwaza (transl. Beck. 42–8), the post-empire ruler of what was left of Mitanni.

26. For accounts of Ugarit's archaeology and history, see Singer (1996), Yon (2006), Bryce (2009: 731–4).

27. As reported in the letter EA 45. The pharaoh was probably Amenhotep III rather than his successor Amenhotep IV/Akhenaten.

28. RS 17.132 = *PRU IV* 35–7.

29. From fragment 28, A iii 11–15, of Suppiluliuma's biography, transl. H. A. Hoffner in *CS* I: 190. Tutankhamun is referred to as Niphururiya in the Hittite texts. This was the Hittite equivalent of Tutankhamun's prenomen Nebkheperure. It should be said that some scholars identify the dead pharaoh as Akhenaten, and

thus the widow as his queen Nefertiti. In the text, she is simply called 'Daha-munzu', a generic term meaning 'wife of the king'. I believe that the evidence, though circumstantial, overwhelmingly supports the identification of the phar-aoh and his widow as Tutankhamun and Ankhesenamun.

CHAPTER 3. THE AMORITE WARRIOR-CHIEFS

The *EA* passages are transl. by or adapted from Moran (1992). There is a view that all the Amurru correspondence should be assigned to Akhenaten's reign.

1. *EA* 71: 16.
2. *EA* 84: 11–21.
3. *EA* 60: 19–29.
4. *EA* 74: 15–19.
5. *EA* 76: 11–16.
6. *EA* 74: 23–30.
7. The reading of the name is uncertain. It is probably the god Ninurta.
8. This and the following quoted passage are from *EA* 74: 31–53.
9. *EA* 81:12–14.
10. Adapted and condensed from *EA* 83: 23–51.
11. *EA* 91: 16–20.
12. *EA* 103: 8–11.
13. *EA* 157: 9–19.
14. *EA* 157: 28–33.
15. *EA* 161: 12–16.
16. *EA* 165: 28–41.
17. *EA* 124: 9–16.
18. *EA* 106: 12–15.
19. *EA* 136: 8–15.
20. *EA* 162: 2–12.
21. *EA* 162: 12–14. The passages cited in the following two paragraphs are also from *EA* 162, Akhenaten's response to Aziru.
22. Thus Westbrook in Cohen and Westbrook (2000: 38).
23. Beck. 36–41.
24. This and the following passages from the letter are taken or adapted from the transl. by Izre'el in Izre'el and Singer (1990: 23–7).
25. A possibility discussed at length by Izre'el and Singer (1990).

CHAPTER 4. THE EMPIRES COLLIDE

1. *EA* 189. The chronological context of the letter is uncertain, and it may have been written prior to Suppiluliuma's attack on Qadesh; see Bryce (2003: 144, n. 33).
2. As we shall see, a remnant of it, called the kingdom of Hanigalbat, survived for a time, first as a Hittite and then as an Assyrian subject state.
3. This and the following passages from Suppiluliuma's biography, composed by Suppiluliuma's son Mursili II and commonly referred to as the 'Deeds', come

from, or are adapted from, the transl. of H. A. Hoffner in *CS* I: 190–1 (whole transl. 185–92).

4. See Chapter 2, n. 29.

5. See Margueron (1995b).

6. The treaties are transl. in Beck. 36–40 and 59–64 respectively.

7. From the comprehensive annals of Mursili. These cover the whole of the king's reign (though parts of them are fragmentary). For a translation of the ten-year annals, covering the first ten years of the reign, see *CS* II: 82–90 (transl. R. H. Beal).

8. Further on the Tette episode, with source references, see Bryce (1988).

9. Extracts from Seti's war monument, transl. Breasted (1906: III, 72–3 §§144, 148). Further on Seti's campaigns, see Murnane (1990).

10. In general on Ramesses' reign, see Kitchen (1982).

11. Qadesh Inscription, extracts from P80–140, after Gardiner (1975: 9–10). The inscription is also transl. by K. A. Kitchen, *CS* II: 33–40.

12. Ramesses conducted two subsequent campaigns into Syria, along the Phoenician coast and into the Orontes valley, between 1271 and 1269, and claimed to have repossessed a number of city-states in the region, including Tyre, Beirut, Byblos, and Tunip. But the occupied territories seem quickly to have reverted to Hittite control after the pharaoh's return home on each occasion; see Kitchen (1982: 68–70).

13. Transl. by Y. Coram in Chavalas (2006: 244–52).

14. For further details of this episode and the letters which Hattusili and Ramesses exchanged about Urhi-Teshub, see Bryce (2003: 213–22). The dialogue between the kings can be reconstructed from passages in the sender's letters quoted by the recipient and specifically addressed in the recipient's replies.

15. For further details on this 'non-event' and the correspondence relating to it, see Bryce (2003: 85–9).

16. S. Öztürk, MD (2006), 'An Early Description of Painful Neuropathy in Hittite Tablets', *Archives of Neurology* 63(2), 2006, p. 296.

17. Beck. 100–3.

18. RS 18.06 + 17.365 (*PRU* IV 137–8), 1'–15'.

19. Scholars have different views on the regnal dates of the Middle Assyrian Kingdom rulers, of whom Shalmaneser was one. I have adopted the so-called 'low chronology' for these reigns.

20. For translations of the treaty, see Beck. 103–7, *CS* II: 98–100 (I. Singer).

21. For details, see Singer (1985), Bryce (2005: 316–18).

CHAPTER 5. THE END OF AN ERA

1. For the letter, with discussion and transl. of the relevant passage, see Bryce (2005: 331–2).

2. RS 17.247 = *PRU IV* 191. Also transl. Beck. 127, no. 21.

3. RS 34.136 (Malbran-Labat, 1991: 29–30, no. 7, lines 5–21).
4. RS 34.143 (Malbran-Labat, 1991: 27–8, no. 6, lines 5–13).
5. *EA* 38: 7–12.
6. RS 34.129 (Malbran-Labat, 1991: 38–40, no. 12).
7. Thus said the pharaoh Merneptah in his Karnak inscription; Breasted (1906: III §580).
8. Nougayrol *et al.* (1968: 85–6, no. 23).
9. Adapted and condensed from RS 18.147 = Nougayrol *et al.* (1968: 87–9, no. 24).
10. Medinet Habu inscription of Ramesses III's 8th year, lines 16–17, transl. J. A. Wilson in *ANET* 262.
11. For the text, see Arnaud (1991: 66–7, no. 30).

CHAPTER 6. THE AGE OF IRON

1. The story is preserved on a papyrus, now in the Pushkin Museum, Moscow. For a translation, see *CS* I: 89–93 (M. Lichtheim).
2. Lichtheim, *CS* I: 89, comments: 'Wenamun stands on the threshold of the first millennium BCE, a millennium in which the modern world began, a world shaped by men and women who were the likes of ourselves.'
3. For a general analysis of Iron Age Syria, see Bunnens (2000: 12–19). 'In chronological terms,' Bunnens comments (p. 19), 'the Iron Age began in Syria in the 11th century BC and reached its peak in the 9th and early 8th century. It began to disintegrate in the late 8th century but survived until, in the 5th and 4th centuries, Hellenism contributed to a reshaping of Syrian culture.' Most chronologies assign a cut-off date of 500 BC to the Iron Age, a conveniently round if somewhat arbitrary figure. I have preferred to deal separately with events of the 6th century in the next chapter.
4. For a detailed treatment of these, see Bryce (2012).
5. Though as we have noted, there is not one single shred of evidence to indicate that the Hittite language survived in the Iron Age either in spoken or written form.
6. In general on the Aramaeans, see Lipiński (2000), Bryce (2012: 163–80).
7. *ANET* 376–8, transl. also in *CS* II: 41 (J. K. Hoffmeier).
8. See Rainey and Notley (2006: 185–9).
9. 1 Kings 14:25–6, 2 Chron. 12:2–9. Sheshonq does not include a conquest of Jerusalem in his own record, or at least not in what survives of it.
10. Thus Taylor (2000: 336).
11. *CS* II 161–2, transl. A. Millard.
12. For a discussion of this and other Neo-Hittite inscriptions found in the Aleppo temple, see Hawkins (2011).
13. For a comprehensive survey of the Canaanites, see Tubb (1998).
14. For a comprehensive survey of the Phoenicians, see Markoe (2000).

CHAPTER 7. THE WOLF UPON THE FOLD:
THE NEO-ASSYRIAN INVASIONS

1. The talent was a measurement of weight, varying from *c.*30 to 60 kilograms.
2. *RIMA* 2: 37, 53.
3. The following account of Ashurnasirpal's operations west of the Euphrates is based primarily on the relevant sections of the king's inscriptions, notably *RIMA* 2: 214–19.
4. This is my suggested reconstruction of the events surrounding Ashurnasirpal's capture of Kinalua, which is only briefly reported in the Assyrian record (*RIMA* 2: 217). The text merely states: 'He (Lubarna) took fright in the face of my raging weapons (and) fierce battle and submitted to me to save his life' (transl. Grayson).
5. The following account of Assyrian campaigns in Syria and Palestine during Shalmaneser's reign is based primarily on the relevant sections of the king's inscriptions, notably *RIMA* 3: 9–11, 15–19, 21–4, 29, 37–9, 48, 54, 67, 69, 118. Readers wishing to correlate these references to the specific episodes to which they refer should see Bryce (2012: 218–38, 242–4).
6. *RIMA* 3:21, transl. Grayson.
7. *RIMA* 3: 21, 29, transl. Grayson.
8. *RIMA* 3: 23–4, adapted and condensed from transl. by Grayson.
9. The biblical account wrongly identifies the man in question as Ben-Hadad (= Bar-Hadad I), who in fact *preceded* Hadadezer on the throne of Damascus.
10. *RIMA* 3: 69, transl. Grayson. Ashur was Assyria's chief deity.
11. For the main sources of information on Assyrian campaigns west of the Euphrates during Adad-nirari's reign, see *RIMA* 3: 203–13.
12. *ARAB* I §§749–60.
13. Our main sources of information on Tiglath-pileser III's reign are provided by the king's inscriptions, ed. and transl. by Tadmor (2007). For specific references in them to the Syrian and Palestinian regions see Bryce (2012: 258–74).
14. For the tribute lists, see Tadmor (2007: 68–9, 106–9), and Bryce (2012: 264–72) for a discussion of the tributaries.
15. *ABC* Chron. 1:73 = Glassner (2004: 195, no. 16).
16. *CS* II: 295, no. 2.118C, transl. K. L. Younger.
17. For details, with sources, of Sennacherib's and Esarhaddon's campaigns in Syria and Palestine, see Grayson (1991b: 109–11, 123–6).

CHAPTER 8. FROM NEBUCHADNEZZAR TO ALEXANDER

1. In general on the history of the Neo-Babylonian empire, see Wiseman (1991). For Egypt's and Babylon's role in Syria and Palestine during this period, with translations of the relevant sources, see Rainey and Notley (2006: 258–64).
2. *ABC* Chron. 3:95 = Glassner (2004: 223, no. 22).

3. The Latin name, meaning 'Way of the Sea', for the coastal highway linking Mesopotamia with Egypt via the Mediterranean coastline, passing through Palestine and coastal Syria before turning east and crossing the Euphrates.

4. So renamed by Necho. His original name was Eliakim.

5. The sources for these events are 2 Kings 23:31–4, 2 Chron. 36:2–4.

6. *ABC* Chron. 5:99 = Glassner (2004: 227, no. 24). In general on the events of Nebuchadnezzar's pre-accession and early regnal years, see Wiseman (1956: 64–75), *ABC* Chron. 5:99–102 = Glassner (2004: 226–30, no. 24).

7. Wiseman (1956: 66–8), *ABC* Chron. 5: 99 = Glassner (2004: 226–9, no. 24), Rainey and Notley (2006: 262).

8. Josephus, *Contra Apionem* 1.137–8.

9. *ABC* Chron. 5:100 = Glassner (2004: 229, no. 24).

10. The sources for these events are Wiseman (1956: 70–1), *ABC* Chron. 5:101 = Glassner (2004: 229, no. 24), 2 Kings 24:7.

11. Most of our information on Jerusalem's fall comes from biblical sources, especially 2 Kings 24–5. For the convenience of those readers who wish to follow up on the specific biblical references, I have included these references in the text, even though the frequency of their insertion may be a little disruptive of the narrative flow.

12. Wiseman (1991: 232–3).

13. Josephus, *JA* 10.108–10.

14. Thus Josephus, *Contra Apionem* 1.137–8.

15. Actually, the claim of a family link between Cyrus and Achaemenes, first made by Cyrus' third successor Darius I (522–486), is almost certainly false. It none the less became an established part of Persian dynastic tradition, as attested in the inscriptions of Darius' successors as well as in Classical sources.

16. Polybius, 16.40/22a (Loeb Polybius, vol.V, 48–51).

17. The designation 'Jews' is generally used of the Israelites after their liberation from their Babylonian exile.

18. The specific references to the authors cited in this paragraph are: Strabo 16.2.20, Arrian, *Anab.* 2.6.3, Josephus, *JA* 11.30.

19. On the famous Eshmunazar inscription, see *OEANE* 2: 261 (G. A. Long). The inscription, carved on the lid of Eshmunazar's sarcophagus, is transl. by P. K. McCarter in *CS* II: 182–3.

20. This was an ultimately unsuccessful uprising initiated by the Ionian Greek cities of Asia Minor against Persian rule. Their cause was taken up by other states in the Greek world, including Athens and a number of Greek cities in Cyprus.

21. Herodotus 3.91. The weight of the Persian talent was *c.*30 kilograms.

22. Making his first landfall on the coast near the site of Troy, where he paid his respects to the Homeric heroes.

23. The Classical sources for Alexander's military operations in Asia Minor are collected and transl. in Kuhrt (2007: 429–36).

24. Our Classical sources for the battle and its aftermath are: Diodorus 17.33–6, Curtius 3.10, Plutarch, *Alexander* 20, Arrian, *Anab.* 2. 6.

25. See Diodorus 17.39.1, Arrian, *Anab.* 2.14. The latter is transl. in Aust. 31–3, no. 7, with useful notes.

26. Diodorus 17.40–6 is our main source for the siege, capture, and destruction of Tyre. See also Curtius 4.2.24–3.1.

27. Diodorus 16.42–5 is our main source for this episode.

28. Arrian, *Anab.* 2.25.4–26.1; 27.7. Batis' alleged fate is recorded in Curtius 4.8–24.

29. For the pilgrimage, see Arrian, *Anab.* 3.3–4, transl. Aust. 35–6. no. 9.

30. For the sources on Alexander's victory at Gaugamela and his subsequent Iranian campaign, see Kuhrt (2007: 446–51).

31. Miles (2010: 157).

CHAPTER 9. THE RISE OF THE SELEUCID EMPIRE

1. For a recent concise treatment of the empire, see Hannestad (2012).

2. For a detailed account of the struggle for supremacy among Alexander's heirs, see Waterfield (2011).

3. For translations of the relevant passages from Arrian and Diodorus, see Aust. 63–5, no. 26. Three notable absentees from the meeting were Antipater, Craterus, and Antigonus, who were engaged in activities elsewhere.

4. i.e. that part of Asia Minor which lay closest to the Hellespont (modern Dardanelles).

5. He had been satrap there since 331.

6. Arrian, *FGrH* 156 F 9 §§34–8, transl. Aust. 71–2, no. 30.

7. Craterus had been killed the previous year in a battle against Eumenes near the Hellespont.

8. Seleucus' entry into office as satrap is recorded in the fragment of the Babylonian Chronicle known as the *Chronicle of the Diadochoi* (*ABC* Chron. 10:115–19 = Glassner (2004: 242–6, no. 30)).

9. Diodorus 19.55.2–5, Appian, *Syr.* 53, transl. Aust. 120, no. 57. According to Appian, the dispute actually began when Seleucus abused one of the local administrators, in Antigonus' presence and without consulting his distinguished guest first; *allegedly* he ought to have done so in deference to the guest's superior status. Furious at this display of lese-majesty, Antigonus then demanded to see Seleucus' accounts. The whole episode might thus have had to do with irregularities in the satrapal finances.

10. Plutarch, *Demetrius* 5.

11. Diodorus 19.91.1.

12. The main source for these events is Diodorus 19.90–2.

13. Diodorus 19.100.

14. Diodorus 19.91.3–4. In Seleucid tradition, Seleucus' return to Babylon marked the foundation date of the Seleucid royal dynasty (April 311, according to the Babylonian calendar, October 312 according to the Macedonian one).

15. *ABC* Chron. 10:118 = Glassner (2004: 247, no. 30).

16. Our main source for the Seleucus–Chandragupta encounter and its aftermath is Appian, *Syr.* 55, transl. Aust. 121, no. 57; see also 123, n. 8. Note Sherwin-White and Kuhrt's comments (1993: 12–13). Strabo 15.2.9 provides the information about the elephants. The 500-figure may well be an inflated one, as Sherwin-White and Kuhrt observe.

17. Appian, *Syr.* 57.

18. Appian, *Syr.* 58 records an interesting story relating to its foundation.

19. Pliny, *NH* 6.122.

20. The most substantial account of the battle is given by Plutarch, *Demetrius* 28–9. See also Diodorus 21.1.4b. Demetrius was later given the epithet Poliorcetes ('Besieger of Cities'), reflecting his year-long siege of Rhodes in 305–304 BC.

21. First attested in the Hellenistic period, the term Coele Syria (literally 'Hollow Syria') here designates the region of the ('hollow') Biqa' valley in Lebanon, extending between the Lebanon and anti-Lebanon ranges. Its northern limit was marked by the Eleutheros river (modern Nahr el-Kebir), which forms the northern boundary of modern Lebanon, and was for long the boundary between Seleucid- and Ptolemaic-controlled territory in Syria. But the term was flexible in its definition. W. G. Dever notes that under the Ptolemies and Seleucids, all of Phoenicia, and even Palestine, could be designated Coele Syria (*OEANE* 2: 41). In later periods, the term was sometimes used to designate the whole of Syria from the Orontes valley eastwards across the Syrian desert to the Euphrates.

22. Antioch, modern Antakya, now lies within Turkey's borders.

23. Our sources for the founding and subsequent dismantling of Antigoneia, and the shift of its population to Antioch, are Diodorus 22.47.5–6 and Strabo 16.2.4.

24. But on the matter of Antioch's status during the first half of the Seleucid empire, note the comments of Grainger (1990: 122).

25. Thus we are informed by Appian, *Syr.* 57, transl. Aust. 121–2, no. 57. Some of his figures are almost certainly inflated ones.

26. Strabo 16.2.4.

27. On these matters, see Arrian, *Anab* 7.4.4, transl. Aust. 48, no. 17.

28. Appian, *Syr.* 62.

29. *ABC* Chron. 12: 121–2 = Glassner (2004: 251, no. 33). See also Sherwin-White and Kuhrt (1993: 21–2).

30. Appian, *Syr.* 62, Memnon of Heraclea *FGrH* 434 F 11 §8, transl. Aust. 290, no. 159.

31. Cf. Sherwin-White and Kuhrt (1993: 29). The information about the uprising is provided in a decree from Ilium (Troy), transl. in Sherwin-White and Kuhrt, and also in Aust. 297–8, no. 162.

32. Appian, *Syr.* 65, Lucian, *Zeuxis* 8–11.

33. The war is poorly attested. For the Babylonian record that is our prime source, see Aust. 299–301, no. 163.

34. Sources for this section include Polybius 5.58.11, Appian, *Syr.* 65–6, Polyaenus 8.50, and the documents transl. by Aust. 312–14, no. 173, and 463–4, no. 266 = *FGrH* 160.

35. Sources relating to Berenice's murder are Polyb 5.58.1, Appian, *Syr.* 65.

36. Justin, *Epit.* 27.2.

37. On the conflict between the two brothers, see Heinen (1984: 428–30), and the refs. in Aust. 321–2, 322–3, 405, nos. 176, 177, 231 respectively, and Justin, *Epit.* 27.2.

38. For an outline of Attalid history and chronology, see Strabo 13.4.1–2, transl. Aust. 395–7, no. 224.

39. Justin, *Epit.* 27.3.

40. Justin, *Epit.* 27.3.

CHAPTER 10. THE SELEUCID EMPIRE IN ITS PRIME

1. Polybius 4.48, transl. Aust. 328–9, no. 180.

2. Our main source for the appointments and the consequences that followed from them is Polybius 5.40–3, transl. Aust. 329–31, no. 181.

3. Polybius 5.42.6.

4. The twin settlements of Seleuceia and Apameia, founded by Seleucus I on the right and left banks respectively of the Euphrates, came to be known jointly as Zeugma, meaning 'junction'.

5. Polybius 5.43.

6. Polybius 5.45.

7. Polybius 5.48.

8. Polybius 5.54 is our source for these events, and those related in the next paragraph.

9. Polybius 5.55 and 56 is our source for the information in this and the following two paragraphs.

10. Polybius 5.56.13, Loeb transl.

11. The information in this paragraph is based on Polybius 5.57.

12. Details are provided by Polybius 5.80–6.

13. Polybius 5.87.3.

14. Polybius 8.20.9.

15. Polybius 8.21.3, Loeb transl.

16. A fragmentary account of these campaigns is preserved in Polybius 11.34 (39), transl. Aust. 337–8, no. 187.

17. Polybius 13.9, Loeb transl.

18. Polybius 11.34 (39),15–16, Loeb transl.

19. Cf. Miles (2010: 162), Sherwin-White and Kuhrt (1993: 200), and see also Shipley (2000: 291).

20. Polybius 15.34–5.

21. As Gruen observes (1984: 615, n. 16), the Fifth Syrian War is 'notoriously ill-documented'; see his references, and add Heinen (1984: 440–2).

22. For a concise treatment of Rome's war with Antiochus, beginning with the latter's invasion of mainland Greece, see Gruen (1984: 636–40). Gruen provides in his footnotes a comprehensive list of the primary sources for the conflict.

23. For details of the peace accord, with documentation of the primary sources, see Gruen (1984: 640–3).

24. Diodorus 28.3, 29.15; Justin, *Epit.* 32.2.1–2.

25. Appian, *Syr.* 45.

26. Gruen (1984: 645) notes that the name was 'hitherto closely associated with the Antigonid dynasty and not previously found among the Seleucids. The choice was deliberate, a sign that the king angled for a revival of relations between the Macedonian and Syrian royal houses that had so frequently held during the third century.'

27. Appian, *Syr.* 39.

28. Appian, *Syr.* 45.

29. Appian, *Syr.* 45. Further on the backing Eumenes provided for Antiochus' assumption of imperial power, see the decree *OGIS* 248, found at Pergamum and transl. by Aust. 370–1, no. 208.

30. See Polybius 26.1, transl. Aust. 371–2, no. 209a and Diodorus 29.32 for an account of his alleged eccentric behaviour, which led to his nickname Epimanes (a play on Epiphanes), 'the madman'. Further on the reports of his eccentricities, and the likely truth or otherwise of them, see Gruen (1984: 662–3), Habicht (1984: 341–2).

31. Diodorus 30.15–16.

32. For a relatively detailed account of the events of this war and the political and diplomatic activities associated with it, with comprehensive documentation of the relevant primary sources, see Gruen (1984: 650–60).

33. There was a Ptolemy VII, who ruled only briefly, in 145 (first as co-regent of his father Ptolemy VI), before he was assassinated by his uncle Ptolemy VIII after his father's death.

34. The main source I have used for this account is Polybius 29.27, transl. Aust. 374–5, no. 211. For other sources, see refs. in Gruen (1984: 659, n. 226).

35. Polybius 30.25–6 is our source for these festivities (25 is transl. by Aust. 376–8, no. 213). The quoted passage is from the Loeb transl. See also Diodorus 31.16.1.

36. Gruen (1984: 660).

37. Davis and Kraay (1973: 209); some of their further observations on this matter are reflected in my following comments.

38. On the extremely sparse sources for Antiochus' final eastern campaigns and his death during the course of them, see Gruen (1984: 661–2, n. 237). See also Habicht (1984: 350–3).

CHAPTER 11. THE MACCABEAN REBELLION

1. Here and in the following paragraph are excerpts from Antiochus III's 'charter of rights' for the Jewish people, transl. Aust. 380–2, no. 215, from Josephus,

JA 12.138–46. Note that the translations from Maccabees are taken from the Revised Standard Version of the Bible and Apocrypha.

2. Hardly likely, says Aust. 382, n. 4, who comments that this applied only to Jerusalem.

3. It was his third visit there. On the first occasion, around 171, he had been warmly welcomed by the people; on the second, during his return from his first Egyptian campaign, he had plundered the treasury and pillaged the temple (1 Macc: 1:20–4).

4. Transl. Aust. 385–6, no. 217.

5. Our other major sources of information for the rebellion and its aftermath are Josephus, *JA* 12.5–13.1, *JW* 1.1.

6. Sherwin-White and Kuhrt (1993: 226).

7. For details and maps of other battles, see Rainey and Notley (2006: 309–17).

8. Cf. Josephus, *JA* 12.313–15, and Rainey and Notley (2006: 311).

9. *HCBD* 635: 'The date of the rededication, 25 Kislev of 164 BC, with the attendant eight-day festivities (1 Macc. 4:52–8), has since that time been celebrated annually as Hanukkah or the "Feast of the Dedication" (see John 10:22).'

10. On both documents, see Habicht (1984: 349–50), and on the question of their chronology Gruen (1984: 745).

11. On Judas' final battles, his death, and the continuing Jewish resistance to Seleucid rule under his brother Jonathan, see Rainey and Notley (2006: 313–17).

CHAPTER 12. THE DECLINE AND FALL OF THE SELEUCIDS

1. Our main source for the information in this paragraph is Polybius 31.2, transl. Aust. 387–8, no. 218.

2. Polybius 31.11–15. See also Appian, *Syr.* 47.

3. Diodorus 31.27a, Appian, *Syr.* 47, 1 Macc. 7:1–4.

4. Diodorus 31.27a, Appian, *Syr.* 45, 47.

5. Polybius 33 frag. 19, Loeb transl.

6. Diodorus 31.32a.

7. For the extensive list of ancient sources that deal with these events, see Gruen (1984: 667, n. 256).

8. Josephus, *JA* 13.80–3, 1 Macc. 10:51–8.

9. He had fled from it as a child on the overthrow of his father.

10. Diodorus 32.9c.

11. This is according to 1 Macc. 11:16; there are other versions of Balas' fate.

12. Diodorus 33.4, transl. Aust. 388–9, no. 219.

13. Sources on Diodotus Tryphon and the events in which he was involved, as outlined here, include Strabo 14.5.2, transl. Aust. 389–90, no. 220, Strabo 16.2.10, Appian, *Syr.* 67–8, Josephus, *JA* 13.143–224, 1 Macc. 11:39–15:37, Justin, *Epit.* 36.1. For a more detailed account of the context in which these events occurred, see Rainey and Notley (2006: 320–7, with refs.); see also Gruen (1984: 668–9, with refs.).

14. Diodorus 33.28, Josephus, *JA* 13.218, 1 Macc. 13:31, Appian, *Syr.* 68, Justin, *Epit.* 36.1.

15. Gruen (1984: 668) observes that 'The Hasmonean dynasts of Judaea often held the balance of power as they deftly manipulated the warring factions for the advancement of their own nation.'

16. Diodorus 33.8, 34.15, Appian, *Syr.* 69, 1 Macc. 14:1–3, Justin, *Epit.* 36.1.

17. He was actually in Rhodes when he learnt of the developments that prompted his return to Syria (Appian, *Syr.* 68).

18. For Cleopatra's motives for the marriage, see Josephus, *JA* 13.222 (Josephus claims that Cleopatra actually instigated it), Appian, *Syr.* 68.

19. Diodorus 34.1, Josephus, *JA* 13.236–44.

20. Justin, *Epit.* 38.10.6.

21. Sources for the Parthian campaign include Diodorus 34.15.17, Josephus, *JA* 13.250–3, Justin, *Epit.* 38.10.

22. Justin, *Epit.* 39.1.

23. Josephus, *JA* 13.268, Justin, *Epit.* 39.1.

24. Josephus, *JA* 13.268, Appian, *Syr.* 68, Justin, *Epit.* 39.1.

25. Appian, *Syr.* 69.

26. Davis and Kraay (1973: 219).

27. It seems to be based in part on an ancient presentation of the prince as a *bon vivant* who entertained daily on a massively generous scale—thus Athenaeus, *Deipnosophistae* 5.210D.

28. Justin, *Epit.* 39.2.

29. Appian, *Syr.* 69, Justin, *Epit.* 39.2.

30. There was also a period between 83 and 69 when Syria was ruled by the Armenian king Tigranes II 'the Great'.

CHAPTER 13. THE COMING OF THE ROMANS

1. Appian, *Syr.* 50, Loeb transl. See also Cassius Dio 37.7a.

2. Josephus, *JW* 1.6–8, Cassius Dio 37.15–16. For a comprehensive treatment of this period in the history of the Hasmonean dynasty, with documentation of sources, see Rainey and Notley (2006: 334–41).

3. The term 'client king' is conventionally used by modern scholars 'to denote a range of monarchs and quasi-monarchs of non-Roman people who enjoyed a relationship with Rome that was essentially harmonious but unequal' (*OCD* 348). Such persons were formally referred to by the Roman Senate as 'king and ally and friend'.

4. Juvenal, *Satires* 3.62–3, transl. C. Plumb.

5. Our main sources for the conflict are Plutarch, *Crassus* 19–31 and Cassius Dio 40.17–27.

6. Plutarch, *Crassus* 33.

7. The most recent earlier civil war, fought between Caesar and Pompey, had resulted in Pompey's defeat and death. Orodes had actually declared his support for Pompey.

8. Our main source for the events in this and the following paragraph is Cassius Dio 48.24–6.

9. Josephus, *JA* 14.365. The law required that the office be held only by those persons whose bodily parts were intact (thus Josephus).

10. Our main source for the events in this paragraph is Cassius Dio 48.39–40, 49.19–21.

11. Josephus, *JA* 14.490, *JW* 1.357, Cassius Dio 49.22.

12. For Herod's reign, with sources, see Rainey and Notley (2006: 342–8).

13. Our main source for the account given below of Antony's eastern campaigns is Plutarch, *Antony* 38–50.

14. Velleius Paterculus 2.101.

15. On the Euphrates as the boundary line, see Strabo 16.1.28.

16. Stoneman (1992: 85).

17. For details of this war and its aftermath, and the relevant ancient sources, see Millar (1993: 70–9), Rainey and Notley (2006: 383–95).

18. Josephus, *JW* 2–7 is our main source for the war.

19. For a more detailed account of these changes, with citations of sources, see Millar (1993: 80–90).

20. During the Roman period, a distinction was drawn between a Greater and a Lesser Armenia. The former included all Armenian territories east of the upper Euphrates, the latter the Armenian territories west and north of the Euphrates, bordering on Pontus to the north and Commagene to the south.

21. Ball (2000: 60) notes that although there were many 'Arabias', only this one, the Provincia Arabia, was an officially designated Roman province; the province 'corresponding to the old Nabataean kingdom, comprised much of the present area of Jordan plus Sinai and the Negev (including Gaza), northern Hijaz, and parts of southern Syria up to and including (for a short while) Damascus'.

22. See Map 10 for the locations of the places mentioned in this and the following paragraph.

23. *OCD* 171.

24. On Trajan's eastern operations, with the relevant ancient sources, see Millar (1993: 90–105).

25. See Cassius Dio 68.17–30 for the overall coverage of these enterprises. The specific references made here are to 68.17.1 and 68.29.1.

26. Stoneman (1992: 89).

27. Ball (2000: 17).

28. For a recent brief account of the fortress-settlement, see Hannestad (2012: 991–3), who notes that the name should more correctly be represented as Europos Dura, since Europos was the Greek name taken from a city in Macedonia and Dura the later Parthian name.

29. As part of his process of forceful assimilation, he may also have banned a number of traditional Jewish practices, including perhaps circumcision, though the evidential support for this is weak. Our only source is the *HA*, Hadrian 14.2.

30. On the Bar Kochba revolt, with the relevant ancient sources, see Millar (1993: 106–8, 372–4, 545–52), Rainey and Notley (2006: 396–9). Bar Kochba was the popular title or nickname of the leader.

31. Eusebius, *Eccl. Hist.* 4.6.3–4. Rainey and Notley (2006: 399) note that according to the Eusebian tradition, Bar Kochba was captured and executed, though legendary depictions present him dying in battle.

32. Cary and Scullard (1975: 441).

CHAPTER 14. NABATAEAN EXCURSUS

1. There were also Nabataean settlements in the region called the Hauran, a large fertile plain in southern Syria, south of Damascus.

2. Strabo 16.4.21.

3. Further on the Nabataeans and their kingdom, see Millar (1993: 400–8), *OEANE* 4: 82–5 (D. F. Graf), Ball (2000: 60–73, with map p. 61 showing the kingdom's approx. limits).

4. According to 2 Corinthians 11:32–3 (cf. Acts 9: 23–5), Paul was living in Damascus, after his conversion on the road to the city, when it again later came under Nabataean control. While there, he fell foul of the local authorities, but escaped the city with the help of supporters who lowered him outside it in a basket through an opening in its walls. This allegedly happened during the reign of the Nabataean king Aretas (IV), but there is some uncertainty about the chronology.

5. But note Millar's comments (1993: 402–3) about the use of Arabic and Aramaic in the Nabataean context.

6. The Arabic origin of their authors is reflected particularly in their Arabic names (by far the greatest number of names recorded in the texts are Arabic in origin) and in a number of Arabic loan words, used for political and legal institutions (thus Graf, *OEANE* 4: 83–4). Graf notes (p. 81) that the majority of the Nabataean inscriptions come from the environs of Petra, from Egra in northern Arabia, and from the Hauran in southern Syria.

7. Diodorus 19.95–8.

8. Josephus, *JA* 4.161.

9. 'The present-day Arab name *Bōsra* corresponds exactly to the Nabataean and Palmyrene written form *BSR*', from the root *bāsar*, "to make inaccessible", when defining, for example, a fort' (J.-M. Dentzer in *OEANE* 1: 350–1).

CHAPTER 15. THE SYRIAN EMPERORS

1. For a recent account of the Roman world in the late 2nd and the 3rd cent. AD, see Goldsworthy (2009: 53–153).

2. The main source for these events is Herodian 2.6–12.

3. Tacitus, *Histories* 4.

4. Herodian 3.4.1–6 gives us an account of the battle and its aftermath.

5. Thus Cassius Dio 79.23.3. Semiramis was a legendary Near Eastern queen. Her historical original was a 9th-cent. BC queen of Assyria called Sammu-ramat, a powerful influence in the court of two successive Assyrian kings, her husband Shamshi-Adad V and her son Adad-nirari III.

6. Our main source for Septimius' trans-Euphrates ventures is Herodian 3.9.

7. The old province of Syria was now divided into two: Coele Syria and Syria Phoenice.

8. Cassius Dio 77.15.2.

9. Herodian 4.8.1–3, Cassius Dio 78.7. He clearly sought to cultivate the image of a latter-day Alexander, and perhaps himself believed that he was Alexander come back to life. Millar (1993: 142) comments: 'Caracalla's imitation of Alexander was no superficial whim but the determining factor in his actions as Emperor.'

10. Cassius Dio 79.1–3.

11. Herodian 4.11.

12. The Loeb translator of Herodian comments that it is quite possible that the emperor was wearing German-style breeches (Latin *bracae*) at the time. Our main source for the emperor's assassination is Herodian 4.13.3–5. Cf. Cassius Dio 79. 5 and *HA*, Caracalla 7.1–2.

13. Cassius Dio 79.23–4.

14. The local version of the god Baal.

15. According to Herodian 5.3.10, Maesa spread the rumour that he was Caracalla's illegitimate offspring.

16. Our main source of information for the events narrated in this paragraph is Herodian 5.3–4.

17. e.g. Herodian 5.3.7–8.

18. As Millar (1993: 147) notes.

19. *HA*, Elagabalus 25.2.

20. Herodian 5.6.1 reports that he executed many distinguished and wealthy men when he heard that they disapproved of and mocked his way of life.

21. Juvenal, *Satires* 3.62–3. The information in the last two paragraphs is based on Herodian 5.7.1–5.8.9.

22. Thus Ball (2000: 415).

CHAPTER 16. THE CRISIS YEARS

1. Classical texts regularly call Ardashir Artaxerxes.

2. Herodian 6.2.1–2 > (= transl. in) DL 1.1.5, p. 16.

3. e.g. DL 352, n. 12.

4. Herodian 6.3.5 > DL 1.2.3, p. 18.

5. Herodian 6.5. > DL 1.3.3, pp. 23–5.

6. Herodian 6.6.1.

7. Herodian 6.6.6 > DL 1.3.3, p. 26 (transl. is that in DL).

8. Millar (1993: 150).

9. Herodian 6.9.8, Loeb transl.

10. Watson (1999: 3): 'During this half century, in excess of sixty individuals laid claim to the imperial purple, and all but one or two of these claims were terminated by the sword. Almost invariably these individuals were put up by the army, or rather by one of the several imperial armies stationed in different parts of the empire, often in opposition to the candidature of another elsewhere.'

11. Millar (1993: 154) notes that Shapur in his inscription (referred to below) 'flatly contradicts the Roman version of the sequence of events which led to the proclamation of Philip as Emperor. For in (the Roman) version it was only after the Roman army had retreated up the Euphrates to near Circesium that Gordian was assassinated and Philip took his place. What is certain at least is that a tomb was built for Gordian at a place called Zaitha near Circesium where Ammianus saw it during Julian's expedition of 363 (Ammianus XXIII 5. 7).'

12. For the central section of Shapur's inscription, transl. by R. N. Frye, see Stoneman (1992: 93–4). The Augustan inscription, the best preserved copy of which is located in Ankara, is commonly known as the monumentum Ancyranum.

13. See Millar (1993: 159).

14. Thus Millar (1993: 159).

15. Stoneman (1992: 11) describes the work as 'an extraordinary farrago . . . which contains a great deal of undifferentiated material of legend and history, in which emperors rub shoulders with demons and talismans'.

16. Passage from Malalas 12 > DL 3.2.2, p. 55.

17. Millar (1993: 160).

18. Millar (1993: 163; with n. 19 for the reference to the letter).

19. Cary and Scullard (1975: 509).

20. See Zosimus 1.32.2, cited also by Millar (1993: 163, n. 21).

21. Firdausi, *Shahnameh* 6.23.2. For a recent translation of Firdausi's poems, see Davis (2006).

22. Zosimus 1.36.1–2 > DL 3.3.1, pp. 61–2.

23. Lactantius, *De mortibus persecutorum* 5 > DL 3.3.1, p. 58.

24. The emperor was seriously wounded in battle in Gaul while trying to quell this movement.

25. *HA*, The Two Gallieni 16.1.

CHAPTER 17. FROM DESERT OASIS TO ROYAL CAPITAL: THE STORY OF PALMYRA

1. *RIMA* 2: 38.

2. John Malalas 18.2.

3. Josephus, *JA* 8.154.

4. Frye (2000: 18).

5. Appian, *Bell. Civ.* 5.9.

6. Polybius 5.79. Zabdibel is not actually called a Palmyrene in this text; but in later inscriptions, the name is attested only at Palmyra.

7. Thus Millar (1993: 35).

8. Ball (2010: 27–8).

9. This list is compiled by Ball (2010: 214).

10. Though Millar (1993: 143) points out that it is not clear whether it was Septimius Severus or his son Caracalla who gave the city this status.

11. Millar (1993: 328–9) comments: 'It does not of course follow that each soldier in a Palmyrene unit in Britain, Numidia or Dacia was literate in both Latin and Palmyrene. But it does follow that such soldiers could (at least) have access to persons who could compose brief texts in Palmyrene, and then have them inscribed.'

12. Stoneman (1992: 67–8).

13. Thus Ball (2010: 222).

14. Stoneman (1992: 65–6).

15. As Bounni notes, *OEANE* 4: 243.

16. Inscriptional evidence dates the marker to the period AD 11–17; see Millar (1993: 34–5).

17. See Millar (1993: 34, with ref. n. 26).

18. Stoneman (1992: 69–70).

CHAPTER 18. SYRIA'S 'KING OF KINGS': THE LIFE AND DEATH OF ODENATHUS

1. The use of capital letters represents the scholarly convention for transcribing Palmyrene words (which were written without vowel sounds).

2. Thus Millar (1993: 158).

3. Though it is possible that by 257/8 he had been appointed governor of the province of Syria Phoenice; see Millar (1993: 162 and 165 with nn. 28, 29).

4. That is how our sources refer to Odenathus' troops; see refs. in Millar (1993: 169, n. 39).

5. Zosimus 1.39 > DL 4.3.2, pp. 74, 75, *HA* Thirty Pretenders 15, Two Valerians 4.

6. Passage from Anon. Continuator of Cassius Dio (*FHG* IV, p. 197) > DL 4.3.2, pp. 75–6.

7. *HA*, Gallieni 3.1–5 > DL 4.3.2, pp. 72–3; cf. Zonaras 12. 24 > DL 4.3.2, pp. 76–7.

8. *HA*, Gallieni 10.5 > DL 4.3.2, p. 73; though the *HA* adds that Odenathus' purpose in sending Gallienus the captured satraps was apparently merely to insult him and display his own prowess.

9. *HA*, Gallieni 3.3 > DL 4.3.2, p. 73.

10. Thus Winsbury (2010: 69).
11. Millar (1993: 169).
12. Its source is a fragment from the writings of the 6th-century lawyer and diplomat Petrus Patricius (Peter the Patrician), transl. in DL 4.1.3, pp. 68–9. Watson (1999: 30) comments that the date of the episode is uncertain, but that it fits in well with the events surrounding the Persian assault on Dura Europos in the mid 250s. He goes on to say: 'Whether it should be taken to represent treachery towards Rome, or merely as an example of the Roman practice of buying off the enemy is debatable.'
13. This has been inferred from the use of the terms *consularis* and *hypatikos* in inscriptions from Palmyra (dated to 257/8) in reference to Odenathus. See Millar (1993: 165, 334).
14. Zosimus 1.39.1–2 > DL 4.3.2, p. 75, and Zonaras 12.24 > DL 4.3.2, p. 77 respectively.
15. Watson (1999: 30).
16. Burns (2009: 208) comments that Odenathus was apparently put in charge of Rome's legions in the region when appointed consul and governor of Syria Phoenice.
17. The inscription is carved on a statue adjacent to another inscribed statue in honour of Odenathus' wife Zenobia, also set up by Zabdas and Zabbai. Both inscriptions are transl. in DL 4.7.2, p. 88.
18. Southern (2008: 69) notes the suggestion that 'Odenathus controlled only Palmyra and the desert zone up to the Euphrates, with no powers in the rest of Syria'.
19. *HA*, Gallieni 3.3. Admittedly the title later appears among those of his son Vaballathus, but it is fairly certain, as Southern comments, that the son did not inherit the title from his father.
20. *HA*, Gallieni 12.1 > DL 4.3.2, p. 74.
21. Southern (2008: 72) notes that Odenathus' son Herodianus is directly attested as 'King of Kings' in a dedication to him of unknown date by Vorodes (Worod) (a man of Persian origin who became Odenathus' chief military officer in his campaigns against Shapur) (DL 4.3.4, p. 77). She makes the point that although in some sources Odenathus is described merely as 'king' (refs. n. 57), 'it is unlikely that Odenathus would have been simply king while his son was King of Kings', but does go on to say that not all scholars agree on this point (ref. n. 58).
22. On the other hand, Southern (2008: 72) sees 'this elevation to supreme royalty' as a deliberate act, noting that there was no hereditary kingship in Palmyra and no tradition of royalty, unlike the eastern states of Emesa or Edessa. Besides, 'The designation King of Kings carried much weight in the east, and would be fully understood by the Persians, who used the title themselves. It was not an attempt by Odenathus to usurp power or to oust Gallienus. He used eastern methods to govern the eastern populations, using titles to which they were accustomed and in which they had faith.'

23. The specific sources, respectively, are a passage from Syncellus > DL 4.5.1, p. 82, Zosimus 1.39.2 > DL 4.5.1, p. 81, *HA*, Pretenders 17.1–3 > DL 4.5.1, p. 81, John of Antioch, *frag* 152. 2 (*FHG* IV, p. 599) > DL 4.5.1, p. 81.

24. This possibility is suggested and discussed by Southern (2008: 80).

25. Zonaras 12.24 > DL 4.5.1, p. 82.

CHAPTER 19. ZENOBIA, QUEEN OF THE EAST

1. Livia was the wife of Augustus and the mother of Tiberius, Augustus' stepson and eventual successor.

2. The relevant section is transl. in Perlmann (1987: 139–50).

3. Southern (2008: 173, n. 3) notes that this name appears on a milestone on the road from Palmyra to Emesa (*Corpus Inscriptionum Semiticarum* II 3971).

4. Thus Southern (2008: 4–5), who discusses briefly the various explanations suggested for the name's appearance in Zenobia's family.

5. *HA*, Thirty Pretenders 30.2.

6. Traditionally, a fortress now called Halabiye on the west bank of the Euphrates, to the north of Dura Europos, and of which there are still to be seen substantial remains of later Byzantine fortifications, was thought to be a defence post built by Zenobia and was in fact known by the name Zenobia—though there is no hard evidence from the site itself of an identification with the settlement Zenobia. Procopius, *De bello Persico* 2.5.4–6 > DL 4.6.2, pp. 85–6 refers to the foundation by Zenobia of a fortress/city called Zenobia on the Euphrates, about three days' journey from Circesium.

7. The Hauran was a fertile plain, *c.*7500 sq km in extent, located south of Damascus, 'between Mount Hermon and the desert with the Jordanian border as its southern limit. The plain is protected from the encroaching desert to the east by the Jebel al-Arab, the Mount Bashan of the Psalms.' (Burns 2009: 289; see this for details of the history of the region.)

8. But as Watson (1999: 54) notes, it was not until the emperor Aurelian arrived in the area in the early autumn of 271 that the Goths, who had already inflicted considerable damage, were actually driven back across the Danube.

9. Ball (2000: 79).

10. For references to these ancient assessments of Longinus, see *OCD* 300.

11. Ball (2000: 79).

12. Southern (2008: 106–7): 'The Roman province of Arabia did not extend over the land that comprises the present-day Arabian peninsula, which remained outside the Roman empire. The Romans called this area Arabia Felix, maintaining some influence over it but not total control. The territory of the Roman province of Arabia was quite small in comparison with the rest of the peninsula, bordered on the north by Syria Phoenice, and on the west by Syria Palestina. The southern boundary is uncertain.' See map in Talbert (1985: 171).

13. The figures are those given by Zosimus 1.44 > DL 4.6.5, p. 87.

14. Probably around the time of the emperor Claudius' death; thus Southern (2008: 114).

15. To adapt a phrase from Stoneman (1992: 160).

16. Thus Millar (1993: 171, with refs. n. 53).

17. Though there is nothing to suggest that during the brief Palmyrene occupation of Egypt Zenobia ever sought to stop its grain shipments to Rome

18. For some suggested reasons for the campaign, see Southern (2008: 117).

19. *HA*, Aurelian 22–4.

20. *HA*, Probus 9.5.

21. For an account of the battle, see Zosimus 1.50–6 > DL 4.8.2, pp. 93–4. This is probably the most reliable version, differing in a number of respects from those of other ancient sources.

22. Zosimus 51–2 > DL 4.8.2, pp. 93–4.

23. According to the *HA*, Aurelian 26.1.

24. *HA*, Aurelian 27.4, in a letter purportedly written by Zenobia to Aurelian. The *HA* subsequently tells us (Aurelian 28.2) that the Persians (i.e. Sasanians) did actually send reinforcements to help relieve the siege, but that these were driven off by Aurelian's forces.

25. *HA*, Aurelian 26.3–4 > DL 4.8.3, p. 96.

26. Zosimus 1.55 > DL 4.8.4, pp. 98–9.

27. *HA*, Pretenders 30.23 > DL 4.8.5, p. 99.

28. Passage from Malalas 12 > DL 4.9.2, p. 101.

29. *HA*, Aurelian 31.2.

30. *HA*, Aurelian 30.1–3, Zosimus 1.56. (2)–3 > DL 4.9, p. 100.

31. For both passages, see DL 4.9.4, pp. 102–3.

32. Burns (2009: 209).

33. The passages which report the rebellion, from the *HA* lives of Aurelian and Firmus, are transl. in DL 4.10.2, pp. 103–5.

34. Zosimus 1.61.1 > DL 4.10.2, p. 105.

35. Transl. in DL 4.10.3, pp. 105–7.

36. Thus *HA*, Pretenders 30.24–6 > DL 4.10.3, pp. 105–6.

37. Zosimus 1.59.1 > DL 4.9.4, p. 102.

38. Passage from Malalas 12 > DL 4.9.2, p. 101.

39. *HA*, Pretenders 30.27. We do not know how many children Zenobia had—as few as one (Vaballathus) or as many as nine (on the basis of numbers totted up from mainly unreliable sources like the *HA*).

40. Passage from Syncellus > DL 4.11.1, p. 109.

41. Eutropius 9.13.2 and Jerome, *Chronica*, p. 223, 1–3 > DL 4.11.1, p. 108.

42. This reconstruction is based in part on a passage from Joan Haslip (1945: 133), quoted verbatim by Stoneman (1992: 193–4).

THE LAST FAREWELL

1. Ball (2010: 31–2).
2. Burns (2009: 10).
3. This famous saying occurs in the Chronicle of Michael the Syrian, a patriarch of Antioch in the 12th century. A 9th-century Arab author al-Baladhuri also has Heraclius saying as he leaves Syria: 'Peace unto thee, O Syria, and what an excellent country this is for the enemy!' My thanks to Dr John Moorhead for this information.

Bibliography

Achtemeier, P. J. (ed.) (1996), *The HarperCollins Bible Dictionary*, New York: Harper-Collins (cited as *HCBD*).

Akkermans, P. M. M. G. and Schwartz, G. M. (2003), *The Archaeology of Syria: From Complex Hunter-Gatherer to Early Urban Societies (c. 16,000–300 BC)*, Cambridge: Cambridge University Press.

Arnaud, D. (1991), 'Une correspondance d'affaires entre Ougaritains et Emariotes (nos. 30–36)', in P. Bordreuil (ed.), 65–78.

Austin, M. (2006), *The Hellenistic World from Alexander to the Roman Conquest* (2nd edn), Cambridge: Cambridge University Press (cited as Aust.).

Ball, W. (2000), *Rome in the East: The Transformation of an Empire*, London and New York: Routledge.

Ball, W. (2010), *Syria, a Historical and Architectural Guide* (rev. edn), Northampton (Mass.): Interlink.

Beckman, G. (1999), *Hittite Diplomatic Texts* (2nd edn), Atlanta: Scholars Press (cited as Beck.).

Bordreuil, P. (ed.) (1991), *Une bibliothèque au sud de la ville. Les textes de la 34ᵉ campagne (1973)* (Ras Shamra-Ougarit VII), Paris: Éditions Recherche sur les Civilisations.

Breasted, J. H. (1906), *Ancient Records of Egypt*, Chicago: Chicago University Press (4 vols.).

Bryce, T. R. (1988), 'Tette and the Rebellions in Nuhassi', *Anatolian Studies* 38: 21–8.

Bryce, T. R. (2003), *Letters of the Great Kings of the Ancient Near East*, London: Routledge.

Bryce, T. R. (2005), *The Kingdom of the Hittites* (new edn), Oxford: Oxford University Press.

Bryce, T. R. (2009/12), *The Routledge Handbook of the Peoples and Places of Ancient Western Asia*, Abingdon: Routledge.

Bryce, T. R. (2012), *The World of the Neo-Hittite Kingdoms*, Oxford: Oxford University Press.

Bunnens, G. (ed.) (2000), *Essays on Syria in the Iron Age*, Louvain, Paris, and Sterling, Va.: Peeters, Ancient Near East Studies, Supplement 7.

Burns, R. (2009), *The Monuments of Syria*, London, New York: I.B. Tauris.

Cary, M. and Scullard, H. H. (1975), *A History of Rome*, Basingstoke and London: MacMillan.

Chavalas, M. W. (ed.) (2006), *The Ancient Near East: Historical Sources in Translation*, Oxford: Blackwells.

Cohen, R. and Westbrook, R. (2000), *Amarna Diplomacy: The Beginnings of International Relations*, Baltimore and London: The Johns Hopkins University Press.

Curtis, J. (ed.) (2000), *Mesopotamia and Iran in the Parthian and Sasanian Periods: Rejection and Revival c. 238 BC–AD 642*, London: British Museum Press.

Davis, D. (2006), *Shahnameh: The Persian Book of Kings*, New York: Viking.

Davis, N. and Kraay, C. M (1973), *The Hellenistic Kingdoms*, London: Thames and Hudson.

Dodgeon, M. H. and Lieu, S. N. C. (1991), *The Roman Eastern Frontier and the Persian Wars AD 226–363. A Documentary History*, London and New York: Routledge (cited as DL).

Durand, J.-M. (1998–2003), *Les Documents épistolaires du palais de Mari*, Paris: Les Éditions du Cerf (3 vols.).

Frye, R. N. (2000), 'Parthian and Sasanian History of Iran', in J. Curtis (ed.), 17–22.

Gardiner, A. (1975), *The Kadesh Inscriptions of Ramesses II*, Oxford: Griffith Institute, Ashmolean Museum.

Glassner, J.-J. (2004), *Mesopotamian Chronicles*, Writings from the Ancient World Number 19, Atlanta: Society of Biblical Literature.

Goldsworthy, A. (2009), *The Fall of the West: The Death of the Roman Superpower*, London: Phoenix.

Grainger, J. D. (1990), *The Cities of Seleukid Syria*, Oxford: Clarendon Press.

Grayson, A. K. (1975), *Assyrian and Babylonian Chronicles*, New York: J. J. Augustin (cited as *ABC*).

Grayson, A. K. (1991a), *The Royal Inscriptions of Mesopotamia. Assyrian Periods*, ii: *Assyrian Rulers of the Early First Millennium BC I (1114–859 BC)*, Toronto, Buffalo, and London: University of Toronto Press (cited as *RIMA* 2).

Grayson, A. K. (1991b), 'Assyria: Sennacherib and Esarhaddon (704–669 B.C.)', *CAH* III.2: 103–41.

Grayson, A. K. (1996), *The Royal Inscriptions of Mesopotamia. Assyrian Periods*, iii: *Assyrian Rulers of the Early First Millennium BC II (858–745 BC)*, Toronto, Buffalo, and London: University of Toronto Press (cited as *RIMA* 3).

Gruen, E. S. (1984), *The Hellenistic World and the Coming of Rome*, Berkeley, Los Angeles, and London: University of California Press.

Habicht, C. (1984), 'The Seleucids and their Rivals', *CAH* VIII: 324–87.

Hannestad, L. (2012), 'The Seleucid Kingdom', in D. T. Potts (ed.), 984–1000.

Haslip, J. (1945), *Lady Hester Stanhope: A Biography*, Harmondsworth: Penguin.

Hawkins, J. D. (2011), 'The Inscriptions of the Aleppo Temple', *Anatolian Studies* 61: 35–54.

Heimpel, W. (2003), *Letters to the King of Mari*, Winona Lake: Eisenbrauns.

Heinen, H. (1984), 'The Syrian-Egyptian Wars and the New Kingdoms of Asia Minor', *CAH* VII.1: 412–45.

Izre'el, I. and Singer, I. (1990), *The General's Letter from Ugarit*, Tel Aviv: Tel Aviv University.

Joannès, F. (ed.) (2001), *Dictionnaire de la civilisation mésopotamienne*, Paris: Éditions Robert Laffont (cited as *DCM*).

Kitchen, K. A. (1982), *Pharaoh Triumphant: The Life and Times of Ramesses II*, Warminster: Aris and Phillips.

Kuhrt, A. (1995), *The Ancient Near East, c. 3000–330 B.C.*, London and New York: Routledge.

Kuhrt, A. (2007), *The Persian Empire*, Abingdon: Routledge.

Kupper, J.-R. (1973), 'Northern Mesopotamia and Syria', *CAH* II.1: 1–41.

Lipiński, E. (2000), *The Aramaeans, their Ancient History, Culture, Religion*, Leuven, Paris, and Sterling, Va.: Peeters.

Luckenbill, D. D. (1928), *Ancient Records of Assyria and Babylonia*, Vols. I and II, Chicago: University of Chicago Press (repr. Greenwood Press, New York, 1968) (cited as *ARAB*).

Malbran-Labat, F. (1991), 'Lettres (nos. 6–29)', in P. Bordreuil (ed.), 27–64.

Margueron, J.-C. (1995a), 'Mari: A Portrait in Art of a Mesopotamian City-State', *CANE* 2: 885–99.

Margueron, J.-C. (1995b), 'Emar, Capital of Aštata in the Fourteenth Century BCE', *Biblical Archaeologist* 58: 126–38.

Markoe, G. E. (2000), *Phoenicians*, London: British Museum Press.

Meyers, E. M. (ed.) (1997), *The Oxford Encyclopedia of Archaeology in the Near East*, New York and Oxford: Oxford University Press (cited as *OEANE*).

Mieroop, M. van de (2004), *A History of the Ancient Near East*, Oxford: Blackwells.

Milano, L. (1995), 'Ebla: A Third Millennium City-State in Ancient Syria', *CANE* 2: 1219–30.

Miles, R. (2010), *Ancient Worlds*, London: Allen Lane.

Millar, F. (1993), *The Roman Near East 31 BC–AD 337*, Cambridge, Mass. and London: Harvard University Press.

Moran, W. (1992), *The Amarna Letters*, Baltimore and London: The Johns Hopkins University Press.

Murnane, W. (1990), *The Road to Kadesh* (2nd edn), Chicago: University of Chicago Press.

Nougayrol, J. (1956), *Le Palais Royal d'Ugarit IV* (Mission de Ras Shamra Tome IX) Paris: Klincksieck (cited as *PRU IV*).

Nougayrol, J., Laroche, E., Virolleaud, C., and Schaeffer, C. F. A. (1968), *Ugaritica V* (Mission de Ras Shamra Tome XVI), Paris: Klincksieck.

Oates, J. (1986), *Babylon*, London: Thames and Hudson.

Perlmann, M. (1987), *The History of al-Tabari*, Albany: State University of New York Press.

Podany, A. H. (2010), *Brotherhood of Kings: How International Relations Shaped the Ancient Near East*, Oxford: Oxford University Press.

Potts, D. T. (ed.) (2012), *A Companion to the Archaeology of the Ancient Near East*, Chichester: Wiley-Blackwell.

Pritchard, J. B. (1969), *Ancient Near Eastern Texts relating to the Old Testament* (3rd edn), Princeton: Princeton University Press (cited as *ANET*).

Rainey, A. F. and Notley, R. S. (2006), *The Sacred Bridge: Carta's Atlas of the Biblical World*, Jerusalem: Carta.

Roux, G. (1980), *Ancient Iraq* (2nd edn), London: Penguin.

Sasson, J. M. (ed.) (1995), *Civilizations of the Ancient Near East*, New York: Charles Scribner's Sons (4 vols.) (cited as *CANE*).

Shaw, I. (ed.) (2000), *The Oxford History of Ancient Egypt*, Oxford: Oxford University Press.

Sherwin-White, S. and Kuhrt, A. (1993), *From Samarkhand to Sardis: A New Approach to the Seleucid Empire*, London: Duckworth.

Shipley, G. (2000), *The Greek World after Alexander 323–30 BC*, London and New York: Routledge.

Singer, I. (1985), 'The Battle of Nihriya and the End of the Hittite Empire', *Zeitschrift für Assyriologie und vorderasiatische Archäologie* 75: 100–23.

Singer, I. (1991), 'A Concise History of Amurru', Appendix III (pp. 135–95) to S. Izre'el, *Amurru Akkadian: A Linguistic Study*, Vol. II, Atlanta: Scholars Press.

Singer, I. (1996), 'A Political History of Ugarit', in W. G. E. Watson and N. Wyatt (eds.), *Handbook of Oriental Studies* (Handbuch der Orientalistik, Abt. 1, *Der Nahe und Mittlere Osten: Bd 39*), Leiden, Boston, and Cologne: Brill, 603–733.

Southern, P. (2008), *The Empress Zenobia: Palmyra's Rebel Queen*, London and New York: Continuum.

Stoneman, R. (1992), *Palmyra and its Empire: Zenobia's Revolt against Rome*, Ann Arbor: University of Michigan Press.

Tadmor, H. (2007), *The Inscriptions of Tiglath-pileser III, King of Assyria*, Jerusalem: The Israel Academy of Sciences and Humanities (second printing of 1994 edition with *addenda et corrigenda*).

Talbert, R. J. A. (ed.) (1985), *Atlas of Classical History*, London and New York: Routledge.

Taylor, J. (2000), 'The Third Intermediate Period', in I. Shaw (ed.) (2000), 330–68.

Tubb, J. N. (1998), *Canaanites*, London: British Museum Press.

Waterfield, R. (2011), *Dividing the Spoils: The War for Alexander the Great's Empire*, Oxford: Oxford University Press.

Watson, A. (1999), *Aurelian and the Third Century*, London and New York: Routledge.

Whiting, R. M. (1995), 'Amorite Tribes and Nations of Second-Millennium Western Asia', *CANE* 2: 1231–42.

Wilhelm, G. (1989), *The Hurrians*, Warminster: Aris and Phillips.

Wilhelm, G. (1995), 'The Kingdom of Mitanni in Second-Millennium Upper Mesopotamia', *CANE* 2: 1243–54.

Winsbury, R. (2010), *Zenobia of Palmyra*, London: Duckworth.

Wiseman, D. J. (1956), *Chronicles of Chaldaean Kings (626–556 BC) in the British Museum*, London: British Museum.

Wiseman, D. J. (1991), 'Babylonia 605–539 B.C.', *CAH* III.2: 229–51.

Yon, M. (2006), *The City of Ugarit at Tel Ras Shamra*, Winona Lake: Eisenbrauns.

Picture Acknowledgements

Index

Achaem. = Achaemenid; Ass. = Assyrian; b. = brother; bibl. = biblical; d. = daughter; dyn. = dynasty; Eg. = Egyptian; emp. = empire; f. = father; Gk. = Greek; grands. = grandson; Hitt. = Hittite; IA = Iron Age; LBA = Late Bronze Age; leg. = legendary; m. = mother; m.c. = military commander; mod. = modern; off. = official; Parth. = Parthian; p. = prince; p'cess = princess; q. = queen; q.v. = see this; Rom. = Roman; r. = ruler (covers emperors, kings, chieftains); s. = son; Sas. = Sasanian; Sel. = Seleucid; w. = wife

Personal names are briefly defined. Page nos. in **bold** indicate main refs. Page nos. in *italics* indicate map locations.